Talking to the Other Side: A History of Modern Spiritualism and Mediumship

Talking to the Other Side: A History of Modern Spiritualism and Mediumship

◆

A Study of the Religion, Science, Philosophy and Mediums that Encompass this American-Made Religion

Todd Jay Leonard, Ph.D.

iUniverse, Inc.
New York Lincoln Shanghai

Talking to the Other Side: A History of Modern Spiritualism and Mediumship
A Study of the Religion, Science, Philosophy and Mediums that Encompass this American-Made Religion

Copyright © 2005 by Todd Jay Leonard

All rights reserved. No part of this book may be used or reproduced by any means, graphic, electronic, or mechanical, including photocopying, recording, taping or by any information storage retrieval system without the written permission of the publisher except in the case of brief quotations embodied in critical articles and reviews.

iUniverse books may be ordered through booksellers or by contacting:

iUniverse
2021 Pine Lake Road, Suite 100
Lincoln, NE 68512
www.iuniverse.com
1-800-Authors (1-800-288-4677)

ISBN-13: 978-0-595-36353-7 (pbk)
ISBN-13: 978-0-595-80790-1 (ebk)
ISBN-10: 0-595-36353-9 (pbk)
ISBN-10: 0-595-80790-9 (ebk)

Printed in the United States of America

To
Grandmother Grace and
Aunt Evelyn in Spirit.

Contents

List of Illustrations xi
List of Tables xiii
Abstract xv
Introduction xix

CHAPTER 1 A History of Religion in America from Early Times through the 19th Century 1
    1.1 Early Times 2
    1.2 European-Jewish Roots in the New World 10
    1.3 The European-Religion Invasion 13
    1.4 African-American Religion 19
    1.5 American-Made Religions of the 19th Century 21
    1.6 Summary 34

CHAPTER 2 A History of Mediumship from Ancient Times to the Advent of Spiritualism in America 36
    2.1 Biblical Accounts of Mediumship 43
    2.2 The Work of Swedenborg 50
    2.3 The Work of Franz Anton Mesmer 55
    2.4 Andrew Jackson Davis, "The Poughkeepsie Seer" 57
    2.5 The Fox Sisters and the Hydesville Rappings 61
    2.6 Notable Works and Personas during "The Era of Great Mediums" 62
    2.7 Summary 67

CHAPTER 3 The Science, Philosophy, and Religion of Spiritualism: An Analysis of its Principles, Beliefs, and Social Policies 70

3.1 The Science of Spiritualism 74
3.2 The Philosophy of Spiritualism 79
3.3 The Declaration of Principles 84
3.4 The Religion of Spiritualism 94
3.5 Social Policy Statements of Spiritualism. 98
3.6 Summary. 101

Chapter 4 Spiritualism and the Phenomenon of Modern Mediumship. 103

4.1 Mental Phases of Mediumship. 106
4.2 Physical Phases of Mediumship 119
4.3 Fraud and Trickery within the Spiritualist Movement 124
4.4 The Séance, Clairvoyant Circle and Healing Circle 130
4.5 Summary. 134

Chapter 5 Statement of the Problem and Purpose of the Study 136

5.1 Introduction 136
5.2 Origins and Rationale 145
5.3 Research Questions 147
5.4 Statement of the Problem 147
5.5 Purpose of the Study 148
5.6 Hypotheses 148
5.7 Significance of the Study 149
5.8 Limitations of the Study 149
5.9 Basic Assumptions. 150
5.10 Definitions. 151
5.11 Summary. 151

Chapter 6 Research Methodology, Procedures, Design, and Data Collection 153

6.1 Research Design and Procedures 153
6.2 Population Sample of Subjects and the Selection Process. 154
6.3 Data Collection Instruments 156
6.4 Ethical Decisions 160
6.5 Summary. 161

CHAPTER 7	Presentation, Analysis, and Discussion of the Data and the Results 163
	7.1 Introduction 163
	7.2 Descriptive Statistics of the Participants' Demographic Data 163
	7.3 Findings and Discussions 175
	7.4 Summary 190

Conclusions and Recommendations 193

Bibliography 201

APPENDIX A	An Abridged Timeline of Modern Spiritualism from 1848-1920 215
APPENDIX B	Hydesville in History: Testimony of Eye-Witnesses 225
APPENDIX C	A Glossary and List of Terms and Definitions Associated with Mediumship and Modern Spiritualism 233
APPENDIX D	The Symbol of Spiritualism: The Sunflower 239
APPENDIX E	The Hydesville Cottage 243
APPENDIX F	Natural Law 245
APPENDIX G	Personal Interview with Rev. Sarah Brown, Spiritualist Medium. 249
APPENDIX H	Personal Interview with Rev. John Lilec, Spiritualist Medium. 261
APPENDIX I	Selected Versions of the "Declaration of Principles" as Used by Spiritualist Organizations throughout the United States and Great Britain. 273
APPENDIX J	Professor Hare's Spiritual Telegraph 277
APPENDIX K	Spirit Manifestations of the Bible 289
APPENDIX L	Definitions of Clairvoyance. 295

APPENDIX M	Testimonial by the Author Regarding his Experiences at Séances and Healing Circles 297
APPENDIX N	Psychometry. 301
APPENDIX O	Spirit Brides and Rag Babies. 309
APPENDIX P	Spirit Guides: Their Importance, Duties, Titles, and Place 317
APPENDIX Q	Morris Pratt Institute Course Listing 323
APPENDIX R	Fieldwork Questionnaire 331

List of Illustrations

Figure 1: Emmanuel Swedenborg *50*

Figure 2: Franz Anton Mesmer *55*

Figure 3: Andrew Jackson Davis *58*

Figure 4: Kate, Margaretta, and Leah Fox *61*

Figure 5: Age and Sex of Subjects *164*

Figure 6: Nationality of Subjects *169*

Figure 7: Years as a Spiritualist *170*

Figure 8: The Years Subjects became Certified *171*

Figure 9: Age Subjects were Aware of their Mediumship *172*

Figure 10: First Experience with Spirit Communication *174*

Figure 11: Percentage of Ordained Ministers as Subjects *184*

Figure 12: Affiliation of Subjects with Spiritualist Associations ... *184*

List of Tables

Table 1: Mental and Physical Mediumship. 40

Abstract

Since its birth in 1848, Spiritualism as a religion, science and philosophy has experienced great highs and lows. At the center of this modern-religious movement are the "mediums"—the people who are able to communicate, in some way, with spirit entities that are no longer on the earth plane. As discovered through empirical research, mediums that purportedly have this gift were raised in a wide range of Christian-based religious backgrounds, and held a variety of belief systems before embracing Spiritualism as a religion. As well, it was found that in their mediumship, these mediums incorporated a variety of methods in their work that assisted them in connecting with those on the other side. Based on three years of fieldwork, and a plethora of data and research collected on the modern Spiritualist movement in America—both primary and secondary—this study focuses upon the ethno-religious aspects of the religion, mediumship and the mediums themselves. Although there are numerous sources of literature on Spiritualism and mediumship as a vocation, the amount of published works and academic studies on the mediums themselves, is severely limited.

The purposes of this study were to determine whether modern Spiritualist mediums were raised in the religion, or actually converted to it from another, more mainstream religion; and if so, what relative factors existed which prompted them to pursue Spiritualism as a religion? Also, what types of mediumship—mental or physical—are most common among Spiritualist mediums and what methods and tools do Spiritualist mediums use to make contact with the spirit world in their readings and daily spiritual routine?

The first half of the study offers an expansive review of the literature encompassing, in great detail, the history of the Spiritualist movement which is popularly regarded to have begun in the mid 1800s, but in fact has its roots in ancient religious traditions dating back to time immemorial. *Chapter 1* centers on the history of religion in America from early times through the 19th century. *Chapter 2* offers a comprehensive account of the history of mediumship from ancient times through to the advent of Spiritualism as a movement. *Chapter 3* thoroughly delineates the principles, beliefs and social policies of Spiritualism as a religion, science and philosophy. *Chapter 4* concentrates on the mental and physical phenomena associated with Spiritualism and mediumship.

The second half of the study comprises the research and data that were compiled and analyzed based on fieldwork investigation, observation, a comprehensive questionnaire, personal interviews, and published literature on the topic of Spiritualism and mediumship. One hundred seventy Spiritualist mediums were initially surveyed, with 48 respondents accepted as subjects in the data collection portion of the study. A number of mediums offered additional research data through consultation and inquiry. The remaining chapters focus on the actual data and research aspects of the study: *Chapter 5* outlines the purpose of the study and the statement of the problem; Chapter 6 specifies the research methodology, procedures, design and the data collection instruments used in this study; Chapter 7 and the *Conclusion* summarize the discussions and conclusions of the study, as well as detailing its implications, offering recommendations for further research.

Acknowledgements

This book had its genesis as a doctoral dissertation for the degree of Doctor of Philosophy (Ph.D.) in Social Science (with a specialization in history) at Empresarial University. The original title of the dissertation was *An American-Made Religion: The History of Spiritualism and Mediumship in the United States—An Analytic Study on the Religion, Science, Philosophy and Mediums that Encompass this Belief System*. The rewording of the title was done for practical reasons and represents the only major change from the original dissertation. This particular version, however, has been slightly edited to include minor changes in grammar and style. Great care was taken not to change the substance or content from the original. Hence, the later chapters that relate specifically to the statement of the problem, purpose of the study, research methodology, and the presentation and analysis of the findings, as well as the discussion of the data and the results, are as they were when it was orally defended before the dissertation committee.

With those caveats in mind, I wish to acknowledge publicly the help and assistance of a number of people who aided me initially in my research. First, I would like to thank my Field Dissertation Advisor (FDA), Dr. Kanako Kitahara who oversaw my research from its inception. When I first approached her about being my onsite advisor, she admitted to me that she really did not know anything about Spiritualism; I told her that made two of us, and that we could learn about it together. Her primary concern was whether or not she could properly advise me. I assured her that her experience and exemplary talent in historical research would serve me well. She is indeed a gifted researcher and is very knowledgeable about ethno-historical issues, which made her an excellent choice to bounce ideas off of and to ask for occasional assistance. With great pleasure I offer my sincere gratitude to Dr. Kitahara for agreeing to take me on as an adjunct student, adding to her already hectic research and work schedule—not to mention her familial obligations—making her a very busy lady.

I am also grateful to all the Spiritualist mediums and ministers that so kindly assisted me in my research and data collection. Without all of their help, it would have been impossible to research this topic. I am most appreciative to The Reverend Sarah Brown who agreed to numerous interviews, endured long discussions, and received nearly weekly telephone calls from me in Japan, inquiring further about areas of Spiritualism I found confusing, or in which I needed additional clarification. Thank you from the bottom of my heart. I would be remiss if I failed to acknowledge the Spiritualist associations which assisted me with my research, either directly or indirectly: The National Spiritualist Association of Churches (NSAC), the Indiana Association of Spiritualists (IAOS), the Universal Spiritualist Association (USA), and the Southern Cassadaga Spiritualist Camp Meeting Association (SCSCMA). I thank all of the Spiritualist mediums who agreed to be subjects in my study, hailing from Camp Lily Dale, Camp Cassadaga, and Camp Chesterfield (a small number of participants from the Universal Spiritualist Association also served as subjects). I extend to these associations and Spiritualist mediums my heartfelt appreciation.

Finally, many people generously offered me boundless support. I sincerely thank all of the individual mediums who took the time to speak with me about Spiritualism throughout the tenure of my study; the administration and mediums at Camp Chesterfield who allowed me to visit church and message services and other gatherings held there; The Reverend John Lilec for indulging me in a tape-recorded interview; the Dissertation Readers of Empresarial University who read my dissertation after its completion; Shingo Ono for his constant encouragement and support; and to my family and friends who endured my obsessive ravings and enthusiasm about Spiritualism and mediumship over the past several years while I researched, and then wrote, the original dissertation. To all of these I am eternally grateful.

Introduction

On March 31, 1848, two young girls, Katie and Maggie Fox, purportedly made a seemingly unlikely, if not unwitting, discovery that literally changed how many people from that night forward would view death and the afterlife. On this night, the two sisters—through an elaborate code of handclapping that resulted in "rappings"—made contact with a disincarnate entity they affectionately called "Mr. Splitfoot." This was the first time in the history of modern mediumship that documented intelligible responses being made and received—not only from those on this side of the veil, but from entities on the other side as well. Almost overnight, word spread of the ghostly discovery and the little hamlet of Hydesville, in upstate New York, was soon inundated with curiosity seekers eagerly wishing to see and experience "spirit communication."

Eventually, these modest beginnings would become a full-fledged religious movement called "Spiritualism." The basic belief system of this purely American-made religion was centered on the "medium" (a person sensitive to the vibrations and energy of those in the spirit world) who could communicate messages from the other side to the earth plane. Some people seemed to be naturally gifted with this ability—seeing, hearing, and feeling disincarnate spirits; these entities seemingly wanted to make contact with those left behind, offering evidential signs and proof in the forms of spirit messages, apports (items from the spirit world), and full-form manifestations of their spirit bodies. This occurred when the energy of the medium and sitters would be transformed into "ectoplasm" (a gooey substance that oozed from all the orifices of the medium during séances) and would take the shape of the spirit entity manifesting.

The roots of Spiritualism, though, go back much further than the 19th century, all the way back to ancient times. Indigenous peoples from all cultures felt a need to attempt communication with spirits not of this world. Every religious tradition since time immemorial attempted some type of spirit contact, whether it was omnipotent and god-like or the spirits of departed tribal chiefs, ancestors, and friends. Even enemies were feared after death that they may come back to haunt those responsible for their demise.

A number of Eastern religions, most principally Buddhism, practice a form of ancestral worship; as well, Native American and African religious traditions incorporate the concept of praying to and communicating with departed family members. All of these traditions served as precursors to mediumship, and ultimately, to the modern religion of Spiritualism.

The religious history of the United States begins well before America was a country. It began with the spirituality of the indigenous peoples who inhabited the whole of the North American continent before the first ships with religious immigrants arrived; then extended to those who would be searching and yearning for religious freedom. In the early days, those who left their countries in search of a new life and religious freedom in the New World, escaping religious persecution, were part of the first religious pioneers that helped to shape the *religio*-psyche of the United States. They brought with them not only a desire to worship freely, but the belief systems that they followed. Over the ensuing centuries, these religious traditions began to change, borrow, and adapt from one another, causing the various religious practices to layer, one onto the other—accepting and negating certain practices and traditions, following and leaving others. These were the common threads in the fabric of American religious history that caused it to grow and mature (a wayward child, of sorts, coming from the traditional parents of mainstream belief systems from across the Atlantic only to be raised by more liberal and distant relatives).

By the middle of the 19th century, however, the wayward child was beyond control; the overall religious condition of the United States was such that changes—economic, social, and spiritual—were about to occur which would affect deeply many of the long held belief systems that had become the norm all across the country. Average citizens had grown tired of the Puritanical belief system and social rules that had occupied their lives for two centuries. They were weary of the fundamental beliefs teaching hell and damnation for even the most minor of indiscretions. People began to question long held religious beliefs, as well as their own spirituality, regarding sin, vicarious atonement, and beliefs about heaven and hell. Being pious and living without "sin" made the task of redemption seem nearly impossible to achieve. The world was modernizing quickly, offering more temptations than ever before. All of this made the conditions ripe for sweeping changes to occur.

First, Mormonism was introduced to the world in 1830 by Joseph Smith, Jr. His new religion was radical in that it offered a history of America back to the time of Jesus Christ, teaching that Jesus had visited North America during his life. As well, his religion advocated new concepts such as personal moral choice, salvation, rejection of original sin, and "spiritual wifery" (plural marriage) as parts of its religious dogma. The majority of Americans at the time were more appalled by the idea of polygamy than they were of slavery, a hotly debated issue of the day. (Krakauer, 6) This did not deter, however, a large number of people from accepting Mormonism and following its leader across the country.

Second, the Spiritualist movement exploded onto the religious landscape of the United States in 1848, adopting some of the more progressive ideas of the Mormons regarding redemption and original sin, but expanding these to include equality of the sexes, a denial of vicarious atonement, and promoting a belief that the resurrection of Jesus was not in the physical sense, but actually as a "spirit entity" that came back to communicate with those left behind on the earth plane. These were very radical ideas, at once shocking the Victorian sensitivities of the day, but still being titillating enough to make people want to pursue them further.

Third, and finally, Mary Baker-Eddy, a former Spiritualist, started her own religious movement—Christian Science—after a personal epiphany that occurred with a miraculous healing she received after reading the Bible. Her religion had its basis in science, but depended upon the power of prayer to heal those who were sick. Both Mormonism and Christian Science have faired better than their cousin Spiritualism. Largely, this was due to the organizational skills of both Smith and Baker-Eddy. They were able to maintain control of their movements autocratically, where Spiritualism, from the beginning, was divided and had no one religious leader or persona to lead it.

These three American-made religions developed within decades of one another, and within very close geographical proximity. The American people were ready for radical religious change and were quite open to and willing to accept new ideas that took away the overwhelming feelings of guilt, shame, and fear of "sinning" that everyone had been led to believe was a necessary part of being righteous in their religious life. People flocked to these new religions, embracing the radical departures in belief that they promulgated, searching for a spiritual path that was more flexible and tolerant.

Spiritualism, and more specifically mediumship, became the religion and practice that would pique the enquiring minds and curiosities of multitudes of people; both would enjoy widespread acceptance and popularity, all the way to the White House, to times of severe crisis where the religion nearly became extinct. Within a few years of the Fox sisters' revelations, mediums all over the country were holding parlor séances in their homes, offering messages from the spirit world and demonstrating both mental and physical phenomenon. The American public was smitten with this new religion that offered not only hope and love, but supposedly evidential proof (through spirit communication) of an afterlife.

At the center of this new religion were the "mediums." These men and women became the toasts of towns far and wide; they were eagerly sought after and then adulated for their amazing gift of talking to the dead. Quickly, more and more people began to claim to be mediums as it was becoming quite financially lucrative for those who could produce, without fail, some type of phenomena. This type of adulation had more than a monetary price; the higher the medium was placed, the farther he/she would fall. The public soon demanded more accurate, as well as fantastic, demonstrations of mediumship by the "sensitives." This constant pressure to perform upon command caused some authentic mediums, and many more fraudulent ones, to manufacture phenomena through trickery and charlatanism, giving mediumship and Spiritualism a bad name. It became clear that some type of organized system had to be created to test and authenticate the validity of the mediumship being done.

This is how Spiritualism first began its odyssey in becoming a full-fledged religion—gradually the movement began to take the form of a religion complete with a list of principles, ministers, churches, and camps. The medium, always remaining the constant force throughout its tumultuous transformation from a movement to a religion, was (and still is) on center stage as the primary vehicle to make contact with the other side. Eventually, procedures were developed that required the medium to prove his/her mediumship through testing and evidential demonstration. As associations began to form, credentials and certifications were becoming more and more the norm in order to distinguish clearly to the public who was "real" and who was "fake." Spiritualist camps began offering development classes and testing procedures to aspiring mediums.

Spiritualism and mediumship have undergone great metamorphoses over the past century and a half. From periods of great interest to times of near dissolution, the religion and movement have survived—sometimes just barely, but nonetheless remaining vibrant. The reason for this continued interest that ebbs and flows in cyclic rhythm is that humans are fascinated with what lies ahead in their futures, and what lies beyond this earth life. As long as there are people, there will most likely be an innate allure to mediumship and the mediums themselves. From ancient times to contemporary times, people have and will continue to seek out the counsel of mediums. It is seemingly an inbred desire or need to know what lies beyond, whether tomorrow, next year, or after the transition known as "death."

The primary focus of this dissertation is Spiritualism and how it relates to mediumship and mediums. Despite its long history, the subject of mediumship has been scantily addressed in the literature available on religious history, particularly in the area of the personal lives and abilities of the mediums. Certain aspects of the religion (*e.g.* Carroll, 1997; Barrow, 1986; Hazelgrove, 2000; Goldsmith, 1998; and Buescher, 2004) have been treated historically, but contemporary studies on mediumship and mediums is lacking. Owens (2000) introduces modern mediumship through experiential means and quasi-case studies, but no study, to my knowledge, has been devoted to or conducted solely on the Spiritualist mediums and mediumship. Modern mediumship and the role of the mediums have been virtually ignored, especially regarding the aspects of why they were attracted to the religion initially, why they decided to become mediums, and the process involved (from the first time they realized their mediumship ability to when they received certification by a Spiritualist organization).

Unlike the well-publicized "psychics" on television and in magazines that have gained in popularity in recent times (*e.g.* psychic hot lines, celebrity psychics, psychic fairs, *etc.*)—where no credentials are offered or even required—Spiritualist mediums do undergo extensive study and a substantial apprenticeship that concludes with an evidentiary testing of their mediumship skills before a panel of their elders (certified mediums). All of this must be done before they are allowed to practice mediumship as a certified Spiritualist medium by the certifying organization. Certified Spiritualist mediums do not garner the same publicity and notoriety as their "psychic" counterparts; unlike those who largely do it for the entertainment value, Spiritualists regard their work with spirit communication as the basis of their religion, something sacred, and something to be revered.

The purpose of this study is to explore this issue—the issue of Spiritualism and mediumship as a sincere religion to Spiritualist mediums—and to determine what prompted them to pursue this religious tradition. Spiritualism is mainly a religion of "converts," comprising people of very different and varied religious backgrounds, hailing from many opposing denominations. As the primary study centers on the mediums themselves, it focuses heavily on issues of religion, belief systems, rituals and the mediumship experiences of the mediums. The overall aim of this dissertation is to explore the mediums' personal backgrounds and interests which led them to pursue Spiritualism as a religion; the type of mediumship; the training and certification process involved; and the rituals mediums use to connect to the spirit world for readings and in their daily life.

An empirical study was done to gather primary research, as well as incorporating a wide range of published knowledge relevant to the topic. The first half of the dissertation serves as an extensive "review of the literature" and is devoted to surveying the history of religion, Spiritualism, and mediumship using largely secondary sources, with some primary and tertiary sources. The second half of the dissertation turns to original investigation, detailing the results of my own research and data expressly generated for the study.

Chapter 1 gives an overview of the history of religion in North America up to the advent of the three American-made religions of Mormonism, Spiritualism, and Christian Science. Chapter 2 deals exclusively with the history of mediumship from ancient times through to the occurrence that started the Spiritualist movement. Chapter 3 examines in greater depth the history of Spiritualism, focusing on it as a religion, science and philosophy, outlining its belief system, principles, and social policies. Chapter 4 delineates the types of mediumship—mental and physical—used by Spiritualist mediums in their work.

While Chapters 1 and 2 constitute an overview of religion and mediumship in general, Chapters 3 and 4 deal entirely with Spiritualism and mediumship as is done by Spiritualist mediums. Chapter 3 gives a linear account of the history of Spiritualism, while Chapter 4 explains in clear detail each form of mental mediumship as well as physical mediumship that sometimes accompanies mediumship work. Building upon the history of mediumship in Chapter 2, and the specificities of Spiritualism as a religion in Chapter 3, Chapter 4 examines how Spiritualism as a religion incorporates mental and physical mediumship into its belief system.

Re-centering the focus of mediumship, Chapter 5 outlines the purpose of the study and offers a statement of the problem. The origins and rationale of the study are also presented along with the specific research questions, significance of the study, limitations of the study, and the basic assumptions of the study. Chapter 6 describes the methodology used in the gathering of the data, as well as specifying the instruments used in the study. Reasons are offered for choosing the particular techniques and design used in the fieldwork portion of this study, and an explanation of the procedures is combined with a discussion of the various methodological issues which arose during the course of the study. Chapter 7 summarizes the discussions and conclusions of the study, as well as stating the implications. The Conclusion summarizes the findings of the research and offers recommendations for further research.

Of course this study has limitations. Carried out using a questionnaire, the sample was rather small. The findings are not necessarily applicable to all Spiritualist mediums and should not be over generalized. This study primarily surveyed mediums living in Spiritualist camps with a small percentage of Spiritualist mediums and ministers living outside of a recognized camp; all in all, this was a fair sampling of all Spiritualist mediums, but it did not distinguish between mediums who lived in camps and those who in fact lived in homes outside of a Spiritualist camp. In the end, the differentiation between the two most likely has no real bearing on the results, but would have been a point of interest as a comparison between the two groups. A more sizeable number of participants would have been preferred, but due to the general attitude of mediums not wishing to participate in these types of studies, I feel fortunate to have generated as many responses as I did. A more detailed study involving a much larger sample was beyond the scope of this dissertation; an open-ended questionnaire, like the one utilized in this study, would not have been possible due to the sheer size of the data it would generate. The smaller sampling does offer more insight, in some ways, than a survey using a checklist or Likert style of data gathering with a larger base of subjects. The comments I received from the subjects often revealed many aspects of Spiritualism and mediumship that I would never have thought of pursuing. Had I restricted the participants' responses by using some type of standardized checklist, the results would not have been nearly as telling.

Aware of these limitations, therefore, the decision was made to concentrate on the available subjects and to exploit the data and instruments to their fullest. In spite of these limitations, it is believed that the study provides a contribution of knowledge in an area which has, as yet, been the focus of little empirical research.

1

A History of Religion in America from Early Times through the 19th Century

In order to appreciate adequately the overall historical religious condition of America, and specifically that of the American-made religion of Spiritualism, it is necessary to return to the roots of American religious traditions to research how and why American religion evolved the way it did. This necessity to delineate, in a factual manner, the circumstances and state of affairs of American religious-life is to provide a proper historical perspective in which to gauge the entire process and development of religions and belief systems in the United States—to understand the historical components that are a part of the whole.

This background knowledge will serve an integral role later on when it will be shown clearly how the advent of Spiritualism arose and formed during the precisely right social, economic, and spiritual conditions of mid-nineteenth century America. In part, Spiritualism was formed due to the layering of religious thought over many centuries that occurred since time immemorial—borrowing, adopting, negating, and adapting the various religious traditions that were originally indigenous to the North American continent, and later those which were brought by the religious freedom-seeking immigrants. All of these religious-based episodes have had a profound influence on America's religious proclivities, synthesizing and fashioning a setting perfect for the creation of new religions that were purely made in America.

In this first chapter, the focus is on the general nature and development of religion in America. Out of necessity, this is a selective historical survey, highlighting pertinent research on the belief systems, religious practices, and denominations which are directly and indirectly related to the topics arising from the primary data that was gathered for this study. The majority of the research in this chapter comes from secondary sources which serve to illustrate and outline the historical background of religious practices in the United States from early times through the nineteenth century.

The New World, and later the United States of America, was viewed as a religious paradise by the early settlers. Throughout the immigration-history of the United States, *America* has represented, and since become synonymous with, "religious freedom." Although immigrants flocked to the New World to escape religious persecution, they oftentimes found new and different hardships with which they had to contend. Religious-life in America did offer early immigrants religious freedom, but conflict with other religions and cultures caused strife among people of different religious beliefs and denominations, as well as within the same denominations.

These obstacles and freedoms both inspired and helped to forge the diverse variety of spiritual practices that are a hallmark of the United States today. The mere idea of being able to practice religion freely offered hope to the immigrant people who were seeking a religious refuge; in time, however, the descendents of these same immigrants who initially sought and fought for their religious freedom would, at times, become intolerant and unbending in their views of others who would be following their own version of religious freedom, condemning those who chose not to follow a mainstream religion and dogma as viewed by the majority, but to pursue their own spiritual truth. These multiple perspectives ranging from widespread acceptance to severe persecution aided in the shaping of the religious consciousness of America, and can only enrich rather than detract from any study of a specific orientation, hence is included as a core element of this dissertation.

1.1 *Early Times*

The huge land masses located between the Asian and Euro-African continents, now known as North and South America, have ancient religious traditions like those of other primal civilizations. These origins date back tens of thousands of years to time immemorial. The indigenous peoples who inhabited the whole of the North and South American continents practiced animistic-based religions that were centered on elaborate ceremonies, some involving ritual, sacrifice, and reverence to nature and supreme beings. "During all this time religious knowledge was transmitted through the spoken word (beliefs and myths) and through imitative behavior (rituals)." (Hulkrantz, 23)

North America (the area known today as Mexico, The United States, and Canada) was home to a variety of indigenous people whose religious traditions often concentrated on the transformation of spirits into gods and guardian spirits (Albanese, 29); nature worship; animal totems; and even blood sacrifice of humans and animals. The tradition of the early peoples serve to illustrate and exemplify how religion has always been an integral and vibrant part of the human experience and is, in a sense, a foundation for later religious traditions which promulgated throughout the New World, based, in part, on these indigenous peoples' ancient observances and practices. Later, modern-religion that will come to the United States from across the Atlantic will also metamorphose to a certain degree, adopting certain aspects, and mirroring others, that are ancient in origin.

The indigenous peoples of North America viewed religion as a way to connect to the divine that is found in all of nature. This animistic belief system focused on ritual and ceremonies that celebrated shamans and their psychic gifts; special dreams were later transformed into ceremonies that were acted out in ritual dramas (Albanese, 29); these interpretive stories were later passed down in an oral tradition, told and retold, for subsequent generations.

The primary purpose of all ritualistic and ceremonial acts of Native Americans was to harmonize with nature:

> Harmony with the natural (and sacred) world, they believed, conferred power in the hunt, in the field, in war, or in government. Power was thought to come from the solemn recitation of origin accounts that brought Indian peoples into harmony with their beginnings. (Albanese, 29)

Belief in a supreme being, the Great Spirit, an almighty creator, is central to many of the belief systems of indigenous peoples. Living a life that revered the sacredness of nature was one way to connect to the divine and to become more spiritually connected to the creator. This reverence to nature is a hallmark of Native American religious traditions and belief systems.

The general labeling of indigenous peoples as "Indians," and later as "Native Americans," is too simplistic to encompass adequately the rich and unique cultural differences that exist between tribes and nations. The various groups of indigenous peoples were (and still are today) comprised of hundreds of tribes, and within these tribal groups, each used their own unique language and had its own societal and religious traditions.[1]

In general terms, the majority of tribes are divided by modern researchers into two basic groups: hunter-gatherer and agricultural. The hunter-gatherer tribes tended to wander the plains, moving easily to follow good hunting; the agricultural-based tribes tended to set up city-like dwellings that were stationary in order to grow and farm agriculture as food.

> The Paleolithic [Old Stone Age] was followed by Neolithic, or New Stone Age, about 10,000 BCE. This was the time when many hunters turned into primitive farmers. In the following millennia pastoral nomadism developed out of this agriculture in places where the cultivated lands met the grasslands and deserts. The world of the farmers and herdsmen is still with us. There is every reason to expect that their religious practices resemble those of their prehistoric predecessors. (Hulkrantz, 23)

Each group, however, had very distinct differences in religion and in how they practiced their indigenous beliefs. These were influenced by their hunter-gatherer or agricultural-based predilections. For instance, the Oglala-Sioux people, who hunted on the plains, "possessed one calendric ritual in the sun dance; for the Hopi [agricultural farmers], every rite depended on the cycle of the seasons. Desire for harmony with nature, in their case, was expressed in ritual harmony with its changing seasons; transformation, so central for all Native Americans, here meant following the movements of nature through cyclic time." (Albanese, 38)

> In the absence of scientific knowledge, ancient civilizations...created mythologies to explain origination (how they came into existence), of good and evil, the natural cycle of the seasons, weather, and the motions of the sun, the moon, and the stars. Such natural phenomena were explained by a body of stories that centered around gods, goddesses, and heroes. (Nelson, 338)

An example of the Sioux peoples' belief system is the mythology of how humans came to be on earth. The Sioux used elaborate traditional accounts to

---

1. It is certainly a misnomer to refer categorically to all Native American people, Native American culture, and Native American religion as one. Historically, this has been done solely for the convenience of contrasting, in general terms, the indigenous people who existed in what is now the United States with their European counterparts who immigrated there. "In reality, about 550 different Indian societies and distinct languages have been identified in North America, and even four decades ago, about 150 Native American languages were still being used north of the Rio Grande." (Albanese, 25)

explain their origins involving Trickster spirits, and a variety of sacred animals, to recount how they came into being:

> The traditional account of the Oglala's [Sioux] origin, like that of many another Indian people, concerns their emergence from the earth—in this case through the intrigues of a Trickster figure, Inktomi the Spider. Through a wolf, Inktomi wooed the people with food and clothing until Tokahe and three strong companions came to the upper world to investigate its virtues for themselves. Here, Inktomi plied them with more gifts and promised them youth, so that they returned to the people in the world below with glowing tales of what they had experienced. Although the old chief and old woman warned of cold wind and the need for hunting in the upper realm, Tokahe led out six families. The results were not as fortunate as they had hoped, and the children cried for food while Inkotmi laughed. Yet all was not lost, for they met the Old Man and Old Woman, who taught them to hunt, clothe themselves, and make tipis. Oglala life had begun: for the tradition, Tokahe and the six families were the first people in the world. (Albanese, 31-32)

This rendition of the beginning of the world is not so dissimilar to other cultures that were being formed half-a-world away, which also incorporated Tricksters, animal totems, and the tug of war between good and evil. The remarkable fact about this is that these stories in the indigenous cultures are seemingly generated independently without direct contact with the other cultures, leading one to conclude that as humanity progressed intellectually throughout the world, the innate need to explain phenomena and facts not easily explained was (and still is) a part of the global human condition. Perhaps a collective world consciousness may explain, in part, why peoples from different ethnic and cultural backgrounds, with no opportunity to exchange ideas, created remarkably similar stories to explain their creation. Some sort of creation-story is the focal point of all ancient religions, including Christianity and Judaism,[2] which offer inspirational and spiritual accounts of how the world began and how the human race came into being.

The Oglala legend, as well as the story of Adam and Eve being cast out of paradise in the Jewish and Christian traditions, illustrates how similar religious philosophy really is. The Judeo-Christian rendition of how humans came to inhabit the earth involved a Trickster (Satan posing as a serpent) which tempted Eve to

---

2. The actual creation story for Jews and Christians has two versions in the Bible. The first account is found in Genesis 1:1-2:3 and the second is found in Genesis 2:4-25. Upon close inspection, these two versions vary greatly from one another.

eat fruit from the forbidden tree.[3] From that moment, all was changed and Adam and Eve were cast out of the Garden of Eden and forced to fend for themselves—the man relegated to toiling and working the hard earth, and the woman enduring extreme pain during childbirth, destined to be ruled by her husband.[4]

In contrast, the Hopi people of the American Southwest have several sacred stories that relate to how people came into being that prominently displays feminine symbolism in a positive light. One such story tells how the Hopi people emerged from the womb of a clearly feminine Mother Earth. "Each Hopi village had its own slightly different version of the origins of things, but there was general agreement on the major motifs. In one version from Oriabi,[5] two Hard Being women (deities of hard objects such as shells, corals, turquoise, and beads) caused dry land to appear and then created birds, animals, a woman and a man." (Albanese, 37)

Again, this closely resembles the Judeo-Christian creation story where God created the heavens and the earth (but in six days and rested on the seventh, making this day holy). God created light, then day, then night; the sky was created to separate the waters from the waters; masses of dry land were created which were separated by the waters, that contained the vegetation, such as trees and plants; the sun, moon, stars and seasons were created; living creatures to inhabit the seas

---

3. The story of the Trickster (serpent) tempting Eve with promises of all-knowing knowledge like that of the gods can be found in Genesis 3:4-5: "And the serpent said unto the woman, Ye shall not surely die. For God doth know that in the day ye eat thereof, then your eyes shall be opened, and ye shall be as gods, knowing good and evil." (Holy Bible, King James Version)
4. The Judeo-Christian biblical accounts of creation and the humanization of Adam and Eve, as well as sagas of floods, famines and other notable world events can be found in other religious traditions, and from much earlier texts. "The biblical tale of the Fall is similar to other legends that contrast humanity's sufferings with an earlier time of perfection, a lost paradise or golden age. The Greeks' Pandora, like Eve, is responsible for the misfortunes of [humankind] because she disobeyed the order not to open the box out of which all the troubles of the world flew. The Blackfoot Indians of North America told of Feather-woman, a maiden who unleashes great ills when she digs up the great Turnip after being told not to do so. For this, she is cast out of Sky-Country. Like all such myths of a lost golden age, the biblical Fall is an attempt to account for the problems of evil and human suffering and a symbol of how humans have always yearned for a better, but possibly unattainable, world." (Davis, 54)
5. Oriabi is a village in the American Southwest that has been continuously occupied since around 1100 AD.

and the sky were created; animals of the earth were created, as well as man (Adam) from the dust of the earth and the breath of life, and from him, God takes a rib while he was sleeping and created woman (Eve), both in his own image. (Davis, 42-43)

Although largely patriarchal, the Judeo-Christian tradition does have prominent female symbolism which is not always portrayed in a positive light.[6] Christians, however, (especially Roman Catholics) hold the Virgin Mary (mother of Jesus) in a sacred and special position as the "Mother of God." In Christianity, just as in ancient primal religions, there seems to be a need to have some semblance of balance between the sexes—the energies of male and female—which offer alternatives to and enhances certain aspects of the particular belief systems. For Christians, Mary represents all that is compassionate and good; for the Hopi, Mother Earth, from which they all came, is the epitome of harmony and nature.

The Hopi tradition also offers a sacred story involving the "Spider Woman" who assists the Hopi with life on earth and aids humanity in creating the sun and moon which became important symbols, as well as objects of worship and reverence to the Hopi people.

> In another sacred story that related subsequent events, the people enjoyed a good life in the world below until evil entered into the hearts of the chiefs and the people, sexuality ran rampant, and hatred and quarreling grew apace. In their plight the chiefs tried to find escape, and they fashioned a Pawaokaya bird, singing over him to give him life. Meanwhile, the chiefs planted a pine tree and a reed beside it to reach the hole in the upper world. The bird flew in circles around the two "ladders," found the opening but found nothing else, and returned exhausted. So, according to the story, the chiefs made a humming bird and then a hawk who, in turn, repeated the search and also came back unsuccessful and exhausted. Finally, the chiefs created Motsni, who flew

---

6. As illustrated before, Eve has basically been blamed for the fall of humankind by tempting her husband Adam with the fruit from the forbidden tree; this is not entirely fair because one biblical version tends to suggest that they were equally responsible for disobeying God's order not to partake from the Tree of Good and Evil. Initially unaware of their nakedness, they unashamedly frolicked in the Garden of Eden becoming "one flesh" until they ate from the tree. At this point they realized their nakedness and hid from God; when God found them, immediately Adam blamed Eve for tempting him with the fruit that he ate from the forbidden tree, which relegated women to a subservient position from that point forward. Other examples of women portrayed negatively as scheming vixens or temptresses in the Bible are Bathsheba (see Holy Bible, 2 Samuel 11:4), Delilah (see Holy Bible, Judges 16:4), Jezebel (see Holy Bible, I Kings 19:2), and Salome (see Holy Bible, Mathew).

through to the upper world, found the site of present day Oraibi, and also encountered, sitting there alone, Masauwuu, or Skeleton. When he heard Motsni's tale, Skeleton explained that he was living in poverty but that people were welcome to join him. So they came, emerging from their plant ladders to the world above. Later, aided by Spider Woman, they fashioned a symbol that turned into the moon and another became the sun. The people had begun to make their way, and given in the story the gift of corn, small though it was, the Hopi were also given an identity. After a series of migrations, the clans arrived at their villages, and life as Hopi knew it began. (Albanese, 37)

There are several interesting correlations between ancient Hopi tradition and other religiously-based myths. First, the Hopi description of the "world below" is not too much unlike the biblical description of Sodom and Gomorrah[7]. Both were good places until human self-indulgence and sinful behavior ran amok, forcing the righteous to flee. Second, the Hopi account of "ladders" into the "upper world" correlates with the Christian story found in Genesis about a dream that Jacob had of a ladder extending from the earth to heaven; on it, angels were going up and down. (Davis, 81) Also, there is an ancient Egyptian belief of ladders reaching into the heavens for those who die to reach the afterlife. "The souls of the dead made their way to their abode in the 'other world' by a ladder, according to a very ancient view, or through a gap in the mountains of Abydos called Peka." (Budge, civ)

Ancient cultures, from Asia, to Africa, the Middle East, to the Americas, used a variety of religious tools to organize their ritualistic and religious ceremonies. Curiously, numbers have played a significant role in religious observance in many cultures and are thematically used in rituals and religious practice. To make sense out of everyday situations, the ancients could easily divide occurrences, like the seasons, and abstract ideas, like good and evil, into separate parts; this was in order to help bring balance and continuity into their lives.

Native Americans used numbers discerningly to show reverence in religious rites; the number four correlated with the seasons (spring, summer, autumn, and winter), and the directions (north, south, east, and west). "The number five was privileged as well, for it added the center to the four corners [of their dwellings

---

7. Sodom and Gomorrah, two cities in Palestine during the time of Abraham (the father of Jewish religion) were renowned for their wickedness and sinfulness. In fact, the modern term "sodomy" is derived from the city's name because both Genesis (19:4-8) and Jude (7) describe the unnatural lusts of men. Sexual promiscuity was so rampant in Sodom that Abraham declared that not even ten righteous men could be found there (Holy Bible, Genesis 18); so God destroyed it with fire and brimstone.

and in their ceremonies]. So, too, was [the number] seven, since to the four directions of the horizontal plane, seven added a vertical dimension: there was the zenith, or highest point, the nadir, or lowest depth, and the center, where the Indian person stood. Understood in this way, religion became a centering process in which Native Americans learned to maintain harmony by living equidistant from all boundaries. For them, life blossomed not just on the edges of society, as transformation had hinted, but also in the middle." (Albanese, 30)

In contrast, euro-based religions tended to divide things into two parts, perhaps in an attempt to balance two opposing forces like good and evil. This practice is similar to the ancient Chinese peoples' concept of "yin and yang" which sought to bring balance into their lives through counterbalancing the two powerful energies of male and female.

> Euro-Americans, on the other hand, tended to see the world in more divided ways. The sacred world of divine power was for them separated from the profane of ordinary existence. God, they believed, had caused the world to be, and his law governed its movements; in that sense, he could be said to dwell within it. Yet for them he also transcended it, and meanwhile his human creatures had increased the separation between God and the world by the fall of the Garden of Eden. In this understanding, sin had entered the world, and it had affected not just human beings, but all of nature. For Euro-Americans, the world had become a three-level affair: God tried to control human beings, and human beings tried to control nature. If there was rebellion in both cases, it only emphasized the fact that the seamless garment of one creation had been, in the Euro-American view, pulled apart. (Albanese, 30)

Religion, whether ancient or modern is not necessarily based on logic or reason; instead, it is an attempt to explain that which is supernatural in the best possible manner according to the historical, societal, and *ethno-religio* circumstances surrounding the people practicing it. The ancients—Greeks, Romans, Egyptians, Celtics, Sumerians, Africans, Native Americans, Aztecs, Toltecs, Incans and Aboriginal shamans—all had the common thread of creating religions with the supernatural to explain what could not be explained in an attempt to fill a spiritual, if not intellectual, void that is universal to all human beings—from ancient times to the present-day.

The proliferation of religion, though, is based on logic and reason in that it spread by individual contact, tradition, word of mouth, and by following set rituals and ceremonies in an organized way. This is what makes animistic, primal religions of America so unique—the rituals, customs, and traditions that were created from the indigenous peoples who sought to make sense of the world around them in the best way they knew how, and to revere a supreme being by offering respect, harmony, and balance to the nature around them.

Although overlapping in some of the more minor details of mythology, the ancient religions of the Native Americans stood in direct contrast, in many ways, to the customs and beliefs of the outsiders who were about to descend upon the East Coast of the North American continent in multitudes. With this imminent invasion came a whole new era of religion in America, that of forced conversion and paranoid suspicion of religious practices that were not mainstream, hence changing the future of religion in the United States of America, forever making it decidedly "Euro-based."

1.2 *European-Jewish Roots in the New World*

When Christopher Columbus first set out to find a new route to the Indies, he had no idea what was in store for him. Even on his deathbed, he never truly realized the magnitude of his discovery—the entire scope of what he happened upon on October 12, 1492. With Columbus' discovery and the determined desire to find riches and gold, came the peripheral obligation to garner converted souls for Christendom. Queen Isabel, the staunch and steadfast Catholic monarch of Spain, wanted the voyage to be that of not only discovery and fortune, but also a means to an end to convert heathen souls into Catholic Christians.

One historical phenomenon that occurred with those initial transatlantic voyages was the migration of Sephardic Jews to the New World. The year 1492 marks a major turning point in human history with Columbus' unwitting discovery, but it also marks a bleaker, more sinister historical occurrence—the Expulsion Edict exiling all Jews who refused to convert to Christianity from the borders of Spain.[8]

In the years leading up to 1492, tensions were rapidly reaching a crisis level in Spain between the Spanish-Jews who had made Spain their home since the Diaspora[9] and their Catholic-Christian compatriots who were in the political, religious, and social majority. To make matters worse, the Catholic Monarchs (King Ferdinand and Queen Isabel) were what could be labeled today as "super-Catholics" who not only dreamed of a united Spain where no foreign invaders lived,[10] but also a wholly Christian Spain where no non-Christians resided.

---

8. The Portuguese issued a similar Edict of Expulsion in 1497; coupled with the earlier Spanish Edict of Expulsion, these acts essentially banished Jewish people of both Spanish and Portuguese nationality from the whole of the Iberian Peninsula.

To avoid religious persecution, many Jews publicly "converted" (*conversos*) to Christianity, but in private continued to worship in the Jewish tradition. (Leonard, 41) These quasi-Jewish/Christians who were insincere in their conversion were labeled *maranos* or "swine" (Crow, 143) by the Spanish and were slowly denied religious freedom by the encroaching and zealous Christians. They were forced to either become sincere Christians or face the wrath of the Inquisition.[11] The Catholic Kings had been tolerant of the Jews who publicly converted, but still observed the Jewish Sabbath and other high holy days because of the wealth they possessed; initially, the Monarchs wanted to make sure that this tax-source remained in the country (Baer, 277). This all changed once the last Moorish stronghold of Granada was retaken by Spanish forces.

A new sense of national pride and an overzealous confidence swept the whole of the Spanish portion of the Iberian Peninsula, giving King Ferdinand and Queen Isabel, as well as a growing legion of anti-Semites throughout the country, more courage to persecute openly and publicly their Jewish comrades. In 1492, all of the anti-Jewish sentiment finally received official, royal approval with the Edict of Expulsion. The much feared and ruthless Inquisition was ready and willing to do what it needed to make these insincere Christians to see the error of their ways; as a way to rectify the heretical situation of "fallen Christians," those Sephardic Jews who had converted to Christianity, but who were accused (oftentimes falsely) of straying from their Catholic faith, reverting back to their Jewish roots, were brought before the Inquisition to repent their sins. Failure to do so often resulted in death.

---

9. The Diaspora was the scattering of the Jewish people from the land of Palestine into other parts of the world; this dispersion of the Jewish people actually occurred over a period of several centuries, but with the "great Diaspora that occurred with the destruction of Jerusalem, these people were forced to roam the Mediterranean basin, settling in several European countries. Spain, because of its seclusion and similar geographical composition, appealed to many of these Jewish refugees, thus becoming a popular location in which to settle." (Leonard, 37)
10. Spain's history is marked with a number of invasions by foreigners; Spain was under Roman, Visigoth and Muslim Rule for many centuries. In 1492, the Catholic Monarchs finally were able to expel the last of the Moorish invaders who had occupied Spain since 711, uniting Spain for the first time in more than a millennium (this period in Spanish history is known as "The Reconquest"). The Catholic Monarchs decided on a policy to "obliterate every trace of Moslem rule from the soil of Spain, so it was incumbent upon them to restore unity of religion within their borders." (Baer, 313)

These *conversos* and *maranos* feared for their lives. As many of these Jewish people began the arduous task of leaving the borders of Spain to scatter around all parts of Europe and the Mediterranean basin (Italy, Turkey and to liberal Holland) and even to Palestine (Albanese, 51), one option presented itself rather serendipitously: escape to the New World.

Even on that historic first voyage of Christopher Columbus, *maranos* were among the crew members who would settle in the New World. A century later, when the descendents of the Sephardic Jews in Holland ventured across the ocean to assist with Dutch settlements in Brazil, did the original *maranos* and new Dutch-Jews intermingle and help to build a prospering Jewish settlement in the New World. When the Portuguese reconquered the Dutch territory, again, the Jews were forced to flee—some to Dutch colonies in the Caribbean, some back to Holland, and some decided to go north to a vibrant new city called "New Amsterdam," a Dutch colony in North America (Albanese, 50).

> Moreover, from the beginning of their history in the New World, the Jews had repeated an age-old pattern of wandering. Moving from place to place through European history, they had no land that, without reservation, they could call home. Indeed their history of wandering was more ancient still…and although the origins of the Hebrew people are shrouded, their earliest representatives were nomads.....this nomadic sense was not only an external condition but also became internalized to shape Jewish religious experience and expression throughout history. Like Native Americans, the Jews were often forced to wander by the misfortunes of history. Like Native Americans, too, they dwelled in small, homogenous communities in which religion and peoplehood were inextricably blended. Indeed, some Americans told tales of a kinship between Jews and Indians. As early as the seventeenth century, stories circulated in the United States [*sic*] describing Native Americans as remnants of the lost tribes of Israel. (Albanese, 51)

These early Sephardic Jews would be joined in the early 1800's by their European cousins, the Ashkenazi, who would usher in a newer and much larger Jewish

---

11. The Inquisition is certainly a black page in Spanish history because it gave the Catholic Church, and the Inquisitors who were largely Catholic clergy, extraordinary powers to seek out and punish any heretics who had supposedly fallen from their faith. "The original victims of the Inquisition were not [practicing] Jews, but *maranos* suspected of having fallen from their new faith. The fact that many of these converts occupied important positions in the medical, professional, banking, tax-collecting, and industrial spheres was undoubtedly one of the reasons for their being hated by the poorer classes." (Crow, 145)

immigration to the United States. "When these German Jews came, there were only about 5,000 Jews in the United States out of a total population of some 13 million. Within the next half century, though, between 200,000 and 400,000 Jews from central Europe entered the country, and the sheer size of their presence transformed Jewish life in the New World," (Albanese, 53) and especially in the young United States of America.

As the original Jewish settlers from Brazil came to escape persecution in the new but sometimes inhospitable land of North America,[12] so did other European groups who wished to find a new kind of religious freedom, far from the shackles of organized religion in the Old World. Thus began a period of Reformation that included a new and unprecedented European-religion invasion from across the Atlantic to a new land—North America.

1.3 *The European-Religion Invasion*

There probably is not an American child of elementary school-age who has not heard or been taught the story of how the Pilgrims came to America to escape religious persecution. Upon their arrival to the New World, they initially came upon terribly hard times and nearly did not make it through that first severe winter. They survived only because they befriended a group of kind Native American inhabitants who helped them provisionally and later taught them how to live, grow and harvest crops, and survive in the inhospitable and unfamiliar environment they found themselves in. The first Thanksgiving to celebrate a bumper harvest after a year of hardship portrays a tale of ethno-religious intimacy between the early English Protestants and the Native American peoples.

> If intimacy is based on common elements between different peoples, the two groups did have something in common. For both, manyness was a social condition in which they lived and a feature of their mental landscape. Native Americans, as we have seen, dwelled in nations that in themselves possessed ethno-religious unity but were surrounded by other, separate Indian nations. English Protestants had left a land in which religious nonconformity meant that they had cultural ties with many of their compatriots but religious differences. (Albanese, 102)

---

12. Further south, on the Florida Peninsula, Catholic settlements were flourishing since the early 1500's. These evangelizing priests originally brought by Ponce de Leon established missions in which to spread the word of God. Although many missions failed, by 1565 St. Augustine had been founded and by the end of the century, tens of thousands of Indians had converted to Catholicism. (Albanese, 74)

What began as a rather congenial relationship eventually turned tumultuous as hoards of Protestant settlers began to invade the land the native peoples had inhabited for thousands of years.

The idea of Protestantism was first initiated by Martin Luther (1483-1546), and later by John Calvin (1509-1564).[13] On many levels, they both had extreme difficulty in accepting Catholic dogma and tradition; they wanted to "reform" the Catholic Church in order to peel away the many layers of ritual that seemed to dominate the Catholic liturgy service.

> ...the Reformers wanted to do two things. First, they wanted to bring about a clear division between extraordinary religion (attempts to reach God) and ordinary religion (aspects of human culture). Second, they wanted to purge Christianity of elements of the idea of correspondence that had crept in, returning to a purer version of the idea of causality. In other words, they wanted to emphasize a gap between the divine order of things and the natural human world. (Albanese, 103)

Strife and conflict plagued the new Protestant religions as vestiges of the old ways often interfered with the more progressive, and at the same time conservative, ideals of some of the worshipers. The Protestant Reformation, now a movement in its own right and already in its second century, was to cross the Atlantic in search of more religious freedom than was allowed in continental Europe; and in search of a new life-style in which to pursue religion as they pleased.

One group that especially identified with the often austere and simple surroundings of the Calvinist tradition was the Puritans. "The Puritans were a varied group of religious reformers who emerged within the Church of England during the middle of the sixteenth century. They shared a common Calvinist theology and common criticisms of the Anglican Church and English society and government." (Heyrman, 2002)

The Pilgrims, who landed at Plymouth Rock in what is now Massachusetts in 1620,[14] were Separatist Puritans (they no longer wanted to be a part of the Anglican tradition that was associated with the Church of England); they are by far the most revered group of religious exiles that ever entered the North American continent. They are the symbolic settlers that hold a special place of honor in Ameri-

---

13. It is interesting to note that John Calvin did not feel that Martin Luther went far enough in his reforms. He had a more austere vision of how a Protestant church service should be: the pulpit in the center-front of the sanctuary and no ornaments adorning the walls except for the Ten Commandments. (Albanese, 106)

can religious history, and are celebrated today every year on the fourth Thursday of November in the United States by families all over America who sit down to partake in the annual Thanksgiving feast with family and friends, reenacting that first Thanksgiving feast between the Pilgrims and the Native American Indians.

The arrival of the Pilgrims was only the first of many invasions by the Europeans looking for a new home in which to practice their religion freely. Unfortunately, with each wave of religious immigration, came more strife and turmoil for those already settled. Disputes between religious sects drove the newcomers further into the wilderness. The worst to fair, however, were the Native Americans and how they were treated by the white invaders; slowly, just because they could, the new immigrants pushed westward, encroaching upon land that had been a part of the indigenous peoples' lives for generations and generations. The initial neighborliness that occurred between the Pilgrims and the Native Americans who helped them was short-lived; as more and more Europeans came from across the Atlantic, the deeper the divide between them and the Indians.

In fact, just ten years after the arrival of the Pilgrims, another group of Puritans arrived and settled in Salem, Massachusetts. These Puritans would clearly set the pace for religious life in New England and early-America which continues to this day. By the end of the century, however, the offspring of these early Puritans who came to escape religious persecution would be embroiled in a religious scandal that would become their religious legacy—The Salem Witch Trials.

The occult, and the belief in occultism, were very much alive and well in America's early history. Although the European invaders were largely fundamentalist Christians, adhering strictly to the Bible and austere moral codes, there was nonetheless a dabbling and belief in the occult—both by learned and less educated people. In particular, belief in astrology and witchcraft was widespread throughout the colonies in the seventeenth and eighteenth centuries.

Astrology had been brought to the New World by Elizabethan subjects in the late 1500's who felt that it offered a scientific basis to explain phenomena more logically than mere superstition. It was embraced by the scholarly elite who repu-

---

14. In a historical side-note, the Pilgrims had originally fled England to Holland in order to escape religious persecution, but found the Netherlands to be much too liberal for their liking, so they petitioned the court of King James I of England to get permission to go to the Virginia Territory in America. Their ship, the Mayflower, sailed way off course and they landed much farther north than Virginia. As a group, they decided to settle there, but before disembarking from the ship, the Pilgrims agreed to and signed the "Mayflower Compact," a document outlining how they were to govern themselves.

diated the old beliefs that had no type of structure or interrelation to the material composition of the universe. (Albanese, 256)

> The colonists inherited this world of the Elizabethans. Like them, they continued to make a distinction between two kinds of astrology. First and most common was natural astrology, which concerned the relationship between the stars and other material things such as the rhythms of nature, the weather, and the human body. Second was judicial astrology, which probed the relationship between the stars and human choice and action. This second form of astrology implicitly challenged the Christian doctrine of freedom of the will, because it suggested to many that the stars controlled human destiny. Thus, it had traditionally been most subject to attack and least accepted. The colonists, however, readily used the ideas that they gained from natural astrology. Among the learned, this material was taught in textbooks used at Harvard and Yale, while it appeared in the private libraries of prominent individuals in the late seventeenth and early eighteenth centuries. Among less educated people, it was spread by means of the almanac, which along with the Bible was found in virtually every colonial household. (Albanese, 257)

Astrology offered people order in their lives and formed the basis for an ordinary religion where they could find some type of pattern in which they could live their lives at any given moment, depending upon the placement of planets in relation to the stars.

In addition to astrology, many colonists actively practiced and believed in witchcraft. Originally brought over by the Germans to the Pennsylvania area, this type of witchcraft most closely resembled paganism (which somewhat resembles the modern Wicca movement) in that it revered nature; this involved ritualistic ceremonies to mark natural events like the summer and winter solstices and equinoxes. "They built bonfires out of trees and bushes, raised ritual chants, and asked sacred powers they invoked to bless the place where they were making a home. The Woman in the Wilderness, as their community came to be called, offered its inhabitants a blend of pagan, Christian, and Jewish elements."[15] (Albanese, 258)

Many of the rituals and traits of these early witches very closely resemble modern day mediums and psychics. Just like modern mediums, the "Cunning Folk" (as they were called) were thought to possess special gifts for divining the future, the laying of hands to heal the sick, the ability to find lost items, and the use of divining rods to find precious metals. (Albanese, 258-259) As well, many were thought to be able to commune with spirits who had passed into transition from this earth plane, making contact psychically. These witches possessed powers that

A History of Religion in America from Early Times through the 19th Century   17

were similar to those of Indian shamans of the time. All of this dabbling in the occult eventually would lead to suspicion of people who were thought to be witches because of eccentric behavior or mannerisms, curious indictments that would become a "witch-hunt"—a term still used today to refer to situations where people are persecuted in the public domain.

In 1691 and 1692, interest in the occult by a group of young Puritan school girls from Salem Village in the Massachusetts Bay colony would have irreversible and deadly consequences for nineteen of the town's people; what initially began as an adolescent's game quickly turned into a nightmare when these young girls began to exhibit strange behavior, prompting their parents to attribute immediately their hysterical episodes to possession by the devil and witchcraft. When urged to identify those who were responsible for bewitching them, they initially pointed their fingers at three local women and a young widower minister. The accusations widened to include hundreds of people, spreading to other Massachusetts Bay communities.

> Events at Salem Village (later Danvers), in the Massachusetts Bay colony, began with Betty Parris, daughter of the town minister, and her cousin Abigail Williams. The two girls, one nine and the other eleven years old, spent many hours with Tituba, a slave from the West Indies, who apparently taught the children something of the magical traditions she had learned. The magic lore attracted other girls in the village, many of them teenagers. Then, when Betty Parris and subsequently Abigail Williams fell into trances—screaming, crying, barking like dogs, and moving on all fours—the diagnosis of witchcraft was pronounced. Neither doctors nor ministers could help, and so events moved to the local courthouse. In a gradual series of escalations, more and more witches were named by the afflicted girls. There was Tituba and then Sarah Good and Sarah Osborne. Before the trials ended, nineteen witches had been hanged, and one, a man, had been pressed to death. (Albanese, 259)

---

15. Today, many Jews and Christians automatically associate "witchcraft" with black magic and satanic cults. In fact, white magic and witchcraft predates Judaism and Christianity by millennia, perhaps back to prehistoric times, before more modern belief systems incorporated a red horned devil named Lucifer. "Modern witches tend to refer to their religion as *wicca*, the feminine form of the Old English *wicce*, which itself means 'witch.' Both male and female followers are known as witches, although the cult itself is decidedly matriarchal, with the High priestess of each coven looked on as a personification (in some rites even the incarnation) of the Great Mother Goddess who is the principal deity of the movement. Consort of the Goddess, personified by the coven's High Priest, is the Horned God, Cernunnos, often quite incorrectly identified with the Devil by those outside the cult." (Campbell, *et al*, 230)

The occult, up to this point, was largely considered to be rather harmless and based more on superstition than any real conjuring of witchcraft. "The Satanic witchcraft of Salem Village was a negative instance of occult religion in the colonies. For others, the old fertility religion of witchcraft had been more benign, and its ordering of life through nature had been a meaningful way to think and act in an agricultural society. Like astrology, it brought ordinary religion to countless numbers of people and directed their everyday lives in ways they desired." (Albanese, 260)

The Salem Witch Trials, however, changed all of this when it was believed that townspeople were casting spells upon the girls. Initially, the trials focused not on people who dabbled in some sort of magical sorcery as much as those that the powers that were believed to be Satanic—witches who made a pact with the devil in order to be able to possess and cast spells on others. Oddly, the Puritans did find religious freedom in the New World, but only for themselves. The Puritans maintained a tight grip over the Massachusetts Bay Colony through fear and intimidation, ruled by an elite and pious minority considered to be living saints. No tolerance—especially religious and social—was allowed.

How an entire community could be swept up into such a religious fervor that they would be so inclined to turn on friends and neighbors, solely relying on and basing their judgments on the hysterical fits of a group of young girls? How could a community of rational, God-fearing people become so obsessed? An underlying economic reason may partially explain why, based upon jealousy "and resentments festering among some Salem Village families who were faltering and falling behind in a society being rapidly transformed by the quest for profit and material comforts." (Heyrman, 2002) Many of the accused were outcasts and pariahs in the community. Later, jealousy and ego would play a part in the widespread accusations, based on spite and envy.

Another possible explanation could be rooted in a misogynistic tendency of the Puritans because a disproportionately high number of the accused were women who stood to inherit property and other assets. (Heyrman, 2002) Also, the clergy of Salem felt that people were losing sight of the important aspects of a godly life, and needed to be reeled in to atone for their indiscretions. In the years leading up to the bewitching, the faithful had been shaken by a series of calamities including disease, famine, and Indian raids on their community. The dictatorship-like theocracy was rapidly crumbling, causing widespread fear and guilt for past indiscretions (hence, they believed that God was punishing them for straying from the path of righteousness, culminating in a weakness that allowed the devil to enter their community and possess their children).

The feelings of sin, shame and guilt that plagued the early Puritans still has its iron grip on American society today. Much of the moral and social code that is a part of American culture can be traced back to this era of religious piousness, intolerance, and blind faith. The Salem Witch Trials broke the power and infallibility of the Puritan clergy, disallowing church officials from meting out judgments based on literal interpretations of the Bible, and administrating civil government based on Puritan ideas of justice. The trials created a new age of individual rights and a sense of rebellion against authority. Never would the Puritans ever wield such religious and social power again. A new age of religion was about to begin.

1.4 *African-American Religion*

Beginning in the fifteenth century, when the first Africans were transported across the Atlantic to serve as slaves in the New World, a rich religious tradition had started. These early slaves brought with them a wide range of local beliefs and practices—products of the diverse cultures, traditions and linguistic groups from which they all came. (Maffly-Kipp, 2000)

> This diversity reflected the many cultures and linguistic groups from which they had come. The majority came from the west coast of Africa,[16] but even within this area religious traditions varied greatly. Islam had also exerted a powerful presence in Africa for several centuries before the start of the slave trade: an estimated twenty percent of enslaved people were practicing Muslims. Catholicism had even established a presence in areas of Africa by the sixteenth century.
>
> Preserving African religions in North America proved to be very difficult. The harsh circumstances under which most slaves lived—high death rates, the separation of families and tribal groups, and the concerted effort of white owners to eradicate "heathen" (or non-Christian) customs—rendered the preservation of religious traditions difficult and often unsuccessful. Isolated songs, rhythms, movements and beliefs in the curative powers of roots and the efficacy of a world of spirits and ancestors did survive well into the nineteenth century. But these were increasingly combined in creative ways with the vari-

---

16. This area of West Africa (and the Congo), where the majority of the African slaves came from, is known as the Angola region. "They included Mandinke, Yoruba, Ibo, Bankongo, Ewe, Fon, and other nations, some of them followers of Islam and many of them practitioners of traditional African religions." (Albanese, 194)

ous forms of Christianity to which Europeans and Americans introduced African slaves. (Maffly-Kipp, 2000)

The religious practices of Africans were in many ways analogous to those of Native Americans, offering sacred accounts of the origin of the world, belief in gods, coupled with elaborate ritual and magical practices. However, before they even arrived, the African slaves had been stripped of all that was familiar to them. Their captors purposefully separated members of families, tribes, and kinfolk in order to keep them from conversing in their own languages and practicing religious rituals. Also, it was feared by their white captors that if the slaves were allowed to speak their own language they could plan a revolt. Being treated as "goods" to be sold, their white captors wanted to ensure that they were beaten into submission in order to follow the strict rules of their new slave-life, making them more appealing to prospective buyers.

> Yet legal fiction could never hide the fact that the slaves were people and not inert objects. More than that, they were *a* people who, although they had been warring enemies in Africa, had also been very much alike. They shared a basic view of life and the relationship of the Gods to the human condition. They spoke for the most part in dialects—although not easily translatable into one another—of perhaps two major languages. So there was much that blacks could mutually affirm as they began to take up the remnants of their lives in the New World. Their fundamental ways of looking at religion and at life had been and would remain similar. Their common experience of servitude would give them another and different set of bonds to share. (Albanese, 196)

Despite the efforts of their white captors to forbid them from maintaining any semblance of their previous lives in Africa, the slaves were able to retain their culture and in the process, an African-American religion was created. "It was built on pieces of a common African past, reconstructed to provide strength and solace in the new situation. It was built, too, on the experiences that the slaves endured in America, mixing their sense of involuntary presence into their religion. And finally, it was built with materials that came to the slaves from the religion of their masters. African-American religion was constructed in part from the Judeo-Christian tradition. Together, these three sources—the West African background, the condition of slavery in the present, the language of European Christianity—provided the elements for a religion to fit the conditions of a distinct people in a new land." (Albanese, 196-197)

> By 1810 the slave trade to the United States had officially ended and the slave population began to increase naturally, making way for the preservation and transmission of religious practices that were, by this time, truly "African-American." This transition coincided with the period of intense religious revivalism known as "awakenings." In the southern states, where the institution of slavery still prevailed, increasing numbers of slaves converted to evangelical religions such as Methodist and Baptist faiths. Many clergy within these denominations actively promoted the idea that all Christians were equal in the sight of God, a message that provided hope and sustenance to the slaves. They also encouraged worship in ways that many Africans found to be similar, or at least adaptable, to African worship patterns, with enthusiastic singing, clapping, dancing, and even spirit-possession. (Maffly-Kipp, 2000)

The slaves were very adept at creating their own style of worship involving signals, passwords, and messages not discernible to whites, incorporating songs with double-meanings in the form of "Negro Spirituals" that often spoke of *religious salvation*, but really meant *freedom from slavery*. (Maffly-Kipp, 2000)

The Emancipation Proclamation, signed by President Abraham Lincoln in 1863, abolished slavery in the South. However, true freedom was not won by the slaves until after the US Civil war ended in 1865. Millions of slaves were freed and with their newly found freedom from their white masters came another equally important newly found freedom—that of "freedom of religion." Black churches were formed all over the South in the decades following the US Civil War, giving the ex-slaves the opportunity to worship as they pleased and in a manner that suited them and their cultural backgrounds.

From the end of slavery and the advent of newly formed black congregations in already existing "white" denominations, a new shift was about to occur in the North that would be of great importance to American-religious history. The mid-to-late 1800's, ushered in a "mini-reformation" of sorts—the creation of "American-made religions" that had their roots not in Europe, but solely in the United States of America.

1.5 *American-Made Religions of the 19th Century*

For the first time in the history of the United States, three major religions would be formed—each as a result of a miracle[17]—in close geographic proximity, and all within decades of one another.[18] Mormonism, Spiritualism, and Christian Science are all American-made religions that, unlike previous religions that were imported,[19] were all founded and created in the context of the American experience. These three main religions would eventually be promulgated from the shores of America to other parts of the world, reversing the earlier trend of modern religions only coming from outside the borders of the United States.

Mormonism

The first religion in the triumvirate to be formed was Mormonism, formally called "The Church of Jesus Christ of Latter-Day Saints," and was founded in 1830, with only six members, by Joseph Smith in upstate, western New York. (Ostling, XVI) Mormons (followers of Mormonism) believe that Smith experienced a true miracle when he found, and later translated, a divinely inspired record of early human history and religion of America. This record is called *The Book of Mormon*, which is considered to be the sacred text of Mormonism, and largely forms the foundation for the religion as a whole, along with Smith's own writings[20] and the Bible. All of these, when combined, form the Mormon scriptures.

> In the Book of Mormon, the scriptures on golden tablets given to Smith by the Angel Moroni, God's biblical work was extended to the Americas, by one leading apostle's reckoning, in the period from 2247 B.C. to A.D. 421. The book tells about Lamanites, Native Americans who are considered by Mormons to be part of the Ten Lost Tribes of Israel.[21] Jesus Christ came to preach to these Indians, the book declares, and for some time, many centuries before Columbus, an American church flourished, then fell into apostasy until the truth and the true church were restored through Joseph Smith. The tablets foretold the prophet's name, Joseph, Jr. (II Nephi 3). Besides giving these new scriptures, God commissioned his American prophet to revise significant por-

---

17. The definition of "miracle," according to Webster's New Collegiate Dictionary, is "an extraordinary event manifesting divine intervention in human affairs." (p. 727) It can also be defined simply as "a remarkable thing." Spiritualists, as a rule, do not accept the belief in miracles; instead, Spiritualists maintain that all occurrences in this world and in the spirit world are governed by Natural Law [See Appendix F.] and there can be no happenings above or beyond this law as it is "God's Law." (Barnes h, 7) The Christian Scientists, following a similar logic, define a miracle as "a divinely natural occurrence that must be learned humanly." (p. 727) For the sake of simplicity, the word "miracle" has been used to describe the fantastical events which accompanied the formation of each of the American-made religions described herein.
18. Mormonism was founded in 1830, Spiritualism in 1848, and Christian Science in 1879.

tions of the Bible that Smith taught had been corrupted by Jews and Christians. (Ostling, XIX)

For the time period, during the early to mid 1800's, these tenets were perceived as being quite radical and extreme (if not fanatical) by those not associated with this new American religion, causing many to view the beliefs and principles connected to this religion with suspicion and contempt. Smith's rendition of religious history of America in the Book of Mormon gave the United States something that it had never had before—the establishment of a biblical past from Hebrew origins that incorporated the indigenous peoples in such a way that made them a part of world-Jewish history, dating back to the time of Jesus Christ. (Albanese, 226)

Apart from the miraculous story of how Smith came upon the sacred scriptures, other beliefs and ideas put forward by the prophet Smith were quite progressive and even welcomed by a certain stratum of society that had become disenchanted with the Calvinistic and Puritanical doctrines that seemed to be inherent in most of the Protestant religions of the day. Mormonism offered a fresh, seemingly modernistic approach to salvation that attracted many people. "It denied original sin and stressed individual moral choice, proclaiming that every human could progress toward godhood. It was a religious version of the American dream: Every man presented with unlimited potential. Its theology

---

19. As mentioned earlier, with the exception of indigenous religions of the Native American people, all organized religions had been brought by immigrants to the New World and to the United States. The majority of the religions being practiced in America during the mid to late1800's were based in belief systems that originated in Europe from the time of the Protestant Reformation—mainly England, France, Holland, and Germany for the Protestant denominations; and of course, Catholicism and Judaism were imported from the time the New World was discovered. The French Huguenots and Calvinists, English Puritans, German Lutherans and Baptists, German Amish and Pennsylvania Dutch Amish, as well as the Hutterites, Shakers and Quakers, were all imports. Once they were brought to America, they of course experienced changes and modifications based on that which precipitated (in many of the cases) the reason why the adherents to these religions initially chose to come to America, which was to escape religious persecution. Another group, the Millerites (and later The Seventh Day Adventists) originated as a "doomsday cult" around its leader, Williams Miller. When the appointed day of the return of Jesus came and gone, the movement waned, but never completely died out. Today, Adventists place an emphasis on the last days and the belief that Christ will soon return.

provided a highly idiosyncratic blend of biblical literalism and strict moralism, a characteristic emphasis on disciplined self-reliance." (Ostling, XIX)

> For Mormons, in the nineteenth century and now, humans were not dependent on God for existence [a belief that was at clear odds with the Puritan interpretation of what constituted piousness]. They accomplished their tasks through their own efforts, through merit and good work, and through achievements that brought its appropriate reward. Mormons said that their souls had preexisted in a spirit realm before entering their present bodies.[22] But in Mormon teaching there was no pronounced dualism between spirit and matter. Things spiritual were seen as a refined essence of the material world—all spirit as matter—so that God, as well as humanity, testified to the sacredness of matter. Moreover, since it was held that Mormons themselves could become "as Gods," they moved toward a polytheism in which divinity, as a principle, would be embodied in many Gods. Likewise, the Gods that the Mormons aspired to become were said to possess material bodies. Because of this teaching, the human body already held a privileged status. Mormon prohibitions of the use of alcohol, tobacco, and caffeine and their sparing use of meat were indications of their respect for the body. (Albanese, 228-229)

Still, though, the majority of people in western New York was skeptical of this new-fangled religion and preferred that the new converts to this belief system move away from their area. So, the Mormons, in an attempt to practice their religion freely and without persecution, kept moving westward from New York to escape the ill-treatment and oppression by neighbors and the general community. First, Smith took his flock to Kirtland, Ohio, then to Independence, Missouri.

---

20. The Book of Mormon was divinely inspired and channeled by Smith. "As Smith told the story, seven years earlier the angel Moroni had appeared before him and told him of a book written on gold plates and buried in a hill outside Manchester, New York. Then on September 22, 1837, after other visitations from Moroni, the plates were turned over to Smith. Over the next twenty-four months, Smith and a few trusted associates, using special, ancient, 'seer' stones, 'translated' the Egyptian hieroglyphics of the plates into English. When they had finished this arduous task, Smith reported, holy fire consumed the plates." (Scott, 2000)
21. It should be noted that "from 1862 on, Mormons, with their accounts of Indian descent from the tribes of Israel, became the most successful among missionaries to the Hopi [Indians]. It was not necessary, though, to abandon Hopi tradition and ceremony to embrace Mormonism...." (Albanese, 42)
22. As will be shown later, this belief is similar to that of Spiritualists.

> From the beginning, Joseph Smith and his followers provoked ridicule for Mormonism's seemingly magical if not superstitious origins, and opposition as a heresy that dared to claim itself "the only true and living church upon the face of the whole earth." Feeling themselves persecuted by their upstate New York neighbors, they organized separate Mormon settlements in Kirtland, Ohio, and in Independence, Missouri. Kirtland was the seat of the prophet where in 1836 the Mormons built and consecrated an elaborate temple. In both places they isolated themselves from their neighbors, and, much as other nineteenth-century religious communitarian groups like the Shakers or the Amish, set up cohesive economically self-sufficient and largely self-governing communities, setting themselves up not simply as a group of worshippers but as a people apart. (Scott, 2000)

It is interesting to compare this isolationist trend of the Mormons to earlier peoples who also experienced persecution, and, in turn decided to isolate themselves from the outside world, setting up self-sufficient, self-governing communities that depended largely on the communal effort of the group—most strikingly, the Puritans. Why was there so much suspicion of those outside the confines of the belief system? Why did these groups distrust the outside world so much?

For both traditions—the Mormon and Puritan—the widespread persecution they experienced made them weary of anyone and everyone who did not follow their belief system. The Puritans believed more, perhaps, that Satan was at the root of all temptation causing them to obsess about the dichotomy between good and evil more fervently than the Mormons; but the Mormons experienced a fear that was more earth-based than ethereal in that outsiders were violent toward them solely because of their unique belief system, and hence made them fear for their lives.

The settlements in both Ohio and Missouri did not offer the Mormon pilgrims the security and freedom to worship as they had initially hoped. (Fraser, 18) By this time, the Mormon movement was gaining in numbers, economic prosperity, and influence—when all combined, this meant (in the eyes of their detractors) they were building an all encompassing power-base, which to those outside the confines of the religion found threatening. Again, the faithful set out to find a new home in which to settle after a fierce attack by the community in Independence, Missouri occurred in 1833. "Opposition also intensified back in Ohio and by early 1838 most of the Kirtland Mormons, led by the prophet, had departed for Missouri, where they joined forces with their Independence coreligionists who settled in a county organized especially for them. Still, the tension between the Mormons and their Gentile neighbors escalated into armed conflict, and the saints were forced to flee once again." (Scott, 2000)

> In the spring of 1839, nearly 15,000 Mormons crossed into Illinois, where they purchased the town of Commerce, which they renamed Nauvoo. Granted a charter that made Nauvoo virtually an independent municipality with its own court system and militia, the Mormon settlement by 1844 had become the largest city in the state. (Scott, 2000)

The year 1844 witnessed a much more ominous occurrence that shook the religion's foundation to its very core. No matter how successful the Mormons were in organizing and prospering their religion, recurrent persecution followed and dogged them wherever they went. Finally, after Smith revealed a plan that organized the Kingdom of God on earth where he would be "king," he was arrested and then taken from jail and murdered by a militia group that was called upon to protect the state against a possible Mormon uprising. Critics regard Mormonism as a cult because it grew around its leader; Mormons categorically consider themselves to belong to a religion. Every religion needs a symbolic reason to exist—Joseph Smith's murder most certainly aided in propelling him to martyrdom. His murder, hence, would not signal the end of Mormonism, but only a new beginning.

> After Smith's murder, the Mormons regrouped and under the leadership of Brigham Young, selected as Smith's successor as prophet and president, undertook the "great trek" westward to the Utah territory, where they established a virtual Mormon kingdom, centered in Great Salt Lake City, which they called the State of Deseret. In Utah, under the long leadership of Young (1847-1877), building on the precepts of plural marriage and patriarchal, prophetic governance promulgated by Joseph Smith, the Mormons established a unique, cohesive, economically sufficient, and thriving society. (Scott, 2000)

Just as Brigham Young was in the midst of settling the Utah Territory, creating a Mormon "kingdom" that would serve forevermore as the center of Mormon thought and the Mormon religion, another occurrence on the other side of the United States would happen in 1848 that would create America's second "homemade" religion—Spiritualism.

Spiritualism

The beginning of modern Spiritualism is often associated with an occurrence that happened in a small cottage in western, upstate New York in a little town called Hydesville, on March 31, 1848.[23] Two sisters, Kate and Maggie Fox, discovered

---

23. For a detailed timeline of Spiritualism, see Appendix A.

that they could summon a rational response from some mysterious rapping noises that had been plaguing them at night for more than a week. On this particular night, they realized that the rapping sounds would respond to their hand-clapping; soon they were able to work out a code by which they were able to communicate with this disincarnate spirit that was haunting their home. They affectionately referred to this spirit-entity as "Mr. Splitfoot."

The Fox Family had desperately tried to figure out how and why these rappings were occurring. Windows were checked, doors were secured. "For more than a week the family had been tormented by the enigmatic sounds, always in the evening after they had gone to bed. On the first night they had gotten up, lighted candles, searched the entire house and found nothing." (Jackson, 1) But on March 31, 1848, the mysterious rappings began to respond intelligently, rather than randomly. When one of the girls would clap her hands, a rapping followed to imitate it. Mrs. Fox, the girls' mother, was aghast with fear and shock, knowing that these sounds were coming from beyond this earthly world.

Together, Mrs. Fox and her daughters began to ask questions.[24] Mrs. Fox first asked the mystery rapper to count to ten—it did. She then asked the spirit to reveal the ages of her daughters—it gave a rap for each year of each girl's age correctly. She asked if it was a human being making these rapping noises—there was no answer. She then asked it to make two raps if it was a spirit—it did. She continued by asking if the spirit had been injured in their home; this question followed with two raps. Mrs. Fox then asked if the perpetrator was still living; again two raps sounded.

> By means of the rappings, Mrs. Fox was able to establish that the "spirit" was that of a male, aged thirty-one at the time of his death. He had been murdered in the house and his remains buried in the cellar. Further, his family consisted of a wife, two sons, and three daughters, all living at the time he was killed. His wife, however, had died two years ago. (Jackson, 4)

Still unable to believe what had just happened, Mrs. Fox wanted to have her neighbors come to witness this supernatural event. Again, the rappings occurred to the disbelief of all those present. Eventually, they were able to work out more details of the deceased person's demise and figured out an exact location in the house's cellar where his body had been buried. They determined that the man was a peddler and his name was "Charles B. Rosna."[25] This is the miracle associ-

---

24. See Appendix B for the transcripts of sworn statements by Mr. and Mrs. Fox and other eye-witnesses.

ated with the founding of Spiritualism—intelligible communication with the spirit world.

Several far reaching features emerged from those initial rappings: 1) it was proven that communication that was intelligible could be made with spirits; 2) certain people, like the Fox sisters, were naturally gifted with the ability to make this communication; and 3) communication could be facilitated by means of a code. The events on this night started a movement of the likes the world had never seen before. Soon, people from all over were flocking to the Fox cottage to witness this supernatural phenomenon. The birth of psychic mediumship, and some time later, the religion known as Spiritualism, had begun.

To non-believers, this whole episode that started the Spiritualist movement seemed a bit fantastical, but to those who had experienced bumps in the night and who had either seen or communicated with spirits, it seemed to be a logical progression of the soul, and only natural that the disincarnate spirit should want to speak and contact those left behind on the earth plane. No logical explanation could be found to explain those mysterious rappings that night, so the practice of communicating with spirits not of this world began to be commonplace. Seemingly overnight, mediums were everywhere, claiming to be able to speak with dead relatives and friends.

> The press loved the story, and Margaret and Catherine's older sister Mrs. Leah Fish, was quick to capitalize on the publicity by turning her younger sisters' ability to communicate with the entity into a stage act. As more and more people came to see the Fox sisters communicate with the dead man, more and more phenomena happened; more "spirits" began to communicate, and the spirits that were communicating gradually became better known and more famous personages (according to *Harper's Encyclopedia of Mystical & Paranormal Experience*, they had the spirit [of] Ben Franklin communicate with them during this time), and physical phenomena would occasionally occur (tables and objects would move on their own, or sometimes float in the air). The Fox sisters' show eventually attracted the backing of the famous P.T. Barnum, who took the girls to New York City and made them nationwide stars.
>
> The fame of the Fox sisters and their tour to promote their "Spiritualist" society encouraged others to discover their own talents for communicating with the dead. It wasn't long before other "mediums" started to appear; and only a short time before most started charging money for their services. These services were rendered in sessions called séances, which typically took place in a

---

25. When the Fox' cellar was finally excavated, indeed human teeth, hair and bones were found buried there.

darkened room with the participants sitting in a circle holding hands. The purpose for holding hands was clear; it prevented anyone from using their hands to falsely produce ghostly phenomena, and, often, the medium would be tied to the chair with his or her legs secured as well. Under these circumstances, sounds were heard, the medium would talk in different voices and languages, small physical objects [apports] would appear and disappear, furniture would levitate or move, and, occasionally, a spirit would "materialize" in a temporary physical form. (Haslam, 2002)

Initially, the work of mediums was done precisely the same way the Fox sisters began their work: traveling to venues to "perform" on a stage. Many Spiritualists in the early years and decades of the movement were "itinerate" lecturers and mediums, traveling from town to town to give lectures on Spirit and to give "spirit messages" to the people in attendance, or to hold séance where manifestations would sometimes occur.

Gradually, the actual religion soon began to take form as a set protocol which outlined mediumship had started to be used; gatherings were organized into "message services" with a lecturer who gave a sermon-like lecture and several mediums who would offer spirit messages to those in attendance. Spiritualist camps[26] were created where mediums could practice their religion and give readings to people who would visit the camps during the high season (summer) and all throughout the year; eventually these camps developed systems to train aspiring mediums (development[27] classes and theology, as well as procedures to test their mediumship abilities under controlled conditions), and also to ordain them as Spiritualist ministers. The numbers began to grow as more and more people felt inclined to seek out and participate in séances and healing circles. In fact, it is rumored that Abraham Lincoln even participated in a séance while president, as well as many other influential and notable personalities of the day.

A huge surge in public interest always occurred after a big war—the US Civil War, World War I, and World War II—because relatives wanted to make some type of contact with their loved ones who had fallen in battle. (Brown, 2003) Spiritualist mediums were able to offer closure and comfort to people who had suffered a loss by reassuring them that the person was all right—this was done via

---

26. The most well-known and successful camps are Lily Dale, New York; Cassadaga, Florida; and Chesterfield, Indiana. All of these Spiritualist camps have long histories and are still thriving today.
27. For a general glossary and list of terms for mediumship and Spiritualism, see Appendix C.

the relaying of a message from the deceased. Also, it helped to reassure the people that there is an afterlife that continues after the physical death.

The decades following the inauguration of Spiritualism were heady days for the religion, attracting multitudes of followers who flocked to séance rooms all across America in hopes of connecting to a deceased grandparent, parent, spouse, child or sibling. Many people who sought out the assistance of mediums, and those who prescribed to the Spiritualist belief system, found great comfort in the "spirit messages" they received. From the very beginning, however, skeptics and critics abounded, charging elaborate trickery and fakery.

Spiritualism was dealt a tremendous blow when the original Fox sisters made claims of fraud within the movement. This accusation occurred many years after the first rappings were heard; Margaret (Maggie) Fox claimed that she and her sister had actually manufactured the rappings by manipulating their toes to snap. "More damning still, in 1888, the Fox sisters made a public appearance in New York in which Margaret stated that Spiritualism was a fraud and an evil, and that herself and Catharine [Katie] had been faking phenomena all the years they had been in practice. The sisters went on tour to expose the fakery of Spiritualism…even though Catharine continued to work as a medium. In 1889, Margaret recanted her confession, but her inconsistent behavior had already damaged Spiritualism's public image deeply. In 1892, Catharine died of alcoholism, and in 1893, Margaret died ill and destitute at a friend's home in Brooklyn." (Haslam, 2003)

Critics of the religion maintain that her confession should carry more weight than her recantation, but true Spiritualists, who themselves have experienced apparitions and phenomena refuse to accept that the whole movement is based on an elaborate hoax that went too far. One of the most strident and ardent supporters and believers of the Fox sisters was Sir Conan Doyle, the reputed author of the *Sherlock Holmes* series. He worked tirelessly, setting aside all other literary endeavors to prove the validity of Spiritualism to the world. The most definitive work on early Spiritualism, *The History of Spiritualism*, was written by Doyle.

From the beginning, Spiritualism offered people a new alternative to the stodgy Puritan inspired Protestant religions that preached hell and damnation, expecting unrealistic piety by its members. Adherents to this new religion liked the idea, and took great comfort in the notion, that once a person's physical body dies, the soul lives on in a form that can be recognized and communicated with by those left behind. Spiritualism attracted many followers because of its unique concept of salvation (*i.e.* all souls are redeemable, no matter how sinful they behaved while on earth); and the negation of certain beliefs (*i.e.* the concept of heaven and hell—Spiritualists regard heaven and hell as states of consciousness and not physical locations); and dogma that were common in the more mainstream religions.[28] One notable person who flirted with Spiritualism would soon break off on her own to start a whole new movement, which condemned mediums and Spiritualism in favor of a more scientifically based approach to healing: Mary Baker Eddy, the founder of Christian Science—the third American-made religion.

Christian Science

The miracle associated with the founding of Christian Science involved Mary Baker Eddy, the founder of the movement, and the ill effects she suffered after a nasty fall in 1866. Previously though, she had been somewhat of an invalid for some time, suffering from chronic back pain and a variety of other physical complaints and ailments. To ease her suffering, she sought treatments that involved many types of holistic-based healing techniques. She finally, after exhausting all known physical methods, began to research mental healing—more commonly known as hypnotism. In 1862, Mrs. Eddy finally found comfort in a technique developed by Phineas P. Quimby,[29] a practitioner of Mesmerism,[30] who helped her overcome her disability. She became a student of Mr. Quimby's until his death in 1866.

> But in 1866, when Quimby died, Eddy felt more bereft than ever. About a month after this traumatic event, she fell on ice and suffered what seemed a

---

28. Chapter 3 will go into more detail regarding the actual belief system of Spiritualism.
29. Phineas P. Quimby was a mental healer. He traveled the country doing hypnotic exhibitions in his earlier years; later he had endeavored to create a new religious philosophy based on a scientific approach to achieve optimum health and personal fulfillment. He believed that this could be achieved through mental healing.
30. Mesmerism is an early form of hypnotism, discovered by Franz Anton Mesmer, a German physician, in the mid 1700's. "According to Mesmer, illness is caused by obstacles to the free flow of fluid—obstacles which can be removed by the sensitive making passes with an iron magnet or (in the case of accomplished practitioners) with the hands and even the nose. Cures often involved putting the patient into a trance, during which he would obey orders and even prophesy the future—although it was observed by critics that on other occasions hysterical convulsions accompanied healing sessions, which collapsed in chaos. Claims about prophecies made in the trance state inevitably led to speculations concerning the relationship between mesmerism and clairvoyance [*e.g.* Spiritualism]. After the master's death, many pupils also claimed to be in psychic communion with him." (Washington, 15-16)

> concussion and a dislocated spine. "On the third day," however, while reading the gospel story of Jesus healing a palsied man (Mathew 9:2),[31] she claimed a profoundly moving experience in which she glimpsed spiritual truth and was instantly healed. She dated the beginning of Christian Science from that moment. (Albanese, 235)

This is the miracle associated with the founding of Christian Science. After her epiphany and healing, she roamed New England from 1866 through 1872, gathering her thoughts and writing about her experience with "prayerful healing." In 1875, she published the book that would make her famous and a cult figure: *Science and Health*. This book would become as important as the Bible to Christian Scientists and would give impetus to the movement in general, not only due to its wide-readership, but because Eddy was attracting a large number of devotees.

Many critics of Eddy maintained that she basically stole all of her ideas from her longtime teacher, Phineas P. Quimby. It was he who had worked to develop the healing system that she adopted to be used as the base-doctrine in Christian Science. If she did not take all of his ideas, she, at the very least, based her system of healing on his basic treatises about mental healing.

Curiously, there is also a Spiritualism connection to Mary Baker Eddy. She was a follower of Spiritualism for some time before she developed her own religion, but worked very hard to distance herself from Spiritualism later on.

> Christian Science emerged from a social context in which Spiritualism enjoyed wide acceptance. Many assumed Eddy to be a medium because she was a woman who healed without medicines or surgery. But, in fact, like her first teacher, the mental healer Phineas Parkhurst Quimby, Eddy viewed her own approach to healing as thoroughly distinct from Spiritualism. Even before she defined her new faith, Eddy addressed "P.P. Quimby's spiritual science healing disease as opposed to deism or Rochester-Rapping Spiritualism" in one of her first public lectures....In spite of her own firm rejection of Spiritualism, she found the first sympathetic audience for her new faith among those whose interest in unorthodox metaphysics drew them to investigate Spiritualism. While committing her new views to paper in *Science and Health*, Mary Baker Eddy lived in two different Spiritualist boarding houses, where politeness compelled her to take a seat at a séance table. At the third Spiritualist home in which she resided while writing *Science and Health*, she converted her hostess to Christian Science. In 1868, Eddy advertised for students in the

---

31. The Holy Bible (King James Version), Mathew 9:2 reads, "And behold, they brought to him a man sick of the palsy, lying on a bed; and Jesus seeing their faith said unto the sick of the palsy; Son, be of good cheer; thy sins be forgiven thee."

> *Banner of Light* [a Spiritualist publication], offering to teach "healing on a *principle of science* [a concept first promulgated by Spiritualism]," using "no medicine, electricity, physiology or hygiene." Nothing in the ad suggested that she was a Spiritualist, but its presence in the *Banner* would at least be in sympathy with Spiritualist practices. (Braude, 183-184)

Eddy's conversion of the Spiritualist woman is quite an auspicious precursor for the movement in general—many Spiritualists would join her new religion, making it one of the most rapidly growing religions of its day. Spiritualism never gained the same type of wide acceptance and appeal as Christian Science enjoyed, nor would it ever have the same amount of wealth.

There are many correlations between the older Spiritualism and the newer Christian Science religion, though, and these similarities is what made it so easy and appealing for people to switch from the older Spiritualism to the newer Christian Science.

> Christian Science addressed the same basic needs that drew investigators to Spiritualism: it provided consolation for the bereaved by denying the reality of death, hope for the sick by denying the reality of disease, and support for the irrelevance of Calvinism by denying the reality of evil. Christian Science, like Spiritualism, claimed to be scientific, making recourse to empirical evidence. Also like Spiritualism, Christian Science consciously opposed itself to the doctrines of orthodoxy in both religion and medicine.... Like Spiritualism, Christian Science further conflicted with regular medicine by encouraging women to become healers and by proposing an egalitarian relationship between healer and patient.... The most significant point on which Christian Scientists concurred with Spiritualists and differed from other Christians was in the belief that there is no change at death. However, Christian Science rejected the Spiritualist view that the continuity of life after death is proved by physical evidence of spirit presence. To answer the Spiritualist assertion that spirit manifestations show that we never really had bodies to begin with, that the only part of the individual that ever really existed was the spirit, before or after death. (Braude, 184)

It can be said, then, that Christian Science was part Mesmerist, part Spiritualist in its inception, but became a unique entity unto itself once Mary Baker Eddy published her best selling book *Science and Health*, cementing and, at the same time, propelling the new movement into a league of its own. Most religions borrow and adapt elements of older religions and belief systems, and Christian Science is no different. But the savvy way in which Mary Baker Eddy was able to cull and glean aspects from earlier religions, manipulating and developing them into a seemingly new set of ideas and dogma, is unique. She quickly became the focal point of the religion, becoming a cult figure.

In contrast to both Mormonism and Christian Science, Spiritualism had no one cult figure in which to build the religion around;[32] Eddy's personality and ability, like Smith and those who first promoted Spiritualism, were able to somehow make the ordinary seem quite extraordinary, which appealed to the general public. "Through the teaching of its founder, Christian Science mined its situation to discover finally what all religions seek as they confront the human situation—a sense of transcendent meaning and purpose. But in the very act of doing so, in the process of turning the ordinary into the extraordinary, Christian Science also made the extraordinary ordinary. Its healings showed believers that the world as it appeared was, after all, malleable. In that conviction Christian Science revealed its American spirit." (Albanese, 240)

1.6 *Summary*

In this chapter, a history of religion in the United States was briefly surveyed from the earliest times when indigenous peoples lived and worshipped animistic-based religions; through to the discovery of the New World when Catholicism (by evangelizing missionaries) and Judaism (by Jews escaping persecution and death) were introduced to the shores of the Americas; to the historical era of Reformation that brought multitudes of Protestants to America as part of the great European invasion; through to the creation of American-made religions that occupied the American religious psyche in the nineteenth century.

The development and evolution of religion has been outlined, along with the links between the ancient and modern belief systems, indigenous and foreign practices, as well as the old-time religions that spawned the new-movements of the nineteenth century. Religion in America developed in stages, each borrowing from the established system that preceded it. Changes were made along the way, adapting the dogma and tenets to fit the social condition and situation of the times.

---

32. Of course, the Fox sisters were the leading figures and "faces" of Spiritualism for many years, but soon the movement began to divide and various factions began promoting their own forms of Spiritualism, detracting from the original figures that started the movement. It was not long until a variety of mediums would be holding séances and promulgating the religion through traveling and itinerate means. The founders of Mormonism and Christian Science held tight control over how the religions were allowed to promulgate, making them more organized and hierarchical.

The linear approach used in this chapter was necessary to give an overview of how religions developed over the course of the history of the New World and America. The view taken in this dissertation is that the religions and belief systems practiced in the whole of the United States were constructed through the layering of prior belief systems and religious traditions from indigenous practices up through the time that America would make its own, unique style of religious traditions in the nineteenth century.

These religions, and the concepts surrounding the various religious traditions, served to shape the American people socially, culturally and spiritually. Even today, remnants of the Puritan ethic are still very much a part of American social-life. The idea of guilt and shame still has its hold on peoples' psyches. The new religions helped to abate some of this, but have not been completely successful as these basic-ideas still permeate people's belief systems and sense of morality.

The American-made religions of the nineteenth century did, however, move America into a new direction where mysticism and metaphysically-based concepts would become more accepted and practiced on a wider scale. Mediumship, then, and its flowery history, became the basis of the most radical and complex of these new religions—Spiritualism—and is the focus of the next chapter.

2

A History of Mediumship from Ancient Times to the Advent of Spiritualism in America

Spirituality has had a profound effect and influence upon all of humanity since the beginning of time. Primitive cave dwellers, who looked at natural phenomena (like thunder and lightening) as being godly signs from a force much greater than themselves, wondered, most likely, at how all came into being. "The thunder rolled, the rains fell and the earthquake rumbled while in his cave, ancient man [*sic*] knelt in fear or prostrated himself in abject terror pleading protection from some unknown power." (Parker-Wakefield, 15)

At some point in time, however, these prehistoric beings began to organize their worship practices by making gods of nature to help make sense of the worldly occurrences happening about them. Eventually, as humanity progressed, these early people began to assign the traits of "good and evil" to the various natural occurrences that were taking place all around them. As these early worshipers began to organize their beliefs, soon rituals and rites were created and performed to celebrate their belief systems. How better to know a divine force than to make that higher force in the image of that which is known? Hence, many of the gods began to take on shapes which resembled that of human beings—including the ability to feel emotions, such as love, hate, happiness, anger, fear, and even carnal desire, making them clearly human in their needs and wants.

> ...then came the belief that the gods were beings in the likeness of man[1] with all of man's likes, dislikes and passions; indeed that they came to earth and walked with men and became fathers of human children. A study of mythology shows that the special favorites of the gods were virgins whose children, resulting from these celestial contacts, were god-men. Mythology teaches us

that all gods and goddesses were once men and women on earth. (Parker-Wakefield, 15)

What initially prompted these early peoples to assign human characteristics to their gods? Could it be that they had glimpsed psychically spirit apparitions around them and hence reasoned that these entities, not of the physical world, must be that of something divine and all powerful? The ancients who saw with their own eyes images of what seemed like people may very well have been a form of physical phenomena[2] which in turn caused them at once to fear and then adore these entities.

In contrast, the Holy Bible offers an alternative Hebrew rendition to how humanity viewed God—a divine being that made man and woman in his own image, rather than the other way around. In Genesis 1:26, God says, "Let us make man in our image, after our likeness..."[3] This is curiously contrastive to how other ancient peoples came to view their gods, and how they reasoned they were supposed to look like. The biblical account offers us a view that is of God making humanity in his image, where in the occurrences in other ancient cultures, it was humankind who initially created the gods to look like them. Of course, because the Bible was supposed to have been divinely inspired by humans, who later passed down the stories orally before they were ever written down,[4] it can be assumed, then, the idea of God resembling humans (at the inception of the Judeo-Christian tradition) is not so dissimilar to that of other, even more ancient cultures, namely the Egyptian culture where many ancient biblical stories have their origin. It is certainly likely that the ancient Hebrews did in fact also create God to fit their image of what a god should look like, hence God's human-like image. "Their value is only historic. The Bible relates to us the

---

1. The patriarchal tendencies of some early cultures, and even in some current belief systems, make it seem as though "mothers" and "daughters" had no role at all to play in the evolution of human-religious history. Contrary to this notion, many ancient cultures in fact revered women and sought out their wisdom and knowledge regularly as sages, shamans, mediums and psychics. Still, unfortunately, women have been largely denied recognition in their pivotal roles of religious and spiritual thought throughout the millennia.
2. For a glossary and list of terms for mediumship and Spiritualism, see Appendix C.
3. In Genesis 1:27, it also states "So god created man in his own image, in the image of God created he him; male and female created he them." (Holy Bible, King James Version)
4. "Despite these realities, many of the Christian people of the world are still taught that the Bible is inerrant or in a literal sense 'the word of God.'" (Spong, 38)

way our ancient forbearers understood and interpreted their world, made sense out of life, and thought about God. Our task is the same as theirs. We must interpret our world in the light of our knowledge and suppositions." (Spong, 33)

Greek and Roman mythology, for instance, offer excellent examples of how the gods once walked the earth, living as humans, before being made divine and omnipotent. As stated previously, even once deified, these gods clearly demonstrated a variety of the human-based conditions and emotions.

> The origin of this belief in gods in the image of man has been traced to what we might call apparitions or psychic phenomena. Our primitive ancestors believed that these apparitions of the dead were gods and that they were behind all the forces of nature. Thus ancestor worship of many years ago is the origin of Spiritualism. When the family became a unit, deceased parents were worshipped. When families became a tribe, the dead ancestors of the chief were worshipped, and when the tribes became nations, the national heroes became gods. Greece and Rome had many gods. (Parker-Wakefield, 15)

Perhaps the origin of some gods, the ones that people claimed to have witnessed with their own eyes, then, could have been merely apparitions of deceased relatives and/or tribe members that appeared to them after their transitional death; not knowing how to rationalize supernatural phenomenon, the ancients assigned duties and human-based stories to them, creating a body of mythology. There has been no time in recorded history of the world where there was not traces found of supernatural phenomenon and recognition of it from humanity. (Doyle, 11) These early beginnings certainly were the precursors to the phenomenon now known as *mediumship*.

What is "mediumship"? How is being a "medium" different from being "psychic"? What are the differences between mediums, psychics and channelers? These questions need to be addressed, and each term adequately defined, in order to avoid confusion later on. First, mediums basically obtain and relay information by physical or mental means from the deceased. (Dreller, 39) These "messages" can be given through clairvoyance,[5] clairaudience[6] and/or clairsentience[7] during a private reading, in a séance or healing circle,[8] or at a Spiritualist church

---

5. Clairvoyance is to see with the spiritual eye or "third eye" located between the physical eyes. Most mediums are given symbols in their mind's eye which they then interpret from the spirit world to the physical world. (Scher, I)
6. Clairaudience is the ability to hear with the spiritual ear or "inner ear." Mediums who hear messages in the form of spirit voices in their heads, or physically, then relay the message from the spirit to the client. (Scher, I)

service where the medium gives messages to those in attendance; messages can be given while fully aware, in semi-trance, or in full-trance.[9] Many mediums are also healers, prognosticators, and spiritual advisors and counselors. A certified Spiritualist medium must ordinarily satisfy an extensive curriculum of study and practicum, including an apprenticeship and the subsequent testing of his/her mediumship skills, before receiving official certification from the particular association for which s/he is seeking certification.

"Psychics" are able to receive and transmit information through Extra Sensory Perception (ESP) and telepathy[10]. Often, psychics are able to go into a person's past, as well as seeing the present and future of the person receiving the reading. Many psychics can pick up on the energy and vibration of objects they handle (psychometry) to gain information psychically about the person who owns it. (Dreller, 39)

A "channeler" is a person who has the ability to receive information from disincarnate entities, from his/her higher self, and sometimes extraterrestrials. The information received is usually in the nature of a religious, spiritual, and/or prophetic vein. The ability to channel is probably the oldest form of spirit communication dating back to ancient times and is most often confused with "mediumship." (Dreller, 39)

Both mental and physical[11] mediumship, the ability to communicate with entities on the other side that have passed over, have their philosophical roots in ancient traditions that go back to time immemorial. Indigenous peoples who inhabited the whole of the earth since the dawn of time have sought out and communicated with those in the spirit world. "Anthropologically, there have

---

7. Clairsentience is to feel intuitively a message which is left on the brain by the spirit entity. Mediums who employ clairsentience give messages from the impressions they feel from the spirit entity. (Scher, I)
8. A séance or healing circle is a gathering of a group of dedicated persons (with one control medium) who sit in a darkened room as one, in hopes of having physical phenomena appear. (Bletzer, 545)
9. A medium who does trance readings is usually in a sleep-like state, and the mind and personality of the medium is completely taken over by the spirit; mediums who do trance readings will have a change in their natural voices when in trance, and almost never remember what message was given or what they did while in trance. The spirit is in full control of the medium. (Scher, I)
10. ESP and telepathy are forms of parapsychology that are experienced by the person without the use of the five normal senses, transmitting thoughts and feelings from one mind to another over a distance without any physical means of intervention. It is also referred to as "precognition" or "psychic cognition." (Bletzer, 210)

always been (wo)men within 'primitive' societies who were looked upon as possessing special knowledge and power. Medicine men, or shamans, had undergone a spontaneous catharsis, or were initiated and felt called upon to maintain contact with the spirit world for the clan." (Rogge, 2000)

World history, and more specifically world religion, offers a rich collection of mediumistic events and occurrences that extend to nearly every society and group that has inhabited the earth. The idea of "ghosts" has haunted the human psyche from the beginning of time, with certain individuals seemingly endowed with special powers to see, feel, and communicate intuitively with these incarnate spirits. "Such a belief has been existent in practically all stages of culture, and in the Roman Empire, manifestations similar to those common to modern Spiritualism were reported." (Larrabee, 51) The mystical[12] experience of these mediums have occurred and been documented since pre-biblical times. In an innate desire by these sages to attempt to transcend the old myths and superstitions that plagued any work in the field of mediumship, many began to incorporate an in-depth approach to explain definitively, and not only in the abstract, proof of continuation of the spirit after the physical occurrence of death.

Table 1: *Mental and Physical Mediumship*

Mental	Physical
Clairvoyance: Vivid mental pictures.	**Ectoplasm:** Diffuses from orifices of the medium's body—mucous membranes; intense trance.
Clairaudience: Hearing messages.	**Telekinesis:** Objects move through mind power.

---

11. Mediumship can be roughly divided into two categories: *mental mediumship*—a more cerebral approach to spirit communication "centered at the base of the brain, the seat of the cerebrospinal nervous system. The visiting spirit entity manipulates the mental faculties and causes the phenomena. The medium's ability to receive and act as the vehicle for spirit communication depends on the medium's physical, emotional, and receptive state. The deeper the meditational trance, the greater the intensity.

    Physical mediumship is dependent on three things: focused trance via the base of the brain; the solar plexus area where the core (gut-level) of intensity cycles with the brain; and third, from the vibrational energy received from the sitters and observers. Physical mediumship is 'state-of-the-art' mediusmhip, and all experts at this level usually have surpassed the abilities of straight mental mediumship." (Dreller, 39-41) [See Table 1 for a list of mental and physical phenomena.]

Table 1: *Mental and Physical Mediumship* (Continued)

Prophecy: Information received from spirits usually concerning future events; can be personal or great events.

Scrying: Clairvoyant receives visions from gazing in [a] crystal ball or water.

Healing: When positive spirit energy is sent through the medium to heal and cure.

Psychometry: Information obtained from handling objects, mainly through clairvoyance and telepathy.

Trance: Deep hypnotic condition in which the medium is controlled by a spirit guide—but not possession.

Automatic Writing and Drawing: When a spirit operator manipulates the muscle reflexes of the medium.

Psychokinesis: Objects move and float because of mind *control*.

Spirit Raps: Spirits bump, bang, and rap furniture, walls.

Apports: Spirits bring objects from their plane—flowers, living animals and objects relevant to séance.

Levitation: Persons, furniture, and objects float or rise.

Materialization: Spirit produced; appears to be solid by sight and touch; can be spirits or objects.

Voices: Direct or indirect voices, comes from the medium, apparition, or "thin air."

Spirit Lights: Singular or hundreds of twinkling lights—all shapes and colors.

Breezes and Drafts: Cold, warm or scented, from spirits.

Musical Instruments, Singing: From spirits.

Table Tipping: Spirit(s) move or rock table back and forth.

Ouija Board: Messages come from Spirit(s).

---

12. Mysticism, in general, is an "esoteric tradition [that] became handed down in spiritual groups, communes, or fraternities. [The adherents to this type of spiritual life resulted in a mutual devotion and] a high degree of perfection comparable to the guilds of craftsmen. In their mystical experiences, they beheld a spiritual reality that could hardly be reconciled with the dogmatic representation given by churches." (Rogge, 2000) Some examples of movements based on mystic traditions include: Grecian mysteries, Eastern philosophy (in the traditions of Confucius, Buddha, Mahavira (India), Zoroaster (Persia), and the prophets of Palestine), Gnosticism, Jewish mysticism and the Kabala, Alchemy, Freemasonry, The Rosicrucian's, Theosophy, Krishnamurti, and the New Age.).

Table 1: *Mental and Physical Mediumship* **(Continued)**

Odors: Flowers, medicines, perfumes, or stench.

Spirit Photography: Spirit images appear on film.

Telephone, Radio, Television, or Tape Recorder Voices: Spirit voices.

(From Dreller, L. (1997) *Beginner's Guide to Mediumship.* York Beach, Maine: Sam Weiser, Inc.)

Mediumsistic phenomena are as old as mankind. Archeological, anthropological and historical literature is full of references to professed intercourse with the spirit world. In the so-called primitive culture, the shaman was a combination of medium, psychic and magician, as were psychics operating from various guises in the ancient Mediterranean world. However, in spite of the ancient phenomena and practices to which Spiritualism is an heir, Spiritualism is itself a relatively new phenomenon, related to the peculiar thrust of Western religion since the late 1600's. The true ancestors of Spiritualism are not the ancient mediums, but the Puritan and Wesleyan conservatives who used psychic phenomena to prove the existence of the unseen world. In the late 1600's, as the polemic against witchcraft grew and Deism, which denied the validity of any intercourse with spirit entities, emerged, the Puritan theologians began to issue numerous accounts of the spirit world. (Melton, 92)

As presented in chapter one, the spiritual realm of occultism and metaphysics was firmly established in the anima of the early-American individual; this occurred not only from early exposure to rituals and spirituality of the indigenous peoples who inhabited the whole of the Americas before the Europeans arrived, but also by the initial outside influence, and eventual homegrown, Puritan tradition. These Christian ancestors of many Americans today demanded that psychic-medium phenomena be demonstrated in response to their own self-doubts about the survival of the spirit after the physical demise of the human body, as well as the existence of the "hereafter." Up to this point in religious history, the demonstration of the survival of the spirit was not a true necessity, nor a major theme in the world of mediumship. People often accepted the notion of spirit communication without hard proof. Hence, it can be deduced, then, that Spiritualism (in an odd sort of way) is the direct inheritor of Puritan-Wesleyan concerns which preceded it. (Melton, 92-93)

In this chapter, examples of mediumship from biblical times will be researched through to the pre-modern period when the idea of supernatural power was first illuminated by Emanuel Swedenborg, a gifted seer and medium, and later, Franz Anton Mesmer, a proponent of psychic healing through animal magnetism and hypnotism. Another notable personality in the metaphysical world at the time was Andrew Jackson Davis, also known as "The Poughkeepsie Seer;" he had a chance meeting with a traveling "Mesmerist" which began his work in channeling spirits as a medium, most notably the spirit of Emanuel Swedenborg. This was a precursory experience to mediumship before anyone really knew what it was and what it entailed. Soon after, the advent of modern Spiritualism occurred with the Hydesville Rappings in upstate New York. It was this momentous event in the history of Spiritualism that demonstrated contact with those on the other side through mediumship, eventually paving the way for the creation of a new American-made religion called Spiritualism, attracting some two million followers by the year 1855, just seven years after the movement began. (Larabee, 51)

When Spiritualism first appeared as a religion, it appealed to a number of people who were exasperated with mainstream religion. This new religion offered believers not only alleged proof of life after death, but a more flexible belief system that incorporated the ideals and truths from a variety of the world's religions. It also allowed women to play a prominent role in religion—a position most nearly always denied by the more fundamentalist-based religions.

The promulgation of the religion and the proliferation of Spiritualism during the period between 1880 and 1920 was a heady time for mediums and publishing houses that were eager to satisfy the insatiable appetite of the public who were demanding information on this new movement and on the mediums themselves. This is also known as "The Era of the Great Mediums." A short commentary on Sir Conan Doyle, an avowed Spiritualist who wrote the definitive and all inclusive tome on the movement, published originally in 1926, will be offered.

2.1 Biblical Accounts of Mediumship

According to the teachings of Spiritualism, both the Old and New Testaments of the *Holy Bible* offer clear instances of mediumship. Perhaps one of the most famous single incidents of mediumship in the history of Judaism and Christianity occurs in the Old Testament, Samuel I: 28.

First, though, it should be mentioned that Samuel was known as "The Boy Medium." As a child he heard his first spirit voice. His mother, Hannah, as fulfillment of a promise she made to God if she were blessed with a baby boy, promised to take the boy to Eli, a priest, so that the child could be raised in a spiritual environment. After Samuel was born, she kept her promise to God and took him to Eli to live in the temple. While growing up, Samuel took initiative and assisted the old priest with duties around the temple because Eli was growing old and was unable to do such tasks.

One night, Samuel was awakened by a voice calling his name. He immediately ran to Eli to see what was the matter. Eli hadn't called him, so he went back to sleep. Again, the voice rang out clearly: "Samuel." This happened three times, and finally Eli realized that a spirit voice had spoken to Samuel. Eli told Samuel to speak to the voice the next time, which he did. Samuel said, "Speak Lord, for thy servant heareth."

The voice did speak again to Samuel and told him that trouble was coming to Eli and to his sons. This was a prophecy that was later fulfilled. This experience with channeling spirit that night made Samuel understand that he had the gift of mediumship. He heard the voice many times and also saw visions from Spirit. News of Samuel's mediumship ability spread quickly and he advised and guided people with the spirit messages he received.[13]

The mediumistic occurrence in Samuel I: 28 takes place in Israel with King Saul. He was to face the Philistines and feared defeat from their powerful army. Through dreams, his royal psychics, and the Urim and Thummim (ancient divination devices), he visited a medium at Endor. He asked her to call up the spirit of Samuel, Saul's departed psychic advisor.

> Sometime after Saul had been made King, the prophet priest Samuel passed into the Spirit World. Saul, had lost his mediumship because he had not valued it as he ought, and thought he could live just as he pleased without listening for the guiding voices of those who would direct him in the right way.
>
> He turned against all mediums and ordered them to be banished from the land. But there came a time when he was very worried. For he was at war with the Philistines and very much afraid they would conquer his people.

---

13. This story appears in the Holy Bible, Samuel I: 28. The version contained herein has been adapted from a published version by Elsie Butler Bunts' in *Old Testament Mediums*, pp 7-8.

> He found out that there was a woman living at a place called Endor who had the gift of mediumship and he decided to go to her for advice. So he disguised himself and when he arrived at her home, she was very much afraid because she knew well enough that he was King Saul.
>
> She told him that she knew him and as he had ordered all mediums to be banished, she did not want to try to give him a message. However, King Saul assured her that he would protect her. While they were talking, the Spirit Samuel appeared to the medium. Then she said to Saul, "an old man is coming and he is wrapped in a robe." Saul recognized the Spirit was Samuel. Then the medium gave him a very true message from Samuel. For Samuel reminded him just how he had been living without regard to right or wrong, until he had lost touch with the spirit guides who wanted to be of help.
>
> He also told Saul that the Philistines would overcome him and his army. This message made Saul weak and faint and the woman hurried to get him something to eat and made him rest before going away from her home.
>
> This kindness showed a forgiving and sympathetic heart, for she was living the Golden Rule[14] in thus trying to help her King. (Bunts b, 11)

This story further offers a glimpse into the types of medium-related occurrences found in the Old Testament of the *Holy Bible*.

The general belief within modern Spiritualism is that many of the seemingly divine occurrences from God that are contained in the Bible were mistaken for messages that were more likely spirits attempting to make communication with those on the earth plane. Many Spiritualists today regard the story in the Old Testament of Moses seeing the burning bush in the desert to have been a type of phenomena or manifestation, not merely a natural occurrence, and the voice calling his name to have been that of the spirit Jehovah (Yah-weh).

---

14. One version of "The Golden Rule" is "do unto others as you would have others do unto you." Similar sayings are found in a variety of other religious scriptures, in nearly every belief system and religion: "You shall love your neighbor as yourself." *Judaism and Christianity*, Leviticus 19:18; "Whatever you wish that men would do to you, do so to them." *Christianity*, Mathew 7:12; "Not one of you is a believer until he loves for his brother what he loves for himself." *Islam*, Forty Hadith of an-Nawawi 13; "A man should wander about treating all creatures as himself would be treated." *Jainism*, Sutrakritanga 1:11.33; "One going to take a pointed stick to pinch a baby bird should first try it on himself to feel how it hurts." *African Traditional Religions*, Yoruba Proverb (Nigeria). (Wilson, 114)

> ...this story in the Bible [about] the spirit that came to Moses, this Jehovah, was a tribal guide and not the personal God that they thought it was. This was a spirit being who sometimes appeared in a kind and helpful way but at other times, lost his temper and was cruel and vengeful, ordering the killing of men, women and little children. (Bunts b, 5)

Spiritualism teaches that the "all loving God" that is at the heart of Spiritualist beliefs would not act in a vengeful, cruel manner. So it is difficult for Spiritualists to accept Moses' channeling of "God" to be that of a highly evolved spirit, let alone that of the Creator. Spiritualists maintain that the spirit conversing and guiding Moses was in fact a lower spirit guide who still must have been working through his own issues while on the other side, not yet fully evolved into a higher entity. Of course, this goes against the accepted belief systems of Judaism and Christianity. Mainstream Jews and Christians believe categorically that God himself spoke to Moses and maintain an inerrant view of the scriptures, rejecting any suggestion that Moses was not conversing actually with God, the Almighty.

To compound this differing of opinions on actual biblical occurrences, Spiritualists view the Ten Commandments given to Moses atop the summit of Mount Sinai as a biblical example of "slate-writing,"[15] and/or an "apport."[16] Again, Spiritualists maintain that the stone tablets and writing were excellent examples of spirit phenomena that appeared not by the hand of God, but by the direct intervention of Moses' spirit guide, Jehovah.[17] It is no wonder then that fundamentalist Jews and Christians are at odds with Spiritualists and categorically disregard such Spiritualist beliefs as being fantasy. Spiritualism, from the beginning, set out to challenge many of the central beliefs of fundamentalist Jews and Christians by following a belief system that explained why events happened (using explanations based on the belief in spirit communication between humans and those who have passed into spirit). Many central beliefs of fundamentalists "make assumptions based upon a literalized view of the biblical narrative that are no longer believable." (Spong, 35) Spiritualists, on the other hand, view the "miracles" of the

---

15. Slate writing, also called "spirit writing," is a form of physical mediumship where the medium does not do the actual writing (unlike "automatic writing" or "inspirational writing" where the spirit works through the medium, inspiring or influencing the medium by dictating, in a sense, what is to be written); the spirit entity does the writing through the use of ectoplasm (an organic compound that is contained in the cells of a person's body that is used by spirits for producing physical phenomena) drawn from the medium.
16. An apport is an actual object that is brought from the spirit world plane to the earth plane.

Bible to be mediumistic occurrences contained within biblical stories that are not so much the result of divine miracles, but more as verified proof of communication with spirits on the other side—a type of spirit-communication with disincarnated spirits.

The New Testament of the Holy Bible, according to Spiritualist teachings, contains many examples of mediumship, especially the gifted mediumship of Jesus. Even before Jesus was born, practicing Spiritualists maintain that the spirit world was working diligently on preparing those whom would be connected to Jesus after his arrival. The archangel Gabriel was originally a spirit "who had advanced in the spirit world to the point where he became a messenger to the earth plane of great importance. To him was entrusted many contacts with Old Testament mediums and those of the New Testament." (Bunts a, 3)

> Zachariah was a priest in the Hebrew Temple. Part of his work was to enter the temple at a certain hour of the day and burn incense while the people stood outside and prayed. One day while attending to this duty, there suddenly appeared a spirit and he became afraid, but the spirit told him that his name was Gabriel and that he had a message for him.
>
> Gabriel told him that he and his wife Elizabeth[18] would have a boy and that he must call his son John. He told him too, that one day his son would "speak in the spirit and the power of Elias" [Elijah[19]]. By this he meant the old Hebrew medium would be his son's spirit guide and would speak through him.
>
> This vision made such an impression upon Zachariah that he became [mute] from the shock, and the people noticed when he came out of the temple that there was something wrong with him. This effect lasted until after the baby

---

17. In the Holy Bible, Exodus 31:18, "And he gave unto Moses, when he had made an end of communing with him upon mount Sinai, two tables of testimony, tables of stone, written with the finger of God." In Exodus 32, the people waiting for Moses to return from the mountain became impatient and decided that they needed a more tangible god than Yahweh (Jehovah), so they beseeched Aaron to give them a tangible god to worship so he made them a golden calf which they used to worship, placing offerings in front of it. "And when the people saw that Moses delayed to come down out of the mount, the people gathered themselves together unto Aaron, and said unto him. Up, make us gods, which shall go before us; for as for this Moses, the man that brought us up out of the land of Egypt, we wot not what is become of him." (King James Version, The Holy Bible)
18. Elizabeth, the wife of Zachariah and mother of John the Baptist, is found in Luke 1:5-66.

John was born. When his little son was placed in his arms, the friends and relatives wanted to call him Zachariah after his father, but the old priest called for writing materials and wrote these words: "His name is John." (Bunts a, 3-4)

This baby would later be known as John the Baptist, the man who baptized Jesus in the river Jordan. John the Baptist was a cousin to Jesus (his mother was a cousin of Jesus' mother Mary). As predicted by Gabriel to Zachariah, Elijah was the spirit guide of John the Baptist. John lived a solitary life, choosing to live in the wilderness, wearing only a camel skin garment. He did preach to the people, encouraging them to live better lives, and those who followed him, he baptized (hence the name "John the Baptist"). "He told his followers that he could baptize them with water, but that when Jesus the medium came, he would baptize them with the Holy Spirit." (Bunts a, 6)

The Spiritualist interpretation of this comment is that Jesus would be able to demonstrate his mediumship skills so ably that they would be completely in awe of his gifted mediumship because he would also help them to use the same spirit power for themselves that he possessed. (Bunts a, 6-7) The Spiritualist portrayal of Gabriel is of a spirit entity turned archangel and messenger, a reoccurring figure in mediumship stories of the Bible. After all, it was Gabriel who appeared to Mary and announced to her the coming of the baby Jesus. Gabriel also appeared to Jesus' father, Joseph, and told him about the baby Jesus which was to be born.

Another famous mediumistic event is found in Mathew 17:3-4.[20] This is popularly known as "The Transfiguration." It is recorded that Jesus and three Apostles were present when two long-deceased figures, Moses and Elijah, appeared and conversed with Jesus. To Spiritualists, this materialization of spirit demonstrates the extraordinary mediumship of Jesus.

Jesus was widely known around Jerusalem, Galilee, and other towns and villages as being a gifted healer and medium. His following began to grow, which

---

19. Elijah was a prophet from Tishbeh of Gilead in the Northern Kingdom. Spiritualists regard his work to be that of a "medium." He performed miracles (I Kings 17:14-16, 17-24); and was taken up to heaven in a whirlwind (II Kings 1:10-12; 2:8). In the New Testament, some thought Jesus to be Elijah (Mathew 16:14; Luke 9:8) and others thought John the Baptist to be Elijah (John 1:21). In the early church, John was regarded as the heir to the spirit and power of Elijah (Luke 1:17).
20. "The Transfiguration" is also mentioned in Mark 9:4-5: "And there appeared unto them Elijah with Moses: they were talking with Jesus. And Peter answered and said to Jesus, Master, it is good for us to be here: and let us make three tabernacles; one for thee, and one for Moses and one for Elijah." (Holy Bible, King James Version)

worried some of the old priests who were threatened by the young, charismatic Jesus. The story of the life of Jesus is extraordinary because of his ability to see into the future, prophesize, have materializations, manifestations, as well as speaking to and seeing spirit. The following rendition of Jesus' work in the area of mediumship is taken from the book by Elsie Bunts, *New Testament Mediums*:

> The wonderful teacher and medium of whom John the Baptist told the people was of course, Jesus. His life stands out more than any other in the *Bible*. In fact, the Christian religion is founded on his teachings. We could spend many lessons studying about him. Many years after his passing to Spirit Life, people began to write stories about him from what they could remember and from what his friends had told them.
>
> Then after a period of time, people began to worship Jesus as a God, and to add to his simple teachings of love and justice, stories they had borrowed from older religions....Having attained his thirtieth birthday, he came down to the river Jordan where John [the Baptist] was busy talking to people and baptizing them, and when he came to speak to John he asked him to baptize him also. This was done and as he prayed he saw a dove, descending from above his head and he heard a voice saying: "This is my beloved son in whom I am well pleased."
>
> This must have been a clairvoyant vision and a clairaudient voice as only John and Jesus witnessed this spiritual manifestation. Some quote as what the spirit said as proof that Jesus was the only son of a very personal God. However, his father Joseph had been in the spirit world eleven years, so it could have been a manifestation from him.
>
> Thus his ministry began with the blessings of the spirit forces resting upon him. He was so sure of the God-spirit within him, that every moment all who came near were helped and healed by his spiritual magnetism.
>
> One day Jesus met a woman at a well where he stopped, thirsty and tired, while some of his friends went into the city to buy food. He asked her for a drink and then he talked with her and gave her a message that proved so true that she knew he was a medium. Surprised, she ran back home and told all of her people about him. Jesus was not only a mental medium, but a materializing medium as well...and the greatest of spiritual healers. He taught that death was only the beginning of life...(Bunts a, 7-8)

The Bible, according to Spiritualists, has numerous examples of mediumship which they believe lend credibility to their movement. Of course, non-Spiritualists easily dismiss such claims as imaginative interpretation of the Scriptures. The issue of the true meaning of the Scriptures may never be solved, which is part of the beauty of the literature contained within the Holy Bible—its complexity and ambiguity. There will always be those who ardently interpret it one way, and others who interpret it another, and never the twain shall meet. At the very least, however, enough references to mediumship-like occurrences are found in the Bible which certainly does, in part, offer the serious researcher and scholar points of reference to explore further. The mere possibility of psychic phenomena in the Bible should be enough to encourage continued investigation by subsequent generations more deeply into the Scriptures and their meanings. Those who categorically deny the possibility may be doing themselves a huge disservice, considering that every culture from prehistoric to ancient times have had people who claimed to have the gift of mediumship.

2.2 *The Work of Swedenborg*

Modern Spiritualism was born in the mid-1800s, but the conditions were made right through the work of Emmanuel Swedenborg (1688-1772).

> Swedenborg was a Swedish scientist, astronomer, and engineer of international repute, who, at the age of fifty-five became so developed mediumistically as to be able to converse at length with evolved spirits, and to travel the spirit realms. This phase of his life began in London in 1744 and continued until his death in 1772. He wrote and published a large number of books descriptive of his experiences, and explaining the philosophy taught to him by his spirit teachers. Probably the best known of his books is *Heaven and Hell*. His teachings, though somewhat theologically biased (his father was a Swedish bishop) were, nevertheless, advanced and revolutionary in the light of the narrow sectarian dogmas of his day. They gave much information regarding the spirit world and its occupants, which was to be substantially confirmed later by the revelations of Spiritualism." (http://www.newage.com.au)

Figure 1.

Emanuel Swedenborg was born on 29 January 1688 in Stockholm, Sweden. The family was ennobled after his father, Jesper Swedberg, became Bishop of Skara. At the University of Uppsala, Swedenborg was educated in philosophy, mathematics, and science, as well as in Latin, Greek, and Hebrew.

In 1710, a year after completing his university training, Swedenborg began a period of travel, during which he studied physics, astronomy, and other natural sciences, as well as learning watch making, bookbinding, cabinetmaking, engraving, brass instrument making, and lens grinding. Over the next few years, he acquired all the knowledge that the early eighteenth century had to offer in the fields of cosmology, mathematics, anatomy, physiology, politics, economics, metallurgy, mineralogy, geology, mining engineering, and chemistry. He wrote extensively on many of these subjects, and was the first person to propound the nebular hypothesis of the solar system. He made numerous original discoveries in a wide variety of scientific disciplines (such as the functions of the cerebral cortex and the ductless glands, and the respiratory movement of the brain tissues), some of which have been confirmed only in the twentieth century. Swedenborg's inventive genius led him to develop plans for a glider-type airplane, a submarine, an air gun, a slow combustion stove, and a mercury air pump, among others.

Throughout the period of his scientific work, Swedenborg had always maintained his interest in spirituality. The aim of much of his research in human biology was to find a rational explanation for the operation of the soul.

During the years 1744 and 1745, Swedenborg experienced a series of visions which had a profound effect on him. Eventually, his spiritual senses were fully opened, and he was able consciously to exist simultaneously in both the natural and the spiritual worlds. He believed that he had been called by God to give a new revelation to humanity, and for the next twenty-seven years, until his death in London at the age of 84, he devoted himself almost exclusively to writing the thirty volumes of theological works which comprise that revelation. In the last month of his life, several of his friends asked Swedenborg to make a final statement regarding the veracity of what he had written. He replied: "I have written nothing but the truth, as you will have more and more confirmed all the days of your life, provided you keep close to the Lord and faithfully serve Him alone by shunning evils as sins against Him and diligently searching His Word, which from beginning to end bears incontestable witness to the truth of the doctrines I have delivered to the world."

Swedenborg himself never attempted to establish a separate ecclesiastical institution, but shortly after his death a small group of people in England organized the Church of the New Jerusalem, also known as the New Church, in order to study, preserve, and disseminate the teachings of the revelation that had been given through him. Today, there are New Church congregations throughout the world, and Swedenborg's theological writings have been translated into a large number of languages. (http://www.swedenborg.net/association/swedenborg.htm)

As a young boy, it has been documented that Swedenborg had psychic visions, but he most likely suppressed them due to his strict religious upbringing and scientific, if not practical, nature and character. Later, he did have a particularly vivid prophetic vision involving "astral-travel"[21] that quickly thrust him into the hazy world of mediumship.

> ...the seer [Swedenborg] observed and reported on a fire in Stockholm, 300 miles away, with perfect accuracy; he was at a dinner party with sixteen guests, who made valuable witnesses. The story was investigated by no less than the philosopher Kant,[22] who was a contemporary. (Doyle, 15-16)

As Doyle noted, "these occasional incidents were, however, merely the signs of latent powers which came to full fruition quite suddenly in London in April of the year 1744....From the day of his first vision he continued until his death, twenty-seven years later, to be in constant touch with the other world." (p.16)

Swedenborg described a kind of vapor oozing from the pores of his body, which initially was vapor-like, but quickly liquefied and fell to the floor. This, reckons Doyle, was "ectoplasm," which, as defined by The Reverend Frances Scher in her book *Spiritualism and Mediumship Studies,* is "a chemical or potion contained in the cyptoplasm of a cell in each person's body...used by spirits for such manifestations[23] as materializations,[24] transfigurations,[25] levitations,[26] *etc*, for physical phases of mediumship phenomena [physical phenomenon]." (p. ii)

---

21. "Astral-traveling" (also called "astral-projection" and "out of body experience") is when one's soul-mind leaves the physical body, enveloped in an astral body, traveling to distant localities. (Bletzer, 44) It is the ability for the soul to leave the physical body to gather information and insights from elsewhere.
22. Immanuel Kant, 1724-1804, was a German metaphysician and one of the greatest figures in philosophy. His numerous writings and publications were read by contemporaries of his, as well as succeeding generations of great thinkers and philosophers in Europe. "The results of Kant's work are incalculable. In addition to being the impetus to the development of German idealism,...Kant's philosophy has influenced almost every area of thought." (Chernow, *et al*, 1450)
23. A "manifestation" is the appearance of spirit phenomena in a form that is evident to the senses (through the act of manifesting by the medium's mediumship) from the Spirit World to the Earth Plane. (Scher, iii)
24. A "materialization" (also called "ectoplasm materialization") is "to bring about, at will, a manifestation of a deceased person, in whole or in part, in a séance setting, using ectoplasm; visible to the physical eye under infrared lighting; ectoplasm that exudes from the medium's body and sitters (in lesser degrees) is utilized by the etheric world intelligence and the person manifesting." (Bletzer, 188)

> ...when he resigned his post and gave himself to the contemplation of spiritual matters, especially to the work of making clear to mankind [sic] the true inner doctrines of the divine Word as he claimed that they were revealed to him by direct insight into the spiritual world after "heaven was opened" to him in 1745. Visions and communication with spirits and angels helped prepare him to set forth the teachings of what he termed the New Church, the inauguration of which he believed to have taken place in 1757 with the second coming of Christ. He claimed to have received from the Lord himself the true sense of the Scriptures.[27] (Chernow, et al, 2667)

Some of Swedenborg's most interesting visions referred to the other world where humans go upon their death. He maintained that the afterlife consisted of a variety of spheres, each representing different degrees or levels that represented the various spiritual conditions possible to humankind. Each person is automatically judged by the totality of his/her life works (he noted that a deathbed confession or an absolution of sins by a member of the clergy made little difference in the whole scheme of one's entire life). (Doyle, 18)

Curiously, Swedenborg envisioned the afterlife to resemble the earth in many respects, containing much of the societal makeup common during the time he lived on the earth plane, with houses, churches, assembly halls, and even palaces where those who were in charge would reside. (Doyle, 19) A number of scholars regard his impressions to have been influenced by his religious and social upbringing. Many of his spiritually based writings have been further illuminated by modern mediums that have had similar visions. Critics, however, maintain that the subsequent visions by later "seers" and mediums that seem to corroborate those of Swedenborg's could merely be backwash intuition from prior knowledge. Proponents maintain that many of the mediums who have experienced

---

25. "Transfigurations" are "changes in the appearance of another's face and body while sitting in a "psychic development circle" [also called a "séance" or "healing circle"] in subdued lighting; the interpenetration of the etheric world guides can be so strong that sitters [people in attendance at the séance or circle] can see changes in the features of others, sometimes taking on the features of the [spirit] guide and sometimes appearances of body movement when the body is still. (Bletzer, 644)
26. "Levitations" are when people or objects are levitated, raised or suspended in the air without the use of any physical means; this is accomplished by the undivided concentration of the subconscious mind or by the [spirit] guides who use ectoplasm and the medium to levitate the person or objects. (Bletzer, 351-352; Scher, iii)
27. Emmanuel Swedenborg's spiritual writings include his expositions of Genesis and Exodus entitled *Arcana Coelistia*; *Heaven and Hell*; *Divine Love and Wisdom*; *True Christian Religion*; and *Apocalypse Revealed*.

similar visions had no prior knowledge or information about Swedenborg's revelations. Metaphysics is an inexact science, making it virtually impossible to prove or disprove conclusively such claims as it completely depends upon the "sensitive" experiencing the visions.

In many respects, Swedenborg is considered to be the true forerunner of Spiritualism because of his descriptions of how the physical death of a human was lovingly assisted and made easy by "celestial beings" who guided the recently departed into the next realm. In addition, an idea that is at the crux of modern Spiritualism is the idea that all souls are redeemable. He found in his visions that there was no eternal damnation; spirits who needed more spiritual-based lessons and experience to achieve a higher level could work their way up to it. As well, those who had lived good lives had no permanent place (*i.e.* heaven), but were also able to work on their souls' journeys by working toward achieving an even higher-state of spirituality. (Doyle, 19)

Swedenborg also described marriage as "a form of spiritual union in the next world. It takes a man and a woman to make a complete human unit. Swedenborg, it may be remarked, was never married in life....Married couples continued together if their feelings were close and sympathetic." (Doyle, 19-20) Some could argue that once people go into transition, why would such a human-based emotion as attraction to a partner, possibly sexual, be of such importance? Would spirits not have more important tasks at hand? Modern Spiritualist thought contends that such human-generated desires, wants, and needs (including the idea of "time") become irrelevant in spirit. Once a person passes into transition, though, the "soul group" or "kindred-spirits" of the person do remain in contact and do maintain similar relationships to those that they experienced while on the earth plane. The difference is that the emphasis on ego-based human emotion is replaced by the divine love of God.

The spiritual work with mediumship that Emmanuel Swedenborg did during his life, although far removed in years from the ancient and biblical accounts of mediumship, helped to raise people's awareness and consciousness regarding the possibility of spirit communication through mediumship. Upon his death in 1772, his followers set out to sustain his teachings. Although not widely known, the devotees of his teachings continued his work and soon another notable person emerged that would also greatly influence the psyches of people, further opening up their minds to even greater possibilities for spiritual development: Franz Anton Mesmer.

2.3 The Work of Franz Anton Mesmer

Spiritualism, then, could be regarded secondarily as the child of the psychic activity of the 18th century, centering on not only the work of Swedenborg, but also that of Franz Anton Mesmer. "Mesmer had, in the 1770's and 1780's, discovered and articulated a form of psychic healing that included both magnetic healing and hypnotism." (Melton, 93) The German healer and physician postulated that there was an all-pervading force or magnetic fluid which linked all beings. "He called this 'animal magnetism' and it was not so different from Hindu *prana* or Chinese *ch'i*. Mesmer's method of laying hands and giving suggestions to patients led to the development of therapeutic hypnotism." (Cambell, Brennan, 151)

Figure 2.

Mesmer studied medicine in Vienna, which in those days was considered the medical center of the world. His family lived in borderline poverty in a small town near Lake Constance. From early records of his life that still exist, psychic investigators conclude that Mesmer was something of a dilettante; it was quite some time before he settled down to just one subject. First, he attended a theological seminary but never graduated. Later he took a degree as Doctor of Philosophy and began to study law. Records show that he was granted a medical degree, but never was interested enough in traditional medicine to practice it.

Mesmer heard stories of Father Gassner's[28] healing powers and came to Klosters to witness the healings himself. As he observed, he was very impressed. He concluded that some unknown force was at work and immediately started work on a theory to explain the cures. The body, he surmised, must have two poles, like a magnet, and must, like a magnet, be emitting an

---

28. Father Gassner was a Roman Catholic priest in Switzerland that practiced faith healing in the 1770's. His method incorporated a crucifix which he used to touch his patients who were seeking a cure. (http://www.psychicinvestigator.com/demo/Mesmr2.htm)

invisible magnetic "fluid." According to Mesmer, disease was due to some interruption or maladjustment in the flow of this "fluid," and it therefore could be cured by correcting the flow.

Mesmer came to the conclusion that only certain people had this gift of being able to control the flow of this mysterious "fluid" and these practitioners had the power to make the fluid flow from themselves into the patient. Furthermore, this could be accomplished indirectly. For example, it could be done by "magnetizing" almost any object, such as a bottle of water. The magnetized objects would then presumably pass on the "fluid" to anyone who touched them.

Pursuing this line of thought further, Mesmer discovered that it was important that there should exist a close interest in, and sympathy for, each other between the physician and the patient. This he described as rapport, French for "harmony" or "connection." This term is still in use in psychoanalytic circles, and describes the relationship in which the doctor has the interest and cooperation of his [sic] patient.

Mesmer had many early successes putting his theories [to work] and carried out many demonstrations of healing. He became a celebrity among the wealthy and was a frequent visitor at the local castles and mansions. His popularity grew, and because most medical men could find no logical basis for his cures, his envious colleagues had the Viennese Medical Council expose him as a fraud. In 1778, Mesmer left Vienna for the more liberal environment of Paris. There he soon established himself and became the talk of the town. The wealthy aristocrats of Paris paid Mesmer large fees; yet it is a matter of record that he treated hundreds of poor peasants for free.

Mesmer used an apparatus which he called a *bacquet*. The bacquet was an oak tub filled with iron filings and broken glass. Protruding from the wooden top were dozens of bottles with the necks pointing in the direction of the patients. Placed inside the bottles were many iron rods whose purpose, according to Mesmer's theories, was to spray magnetic rays on the subject. These bottles were filled with supposedly magnetic water.

The assembled patients gathered around the baquet, each holding the hand of the patient on either side, the whole party forming a kind of "magnetic ring." Ethereal soft music would play and the lights [would be] dimmed. Some of the patients would start singing during these strange séances. Inevitably, a few patients experienced spasms or a "crisis" after which they would emerge from the experience feeling improved in health. Occasionally young aristocratic women would return for the pleasure of the experience even though they no longer had any medical condition to treat.

> Despite widespread skepticism of Mesmer's methods, he was certainly the first person to draw the attention of the world to the important fact that mental treatment can have a direct bearing on illness of the body, and that the proper use of mesmerism, or hypnosis, can have immense benefit to psychic investigators. (http://www.psychicinvestigator.com/demo/Mesmr2.htm)

In 1784, at the age of 54, Mesmer left Paris in disgrace, eventually settling back in Lake Constance where he was born. (Morgan, 2003) He was publicly denounced and humiliated by the French Academy for his work in the fields of life force energy ("animal magnetism") and hypnotism. (Melton, 93) He lived a quiet life, dabbling in a little medicine, but remaining largely disconnected from the social life and world he enjoyed while being a celebrity hypnotist in Paris, until his death on 15th March 1815, at the age of 85. He never changed his views on animal magnetism but did return to the Catholic Church from which he had lapsed for most of his life. (Morgan, 2003)

Although Mesmer died in disgrace, his students continued his work and took his theories on magnetic philosophy and hypnotism to England and the United States. "As a result of the publication of the *Progress of Animal Magnetism in New England* by Charles Poyen in 1837 and widespread lecturing by him and other magnetic students, the issue of man's [*sic*] nature was raised across the country in the early 1840's. In 1843, one of these roving Mesmerists spurred interest in a young shoe-maker apprentice, Andrew Jackson Davis." (Melton, 93) With this chance encounter with the traveling Mesmerist, it can be said that the movement of Modern Spiritualism truly began.

2.4 Andrew Jackson Davis, "The Poughkeepsie Seer"

Andrew Jackson Davis was born in Blooming, New York in 1826, and died in Boston, Massachusetts in 1910. He grew up in abject poverty, the son of uneducated parents—his father was a weaver and a shoemaker. He has been called the "John the Baptist" of Spiritualism due to the profound influence he had on spreading the movement (once it started a number of years after his initial encounter with the traveling Mesmerist). After all, it was he who initially predicted the advent of the Spiritualist movement.

> Young Davis showed signs of clairvoyance and heard voices very early in life and, on the advice given from Spirit, he convinced his father to move to Poughkeepsie in 1838. In 1843, Dr. J. S. Grimes visited the city and gave a series of lectures on mesmerism (hypnosis). With Davis's curiosity getting the

better of him, he attended one of the lectures and was tested as a subject, with no results. Later, a local tailor named William Levington helped induce upon Davis a state of mesmeric trance and found that in this altered state of consciousness, he (Davis) could accurately diagnose medical disorders. In this condition, Davis described how the human body became transparent to his spirit eyes; this seemed to come from the center of the forehead. Each organ stood out clearly with a special luminosity of its own which greatly diminished in cases of disease.

Figure 3.

In 1844, Andrew Jackson Davis had an experience which was to change the course of his life. On the evening of March 6th, Davis was suddenly overcome by some power which led him to "fly" from Poughkeepsie, where he lived, and hurry off in a semi-trance state, upon a rapid journey. Upon gaining full consciousness the next morning, he found himself amidst the Catskill Mountains, some 40 miles away. Here, he claims to have met two very distinguished men, whom he later identified as the philosopher Galen, and the Swedish seer Emanuel Swedenborg, both of whom were, of course, dead. He also claimed to have experienced a great mental illumination and revelation.
(http://www.geocities.com/CollegePark/Quad/6460/bio/D/avisAJ.html)

Andrew Jackson Davis was known as "The Poughkeepsie Seer" and continued the work of Swedenborg through his naturally mediumistic trance channeling sessions. Swedenborg was able to resume his work through Davis, by channeling dictated philosophical books. Davis also predicted, via Swedenborg in Spirit, the advent of Spiritualism.

As defined earlier, is it possible that Andrew Jackson Davis experienced a "levitation" or "astral-travel"? He was physically in the Catskill Mountains, making astral-travel unlikely. The speed in which he arrived at his destination, at a time when the only mode of transportation was by horse, leaves one to question how this occurred. Regardless of how he arrived 40 miles away from his home in the course of one night, this experience profoundly changed his life. He began in earnest his study of things metaphysical and began lecturing and teaching publicly, traveling around the area to promote what he had experienced.

> From that time onward, he traveled extensively, giving public lectures and teachings. In the course of a teaching tour, Davis met Dr. Lyons and Rev. Fishbough. Dr. Lyons was a qualified mesmerist and often induced the trance state upon Davis. During these episodes, a wealth of material came through, all of which was transcribed by Rev. Fishbough. In November, 1845, Davis began dictating his great work, *The Principles of Nature: Her Divine Revelations and A Voice To Mankind*. The dictation lasted for 15 months, with many enthusiastic people bearing witness to these trance utterances. (http://www.geocities.com/CollegePark/Quad/6460/bio/D/avisAJ.html)

The *Principles of Nature*, considered by many to be Andrew Jackson Davis' greatest work, is remarkable in its comprehensiveness. In it, he discusses the cosmos, the solar system, creation, Earth's history, the origin of the human species, and the primitive history of humans from psychic sources. Even more remarkably, perhaps, is that he described a philosophy that in effect was modern Spiritualism, before Spiritualism was even a movement. He, too, wrote about the redemption of everyone, no matter how wicked they were on the earth plane; everyone has a chance to redeem his/herself once in spirit.

> The doctrine, in a word, was that the world beyond is as natural as this world of ours; that it is neither the heaven nor hell of official Christianity; that it is simply this world spiritualized, and that men and women in their psychic bodies are as men and women here in body and flesh, but with better opportunities of progress and a far better environment. They are encompassed by helpers innumerable, so that those even who pass from life of earth in a state of hardened criminality have every encouragement to amend and ultimately never fail to do so. In a word, the gospel of Davis, in common with that of Spiritualism, cast out all fear concerning the life to come. (Davis, viii)

This notion of redemption for every soul is similar to that of Emmanuel Swedenborg. In fact, many people during the time he channeled this information felt that it resembled the work of Swedenborg not only in content, but also in its style. Critics would maintain that such a coincidence could be only the result of his reading Swedenborg's material beforehand; adherents would counter that Davis was channeling the spirit of Swedenborg, so, of course, the materials resemble one another. Also, Davis' proponents pointed out that he was not an educated man and could not have studied it prior to his channeling of it:

> ...much of the teaching that was given through Andrew Jackson Davis is similar in style and content to that of Emanuel Swedenborg; yet Davis was not at all an educated person during his earlier years. It is this fact, we feel, which makes the revelations of Davis so very interesting. Here we have two seers, Emanuel Swedenborg and Andrew Jackson Davis. Each came from totally different social, economic and educational backgrounds, yet both were channels for some of the most profound and esoteric philosophies and teachings to come out of the eighteenth and nineteenth centuries. (http://www.geocities.com/CollegePark/Quad/6460/bio/D/avisAJ.html)

Sir Arthur Conan Doyle, in his book *The History of Spiritualism*, also comments on the similarity of visions of both Swedenborg and Davis. He does not allude to or insinuate that Andrew Jackson Davis borrowed his ideas from Swedenborg, and only has praise for Davis and describes him as "very humble minded, and yet he was of the stuff that saints are made of." (p. 56) Andrew Jackson Davis was a gifted medium that was able to predict innumerable events. Perhaps his most famous prediction was when he prophesized the beginning of the movement of Modern Spiritualism. As included in his book, *The Principles of Nature*, published in 1847 (a year before the Hydesville Rappings which spawned the movement) Doyle quotes the following of Davis:

> It is a truth that spirits commune with one another while one is in the body and the other in the higher spheres—and this, too, when the person in the body is unconscious of the influx, and hence cannot be convinced of the fact; and this truth will ere long present itself in the form of a living demonstration. And the world will hail with delight the ushering in of that era when the interiors of men will be opened, and the spiritual communion will be established. (p. 54)

Andrew Jackson Davis played a significant, if not pivotal role, in the promulgation of Spiritualism. His work prior to the advent of Modern Spiritualism laid the foundations for the movement. As Doyle noted:

> He was clearly destined to be closely associated with it, for he was aware of the material demonstration at Hydesville upon the very day it occurred. From his notes there is quoted the sentence, under the vital date of March 31, 1848: About daylight this morning a warm breathing passed over my face and I heard a voice, tender and strong, saying, 'Brother, the good work has begun—behold, a living demonstration is born.' I was left wondering what could be meant by such a message." (p. 56-57)

A History of Mediumship from Ancient Times to the Advent of Spiritualism in America 61

It was at that moment, in an unpretentious cottage not far from where he lived, in Hydesville, New York, did communication with an apparition take place between two young girls named Katie and Margartta Fox, thus heralding the movement of modern Spiritualism, an American-made religion.

2.5 The Fox Sisters and the Hydesville Rappings[29]

> The event to which most American Spiritualists look more than to Davis as the birth of their faith occurred on March 31, 1848. Then Kate Fox [and her sister Margaretta, two young women], began to get rational response from some mysterious rapping noises in [their] home in Hydesville, New York. Kate and her [sister] discovered that the rapping would respond to their hand clapping. With a little practice, they were able to work out a code by which they were able to communicate with Mr. Splitfoot, as they called him, a disincarnate entity. Mr. Splitfoot rapped out his name as Charles B. Rosna, and told them he had been murdered in that house some years previously. Neighbors came to witness the rapping....News of the Fox sister's mediumship spread, and soon other psychics who could communicate began to appear. Some were slate mediums: the spirits wrote their messages with chalk on slates. Other mediums tipped tables. Still others went into trances and allowed spirits to use their voice boxes. Physical mediums, who could produce materialized images of the spirits, appeared. Within a decade of the US Civil War, what was to become a Spiritualist movement was developing. (Melton, 94)
> **Figure 4.**

The rappings heard by Kate and Margaretta started out as a kind of game.[30] They asked the mysterious phenomena to respond to their questions—the response

---

29. In chapter 1, a very detailed account of the "Hydesville Rappings," and Spiritualism, in general, are included in section 1.5, "American-Made religions of the 19th Century." The information included in this chapter is abbreviated in order not to be redundant. See Appendices B and E for more detailed accounts of the rappings by eyewitnesses.

was immediate and definite. It became quite clear that some kind of intelligence was manifesting. "A Committee of Investigation was formed, a definite code of signals agreed upon, and it was then established that the communicator was one Charles B. Rosna, a peddler who had been murdered by a previous occupant of the cottage and buried in the cellar. This information was subsequently verified." (http://www.newage.com.au/)

2.6 Notable Works and Personas during "The Era of Great Mediums"

The years between 1880 and 1920 is considered to be "The Era of Great Mediums." This period in Modern Spiritualism's history was a banner time for mediums and Spiritualist-related publishing. Numerous books were written which were channeled works by mediums from all walks of life. Perhaps one of the most important works produced during this time, for modern Spiritualists, was the *Aquarian Gospel of Jesus the Christ* by Levi H. Dowling. This book continues the story of Jesus where the New Testament left off; specifically, it explains how Jesus attained the Christ consciousness open to all, and offers a complete record of the "lost" eighteen years strangely absent in the *Holy Bible*. The *Aquarian Gospel* relates an active period in Jesus' life of traveling and learning from masters, seers, and wise men in temples and schools in Tibet, Egypt, India, Persia and Greece. (Dowling, 1907)

The book, *Universal Spiritualism*, written by W. J. Colville and published in 1906, was intended to be used as a class textbook by aspiring mediums during their mediumship training. In it, he delineates the teachings of immortality in other religious traditions including Egyptian thought, the Jewish Cabala, the Persian theory of religion, Greek and Roman views, Hindu writings, Chinese and Japanese philosophy, Scandinavian beliefs, Etruscan and Mohammedan beliefs, and psychical research as done in England, and Europe, contemporary to the time it was written. (Autry-Smith, in Colville, 1987)

The Rise of Victorian Spiritualism, written by Frank Podmore and published in 1902, consists of eight volumes that painstakingly detail many aspects of Spiritualism, most notably individual examples of phenomena. In Volume 2, *Modern Spiritualism: A History and a Criticism*, focuses on Spiritualism as it was exported

---

30. Leah Fox, an older sister of Kate and Margaretta, was instrumental in helping them attain notoriety by arranging public demonstrations where her sisters would give spirit messages and demonstrate their mental and physical mediumship.

to England—one of the first times an American religion was exported from the United States and not merely imported to America—and topics such as private mediumship, physical mediumship, materializations, spirit photographs, clairvoyance, trance, science and superstition, and problems of mediumship during the time it was written. These books were intended to document the many mediumship experiences of the people of the day including the famous British-American medium, Daniel Dunglas Home.[31]

Three earlier works that were written before the time period of "The Era of Great Mediums," but were nonetheless quite influential in the thought processes of the people in the late 19th and early 20th centuries, were books by Andrew Jackson Davis, Allan Kardec, Robert Hare, and William Crookes.

The books written by Andrew Jackson Davis truly did help to initiate the entire Spiritualist movement in its infancy. His *The Harmonial Philosophy: A Compendium and Digest of the Works* is a compilation of his most noted writings that outline topics such as death and the afterlife, Summerland,[32] spirit mysteries, and a myriad of other topics that specifically pertain to spirituality, which would later be adopted by Spiritualists in mass as being the basis of their new religion.

A book published in 1874 by Allan Kardec quickly became an indispensable item for aspiring mediums—*The Book of Mediums: Guide for Mediums and Invocators*. This instructional book helped guide novice mediums through the proper steps of honing their gifts. The book is comprehensive and extremely detailed in its presentation of mediumship development, manifestations, the means of communicating with spirits, and most importantly, perhaps, the difficulties and dangers that can be encountered in the practice of mediumship. He cautions aspiring mediums to beware of inferior or lower spirits who may act as tricksters, who like humans, exist at different levels, some being good and some being bad.

---

31. Daniel Dunglas Home, 1833-1886, "a Scottish-American Spiritualist medium, he was taken to the United States when a small child. At the age of 13 he claimed to have discovered his gifts for dealing with spirits, and from 1850 to his death he had a triumphant career as a medium, always retaining his amateur status by refusing money, although he did accept expensive gifts. In his drawing room séances, furniture moved with no apparent cause, ghostly hands appeared, and furniture and Home himself would levitate in the air. There was much dispute about the validity of these highly physical manifestations of spirits. Though numerous efforts were made to expose him, none were successful." (Chernow, et al, 1260)
32. "Summerland" is a name coined by Andrew Jackson Davis during one of his channeling sessions which refers to the Spiritualist idea of paradise. It is a place where spirits go in the etheric world upon transition; it looks like the earth plane, except it is far better and superior to life on earth.

Two books that were written before 1880 by two different authors focused primarily on the research into the scientific side of Spiritualism: *Experimental Investigation of the Spirit Manifestations: The Existence of Spirits and Their Communion with Mortals* by Dr. Robert Hare, MD, and *Researches in the Phenomena of Spiritualism* by William Crookes. The main focus of these books is to highlight the scientific side of proving the existence of spirit communication through apparatus' and seemingly scientific methods. This was a very important aspect of early Spiritualism—to show definitively through scientific means that communication with spirits from the other side is real and to prove the existence of physical and mental phenomena.

However, early on when the movement was in its infancy, photography was thought to be a way to prove categorically the existence of spirit manifestations. As with any early science, it was inexact in that something as benign as a worn camera sheath that had a hole the size of a pin could allow light to expose small orbs on the picture. Believers thought these were "spirit orbs" around the people, but in fact were most likely light-generated exposures that had inadvertently come into contact with the film. Tin plate pictures sometimes would allow double-exposures to occur which appeared to be spirits hovering around the person.

Today, the sophistication of the general public of the 21st century that routinely use modern appliances can logically explain such occurrences, but people of the mid-19th century who were less experienced in the areas of gadgets did not allow for such clarity. As well, unscrupulous people, in an effort to enrich themselves by duping unsuspecting believers, would also purposefully manipulate photography in an effort to ply their craft more widely. These attempts at fakery cast a dark light on the entire movement since there was no organizing body that could regulate the movement in a strict and consistent manner. Eventually, to combat widespread fraud being perpetrated by corrupt swindlers against the public, organizations began to be formed to help regulate mediums and to test their mediumship through lyceums or schools as a form of "accreditation."

Sir Arthur Conan Doyle, the creator of the world's most rational fictional detective, Sherlock Holmes, was "himself fascinated by the irrational and mysterious. He was a keen student of the psychic and paranormal for almost half a century and in the last twelve years of his life was an active exponent of Spiritualism." (Campbell, Brennan, 71) Raised as a Roman Catholic, Doyle became an agnostic and originally became interested in Spiritualism when a university student—as a firm skeptic. Some sources report the year 1917 as the year he publicly declared his belief in Spiritualism, others report it as being 1918. In either case, Doyle was in his late forties when this occurred and it changed his life, giving him a burning mission and taking him on international lecture tours. He collected data and documents, wrote voluminously on the subject and absorbed all he could about spiritual phenomena. (Pakenham, 18) He actively lectured on Spiritualism and participated in Spiritualist related organizations until his death in 1930. His two volume book, *The History of Spiritualism*, is an exhaustive account of Spiritualism's history, written in painstaking detail, covering all aspects of the movement, including biographical and evidential information on specific mediums and notable Spiritualist personas who were involved in promulgating the religion in America and overseas; also, research and investigation into proving physical phenomena are real are also included.

A book written in the latter half of the 1800's by M.H. & E.W. Wallis, entitled *A Guide to Mediumship and Psychical Unfoldment*, is yet another guide to assist people in unlocking their own psychic powers and gifts of mediumship. The authors divided their guide into three main "Parts," with each of these being subdivided even further. Principally, the book explains mediumship, how to develop it, and how to cultivate one's psychic abilities. The theme of "self-help" or "how to" was very popular during the years at the end of the 19th century. Obviously, publishers were eager to publish books on the subject of Spiritualism because they were in great demand. The plethora of books published, during a time when publishing a book was expensive with regards to not only money, but also the inordinate amount of time it took to publish a book, attests to the public's desire to know more about the movement and to learn how to dabble in spirit communication themselves.

Many of the books published during this time contain scientific references and allusions which are clearly not relevant in light of modern scientific knowledge, but all had a profound impact upon American society of the late-19th and early-20th centuries. A book entitled *Clairvoyance* by C.W. Leadbeater, first published in 1899, is a good example. The most recent edition cautions readers with a similar disclaimer, but quickly points out that the basic material contained still has great spiritual value and is still in print after more than one hundred years.

Leadbeater teamed up with Helena Petrovna Blavatsky to form The Theosophical Society after becoming disillusioned with Spiritualism. She published a number of books, one being *The Key to Theosophy*, which explains Thesophy in layman's terms. In the preface, Madame Blavatsky offers the following:

> The purpose of this book is exactly expressed in its title, "The Key to Theosophy," and needs but few words of explanation. It is not a complete or exhaustive textbook of Theosophy, but only a key to unlock the door that leads to

> the deeper study. It traces the broad outlines of the Wisdom Religion, and explains its fundamental principles; meeting, at the same time, the various objections raised by the average Western enquirer, and endeavoring to present unfamiliar concepts in a form as simple and in language as clear as possible. (p. xi)

Many of the books published during this period emphasized the fact that novice readers, and those who have a casual interest in metaphysics, would be able to read, understand, and implement the techniques easily themselves. This is perhaps why the movement of Spiritualism, Theosophy, and Christian Science gained such wide followings in such a short amount of time. A number of splinter groups developed (including Christian Science and Theosophy).

Spiritualism offered women a greater role in religion (traditionally denied to them by the mainstream religions); it also empowered them to create their own movements, which ultimately took followers away from Spiritualism. Both Mary Baker-Eddy (Christian Science) and Madame Blavatsky (The Theosophical Society) were somehow connected to Spiritualism and broke off to create their own movements. Ironically, in many ways, both of these splinter movements have been more successful than Spiritualism over the past century or so in maintaining the movements, enjoying a wider base of followers. Although revivals occurred in Spiritualism after each of the great wars, it has not faired so well historically with regards to the numbers of active members and churches.

Today, vibrant Spiritualist camps exist, as well as Spiritualist churches that thrive in pockets around the United States, but it has not enjoyed for many decades the numbers of followers it once did during its heyday. Perhaps because the splinter groups had centralized organizations led and controlled by autocratic leaders helped them to organize and move forward; Spiritualism was never centered on a particular personality, but was comprised of independents that tended to go about and do their own style of mediumship.

In hindsight, this most likely served to impair the movement. Instead of a centralized figure that represented the religion, many competing societies were formed that were built around churches that featured resident mediums. Once that star medium passed into Spirit, often was the case where the church slowly lost its members and eventually died. To compound this problem was the fact that Spiritualism proudly asserted that it had no dogma (perhaps in an effort to set itself apart from the traditional, mainstream religions). In contrast, the other American-made religions, as well as the newly formed movements that had splintered off of the Spiritualist movement, clearly set out theological doctrines that were strictly adhered to by their members (*i.e.* Joseph Smith and his *Book of Mor-*

mon for Mormonism; Mary Baker-Eddy and her *Science and Health* for Christian Science; and Madame Blavatsky and her writings, most notably *Isis Unveiled*, *The Secret Doctrine*, and *The Key to Theosophy* for The Theosophical Society).

The independent inclination of Spiritualism allowed initially for a variety of Spiritualist societies and associations to form, each following a loosely interpreted set of Spiritualist teachings and beliefs of the religion, but more often than not, following their own individual set of criteria for organizing churches, camps, and educational systems for certifying, testing and evaluating mediums in their organizations. It is an interesting side note that two of the more successful and powerful of the splinter groups—Christian Science and Theosophy—were started by people disgruntled with the loose organization and varying set of principles and credos of the Spiritualist movement, hence they started their own.

2.7 Summary

In this chapter, the history of mediumship was surveyed from pre-biblical and biblical times, citing a variety of instances from the Holy Bible which suggest the mediumship of notable biblical personas. The terms mediumship, psychic, and channeling were defined in the sense in which these terms will be referred to in this dissertation The development of each was outlined, and the connection between these terms were explored.

With some reservations, I have followed a somewhat linear approach to outline mediumship throughout history, advancing immediately from biblical mediumship to that of the gifted mediumship of Emmanuel Swedenborg, a noted figure in the history of mediumship who was the first to write down systematically his experiences with spirit communication. The metaphysical and scientific work of Franz Anton Mesmer was summarized in order to give sufficient background information to the general societal condition which made the United States more conducive to accepting the eventual revelations of spirit communication through mediumship, and to offer some historical perspective as to why Andrew Jackson Davis would be interested in Mesmerism.

Andrew Jackson Davis, and his chance meeting with a Mesmerist which helped him to realize his own psychic gift, can be regarded as the primary impetus in exposing the general public to the idea of spirit communication through mediumship through his writings and lectures. Once the Fox sisters made contact with the spirit entity in their house, producing physical phenomena that were clearly heard by not just the control medium, but by numerous witnesses who were present, did the movement truly begin. Davis' tireless work prior to the Fox sister's revelation helped to pave the way for the movement, fostering its progress through his teachings, writings and extremely accurate clairvoyant insights.

The period between the years of 1880 and 1920 produced a multitude of interest by the general public who were intrigued with the idea of communicating with loved ones who had passed and with guardian spirits. This insatiable appetite by the public at large legitimized the religion in many respects, attracting a huge following that made Spiritualism seem "mainstream." This "Era of Great Mediums" produced a number of published works which brought Spiritualism to the average person and to the forefront of American society. The sheer number alone of converted people attests to its popularity. These ordinary people were guided by their desire to connect spiritually and physically with departed loved ones, and the influx of published materials geared toward the average person made developing one's own psychic ability to communicate with spirit accessible and possible.

Most notable, perhaps, was Sir Conan Doyle, a staunch believer and follower who championed the Spiritualist cause by lending his expertise in writing and impeccable reputation for honesty and detail to the movement. His book, *The History of Spiritualism,* is the definitive work on the Spiritualist movement and is still considered to be so today.

The most striking difference, perhaps, between ancient mediumship and modern Spiritualism is the fact that it was not until the mid-19th century that mediums organized and formed groups to share with a larger stratum of people their abilities to communicate with those in the spirit world. Many cultures around the world, prior to the advent of Spiritualism, did have traditional shamans, who offered spirit communication, but these were considered indigenous to the regions they were from; Spiritualism brought mediumship to the forefront of society. This difference made it unique and separated it from other traditional systems of mediumship.

The ability to commune with spirits is as old as time itself—the organized effort to speak to those in spirit using a code offered evidence that was never before seen. On March 31, 1848, when the Fox sisters made contact with the disincarnate they playfully called "Mr. Splitfoot," changed mediumship forever, bringing it out into the open and into the hearts and minds of people from all walks of life.

The advent of Modern Spiritualism did, however, pose a serious dilemma for those most closely involved in it: How was it going to be organized? How would it grow and prosper? Slowly, as more mediums began to appear, the movement began to take shape in the form of a truly organized religion with churches, ministers, camps, and associations. The young movement was coming of age and a system was needed to clearly define its principles, hence the Science, Religion, and Philosophy of Spiritualism are the focus of Chapter 3.

3

The Science, Philosophy, and Religion of Spiritualism: An Analysis of its Principles, Beliefs, and Social Policies

Often, people confuse the terms *Spiritualism* and *spirituality*. The two are somewhat connected, in the sense that most Spiritualists would readily consider themselves to be "spiritual;" the majority of people, however, who regard themselves as spiritual, are not "Spiritualists." Spirituality tends to focus on a person's personal belief system and "soul" desire, which usually incorporates an acceptance of a higher power that is divine and all-knowing, unlike mere mortals—one that is not corporeal or tangible, but ethereal and spirit-like, forming the basis from which the person's sense of sacredness and/or religion is made.

Similarly, Spiritualism holds the "soul" in the same relevance, as well as the belief in a divine force (referred to as *Infinite Intelligence* by practicing Spiritualists), but this is where the similarities end. In contrast, Spiritualism's primary focus is to promulgate the belief that the dead survive their physical death as spirit entities which can indeed communicate with those on the earth plane who are still living. This communication occurs through a sensitive-intermediary called a "medium" which can make contact with and relay messages from those who have passed over to the other side.

With that clarification rendered, the questions that still beg for further elucidation are: What is Spiritualism? Is it a religion? Or is it a philosophy? In what way is it considered to be a science? Simply answered, according to the *National Association of Spiritualist Churches Spiritualist Manual*, it is a combination of all three. "Spiritualism is the Science, Philosophy, and Religion of continuous life, based upon the demonstrated fact of communication, by means of mediumship, with those who live in the Spirit World." (p. 35) "Continuous life" refers to the proven communication with entities in the spirit world who have experienced the change called death. (Faubel, 7)

Since March 31, 1848, when the Fox sisters, Margaretta (Maggie) and Catherine (Katie) experienced the "Hydesville Rappings" (the name associated with the first occurrence of spirit communication that started the movement),[1] those who became the early adherents of the movement worked very hard to distance their new-found religion from mainstream religions of the day (mainly the Protestant denominations of Christianity). The belief system developed as a viable alternative to those "other" religions, offering not only a religion, but a philosophy to live by, and the use of science to prove its claims.

The United States of the mid-19th century was in the end-days of the industrial revolution which was having a huge impact upon the way people lived and viewed social and economic changes that were taking place in America and in Europe. Perhaps the term "revolution" is a misnomer in that there was no violent or sudden change in the way society was affected by the use of machinery, but rather it was a gradual development, and then, acceptance of mechanical technology. All of this did, however, help to lay the foundation for the possibility of technology being able to be used as a form of "science" to prove the existence of life after death in the form of spirit communication.

Around this same time, the science of photography was becoming more and more prevalent, and this was also thought to be a mode in which to prove definitively, through photographs, the existence of spirits.

> Spiritualists found inspiration in the invention of photography, which Louis Daguerre had first exhibited in 1839. Photography bridged the gap between different times and places (the past and the present, the distant and the near), analogous to the Spiritualists' bridge between heaven and earth. Photography appeared to offer proof that the intangible could act upon the tangible that spirit could inform the world, or even that mind could act directly upon matter.
>
> ...Spiritualists hoped it would serve not only as a means of collecting objective evidence that could prove to others the existence of the spirits seen at a séance but also as a means of investigating the invisible spirit realm by registering on photosensitive material images that the eye was otherwise incapable of apprehending.[2] (*Photographing Heaven*, 2002)

---

1. See Appendix B for a detailed account of this occurrence.

A book written by a Dr. Robert Hare, MD in 1855, when Spiritualism was still in its infancy, was solely dedicated to the experimental investigation of phenomena. *Spiritualism: Scientifically Demonstrated* offered readers of the day scientifically based information to collaborate the existence of spirit communication, including diagrams of scientific contraptions[3] used to prove the continuance of life after death. On the title page of his book, Dr. Hare lists his credentials—Emeritus Professor of Chemistry in the University of Pennsylvania, graduate of Yale College and Harvard University, Associate of the Smithsonian Institute, and a member of various learned societies—which illustrates, in part, how seriously the movement was regarded by not only common folk, but also by academia and the educated classes. The need for scientific proof was great in the psyches of people at this time because it seemed possible to be able to fuse religion, science and philosophy together. For the first time in human history, Spiritualism offered people a religion founded not solely on divine revelation, but upon scientific investigation.

In addition, Spiritualism provided people with a renewed sense of hope philosophically, that there was something beyond this earthly experience; that loved ones lived on in the spirit realm indefinitely; and no matter how sinful a person

---

2. Although early photography lacked the sophistication it does today, people were still able to manipulate it to produce fraudulent images. This type of trickery hurt the movement when the ruses by the deceivers were found out. There were earnest attempts to use photography in scientific ways without conscious deception; unfortunately, oftentimes small holes that had naturally worn into the sheath of the camera would produce supernatural-like images behind or in front of the people sitting for the photograph. These were considered to be verifiable proof of spirit orbs, spirit lights, and spirit entities (because they did have a "ghost-like" appearance to them). Also, another problem that sometimes occurred was that residual images from the plates used in the camera would sometimes bleed through onto the next photograph; these images appeared to be transparent, appearing above or beside the people sitting for the actual photo. To the untrained eye of the time, without being able to scientifically prove otherwise, it did appear to be spirit entities lurking about. Modern science has shown that the majority of these "spirit photographs" that were not intentionally manipulated were indeed not of another world, but of light entering the shutter from the side of the camera or from residual images from a prior photograph. It is interesting to note, though, that not all of these photos can be explained away so easily and modern photography, as well as video, has captured unexplainable phenomena that cannot be completely discounted.
3. See Appendix J for an essay by Julia Schlesinger (written in 1886) regarding Dr. Hare's experiments into proving paranormal activities; included are sketches of his contraptions.

was in life on earth, salvation and redemption was at hand for those who were willing to work toward it in spirit. Also, people were attracted to other facets of Spiritualism which were more philosophically and religiously-based, such as the denial of many of the entrenched Christian-based beliefs. For example, Spiritualists do not adhere to the Christian beliefs in original sin, vicarious atonement, the God-like divinity of Jesus the Christ, and the existence of Heaven and Hell as locations.[4]

These differences, all of which will be expanded upon later in this chapter, set Spiritualism apart from mainstream Christianity. People in the mid-to-late 1800s welcomed this more relaxed view of religion. It offered them hope for salvation that was reasonable and possible, much unlike the fundamentalist religions which preached fire and brimstone messages, expounding the importance and need to live sinless lives built on an unattainable sense of human perfection, making it seemingly impossible to fulfill. Spiritualism offered an alternative to the mainstream, countering that as humans, all are bound to sin at some point, and *that* is a part of the divine order of things and is a necessary part of one's soul's purpose and journey—to experience the unpleasant as well as the pleasurable in order to learn spiritually.

It is interesting to note, though, that Spiritualists did have, and many continue to have to this day, a strong appreciation for and predisposition to Christianity. Perhaps this is largely due to the fact that early Spiritualists, as well as modern-day Spiritualists, came from Christian backgrounds. Spiritualism primarily is a religion of "converts," even though it is well over 150 years old. Today, there is a small percentage of Spiritualists who grew up within the religion from childhood, with the majority of practicing Spiritualists who currently adhere to this belief system having converted to it as adults. Of this percentage, an overwhelming number of Spiritualists were raised in either a Protestant or Roman Catholic Christian tradition.[5] For this reason, then, a goodly number of Spiritualists find much comfort in the teachings of Jesus,[6] as well as preferring to use the

---

4. Spiritualists view these as "conditions;" Heaven is going to the light, advancing spiritually by living as spirit; Hell is the unhappiness one makes for oneself in this life and at death will gravitate to a "plane of consciousness which [his/her] earth life prepared [him/her] for. But if [he/she] chooses to drift and refuses to make an effort to progress, [he/she] weaves about [himself/herself] a mantle of darkness which shuts out the life giving light. This will be [his/her] Hell. This knowledge is based on the testimony of those who have passed on to the spirit side of life." (Faubel, 9-10)
5. The statistics for this data will be expanded and explained in detail in Chapter 7.

Holy Bible as a tool in their mediumship work, in their rituals, and in their church services.

In this chapter, the science, philosophy and religion of Spiritualism will be clearly explained. As well, the religion's principles and beliefs will be delineated showing the similarities and differences in the belief systems between it and mainstream Christianity. Finally, a review of Spiritualist social policy statements will be included in order to illustrate unambiguously the belief system and social attitudes of this American-made religion.

3.1 *The Science of Spiritualism*

Spiritualism is considered to be a "science" because it purports to investigate, analyze, and classify proof of spirit-communication and physical phenomenon (NSAC, 35).

> ...the fact that it is a science has been proven by physical phenomena. It is demonstrated through mediumship, in a physical way, which absolutely is ruled by Natural Law.[7] (Brown, 2004)

---

6. Although Spiritualists do not regard Jesus as the only "son of God" (all people are sons and daughters of God, possessing equal divinity, according to Spiritualist teachings), they do, however, hold him in very high esteem as a man who walked the earth plane, ministering, healing, and teaching great lessons in compassion, love, and kindness to the multitudes. Spiritualists view Jesus as a wonderfully gifted medium, healer, and teacher who is a master-teacher. As stated in an informational packet from the Indiana Association of Spiritualists at Camp Chesterfield, Indiana, entitled *What is Spiritualism?*, "...Jesus was, as the Bible states, 'a supreme master of God's Laws.' His life was an example to us of what we could become for he stated in John 14:1, 'Verily, verily, I say unto you, he that believeth in me, the works that I do shall he do also; and greater works these shall he do.' He demonstrated many of the spiritual gifts and most importantly the continuity of life after death. His teachings of brotherhood, love, humility and service are the basis of the philosophy of Spiritualism." (2002)
7. According to *The Fundamentals of Spiritualism* by Peggy Barnes, "Natural Law is the law God set into motion to govern all. It is immutable and unchangeable. There is no record of it having been changed to suit the whims of anyone. There is law that controls organic life and a law that controls spiritual life. Both are so correlated that one reacts upon the other. Today, we are coming to a realization of the fact that we may control our own destiny with Natural Law. Through right living, we may create health, happiness, and for ourselves prosperity." (p. 43) [See Appendix F for a list of Natural Laws.]

The Science, Philosophy, and Religion of Spiritualism: An Analysis of its Principles, Beliefs, and Social Policies

In his book, *The A.B.C. of Spiritualism* (1920), B.F. Austin explains the science of Spiritualism as that "which affirms the existence of Spirit and the Origin, Sustainer and reality in all the forms of Nature in all the expression of life. According to its teachings, the Universe is spirit-built and constitutes a Divine revelation of Spirit (God). Spirit manifests in all that is True, Beautiful and Good." (p. 4)

The primary problem, however, with these explanations is that they, in essence, offer little scientific "proof" that is irrefutable in the eyes of critics and skeptics. Or do they? What exactly is the science of Spiritualism? Could the "proof" be in the perceiver more than in the elaborate experiments that early believers and skeptics tried to perform to prove definitively the existence of physical phenomena and spirit-communication? Part of the problem, perhaps, had to do with the way Spiritualism was offered to the public. By announcing confidently, as Spiritualism does, that it is a "science" (as well as a philosophy and religion) encourages scrutiny and leads people to demand scientific proof—a proof that is tested under proper conditions and verified by a totally objective panel of experts using scientific means to do so. For Spiritualists who have experienced phenomena and received messages from loved ones, this is all the proof they need. It is irrefutable and definitive in their eyes. By experiential means, they are satisfied with the end results. True believers have all the proof they need; non-believers will most likely never have enough proof.

In the early years of the Spiritualist movement, as the world embraced science and new technologies never before seen in the history of the world, many attempts—some successful and verifiable, some not so convincing—took place to offer scientific proof of spirit communication. These often included some rather odd-looking and dubiously constructed contraptions[8] that were designed for the sole purpose of testing and proving categorically the existence of spirit and spirit communication. Many outstanding and reputable academicians set out in earnest to prove, and often to disprove, the existence of spirit.

Two of the most well-known among these were Sir Conan Doyle,[9] best remembered for being the author of the Sherlock Holmes series of detective stories and who also believed wholeheartedly in Spiritualism and spirit communication. He was determined to prove to the world its veracity and authenticity. The other man was Harry Houdini,[10] the famed escape artist and magician who was convinced that all mediumship was based on fraud, parlor tricks, and elaborate hoaxes. These two men had a love-hate relationship, largely based on mutual respect in the beginning, and finally with mostly mutual disdain in the end.[11]

---

8. See Appendix J to see two examples of these machines.

Because of their leadership in opposing camps, Houdini and Doyle were much aware of each other. The earliest surviving letter in what became an immense correspondence was dated March 15, 1920. In the spring of 1923, they were on tour in the United States, and met in Denver, Colorado. Their friendship continued and grew, with exchanges of long letters and extensive visits that included both their wives.

In October 1922, Houdini expressed his views in the New York Sun. "I am perfectly willing to believe, but…I have never seen or heard anything that could convince me that there is a possibility with communication with the loved ones who have gone beyond."

Meanwhile, Conan Doyle continued to spend a vast amount of time and money on "psychic" phenomena—hypnosis, auras, table tipping, spirit channeling, séances, spirit photography, ectoplasm and the like. He was highly sympathetic to such claims—even those proved fraudulent—and believed passionately in communication of spirits from the afterlife.

At the height of their friendship and correspondence, Conan Doyle again and again asserted Houdini had—and his performances used—"wonderful occult power," although Houdini utterly repudiated the idea. In the early 1920s, Houdini began abandoning his performances in favor of lectures and demon-

---

9. "Arthur Conan Doyle was born in Edinburgh, Scotland, on May 22, 1859, earned an MD degree and practiced medicine in England until he became one of the most popular and successful authors in the English language, beginning with *A Study of Scarlet*, the first of the Sherlock Holmes detective stories, published in 1887. He covered the Boer War and World War I as a newspaper correspondent and was knighted in 1902 for his journalism. Raised a Roman Catholic, he became an agnostic and originally became interested in Spiritualism when a university student—as a firm skeptic. He publicly declared his belief in Spiritualism in 1917, at 48. It changed his life, giving him a burning mission and taking him on international lecture tours. He collected data and documents, wrote voluminously on the subject and absorbed all he could about spiritual phenomena." (Pakenham, 2001)
10. Harry Houdini was born Erik Weisz in Budapest on March 24, 1874, to a rabbi who brought his family to the United States in 1878. From childhood, he was fascinated with magic tricks. When he was sixteen, he took the name Houdini, based on the great French conjuror Jean-Eugene Robert-Houdin (1805-1881). He worked beer halls and small theaters as an apprentice and became spectacularly successful as a stage magician. A serious self-made intellectual, he accumulated a huge library on magic and mysticism and wrote widely. By 1900 he was known worldwide, especially for his escape tricks. He became the highest paid entertainer of his era. He scorned any suggestion of the occult in his work." (Pakenham, 2001)

strations devoted to debunking Spiritualism, just as Conan Doyle intensified his own lecturing.

Ultimately, as their differences grew, they became bitter critics of each other and their work. By 1925, Conan Doyle was writing of Houdini as an unconscionable self-promoter and defamer of psychic occurrences and "a very discredited man." Houdini, whose life had become an anti-Spiritualist crusade, wrote: "My opinion of Sir Arthur Conan Doyle is that he is a menace to mankind, because the public thinks that he is just as great a man in (the) spiritualistic field as he is in writing stories...He has not enough mentality left to use good judgment."

They never reconciled. Houdini died on October 31, 1926, from internal damage caused by a student punching him in the stomach, ostensibly as a test of his strength. Conan Doyle lived until 1930. (Pakenham, 2001)[12]

The rivalry between Conan Doyle and Harry Houdini illustrates how seriously people took the idea of "proof" in the early years. This overwhelming need in the early decades of Spiritualism by both believers and nonbelievers to substantiate their points is an interesting, if not unique, aspect of Spiritualism. Most religious traditions offer their adherents less "proof," and yet expect them to have blind faith in the unseen and the unknown, based solely upon their own spiritual understanding and personal religious experience and epiphany.[13]

---

11. For a detailed look at the relationship between Doyle and Houdini, please see *Final Séance: The Strange Friendship between Houdini and Conan Doyle*, by Massimo Polidoro (published by Prometheus, 2001).
12. "In spite of staged, fraudulent demonstrations and mediums of questionable honesty, Spiritualism continued to flourish. Indeed, especially during World War I's horrific carnage, séance mediums and Spiritualist churches were consulted more than the older, firmly-established religious institutions. Many startling spirit contacts were made with deceased soldiers and sailors, revelations to this day that have been hard to discredit. Rudyard Kipling and Arthur Conan Doyle became spokesmen of Spiritualism because of contacts with the other side." (Dreller, 45)
13. Interestingly, Christians accept without question the divinity of Jesus Christ. It would seem absurd to a Christian to be asked: "Prove that Jesus is the son of God scientifically—not referring to the Bible, but through scientific means." The response most likely would be one of disdain. Religions do not have to prove themselves, and most people follow a particular religion without any proof at all. Those who demand proof might do well to do some self-reflection and to demand proof from their particular belief system. The point is the question is moot because it is a *religion*. The "proof" of any religion comes from within the person who is a follower.

Spiritualism, though, from the beginning offered as part of its attraction the idea that it was in large part based on science and could be proven. Spiritualist mediums today feel less inclined to prove to others their abilities to communicate with spirit. In part, this could also be due to the fact that many adherents today are more discerning and are able to decide on their own accord what is genuine and what is not.

After all, the average citizen of the 21st century is much more savvy and aware of scientific progress in the areas of radio waves, microwaves, satellite communication, electronic mail, and all of the other "unseen" technology and scientific wonders that are a part of daily life. No one today questions why a mobile phone is used without being hard-wired to a pole; or why a microwave oven can cook an entire meal in a matter of minutes. It is all a part of living in an age where maybe science has finally caught up with Spiritualism.

Adherents of Spiritualism in the 1800's and 1900's could never have imagined the type of technology that is used without conscious thought today—all seemingly done invisibly. In those days, physicians denied certain basic premises of medical science because it could not be seen by the naked eye or with the unsophisticated microscopes of the day. Much progress has been made, but to them, verification and proof was a seeming necessity. The following is an excerpt from an interview given to this researcher by Reverend Sarah Brown, an ordained minister and Spiritualist medium:

> You see, we don't find it necessary [to subject ourselves to scientific tests], and not because I accept it on blind faith, because I don't; but I don't worry about proving my religion in a scientific way. I have just seen phenomena and I have seen it happen and I know what I see and I know what I hear and I know what I smell. And I don't find it necessary to prove it. It seems that in order for it to be accepted in the last century, that they prove that scientific part of it.
>
> …We don't set ourselves up to be tested anymore as much as the old mediums did. It was not unusual at all for a poor thing to subject herself to be tied up or stripped naked, to prove that what she was doing was real. Well, the American public is sophisticated enough now that they are going to pretty well know if what you are doing is genuine or fraudulent.[14] (Brown, 2004)

In the *National Spiritualist Association of Churches Service Book*, a question and answer section is included. One question of interest asks, "What should convince me of [Spiritualism's] truths? The answer simply states: "your own reason and

---

14. For the complete transcript of the interview, see Appendix G.

common sense after a thorough and scientific investigation." (p. 81) Again, the idea of scientific investigation is expressed. Perhaps therein lays the dilemma: What is *science*, in the context of Spiritualism? According to Webster's New World dictionary, science is basically the "systematized knowledge derived from observation and study." (p. 526) With this definition in hand, then, an empirical study is all that is necessary to offer an individual proof of spirit communication (*i.e.* a sitter at a séance receives a message from a loved one or sees some type of physical phenomena; as long as the person is discerning in the observation and has done research beforehand about spirit communication, and can vouch for the conditions of the sitting).

Basically, it comes down to what a person decides to believe for him or herself; and to decide *what is scientific and what is not*? A person who witnesses and experiences personally some type of physical phenomena via mediumship has all the necessary proof he/she needs to accept or reject spirit communication. Those who have not experienced phenomena most likely will not accept it as it is not within their personal realm of experience.

A person's spiritual belief system is personal and, for the most part, is experiential—regardless of whether one is an adherent of Spiritualism, Christianity, Judaism, Islam, Buddhism, or any one or more of the many other religious traditions that make up and are a part of world religion. Each person belongs to or is attracted to a religion for a reason—it may be because one was raised in a certain tradition, or married someone or has a partner who is a follower of a particular belief system, or searched and sought out a spiritual practice from within, that resonated with the person on some level.

The point is: Few religions (if any other than Spiritualism) are subjected to such intense scrutiny to show "proof" that is scientifically verifiable. Most people know from within what is true for them and in turn follow a spiritual path that is based on this intuitive knowledge. This is based largely on personal experience, a feeling (the knowing from within), but it is also usually based on a philosophy. Spiritualism is no different; it not only is a religion and a science, but it is also a "philosophy."

3.2 *The Philosophy of Spiritualism*

The "philosophy" of Spiritualism is much easier to delineate concretely than the "science" portion of its treatise. The primary philosophy of this religion is belief in an "Infinite Intelligence" that pervades all and is in control of the universe and its workings. This Great Force has no form or shape and is impersonal, omnipresent and omnipotent. (NSAC, 39) This concept is in direct contrast to the mainstream view of God being an all knowing, omnipotent being on a throne, meting out judgments at will—some as tests, some as punishments, and some as rewards for good behavior.

> We have for many years visualized our God as a glorious man and placed Him in a body similar to our own. By so doing, we have limited our understanding of Him and of His manifestations, in spite of the fact that we have asserted that he is omnipotent, omnipresent and omniscient. We have placed him in a literal heaven which we have asserted to be in the skies, and thus we have built a wall between our creator and ourselves. This wall is one of ignorance and in spite of the fact that God and the ways of life are still to a great extent incomprehensible to us, we have learned much through Divine Revelation, and the findings of science. (Barnes b, 5)

The anthropomorphic God of mainstream religion is replaced by a more spirit-like presence that has no particular appearance or gender for Spiritualists. It is important to note, however, that much of the material written about Spiritualism by avowed Spiritualists refer to this Infinite Intelligence at times with masculine pronouns (*i.e.* He, Him, the Father, *etc.*). Current political correctness, however, has started to infiltrate the religion and recently terms such as "Heavenly Father, Mother God" are being used to incorporate the idea that God is neither masculine nor feminine, but both. Other terms that are used are: Creator, Almighty, All-Knowing, Oneness, and of course, Infinite Intelligence.

Spiritualists view the universe and its origin as being unknown without direct bearing on one's moral conduct. "The universe is an aggregation of forces and matter, which always moves and acts in the same manner under the same conditions and is not capriciously governed." (NSAC, 39) Spiritualism does not discount evolution like fundamentalist-Christians tend to do; instead, Spiritualists accept the Law of Evolution as being the natural order of things that can be proven scientifically as fact and thus accepted as such.

> In Genesis [Genesis 1:1] we read the story of the creation is written by Moses, and after studying the findings of our present day scientists in regard to the theory of the evolution of organic matter, and making a comparison of the two, we find a certain harmony between the Bible story and the different steps and eras in the theory of evolution. Nothing is created, in a literal sense of the word, for all is in the process of being created. Constant change and constant growth onward and upward is the law of the universe. (Barnes b, 6)

The idea of the earth being created in seven days goes against scientific understanding. The Book of Genesis uses "seven days" as a literary tool, that is symbolic of the different cycles of evolution, rather than confined to what we consider to be a week in actual time (from Sunday to Saturday incorporating seven earth days). The gradual manifestation of "all that *is*" has occurred over a long period of time, and is still in the process of evolving, according to Spiritualist beliefs.

The conviction that humans were created perfect, and then retrogressed to imperfection is a difficult ideology for Spiritualists to accept. Instead, it makes more spiritual sense to adherents of Spiritualism that all (including humans) were created from a single cell and have gradually progressed and evolved upwardly to the status of intellectuality, spirituality and integrity that people possess at any particular time or moment—and will continue to progress, on all levels, indefinitely. "[Humans are spiritual beings], evolved from the lower forms of life, up through the period of consciousness, to the state of the higher moral and spiritual faculties, which survive, unaffected, the decomposition of the physical body." (NSAC, 39) The "soul" or "spirit" of the person is what lives on and is unchanging accept for the fact that it can progress and evolve spiritually to become more enlightened. The vessel or body of the person is in many ways inconsequential in that it is only a vehicle for the spirit while on the earth plane; once the physical body is no longer alive, the spirit leaves the body and goes into the spirit-realm.

> The spirit of man, that which is a part of God, must of necessity be perfect as God is perfect. There is an intermediate principle between the Spirit and organic man which we call the soul or celestial body…thus man becomes a trinity—body, soul, and spirit. At the time of so-called death, the soul and spirit leave the organic man and the soul or celestial body forms over the physical body by a cord, similar in nature to the umbilical cord that connects the mother and her child before birth, only in this instance the cord is made of a more spiritual substance. Death, so-called, does not occur until this cord is severed, and then the soul and spirit pass into the next expression of life and the organic body now discarded, and no longer animated by spirit, goes back into the chemicals and dust from which it came. (Barnes b, 7)

In accordance with Spiritualist beliefs, the primordial duty of humans on the earth plane is to begin the process of gaining and attaining knowledge based on universal truths. In so doing, people are able to steadily develop their character and basic nature to harmonize eventually with the fully unfolded spiritual state. This is not limited to one's spirituality, but also moral conduct and mental attitude toward life and spirit. Related to this concept are the ideas of "brotherhood" and the importance of serving and loving others.

> By virtue of similar qualities, conditions, wants and aspirations, mankind is a brotherhood; and in this life, at least, cannot escape the good or evil effects of contact and conversation. It is, therefore, necessary that this brotherhood be promoted by the more fortunate ones for the betterment and upliftment of the less fortunate. (NSAC, 39)

This learning process then continues on once a person goes into transition, retaining his/her individuality and issues that were a part of the life drama and episode he/she had on the earth plane. The continuous unfolding of a person's moral, mental, and spiritual capabilities continue on while in spirit.

> After the spirit has severed its relations with the physical body, man's moral status is the same as immediately before the change and he enters into a high or low estate according to his attainments in this world. By a subtle law, both the good and the evil he has done are fairly weighed; he himself holds the scales and renders the judgment. (NSAC, 41)

The Hindu belief in *karma*[15] is related to this concept. In Spiritualism, it is referred to as the Law of Compensation—the law that metes out automatically to humans just payment for the acts they perpetrate, whether good or bad, exacting both punishment and reward. (Barnes b, 8)

> Good deeds, springing from a good heart, have a creative force in building pleasant abodes in spirit life, and conversely the sinful create their own unhappy habitations. The wicked must compensate for their evil deeds, here or hereafter, and attain a state of justice before they are prepared to enter upon the path which leads to spiritual happiness and progression. (NSAC, 41)

The most important philosophy of Spiritualism, perhaps, is the belief in the continuity of life. Spiritualists, through mediumship,[16] make contact and communicate with those who are on the other side. The primary purpose of medium-

---

15. "*Karma* is the principle that makes every man or woman the cause of their present global location, lifestyle, intelligence, relatives and physical body condition; this principle is governed by one's entire activities, thoughts, and emotions throughout all incarnations." (Bletzer, 334) It is also called the Law of Cause and Effect—for every action, there is a reaction.

ship is not to have physical phenomena, but to make contact with spirits and to communicate messages to those on the earth plane from these spirits, therefore giving people hope and proving that life indeed does go on. (Brown, 2004) Often is the case where physical phenomenon will occur, but a medium does not necessarily expect it to happen. The main focus is to receive a message and relay it to the intended person present, whether it is in a circle, a private reading, or at a message service in a Spiritualist church.

> Mediumship does not depend upon belief or goodness. It has been manifested in all ages, to men [and women] of all faiths, to the good, the bad and indifferent. Goodness and character are the result of individual effort, self control and earnest desire. The truths of Spiritualism have been established after much questioning, much examination, much comparison and much testing. They have come for many years through mediums all over the globe and from many different spiritual sources, with wonderful unanimity; and they satisfy our reason and sense of justice. (NSAC, 42)

Spiritualists have a very magnanimous attitude toward all people and all religions, accepting any spiritual tradition that is sincere, genuine and has only the highest good as its intention.

A major difference between mainstream Christianity and Spiritualism, as well as the concept of Divine Order, is explained by Reverend Sarah Brown, as follows:

> …we are free thinkers.…And this sounds rather self-serving—but I don't think we are as judgmental.…moral living is hoped to be obtained by all of us, but what is right for me may not be right for you. As long as I'm not hurting anyone, it is not my right or your right to judge each other. What I consider to be moral you may not, but of course, morals differ from culture to culture, country to country, and generation to generation. We, as Spiritualists, do not have a set of rules; of course, abiding by Natural Law…and the Ten Commandments are good rules to live by, but a lot of religions go to places, that in my opinion, they don't belong—you shouldn't drink coffee, you shouldn't do this, you shouldn't do that—they get into "rule" making and that's where I have the freedom as a Spiritualist. Now, I must abide by the laws of the land I am living in, and I must strive for high moral character, but what that means

---

16. "A medium is one whose organism is sensitive to vibrations from the Spirit World, and through whose instrumentality intelligence in that world is able to convey messages and produce phenomena of Spiritualism." (NSAC, 35)

to people varies from person to person. A good thing, above all, is do no harm, in my opinion.

I do believe that there is Divine Order and a Divine Plan, but that does not take away our freedom of choice and our freewill. Otherwise, we would just be robots. I do believe that all is in Divine Order until we, with our freewill and free choice, change that. And if it is divine, it must be of the highest and the best. Where I get into trouble is when I step in and insert my own will and freewill. But it is not always wrong [to do so]....As we evolve, hopefully our choices and our freewill will lead us to a higher level. I make mistakes. Of course, how else would I learn? I do not believe that God tests us. I do not believe that God punishes us. I think we do quite a fine job of that for ourselves. But, I think things happen in Divine Order because I was supposed to learn for some reason. (Brown, 2004)

In her commentary, the Reverend Brown mentioned that Spiritualists do not have a "set of rules." There is, however, a list of beliefs entitled the *Declaration of Principles*. These are not considered by practicing Spiritualists to be dogma or a creed. In fact, Spiritualism prides itself as being a "creedless" religion. If the Declaration of Principles is not a creed, then what is it?

3.3 *The Declaration of Principles*

"Spiritualism believes in Natural Law, which provides for a philosophy of life. The Declaration of Principles is a general set of principles that Spiritualists believe in and go by. The principles are not dogma or creed." (Loffredo, 2001) Some might argue that a set of written principles do, indeed, constitute dogma and are in essence a "creed." The *Webster's New World Dictionary* defines a "creed" as being a brief statement of religious belief, especially one that is accepted as authoritative by a church; or any statement of belief or principles. (Neufeldt, 143) This definition certainly suggests that Spiritualism's Declaration of Principles is a creed. In contrast, "dogma" tends to purport a set of doctrines that are strictly adhered to by the believers. (Neufeldt, 177) Both of these definitions of creed and dogma seem to suggest that, in fact, the Declaration of Principles, as laid out by Spiritualist organizations, is a type of creed and is dogma.

This distinction that is made by Spiritualists is most likely a result of the early organizers of the Spiritualist movement trying to do all they could to distance themselves from mainstream-Christian doctrine. It is certainly a question of semantics as the terms creed, dogma, and principles are so closely related that they could be easily interchanged with one another. Perhaps the need to stand apart from other established religions, as well as the dogma they espoused, can help to explain why a stated differentiation was made, and still today is voraciously defended when there is even the slightest suggestion (by outsiders looking in) that Spiritualist principles are a type of dogma or creed.

In Christianity, the Apostles Creed (c. 650) is used by both Roman Catholics and Protestants. It begins with "I believe in God the Father Almighty, Creator of Heaven and Earth. And in Jesus Christ…." (Chernow and Vallasi, 679) Since Spiritualists do not believe in a personal God, the sole divinity of Jesus as the only son of God, or in Heaven or Hell, this statement in its totality conflicts with their general belief system. The Nicene Creed (c. 325) is similar, but states "I believe in one God the Father Almighty, maker of heaven and earth, and all things visible and invisible, and in one Lord Jesus Christ…." (p.678) This also clashes with Spiritualist beliefs because they do not adhere to the supernatural belief in the creation of all things animate and inanimate. Instead, Spiritualists believe in the natural progression of everything, including the earth and all that inhabits it, in accordance with Natural Law[17] and the Law of Evolution.

> The main reason the Spiritualist does not claim that the Declaration of Principles is a Creed is that our Declarations are not subservient to an already established form of worship. They are not approached through the channels of the Christian Bible alone, but normally and naturally, through the channels of science and philosophy. The value of their application personally, is developed through Natural Law, a force and power as eternal as time. Self Realization does not come through an outside channel, such as the many times translated Christian Bible, nor a personalized God, but through the combination of natural forces inside and outside of every individual. It is the result of EFFORT and the recognition of CAUSE and EFFECT. While the Orthodox Christian church promises reward and salvation through Vicarious Atonement by supernatural means, our Declaration of Principles becomes simply a mirror in which we see reflected not only ourselves but an ability to use for ourselves the never changing qualities of Natural Law. Our problem becomes our own individual problem; we cannot shift that problem to any other human being or to an anthropomorphic God. Our Declaration is not a creed; it places all dependence on self as the channel of Infinite Intelligence; God speaks to man through man, this is actual and it is factual, it is the noblest pattern for life, here and forever. (Myers, 5)

The Declaration of Principles of the National Spiritualist Association of Churches (NSAC) was originally adopted by an earlier organization, called the

---

17. See Appendix F for a list of Natural Law.

National Spiritualist Association. Sections 1-6 of the Declaration of Principles were first adopted by the organization in Chicago, Illinois in 1899, over fifty years after the Hydesville Rappings. Sections 7-8 were formally adopted in Rochester, New York in 1909, which is geographically near to the first spirit communication occurrence of the Fox sisters. Lastly, Section 9 was adopted in St. Louis, Missouri in 1944. (NSAC, 32) The following are the nine principles as outlined by the National Spiritualist Association of Churches (NSAC)[18]:

1. We believe in Infinite Intelligence.

2. We believe that the phenomena of nature, both physical and spiritual, are the expression of Infinite Intelligence.

3. We affirm that a correct understanding of such expression and living in accordance there with, constitute true religion.

4. We affirm that the existence and personal identity of the individual continue after the change called death.

5. We affirm that communication with so-called dead is a fact, scientifically proven by the phenomena of Spiritualism.

6. We believe that the highest morality is contained in the Golden Rule: "Whatsoever ye would that others should do unto you, do ye also unto them."

7. We affirm the moral responsibility of individuals, and that we make our own happiness or unhappiness as we obey or disobey Nature's physical and spiritual laws.

8. We affirm that the doorway to reformation is never closed against any human soul here or hereafter.

9. We affirm that the Precepts of Prophecy and Healing contained in all sacred texts are divine attributes proven through mediumship. (NSAC, 32)

---

18. Other Spiritualist organizations either accept the Declaration of Principles as adopted by the National Spiritualist Association of Churches, or they have adopted a portion of these and revised the rest. See Appendix I for several alternative versions of the Declaration of Principles as used by other Spiritualist organizations and associations.

The *Spiritualist Manual* for the National Spiritualist Association of Churches (NSAC) offers an interpretation by Joseph P. Whitewell of the above Declaration of Principles:

1. **We believe in Infinite Intelligence.**

   By this we express our belief in a supreme Impersonal Power, everywhere present, manifesting as life, through all forms of organized matter, called by some, God, by others, Spirit and by Spiritualists, Infinite Intelligence.

2. **We believe that the phenomena of nature, both physical and spiritual, are the expression of Infinite Intelligence.**

   In this manner we express our belief in the immanence of Spirit and that all forms of life are manifestations of Spirit or Infinite Intelligence, and thus that all men are children of God.

3. **We affirm that a correct understanding of such expression and living in accordance therewith, constitute true religion.**

   A correct understanding of the laws of nature on the physical, mental and spiritual planes of life and living in accordance therewith will unfold the highest aspirations and attributes of the Soul, which is the correct function of True Religion.

4. **We affirm that the existence and personal identity of the individual continue after the change called death.**

   "Life here and life hereafter is all one life whose continuity of consciousness is unbroken by that mere change in form whose process we call death." Lillian Whiting.

5. **We affirm that communication with so-called dead is a fact, scientifically proven by the phenomena of Spiritualism.**

   Spirit communication has been in evidence in all ages of the world and is amply recorded in both sacred and profane literature of all ages. Orthodoxy has accepted these manifestations and has interpreted them in dogma and creed in terms of the supernatural. Spiritualism accepts and recognizes these manifestations and interprets them in the understanding and light of Natural Law.

6. **We believe that the highest morality is contained in the Golden Rule: "Whatsoever ye would that others should do unto you, do ye also unto them."**

This precept we believe to be true. It points the way to harmony, peace and happiness. Wherever tried it has proven successful and when fully understood and practiced, will bring peace and happiness to man on earth.

7. **We affirm the moral responsibility of individuals, and that we make our own happiness or unhappiness as we obey or disobey Nature's physical and spiritual laws.**

Man himself is responsible for the welfare of the world in which he lives; for its welfare or its misery, for its happiness or unhappiness and if he is to obtain Heaven upon Earth, he must learn to make that heaven, for himself and for others. Individually, man is responsible for his own spiritual growth and welfare. Sins and wrong-doing must be outgrown and overcome. Virtue and love of good must take their place. Spiritual growth and advancement must be attained by aspiration and personal striving. Vicarious atonement has no place in the philosophy of Spiritualism. Each one must carry his own cross to Calvary's Heights in the overcoming of wrong-doing and replacing them with the right.

8. **We affirm that the doorway to reformation is never closed against any human soul here or hereafter.**

We discard entirely the terrible wrong and illogical teachings of eternal damnation and in place thereof we accept and present for consideration of thinking people the thought of the continuity of life beyond the change called death.

9. **We affirm that the Precepts of Prophecy and Healing contained in all sacred texts are divine attributes proven through mediumship.**

We thus affirm our belief in and acceptance of the truths which are contained in the Bible and assert that Prophecy and Mediumship are not unique nor of recent occurrence alone, but they are universal everlasting and have been witnessed and observed in all ages of the world. (NSAC, 32-34)

In addition, scientifically, Spiritualists accept the idea of the Law of Evolution and that the age of the universe and earth is in fact billions of years old and not just thousands. All is believed to be in Divine Order, having a natural progression that is right and just. The idea of a "heaven" and "hell" as locations is a foreign concept to practicing Spiritualists—they are considered conditions or states of consciousness. Individuals, through their actions—good and bad, noble and dishonorable—create their own heavens and hells for themselves on earth. (Brown, 2004)

Spiritualism does not depend upon any former revelation (*i.e.* The Holy Bible) to prove its credentials. (Austin, 9) "The Bible so far as it is inspired and true is based upon Mediumship and therefore, both Christianity (the simple and beautiful teachings of Jesus—real primitive Christianity) and Spiritualism rest on the same basis." (Austin, 9)

Both [Christianity and Spiritualism] originated through Mediumship.

> Both teach the spiritual nature of man; both teach and illustrate the continuity of life after death; both teach salvation by knowledge of, and obedience to, the Truth; both teach the intercommunication of two worlds. The conflict, if any, is between Spiritualism and the Spurious Churchianity of today, which has usurped the place of truly spiritual teachings of Jesus, and is teaching what Jesus never taught and is not teaching what Jesus did teach. (Austin, 9)

This, of course, is the Spiritualist comparison of the two religions. Fundamentalists and even some mainstream Christian denominations might not see the similarity between the two traditions. First, Christians do not consider the divinely inspired communications received by the biblical figures in both the Old and New Testaments to have been "spirit communication." Many Christians tend to lump such spirit communication activity into the "it must be the work of the devil" category. This is unfair, because there are numerous examples of mediumship in the Bible. Many Christians accept readily the ability to be able to communicate with God, and Jesus Christ; Roman Catholics converse with anointed Saints. Why is Spiritualism's practice of speaking with the dead so scorned by mainstream religions? According Reverend Brown, it is largely based on fear of the unknown:

> ...people fear what they don't understand. They have been taught to fear. You most often hear it referred to as "consorting with spirit." They will pray to the spirits of the Father, and Son, and Holy Spirit...even Catholics talk about the communion of saints in the other world. They are talking about spirit. For some reason it is OK to talk to martyred or anointed or sanctified spirits, but it is not OK to talk to your mother or grandmother. I think it is mostly fear and a lack of understanding. Ignorance breeds fear. [Fundamentalists] love to quote the Bible that you are not supposed to seek out mediums and fortune-tellers. We are not fortunetellers; we are prophets and mediums. (Brown, 2004)

It is no wonder why fundamentalist Christians reject the majority of Spiritualist beliefs because Spiritualism denies many of the sacred beliefs that form the core of Christianity[19]—beliefs that Christians view as factual, true and nonnegotiable: 1) an inerrant view of the Holy Bible (Spiritualists view the Bible as being a rich literary work, filled with wonderful allegorical stories based on legend and myth); 2) original sin (Spiritualists do not accept the notion that people are born with sin, meaning that they are tainted from birth due to the indiscretions of Adam and Eve in the Garden of Eden when they ate from the Tree of Knowledge; this story is metaphorical, not factual, to explain the beginning of life, expressing the idea that as humans, we were unenlightened); 3) baptism (Spiritualists, in general, do not accept baptism as a way to cleanse one's sins; the Law of Compensation makes it incumbent upon the actual person to compensate wrongs with rights); 4) Immaculate Conception (Spiritualists do not believe in the miraculous birth of Jesus because it goes against Natural Law, which are the Laws of God and are immutable—Spiritualists do believe Jesus was born and lived a life on earth and had attained a "Christed" state); 5) Vicarious Atonement (Spiritualism teaches that each individual has his/her own moral obligation to right the wrongs that he/she commits in life, accepting complete responsibility for his/her actions); and 6) Resurrection (Spiritualists believe that Jesus was seen after his death, as witnessed by numerous people, but this was not his physical body, but his spirit which manifested fully to them).

As delineated above, there are many differences between Spiritualism and Christianity which serve to widen the divide between the two traditions. Although some parts of the religions overlap, the actual beliefs and interpreta-

---

19. There are Christian Spiritualists, which to some Christians and Spiritualists alike, seems like an oxymoron. A certain percentage of Spiritualists, though, do believe in Jesus Christ as the Son of God, and redemption of one's soul can only occur through belief in him (as well as other aspects of Christianity).

tions of occurrences are quite different. Spiritualists readily accept Jesus as "The Christ," and completely admire his work in the ministry, his healing and teaching, considering him to be a wonderfully gifted medium and master-teacher.

> Christ was not his last name. Christians mistakenly, in my opinion, call him "Jesus Christ," thinking that it is a part of his name. If you ask most Christians what that word [Christ] means, they usually tell you it is his name. What happened was the "Christed" state, when one reaches a state of perfection. The Christ Spirit is when you have attained the ultimate of human life; you are in a "Christed" state. I think that the historical Jesus actually lived, as most Spiritualists do. We never argue the fact he existed and was a great prophet and that he was a master-teacher and that he had attained that "Christed" state...but I still think he was human.... Being in the human state, he may well have been married, and may well have lived a human life like we all do, even traveling and learning other religious traditions.[20] (Brown, 2004)

Noticeably absent in the Holy Bible is a long period of Jesus' adult life. Some Spiritualists believe that Jesus traveled, studied other religious traditions and probably even married, during these lost years. Given the time period, it would have been very unlikely had Jesus reached adulthood not to have been expected to marry and have a family.

Although independent of one another, Christianity and Spiritualism do share similar aspects on some level—the interpretation of these, however, differs. For instance, mainstream Christianity views a variety of supernatural occurrences as being "miracles;" instead of considering these as "miracles," Spiritualists believe they occurred in accordance with Natural Law and offer further proof in the form of physical phenomenon.

> If the early miracles really happened—such as the healing of the sick, the gift of tongues, the lights and sounds of Pentecost, the remarkable deliverances of the followers of Jesus, *etc, etc*—it is evident they occurred in natural order, and therefore, may happen in our time....

---

20. "Frequently, the term—'Jesus Christ'—is used whereas it should be—'Jesus, The Christ.' Christ was originally a heathen title, later adopted by the Gentiles, but common in many countries. The Chaldeans called it Chris; the Hindus said Chrisna; the Greeks, Chrest; while the Christians termed it Christ. In order to distinguish this Christ from the others, he was called: Jesus, the Christ, of Nazareth. 'Christ' means anointed. It was not, however, of his endowment as a preacher, but because of his office as king, that Jesus came to be called 'Christ' or the 'Anointed One.'" (Milburn, 72)

> ...The vast majority of Spiritualists, including all their representative writers, accept Jesus as an historical character. They do not deny his miracles, though they hold it impossible to make certain to human minds the happenings of two thousand years ago. Spiritualists as a body venerate the name and character of Jesus and regard him as the world's great Teacher and Exemplar.
>
> ...Spiritualists believe in the divinity of all men. Every man is divine in that he is a child of God, and inherits a spiritual (divine) nature. Just as a man develops his intellectual and spiritual nature and expresses it in life, he is "God manifest in the flesh." Since Jesus attained to the manifested in a very unusual degree, the divine attributes of Spirit, no Spiritualist would question his divinity. (Austin, 10)

Hence, Spiritualists do accept Jesus completely, but as one of many "Savior Christs" who have lived on the earth plane at different times, in different parts of the world, to teach and show by example the way to truth and enlightenment. Unlike Christianity, though, Spiritualists do not require adherents to believe in him divinely as the only Son of God as a prerequisite to entering heaven and eternal life. Spiritualists do place him in an honored position and hold him in very high esteem for the work he did, the progress he made while on earth, and for his remarkable mediumship and healings that he did. He is placed alongside a number of other great teachers, healers, saviors, and enlightened beings, such as (but not inclusive of): Vardhammana, Confucius, Buddha, Lao Tse, Osiris, Zoroaster, Abraham, Muhammad, and Zeus.[21]

Having knowledge of and accepting spiritual truths from a variety of enlightened teachers allows Spiritualists to decide for themselves which ones to look to for inspiration and spiritual upliftment. The idea of being "saved" in Spiritualism is quite different than that of mainstream and fundamentalist-Christian traditions. For Spiritualists, knowledge of and accepting Natural Law and spiritual truths can ultimately save people; and this can be done by using Jesus as an example of truth and goodness in how he lived his life and ministered to the people through prophecy and healings. This, in the end, helps people to be set free, thus

---

21. These particular masters were delineated here because they are immortalized in sculptures on the grounds of Camp Chesterfield, the Spiritualist Camp of the Indiana Association of Spiritualists, located in Chesterfield, Indiana. The area where the statues of these masters and teachers can be found is on "The Trail of Religion," in which the busts of these masters have been placed in a semi-circle configuration. For a more complete introduction of these master-teachers, see the book entitled *Trail of Religion*, compiled and edited by Esther Milburn.

saving them...but so does following the great teachings of other avatars and saviors like Mohammad, Buddha, Zoroaster, Confucius, and any number of other great teachers who have come before and after Jesus, The Christ.

One primary difference, also, between Christians and Spiritualists is the notion of Vicarious Atonement—the belief that Jesus died for the atonement of humankind's sins. Simply, Spiritualists do not accept this belief. Related to this is the Christian belief that the only way to salvation is through complete devotion to and belief in Jesus as the Savior, Lord, and only Son of God. Again, Spiritualists believe each person is a son or daughter of God and is personally responsible for his/her own salvation; "saving" oneself can best be achieved through right living, following a high moral path which is nonjudgmental, tolerant and accepting of others' beliefs and traditions.

A basic, fundamental philosophy of Spiritualism includes the acceptance of all religious traditions, sacred texts and writings, and master-teachers of the world. Although a large number of Spiritualists have an affinity to Christianity because they were raised in the religion, a number of Spiritualists hail from other traditions and backgrounds.

> We believe that there is truth in all religions. And basically all religions teach the same things about right living: "Do unto others as you would have them do unto you." That [belief] is in every religion.…We have Catholic nuns who attend our services. We have Tibetan monks that come to Spiritualist Camp. We have one ordained Methodist minister who is also an ordained medium…. There are people from all religions who come to see the Spiritualists. Most of them are curiosity seekers. Some of them, though, are seriously seeking because maybe something is missing from their own religion. (Brown, 2004)

The philosophy of Spiritualism developed, in part, as complimentary facets of older religions, but also that which is separated and stands apart. In a sense, Spiritualism can be regarded as a wayward cousin of Christianity; although it comes from the same family tree, for the most part, it is considered to be a "black sheep" amongst the more fervent and fundamentalist Christians. The basic philosophy of Spiritualism can be summed up in its Declaration of Principles—a guide for right living, that encompasses the basic tenets of this modern day religion.

3.4 The Religion of Spiritualism[22]

Spiritualism considers itself to be a religion "because it strives to understand and to comply with the Physical, Mental, and Spiritual Laws of Nature, 'which are the laws of God.'" (NSAC, 35) From research done for this study, it has been found that one of the most characteristic aspects of Spiritualism (as a religion) is not its beliefs so much as its attitude towards pursuing them. Spiritualism encourages "free thinking," allowing adherents to mix and match, accept or reject a variety of belief systems, ultimately giving the believer the personal power to follow their own personal beliefs as they see fit. Spiritualists are encouraged to seek out all religious truths and spiritual knowledge from any and all traditions.

> ...Spiritualism is trying to bring out all of your abilities, all of your capabilities, to make you a bigger and a greater person; to teach that you are responsible for that which you are, and that which you may become. Other religions, on the basis of trying to get people and keep them together, try to see to it that they don't learn anything else which might interfere. Now think of the pattern. In the meantime, they are all teaching the same thing, 250 different denominations, all based on verses of the Bible, and they can't even agree among themselves. (Wilson, vol. 1, 16-17)

Religions basically share three common aspects; the belief in and worship of a higher power (most commonly referred to as "God") with a specific system of beliefs; the power of prayer; and a code of ethics in which to live harmoniously.

> Spiritualism recognizes the omnipresence of Spirit—finds its manifestations and divine revelations in heaven and earth, in man and beast, in rock and flower, and thus the truly awakened Spiritualist if [sic] ever "face to face" with God.
>
> Spiritualism recognizes the efficacy and value of prayer, explaining in its lucid and inspired teachings how every expression of man's desire for the True, Beautiful, and Good, causes the soul to "mount up on wings like the eagle," through the operation of natural law; and how prayers are often specifically answered through the ministering angels and our arisen friends.
>
> Spiritualism in all its literature and inspired teachings has ever affirmed the absolute failure of all creeds, ceremonies, sacraments and ecclesiastical services

---

22. The symbol of Spiritualism as a religion is the "sunflower." This is based on a variety of reasons which are outlined in Appendix D.

> to bring peace and comfort to mankind until the individual, through knowledge of the truth and loyal obedience to the truth, has brought his thoughts and affections into harmony with the great laws that govern the spirit realm. Salvation from the viewpoint of Spiritualism is found only in that knowledge of, and obedience to, truth which brings man's life into perfect adjustment with Nature and with God. (Austin, 4-5)

A basic tenet of Spiritualism can be summed up in the biblical saying "one reaps what one sows," meaning that individual conduct is what will result in the type of reward in Spirit one will receive, or regret. These souls will all have an opportunity to be redeemed. Which is another premise of Spiritualism: that as souls we live eternally, and once on the other side, mediums can act as intermediaries to speak with those left on the earth plane. The basic understanding of these concepts has been received by mediums, through spirit communication.

> Spiritualism receives authority for its statements from progressed souls of Etheric Planes (Spirit World) who through mediums bring their knowledge to earth in order to free humanity from out-dated creeds and superstitions. They give us a religion by which we may live each day; in fact, they say—Religion is right living. Right living is encompassed in its entirety in the "Golden Rule," as declared by Jesus, the great teacher. Living one's religion, as taught by spirit teachers, involves "Love thy neighbor as thyself," and "Do unto unto others as you would that they should do unto you." Loving one another, tolerance of the thoughts, opinions and conduct of those about us, charity for all, these are the leading thoughts concerning our relations with humanity in general. (NSAC, *Foundation facts Concerning Spiritualism as a Religion*, revised 1999)

The medium is at the heart of Spiritualism. The professed communication between those on the earth plane and those who have passed into the spirit realm by Spiritualist mediums is the basis of this modern-day religion.

> Spiritualism teaches that, under certain conditions, there can be interchange of thought between souls of earth and those of Spirit Planes. This communication is usually carried on by means of sensitives called mediums whose nervous system is sufficiently refined and harmonized with souls of similar conditions of the Spirit Planes, that individuals may receive proof of the continuation of life after so-called death. Teachers from the Spirit Planes, speaking through mediums, whose powers they may use, bring to us many facts concerning the continued life. (NSAC, *Foundation facts Concerning Spiritualism as a Religion*, revised 1999)

The role of the medium within the religion, many of whom are ordained ministers, then, is to minister and to offer hope to those who want and need reassurance that a loved one is indeed in spirit and is doing well. Also, the mediums can ask questions to those in spirit about what it is like on the other side via communication received by the spirit entity.

> The Spirit Plane furnishes all conditions which any soul may require for its comfort, pleasure, even delight, all free for the taking. To be sure, we must learn first to desire and then to help ourselves to these conditions. We must learn to provide from materials at hand, all we need for sustenance, clothing, homes, furniture. The soul meets former friends as well as teachers. To the progressive soul, all things which are desired shall be attained when they are earned. (NSAC, *Foundation facts Concerning Spiritualism as a Religion*, revised 1999)

Critics of Spiritualism may point out that this idea of the spirit world seems a lot like the Christian idea of "Heaven," in that all is provided for "comfort and pleasure, free for the taking." These earth-based desires and wants would seem irrelevant in the spirit world, as these are physical-based needs, rather than spiritual. A soul seeking enlightenment would not be interested in pursuing earth-based pleasures as they will have reached a higher level by merely passing into the spirit realm. There would be no need for sustenance, clothing, homes or furniture.

In conversations with Spiritualists, these specific points were countered with the idea that it is easier for people to imagine a world that is relative to their understanding; hence, for people to better form a mental picture of how perfect the other side is, symbols from their earth-based existence are used to help them to visualize it. Often, spirits are perceived in clothing of different periods, as well as with objects from that period. This, in part, is due to the same reasoning; in order for the perceiver to better interpret the spirit's message, the spirit will use symbols and wear clothing that is recognizable by those on the earth plane.

Through mediumship, Spiritualism as a religion teaches that the earth-life people experience is only a precursor to a life beyond—a preparation of sorts for entrance into a continued existence. However, in order to understand this preparatory existence, one must seek out the truths contained in Natural Law and spiritual knowledge. The idea that humans are personally responsible for their own soul, and will not be redeemed through the sacrifice of another (*i.e.* Jesus dying on the cross for the sins of humankind) is a central belief to this religion.

Furthermore, the idea of a red-horned devil named Lucifer or Satan is not a part of Spiritualists' idea of Hell or "evil." Instead, the adherent must recognize the propensity of sin, whether it is of an evil nature, a temptation, or a misdeed, from within and work personally on countering these impure acts and desires. In other words, the devil does not make one do anything; innermost desire does, hence putting the responsibility upon the person perpetrating the act or desire, and not upon some outside, unseen evil force. Taking personal responsibility for one's physical, mental, and spiritual well-being is a cornerstone of the religion.

> Our own conduct leads to our rewards or negative situations and produces thereby our own heaven or hell. In this sense, heaven being a state of contentment, of satisfaction with results reached. Hell is a state of ignorance of possibilities, sometimes called darkness, a state of dissatisfaction, of restlessness, of continued obstinate refusal to desire improvement, and often distinct unhappiness or even mental and spiritual agony caused by the results of our own conduct.

> Therefore, they say: Prepare, there is no death of aught lives. We proclaim in words of light, prepare to live evermore: prepare to live well, in happiness and joy, both on Earth and on the Spirit Plane. This plane is neither Heaven nor Hell except as each soul makes it so for themselves, which is also true of Earth and your homes there. Every degree of pleasure or of sorrow is dependent upon the individuals in the home and according to their conduct, your Earth life is happy or unhappy. (NSAC, *Foundation facts Concerning Spiritualism as a Religion*, revised 1999)

Once on the spirit plane, the soul leaves behind all physical ailments and conditions and is free to make its own conditions. Spirit helpers and teachers who are a part of the person's soul group are near and will assist the recently arrived spirit to seek out and recognize the areas which need improvement and those talents which can be developed and strengthened for the good of the soul. Spiritualists maintain that if one were to succumb to desires in their incarnation on earth, rooted in sin (whether it is evilness, temptation, wickedness, or simple transgressions and misdeeds) that these too are a part of the soul's journey and is a valuable learning experience on a spiritual level. In turn, the bad deeds done will create negative cycles for the person with a karma-like result. This, as mentioned before, is the Natural Law of Cause and Effect.

> Spiritual education is a most important preparation for spiritual progress, the progress which leads to happiness here and hereafter. For the spiritual evolution of our own soul, we must practice self-control, self-reliance, as well as reliance upon the instructions of our teachers. We must acquire the perfect faith which leads to knowledge; faith and knowledge lead to serenity, to peace of

mind. If we know what we believe, then under all trials, tests and sorrowful conditions, we will be at peace, serene in our wisdom and protective power of our faithful but invisible friends. (NSAC, *Foundation facts Concerning Spiritualism as a Religion*, revised 1999)

The religion of Spiritualism is guided by the Laws of Nature which form the basis for a physical, mental and spiritual understanding of the religion's belief system; it is also guided by the Declaration of Principles which lays out the recipe for "right living,"—a central hope and desire of all Spiritualists. In addition to the science, philosophy, and religion of Spiritualism, like many other belief systems, an official set of organizational attitudes toward social policies are a part of its religion

3.5 Social Policy Statements of Spiritualism

Like many religions, Spiritualism has developed a general consensus toward social issues that further offers insight into the religion as a whole. The National Spiritualist Association of Churches developed a policy statement that reflects the general opinions of its members on the official Spiritualist position on a wide range of controversial topics that have been and still are debated in all strata of society. These social policies were originally developed and published to offer people an understanding of Spiritualism's stance on social issues. It clearly stated that the statement in no way was meant to "bind the conscience of any individual, but to address the social conditions of society, and the world to express the majority consensus of the delegation as adopted at the National Spiritualist Association of Churches 100th Annual Convention in St. Louis, Missouri, in October 1992. As far back as 1900, many of these statements were adopted as resolutions at previous delegate conventions of the NSAC." (NSAC, *Spiritualism Social Policy Statements*, 2001)

Therefore, the NSAC:

Religion—Demands freedom of religious thought and expression as the cornerstone of all lasting good in the world.[23]

---

23. This idea refers to the "free thinking" attitude of Spiritualists which allows adherents to follow the religious path they so desire. Then, any path chosen is in compliance with Spiritualist teachings and beliefs.

Discrimination—Promotes and provides an environment free of all discrimination based on race, color, sex, national origin, disability, age, or sexual orientation.[24] (Adopted October 2001)

Ministry—Affirms that our Ministry has the right, honor and privilege to perform all life celebrations.[25] (Adopted October 2000)

Equal Rights—Recognizes the purifying and uplifting power of woman in both public and private life. We demand for her all the privileges political, social and industrial that are accorded to her brother man.[26]

War—Abhors in any form and supports every effort by any nation or group to maintain peace in the world. We do support our nation's young men and women who serve in the armed forces but do not support the war itself as a method of resolving disputes and differences. Wars at any stage of human progress are brutal and morally injurious to the welfare of society, and that all international disputes should be settled by boards of arbitration, thus ushering in the era of universal peace on earth, good will to all.[27]

---

24. In general, Spiritualists have no problem with gays and lesbians being open about their sexuality; many Spiritualist camps have resident mediums that are openly gay and lesbian. These members serve vital roles in all facets of the ministry, even being ordained as ministers and healers. Unlike many mainstream religions which denounce homosexuality as an abominable and sinful, Spiritualism embraces homosexuals, welcoming them into their churches and ministries with open arms. The ideas of love, compassion, tolerance and acceptance—all of which were taught by Jesus and touted by Christians as being the basis for their religion—are practiced on a daily basis by Spiritualists. Gays and lesbians are simply just a part of God's huge, extended, and all inclusive family.
25. This very well could have been adopted in response to "commitment ceremonies" between members of the same sex, thus allowing clergy to perform these officially.
26. From the very beginning of the movement, Spiritualism has served to empower women to be independent and has given them a platform in which to pursue a professional life as clergy, mediums, and businesswomen. The movement has always treated women equally, and many Spiritualist women were instrumental in demonstrating to get the right to vote for women during the Suffrage Movement in the United States.
27. Interestingly, immediately after the major US wars—The United States Civil War, World Wars I and II—Spiritualism enjoyed a surge in popularity from family and loved ones who desperately wanted to make contact with soldiers who had fallen in combat.

Justice—Stands shoulder to shoulder with those who are opposing grafters, high and low, and works to secure justice for the oppressed of the earth; we condemn child labor, the sweat shop and industrial oppression and the practical and political disenfranchisement of all. We will work ceaselessly to make this nation in reality a government of the people, by the people, and for the people.

Capital Punishment—Considers it a disservice to humanity to support capital punishment. Crime is but the result of ignorance and a diseased mentality and capital punishment a relic of a partially civilized age. Knowing of the continuation of life after so-called death and that the individual carries with them the same type of mentality that was expressed before leaving the physical world, we know that minds of different thought exist on the Earth Plane and can be influenced by this mentality, thus the crime can be compounded. We support reform measures in the penal system and humane treatment of inmates. Through treatment and education, the criminal is given the opportunity to reform. We heartily commend those states and nations which have abolished this practice.

Life and Death with Dignity—Affirms the right of each individual to determine for self, or through a guardian, the extent through which the medical community or family may interfere with the treatment of a terminal, or irreversible condition, by the use of Living Wills, Advanced Directives and Durable Power of Attorneys, available in all states in various form. We, as Spiritualists, are bound to follow the law. If we, as individuals, would have the current law changed or extended beyond their present scope, it is our individual right to work for this through the proper channels.

Medicine and Spiritual Healing—Recommends that all medical cases pronounced incurable or terminal by medical doctors to be submitted to one or more spiritual healers.

Parenthood—Advocates planned parenthood and the widest dissemination of sex and hygiene knowledge to the end that poverty and social diseases may be eliminated.

Abortion: Informed Choice—Stands on the premise that the individual is responsible for her own happiness regarding abortion. It is not the prerogative of organized religion to mandate what constitutes happiness to an individual. It is the individual's right to make an informed choice in the matter as she alone would be responsible for her actions. This statement does not say we are pro-choice, it states we are in favor of Informed Choice.

Legitimacy of Birth—Denounces the cruel and heartless custom of designating any of God's children as illegitimate because of circumstances of their births.

World Peace—Recommends the interchange of students between colleges and schools of the nations of the world to the end that foolish, local prejudices be broken down by simple expediency of young people living and learning together as citizens of the world. (NSAC, *Spiritualism Social Policy Statements: Consensus Resolutions on Current Issues*, 2001)

The above statements show how progressive Spiritualism has been from the beginning; and it continues to be on the cutting edge of policy regarding issues that are of great importance. The majority of these issues are heatedly debated currently within societies, communities, and church denominations. The enlightened attitude found in these statements offers much credence to the Spiritualist concepts of "free thinking" and "nonjudgmental" attitudes toward fellow human beings. Much of the information contained within the statements reflects the basic Spiritualist belief in the Universal Law of Cause and Effect; each person must be judged first from within, and then when in the spirit world, for actions and behaviors perpetrated while on the earth plane. Each person's individual choices are his/her own responsibility.

3.6 Summary

In this chapter, the science, philosophy and religion of Spiritualism were individually and thoroughly defined. Spiritualism is unique in that it claimed proudly from the beginning to be scientifically based, being able to prove spirit communication, in addition to being a philosophy and religion. This claim would serve to cause consternation between adherents, between adherents and skeptics, and from other religions, most notably Christian-based faiths. To the Spiritualist who has experienced phenomena personally, that is all the proof necessary. For skeptics, who fervently charge that the movement is based on fraud and trickery, only hard science that is irrefutable under proper test conditions will prove to them its validity.

Perhaps this is an area where Spiritualism went wrong; the science of the mid-nineteenth century, although seemingly advanced at the time, was actually rather unsophisticated. Today, technology is continuing to discover never before seen advances in quantum physics, medical sciences, engineering and chemistry. Perhaps one day science will catch up with Spiritualism, proving scientifically beyond any doubt that spirits do surround us and do communicate with those of us on the earth plane that are gifted with mediumship. Currently, however, the proof is rather experiential leaving many outside the movement to look at it askance and with suspicion. For those who have experienced true spirit-communication and who have seen phenomena, nothing could be truer. Science and religion in many ways is like oil and water—perhaps the twain shall never meet. Currently, no religion can be scientifically proven in the context of how science is regarded in today's society. Part of the appeal of religious belief is the fact that much of the belief comes from an inner feeling, an innate knowing.

As well, the basic belief structure of the religion was reviewed, concentrating on the *Declaration of Principles* which is used as a guide by Spiritualists for "right living." These principles lay the foundation for the religion. A comparison was made between the belief system of Spiritualism and that of Christianity. Although they seemingly have similar roots, and overlap in ideals, the interpretation of the actual beliefs is quite different. The basic tenets of Christianity dealing with the divinity of Jesus, vicarious atonement, baptism, original sin, and the physical resurrection of Jesus are clear departure points for Spiritualists who do not interpret them in the same manner.

Spiritualism is based on Natural Law, that which is immutable and unchanging—the Law of God. Within the realm of Natural Law is the belief in spirit communication as proof of the continuation of life after the physical death of a person. This communication is achieved through the ability of a medium to make contact and relay messages from the spirit world to those on earth. This basic belief is at the heart of Spiritualism—communicating with those in the spirit world, hence claiming to offer proof of the continuity of life. The intricacies of this, the mental and physical aspects of the phenomena of modern mediumship, are the focus of the next chapter.

4

Spiritualism and the Phenomenon of Modern Mediumship

Mediumship or the ability to communicate with those who have passed from this earth life, is the primary purpose of the American religion of Spiritualism; and is the ultimate goal of Spiritualists—to communicate with those in the spirit world. Although mediums and mediumship have existed since ancient times, it has only been since the mid-1800s that this ability was organized into a religion. The main difference between Spiritualism and every other organized religion, and the most noticeable distinguishing factor that sets Spiritualism apart from all other religious traditions, is the emphasis it places upon the continuity of life in the spirit world and the ability of the medium to communicate with spirits.

All religions have a belief in a Supreme Being(s), and all religions promote the belief in a hereafter. Only Spiritualism, however, actively practices and advances the belief in spirit communication with loved ones and those in spirit through a sensitive called a "medium."[1] Also, another key concept in Spiritualism is the idea that the personality of the person during life on earth follows that person into spirit, as well as any issues or lessons that the person experienced in life; a fun-loving, jovial person in life retains these qualities in spirit (if a person had emotional and spiritual lessons to be learned in life but was unable to finish these before his/her transition, so must he/she continue to work upon these on the other side).

To those who believe, mediumship offers them a doorway or window onto the other side, offering hope and comfort in knowing that there is something beyond

---

1. "Some religions believe in spirits, but only in a saintly fashion. Fundamentalist Christians believe that to attempt communication with spirits is to solicit contact with the devil. Spiritualists, on the other hand, center their religion around communication with the spirit world." (Owens, xiv)

this earthly existence—a spiritual life where people go when the transition of death occurs, allowing the spirits of these people to continue along their souls' journeys. Believers find spirit communication to be just another phase of the natural progression of life, providing a limitless source of truth to those willing to accept it; hope for those willing to ask for it; and profuse possibilities to elevate and perfect their souls' desires toward the eventual goal of enlightenment.

To nonbelievers, categorical rejection of the possibility of spirit communication is at the center of their argument and disbelief in mediumship. Oftentimes, the mere idea of "speaking to the dead" is regarded as nothing more than a form of either witchcraft[2] or the fanciful delusions of a charlatan based on trickery and hocus-pocus fakery. To these disbelievers, the earth life humans experience in the here and now is all that is; once the physical body ceases to sustain life, there is no more. Non-adherents to spirit communication, but those who do follow a religious tradition such as prescribed by Christianity or Judaism, often use scripture from the *Holy Bible* to bolster and corroborate their claims.

> For the living know that they shall die; but the dead know not any thing, neither have they any more a reward; for the memory of them is forgotten. Also their love and their hatred, and their envy, is now perished; neither have they any more a portion for ever in any *thing* that is done under the sun....Whatsoever thy hand findeth to do, do *it* with thy might; there *is* no work, nor device, nor knowledge, nor wisdom, in the grave, whither thou goest. (Ecclesiastes 9:5-6, 10, *Holy Bible*, King James Version)

Just as nonbelievers can quote scripture against spirit communication, so can Spiritualists cite biblical verses to corroborate their beliefs:

> Now concerning spiritual *gifts*, brethren, I would not have you ignorant....Now there are diversities of gifts, but the same in Spirit. And there are differences of administrations, but the same Lord. And there are diversities of operations, but it is the same God which worketh in all. But the manifestation of the Spirit is given to every man to profit withal. For to one is given by the Spirit the word of wisdom; to another the word of knowledge by the same Spirit; To another faith by the same Spirit to another the gifts of healing by the same Spirit; To another the working of miracles; to another prophecy; to

---

2. To the uninformed, this may seem to be the case. In fact, however, Spiritualism and mediumship is in no way related to "black magic" or the "conjuring of evil forces or dark spirits." Spiritualists believe strongly in God and only work with entities that are benevolent in nature, from the light of the Creator, that wish to offer love and healing to those on the earth plane.

another discerning of spirits; to another *diverse* kinds of tongues; to another the interpretation of tongues; But all these worketh that one and the selfsame Spirit, dividing to every man severally as he will. (I Corinthians 12: 1, 4-11, *Holy Bible*, King James Version)

Also, in I Corinthians 15:44-49, the *Holy Bible* clearly distinguishes between an earthly body and a spiritual body:

It is sown a natural body; it is raised a spiritual body. There is a natural body, and there is a spiritual body. And so it is written, the first man Adam was made a living soul; the last Adam was *made* a quickening spirit. Howbeit that was not first which is spiritual, but that which is natural; and afterward that which is spiritual. The first man *is* of the earth, earthy: the second man *is* the Lord from heaven. As *is* the earthy, such *are* they also that are earthy; and as *is* the heavenly, such *are* they also that are heavenly. And as we have borne the image of the earthy, we shall also bear the image of the heavenly. (*Holy Bible*, King James Version)

Christians who believe that once the body is dead, waiting until the Second Coming of Jesus to be resurrected, Spiritualists query: What becomes of the soul—the spirit—during this period of time? The above delineated scriptures from I Corinthians suggest clearly that the spirit is alive and active. As I Corinthians 15:55 states: "O Death where is *thy* sting? O grave where *is* thy victory?" This suggests that the end is not when the body dies, but that there is continued life, which Spiritualists maintain is in the form of spirit entities that can have intelligible communication with those left behind on the earth plane. The essence of the person—its soul, its life-force energy, its spirit—departs the body and is thus released. It is energy, which is constant, and must be somewhere. It cannot be in a stagnant state, according to Spiritualists, dormant and waiting to be resurrected. Instead, it is active, alive, and anxious to make contact with those left behind.

It is, in many respects, a moot point to use the *Holy Bible* to either persuade or dissuade anyone in believing or not believing in mediumship and spirit communication. The *Holy Bible* is a literary masterpiece, both ageless and dated at the same time, perhaps inspired by God, but made by humans after being passed down orally (in some cases) for hundreds of years before being put down onto paper. Its ambiguity is what makes it unique and distinctive. For Spiritualists, the interpretation is as clear and unambiguous as it is to fundamentalist Christians and Jews who interpret the same passages quite differently. The scriptures have always been, and will always be, a source of great debate between followers of different traditions.

The National Spiritualist Association of Churches define a "medium" as "one whose organism is sensitive to vibrations from the spirit world and through whose instrumentality, intelligences in that world are able to convey messages and produce the phenomena of Spiritualism." (NSAC, 35) It continues on to define the "phenomena of Spiritualism" as that which "consists of Prophecy, Clairvoyance, Clairaudience, Gift of Tongues, Laying on of Hands, Healing, Visions, Trance, Apports, Levitation, Raps, Automatic and Independent Writings and Paintings, Voice, Materialization, Photography, Psychometry and any other manifestation proving the continuity of life as demonstrated through the physical and spiritual senses and faculties of man." (NSAC, 35)

In this chapter, a sampling of the above examples of spirit-communication and phenomena will be focused upon and divided into two parts: The *Mental* and *Physical* Phases of Mediumship. Trickery and fraud have plagued Spiritualism from its earliest beginnings until currently; these issues will be addressed fully demarcating the types and methods of fakery historically used by those posing as mediums, attempting to capitalize on the weaknesses of people searching for closure and hope in knowing about loved ones. In addition, an in-depth explanation of séances and healing circles will be given along with personal commentary by this researcher on how these are conducted and the kinds and types of spirit communication and phenomena that were experienced during these sessions.

4.1 Mental Phases of Mediumship[3]

Mediumship—as a process—is when the medium receives messages and acts as a channel for spirit beings wishing to communicate to those on the earth plane; this ability to communicate with spirits is not reserved for a select few with special psychic gifts and talents, but to some degree is possessed by all humans in varying intensities. Mediumship can be developed through concentrated instruction, self-discipline and a practicum that allows ample opportunity to hone the skills involved in receiving and deciphering messages from the other side. Not everyone has the needed perseverance and practical know-how to become proficient in spirit communication; it takes a long time to develop with hard work and much dedication.

---

3. For a list of the different types of mental and physical mediumship, see Table 1 in Chapter 2.

Spiritualist mediums are required to undergo an extensive developmental process and apprenticeship before being certified by a Spiritualist organization. A mediumship "test" is often performed under prescribed conditions to make sure that the aspiring medium is indeed connected to spirit and can offer messages to others that are correct and informative to the receiver, often including specifics such as names and events.

Prophecy

The gift of prophecy has been practiced since prehistoric and ancient times. It is central to many of the world's great religions. In the course of human history, there have not only been true prophets, but also false prophets. Spiritualists concur that whenever there is authenticity in any endeavor, so shall there be dishonesty and deceptiveness in an attempt to mimic that which is true. In order to have fakery, there must be a model of the genuine in which to base the insincere. (Brown, 2004) Such is the case with Spiritualism—there are those who try to pass themselves off as genuine mediums for self-gain and profit.

> Prophecy has been practiced for many centuries in connection with many religions. There have, of course, been false prophets as well as true prophets. But there are also good and bad men, honest and dishonest, false and fair, in every human calling. The existence of the false is no good or logical reason for attempting to hinder, stifle or destroy the true and honest. Because there are imposters and pseudo-mediums is no good reason for passing laws to silence the voice of honest mediums. The false and dishonest persons engaged in any legitimate work or businesses are only a small percentage of the whole number; and, therefore, it must appear an unwise policy, nay more, an unjust and oppressive procedure, to legislate the whole body out to their calling or employment because of the wrongs of a few. There are always weeds or tares among the wheat. (NSAC, 55)

From interviews and research done for this study, it is clear that Spiritualists are very concerned about their image and do work hard toward "weeding out the tares among the wheat" within their particular organizations. Accusations of fraud are taken very seriously and are promptly investigated; if the medium is found to be using false tactics or trickery that is passed off as genuine spirit communication or phenomena, then the medium that is in noncompliance is asked to leave the association, organization, or church and to desist in practicing their mediumship under the banner of the Spiritualist organization.[4]

With these caveats in mind, two questions present themselves: Why is prophecy such an integral part of this modern-day religion? And why do people seek out the assistance of prophets and mediums? The National Spiritualist Association of Churches lists four specific reasons which serve to answer these questions:

> First, to learn from them moral lessons. And these are sometimes impressed as forcibly by those who still inhabit the lower spheres as by those who have advanced to higher ones; even as we are, in this life, sometimes more quickly moved to moral effort by the conditions and sufferings of the sinful than we are by the precept and example of those who live pure and upright lives.
>
> Second, to receive instructions from spirits in regard to the laws, structure, and character of the spirit world; just as we would try to learn of these things in regard to any country on this earth to which we expected to travel.
>
> Third, to hold communion with our beloved ones over there for the mere pleasure that such communion imparts, in exchanging assurance of continued love, just to do in this world, by visiting and writing to the objects of our love and affection.
>
> Fourth, to seek the advice of spirits in matters affecting our mundane welfare. But in so doing, we do not accept their advice as always infallibly correct, since we realize that the judgments, points-of-view, and ability to foresee differ among the wise and experienced denizens of the spirit world as they do among those of this earth; however we feel assured, from our own experiences in holding converse with spirits, that they are often better qualified to prophesy for us and have a keener insight into the future than our earthly friends, and thus are often in a better position to give us suggestions for our consideration in connection with our plans and conduct for the future. (NSAC, 54-55)

---

4. In the course of the research for this study, this researcher was privy to a situation which occurred where a medium was found to be falsifying phenomena; promptly, the medium was investigated and the medium's credentials were rescinded by the parent organization. Critics of Spiritualism oftentimes assume that such instances are rare where a medium is, in effect, excommunicated. Over the course of three years of onsite research and personal observations, I found that the Spiritualist organizations used in my study were very concerned with any hint of impropriety and immediately investigated it to conclusion. As it was explained to me, it is necessary for the movement as a whole to keep the mediumship standards beyond reproach, and the quality of the mediums engaged in this work high; not doing so would be detrimental to the organization, and ultimately, to the religion.

On the fourth point, critics may contend that if a message indeed comes from the spirit world, should it not be infallible? Spiritualism advises that if one is not able personally to receive messages directly, and hence seeks out a medium to assist in this task, then it is up to the seeker to discern wisely in choosing a person who has the best qualifications to accomplish this task. Anytime a person purports to be able to speak to those in the spirit world, it must be remembered that the medium is human, and as a human, can make mistakes. No medium is endowed with perfect judgment in matters of his/her physical life or mediumship. An example offered by the National Spiritualist Association of Churches likens it to people erring in selecting their medical doctors, legal advisors, politicians, business associates or even friends—seeking spiritual advice is no different, there are honest as well as dishonest mediums; good as well as bad mediums; accurate as well as inaccurate mediums.

> …the Spiritualist claims the right to act for himself without let or hindrance from those who differ from him in religious views. If he makes a mistake which causes him loss or suffering, it must be remembered that even Jesus, with his extraordinary psychic powers, made a mistake when he selected Judas Iscariot as one of the Twelve. If it be said that this seeming mistake was part of a divine plan, then it may be also said that the Spiritualist's seeming mistakes may also be a part of a divine plan. (NSAC, 55)

This type of reasoning—that messages clearly wrong or irrelevant may be a part of divine order—may seem a bit too convenient to skeptics who demand accuracy in order to prove one's mediumship skills; they maintain that this is an easy way out for mediums to explain away their erroneous or faulty predictions. Upon deeper inspection, though, is it reasonable to expect the medium to have 100% accuracy in matters of prophecy? In defense of matters of spirit, it, after all, is not an exact science and even scientists rarely are able to have 100% results in their work; readings largely depend upon a variety of extraneous factors, most notably the physical and mental condition of the medium as the "reader," and the person receiving the reading's openness to receive and ability to interpret the message given. As stated before, mediums are human, a fact stressed by Spiritualists, and making mistakes are inevitable; in addition, spirit-messages sometimes are symbolic and it is up to the medium to give the message received, interpreting the best way he/she can; it is up to the receiver to further interpret the message, taking from it what he/she needs, and leaving the rest in the reading room.

Primarily, a medium's role in prophecy is basically to offer comfort to the bereaved in order to lessen the pain or even guilt; to assist in prayerful devotion in helping the departed soul in its transition; to gain knowledge of that which is not easily understood; to negate the fear of death in order to establish peace of mind for those on the earth plane; to have open dialogue with the spirit world; to reveal to those left behind that there is a cause and effect relationship related to one's actions which can result in more spiritual work when in spirit or rewards for good deeds done while on earth as a mortal; to heal; and finally to develop the gift of prophecy. (Dreller, 2)

Clairvoyance and Clairaudience

Under the umbrella of "prophecy" is clairvoyance and clairaudience. These two abilities are perhaps the most common types of mediumship. Clairvoyance (literally *clear seeing*) manifests visually as an impression or perception received in the "mind's eye" or "third-eye" chakra located between the eyes, in the middle of the forehead.

> There are several types of clairvoyance, varying according to the mental and physical make-up of the medium. These are: (1) x-ray clairvoyance enabling the medium to see through opaque objects; (2) subjective, impressionable or mediumistic clairvoyance, by means of which the communicating spirit registers the thought upon the mind of the medium through vision, symbol, or impression, or the taking on of conditions; and (3) objective clairvoyance, wherein the medium is able to see, objectively, spirit entities and their surroundings as they actually exist in the spirit world. This form of mediumship may also be referred to as soul sight. (King, 15)

Clairaudience, similarly, "is a mental form of mediumship closely allied to clairvoyance. Clairaudience is known as *clear hearing*. The impressions appear to be heard rather than seen. The two phases may often manifest in the same medium at the same time." (King, 15)

In a book entitled *Clairvoyance* (written by C.W. Leadbeater and first published in 1899) divides clairvoyance into a variety of categories: simple clairvoyance—full and partial; clairvoyance in space—intentional and semi-intentional, as well as unintentional; and clairvoyance in time—the past and future.

"Simple clairvoyance—full" involves the ability of the medium to see whatever may be present around him/her on different, but corresponding, levels (but nothing at great distances).

> We find among sensitive people all degrees of this kind of clairvoyance, from that of the man who gets a vague impression which hardly deserves the name

of sight at all, up to the full possession of etheric and astral vision respectively (p. 32).

"Simple clairvoyance—partial" pertains to the medium's ability to see only partially in degree, variety, or in permanence a vision:

> Sometimes, for example, a man's clairvoyance will be permanent, but very partial, extending only perhaps to one or two classes of the phenomena observable; he will find himself endowed with some isolated fragment of higher powers of sight which ought normally to accompany that fragment, or even to precede it (p. 57).

Leadbeater describes "clairvoyance in space—intentional" as a "capacity to see events or scenes removed from the seer in space and too far distant for ordinary observation" (p. 67). In contrast, he defines "semi-intentional" clairvoyance as when the medium tries to will him/herself to see something, but then has no control over the sight after the visions start; being receptive to receiving, but simply waiting for a message in the form of a vision to appear (p. 99).

An "unintentional" clairvoyance episode in space is when the medium picks up a vision of some event taking place in a distance, but is seen quite unexpectedly and without any conscious preparation to receive them.

> There are people who are subject to such visions, while there are many others to whom such a thing will happen only once in a lifetime. The visions are of all kinds and of all degrees of completeness, and apparently may be produced by various causes. Sometimes the reason of the vision is obvious, and the subject-matter of the gravest importance, at other times no reason at all is discoverable, and the events shown seem of the most trivial nature. (p. 104)

Finally, Leadbeater categorizes clairvoyance into "past" occurrence and "future" events. These clairvoyant visions offer a glimpse into these spaces of constant time to see events that have happened in the past and will happen in the future.[5]

Clairaudience "is the psychic state in which conscious interchange of thought between medium and spirit entities results from the ability of certain sensitives to *tune in* mentally with disembodied entities. (King, 16) This form of mental mediumship allows the medium to hear "through the etheric body system impressed on their inner listening ear—or objectively—as an externally heard physical vocalization." (DeSwarte, 27)[6]

---

5. See Appendix L for a list of definitions for clairvoyance.

Clairsentience, also known as the "sixth sense," literally means *clear sensing*. It basically entails the ability to perceive spirit communication by sensing intuitively what the message is (from the spirit entity). Although similar to clairvoyance and clairaudience in that the medium must do a fair amount of interpretation of the information received, in clairsentience it is especially necessary that the interpretation of the information is done correctly.

> Clairsentience also has some of the qualities of psychometry (reading of objects), intuition, telepathy, and in fact, of all supernatural mental vibrations that impinge upon the realm of spiritual discernment. There are countless variations of the vibrations entering the consciousness of the receiver. (King, 17)

This form of mental mediumship is related to being able to discern the spirit-world using one's intuition in conjunction with the five physical senses (hearing, seeing, smelling, touching and tasting). It is the "hunch" a person gets but cannot explain why this intuitive knowing occurred. It is an intuitive "knowing." (Greer, 2)

In my research, I observed that mediums often used a combination and variety of techniques in their mediumship-work that involved not only clairvoyance and clairaudience, but also clairsentience. Particularly, mediums have to learn to decipher and interpret messages. Some messages come in the form of symbols. For instance, a "rose" that is seen psychically by the medium could relate to a favorite flower of the person in spirit, or of the person receiving the message, or as a name of someone living or dead. A good medium will throw out whatever symbols come through from spirit to allow the person receiving the reading to assist in their interpretation. The symbols may mean nothing to the medium, but the sitter may know exactly what they refer to in relation to his/her life and experience with the person coming through. This can be a secret code, of sorts, between the sitter and the entity attempting to make contact.

Other times, the medium is able to work out a set of symbolic definitions with his/her spirit-guide which signal to him/her a particular message involving a family member or event for the sitter. For example, a medium that perceives a "soldier" as a message could refer to the person in spirit and how he/she passed, or is a source of pride for the person in spirit as a form of "proof" to the sitter, or could

---

6. In the primary data gathered for this study, the majority of respondents who are licensed mediums through Spiritualist associations and organizations claimed to be clairvoyant; second was clairaudient.

relate to a current person in the military. The medium works out how the symbols relate to him/her and the sitter, through trial and error and years of experiential readings, to connect those symbols to actual messages that can be understood easily by the sitter.

Aural messages can also occur either independently, or in conjunction with a visual message. Some mediums report hearing an actual, independent voice that appears to be coming from far away; others report experiencing a voice from within their mind that sometimes resembles their own voice. In either case, the voices often offer information that give proof to the sitter of the identity of the spirit who is attempting contact. The most convincing, perhaps, is when actual names are offered that are somewhat unique (*i.e.* not Mary, John, or Bill—common names that almost every family has at least one member with the same name somewhere in their family tree).[7]

Clairsentience is similar to clairvoyance and clairaudience in that the medium often will (through practice and experience) be able to interpret feelings he/she receives during a message. Often mediums will work out a system with his/her spirit guide in order to know who and what type of spirit is attempting to make contact. For example, a medium can work out a system where if he/she feels tingling on the left side of the body, this could be in reference to a male figure, the right side, a female, or vice versa. The same is used in trying to figure out if the entity is a relative or loved one, friend, neighbor or teacher, *etc*; or if it is someone completely unrelated just trying to get through (even though there is no familial or friendly connection between the sitter and the spirit). Often, as explained to me by practicing mediums, spirits clamor to get through in any way they can and when an open channel is noticed, an attempt may be made. When this occurs, the medium asks the spirit entity to step back and another attempt is made to make contact with someone familiar to the person receiving the reading.

Added to this is when spirits attempt contact but the sitter is unaware, has forgotten, or is in such an emotional or mental state that he/she cannot clearly discern who or what the entity is.[8] It is important in these instances for the sitter to take what he/she needs and to leave the rest; the reason (or spirit) behind the message may present itself later and clarity may ensue around the message once contemplation is made upon the information given or after consulting with other family members about confusing symbols or names contained within the message.

---

7. For a testimonial of a séance experience by this author, see Appendix M.
8. For an example of this, see Appendix M.

Psychometry[9]

The phase of psychometry is when a medium is able to hold an object and subsequently receives a message merely by touching it. It is thought that the object itself has energy and this causes the object to give off the vibration of previous owners of the object or of people who have come into contact with it.

> Upon contact with a physical object a medium may be able, on feeling the vibrations emanating from it, to learn its origin, its natural surroundings, and receive a glimpse into the characteristics of those who have touched it. Some people accept psychometry as only psychic, not necessarily spiritual. Others classify the term as a blending of mental and physical faculties. Leading contemporary scientists consider it to be a purely mental type of mediumship. (King, 25)

This technique is based on the idea of a "universal consciousness" which records all events of the past, present and future. A person gifted with psychometry can tap into this consciousness and history of an object, therefore giving information about the people who were in contact with it. It is believed that the vibrations of the object impress themselves on the medium's brain, thus allowing the sensitive to give a reading based on these impressions. This notion is somewhat related to karma in that many New Age followers believe that like people, objects (*i.e.* jewelry, houses, pieces of clothing) have their own karma which details the histories of all of those who have owned them in the past.

> ...Because the impressions coming from the object observed and the thoughts from the medium's own mind are closely blended, great care must be taken on the part of the medium to learn to recognize the distinction between the two ways of receiving information. With practice and care, the medium may learn to separate what is coming from spirit sources from what is coming from himself. (King, 25-26)

---

9. Psychometry was discovered by Joseph Rodes Buchanan (1814-1899). "He believed that humans leave psychic energy on objects they touch as a kind of residue, and that the sensitive psychic could read the collected energies on an object as an imagined narrative history of its use. This was used by psychics to produce descriptions of ancient civilizations through touching recovered artifacts. It was also used by psychic 'healers' to diagnose the illnesses of people who had sent them a lock of their hair and a dollar in an envelope." (*The Organ of Spirituality*, 2002) To read further about Joseph Buchanan, an article he authored, and his work, see Appendix N.

Psychometry, then, is perhaps the hardest to decipher for the medium because he/she must be able to know intuitively which information is a form of the subconscious, and which is authentic spirit communication. "Perfect good faith, however, is not incompatible with this source of error, the psychic may faithfully describe the vision which arises before him, and yet it may be nothing but a dream-structure evolved by his subconscious, and clearly revealing, to those who know how to look for them, his own repressed wishes and anxieties."[10] (Fortune, 188-189)

Trance

Although "trance" mediumship is often placed in the subject area of the mental phase of mediumship, it does sometimes take on the appearance of being a form of the physical phase of mediumship in that the medium often does change in appearance somewhat and the medium's natural voice is replaced with that of the spirit entity. Initially, though, the medium must release completely from his/her physical surroundings—a withdrawal of consciousness from the objective world (this is so the ego can be released from any limitations that is placed upon it in the physical world, allowing it to enter into another higher plane of consciousness). (Fortune, 70)

> Although there are considerable differences in degree, trance is spoken of as *going under control*. It resembles a *sleep state* in that there are various stages of unconsciousness....As in sleep, trance has its preparatory stages of lulling to sleep, deep trance assuming the condition induced by an anesthetic, and the return to consciousness similar to emerging from a sleep state. The mental organization of the medium is manipulated by the spirit control in order that the desired thought may reach the mind of the medium, but never does the guide actually enter the physical body of the medium.
>
> ...The receptivity and sensitivity of the medium, as well as the extent to which he or she may be used as an instrument of communication, expands under trance. The instrument is more capable of transmitting a message or thought going far beyond the ordinary perceptive powers. Indeed, trance does not harm one's individuality. Rather, the opposite is true. Through trance, the medium gains a greater awareness and a deeper knowledge and understanding of the mighty universe than could have been possible otherwise. (King, 21-22)

---

10. In all of the primary research done for this study (including interviews and surveys of dozens of Spiritualist mediums) I did not come across any medium who actively does psychometry on a regular, consistent basis in his/her mediumship work.

There are those that have a natural gift for trance and those who must train themselves to do it at will. For people who have a natural gift, it is believed by people who subscribe to the concept of "reincarnation" that the person trained in the occult or spiritual matters extensively in a previous life, hence this past-life memory accompanies them into this life making them more susceptible to trance mediumship. People who must train themselves to go into trance have to work diligently over a long period of time in order to become proficient at it.

Basically, there are three primary types of trance which mediums go under: *Trance of Projection*, *Trance of Vision*, and *Mediumistic Trance*. Each of these requires the medium to experience a disassociation of the self, separating the different levels of consciousness.

> *Trance of Projection* [is called such] because the Self is withdrawn from the physical body and functions independently.... The second type of trance...—*Trance of Vision*—[is called such] because in this case the soul does not withdraw from the body, but, inhibiting the physical senses, appears to open up the senses of super consciousness which can perceive the subtler planes of existence.... In the third type of trance, which is called the *Mediumistic Trance*, disassociation takes place between Personality and the Individuality; that is to say, the whole of the Self which has been built up by the experiences of the current incarnation is left to ensoul [*sic*] the body, while the Higher Self, as a whole, withdraws. (Fortune, 66-67)

The control that the spirit guide exercises over the medium is done mentally and not physically. Unlike that which is portrayed in movies and on television, the actual organism of the medium is never taken over by an outside force (*i.e.* possessed); instead the spirit enters the medium's energy field (aura) that surrounds everyone's physical body and merely blends with it, taking control of the thought processes of the medium. (King, 21)

Inspirational Speaking and Writing

This form of mental mediumship is somewhat related to trance, but in this phase of mediumship the medium is never completely unconscious or unaware, and is able to control his/her body at will. The medium is very much aware of everything that is being said and all that is taking place around him/her. Simply, by controlling the medium's flow of thoughts, the spirit can "inspire" the medium through speech or written prose without any effort on the medium's part. In order to do this, all the sensitive has to do is to ask earnestly and sincerely to be an instrument of the spirit guide, and the inspiration begins to gush forth.

This is perhaps one of the most common forms of spirit communication between a novice medium and spirit entity initially; the aspiring medium is inspired through writing regarding spiritual truths and wisdom that is not a part of the person's learned knowledge base. Also, it is believed to encourage the flow of energy without the interference of the medium's personal thoughts about life and work, helping the medium to become more adept at spirit communication. This is best accomplished when in a quiet or meditative state.

> The instrument may be used by more than one spirit being on a single occasion. The thought intention of the personality in spirit is projected into the subconscious mind of the medium who then frames it into words by voice or writing. There is a blending of the mentalities of the sender and receiver. (King, 23)

Related to inspirational speaking and writing is "automatic drawing." This is done by mediums (even those with no artistic ability at all) who can draw portraits of spirit guides and people they have not yet met. It has been described as being as if someone else was doing the drawing, but with the person's body.[11]

Spiritual Healing

Spiritual healing is an important aspect of Spiritualism. This practice, though, was not developed by Spiritualists but instead has been a part of collective human history for millennia. Notable healers throughout history include Buddha (who believed that illness was actually rooted in people's minds); Zoroaster (who taught his followers that prayer had powerful curative effects); Elijah and Elisha (Hebrew prophets who were renowned healers during their time); Jesus, perhaps the greatest healer who ever lived, healed many during his lifetime; and Moham-

---

11. During a message service at a Spiritualist camp I attended while researching this topic, I witnessed this form of mental/physical mediumship. The medium sat at the front of the church with a drawing pad of blank paper and a variety of colored pencils; during the service she feverishly drew portraits while occasionally gazing out toward the audience, but not really focusing on any one person. At the end of the service she gave a message from the spirit world, along with a drawing of the person's spirit guide, to a number of people in attendance. Of course, it is impossible to know if the portraits are accurate, but interestingly each one had smaller sized images around the peripheral edges of the paper. After the service, a number of people commented that those smaller portraits indeed resembled family members who were in the spirit world.

med who had a healing touch and healed many who suffered from a variety of health problems (Harris, 137).

This is also known as the "laying of hands" where the hands of the medium are placed upon the physical body; curative energy from the spirit world passes through the medium's body and out of the hands to heal the illness or disease affecting the person's body. The medium acts as a vehicle for the healing and the spirit world does the actual healing. The energy that passes through the medium is a vibratory force. "This force enters the etheric body of the patient and stimulates the vitality, soothes, and builds up the tissues of the sufferer, thus placing the body in a state of harmony. These spiritual forces operate through a spiritual healer." (King, 19)

The purpose of a healing is not to produce a "miracle" because Spiritualism does not subscribe to the belief in miracles—everything is based on Natural Law, which is God's Law. Instead, a spiritual healing endeavors to bring about a harmonious balance between an overabundance of vital energy and an insufficient amount (King, 19).

> Healing is brought about by working through the medium to vitalize the diseased portion of the patient's body with curative fluids and energy; through illumination by spirit of the brain of the healer so that he may know the nature of the disease and its cure; and by absent treatments whereby the patient may be healed without being in the presence of the healer....The healing force emanates from higher spiritual planes and contacts the etheric body of the individual being treated. The etheric body, in turn, dwells within the physical body. The physical and mental bodies are both acted upon. This is accomplished through the laws of attraction and vibration. (King, 19)

A necessary part of the healing depends upon the person being healed. A sincere desire on the part of the person being healed to have a spiritual healing is a component in the overall healing process. If the person passively receives the healing without a sincere desire to become healed, then the affect of the healing is lessened. In order to attract the vibrations needed to affect a healing, the receiver, as well as the giver, needs to cooperate in the process in order to achieve a successful outcome.

4.2 Physical Phases of Mediumship[12]

Physical mediumship that produces physical phenomena (like materializations, transfigurations, apports, rapping, *etc.*) is much rarer than mental mediumship that produces clairvoyant, clairaudient, and clairsentience phenomena. This is, in part, due to the fact that physical mediumship requires much more precise conditions for phenomena to occur. As mentioned earlier, in mental mediumship the medium's ability to receive and act as a vehicle for spirit communication is dependent upon the medium's overall physical, emotional and mental condition; this is true for physical mediumship. However, "physical mediumship is dependent on three things: focused trance via the base of the brain; the solar plexus area where the core (gut-level) of intensity cycles with the brain; and third, from the vibrational energy received from the sitters and observers." (Dreller, 41) This type of mediumship requires much more effort and ability by the medium as compared to mental mediumship. This is not to suggest that one form of mediumship is superior or better to the other; quite the contrary. Each method has its merits and some mediums are more adept at performing one type over the other. Also, much depends upon the spirit world and which mode of mediumship they choose to make contact during a séance or reading.

Materializations[13]

Materializations occur when spirits appear to those present, as actual physical beings to the sight and touch. This can include objects as well as entities, and should not be confused with other types of apparitions such as ghosts or phantasms. Spirits that form in materializations during a séance or healing circle do so by using the energy of the medium and those in attendance to appear as physical phenomena. Materializations will sometimes occur when a group of people gather as one accord for séance work over a long period of time, building up energy each time which makes the conditions more suitable for this type of physical phenomena to occur.

---

12. For a list of the different types of mental and physical mediumship, see Table 1 in Chapter 2.
13. For examples of materializations and other physical phenomena as experienced by an ordained Spiritualist minister and medium, see Appendix H, an interview with The Reverend John Lilec.

Full-form materialization is rare. Nevertheless, it is a most impressive form of mediumship, especially convincing to the senses and emotions of the sitters. To produce these phenomena, the vibrations of the spirit entity wishing to manifest are slowed down by the use of ectoplasm[14] drawn from the medium and sitters until the form becomes visible to our physical eyes. The ectoplasm is molded by the spirit entity through the power of thought until it is solid enough to resemble the former physical body. To accomplish this, the manifesting spirit has to recall how the physical body looked. Memory may not always be perfect in every respect.

To demonstrate the phenomenon of materialization the séance room must have just enough light for the forms to become visible. A cabinet is set up, usually with black curtains, in which the medium sits entranced while the spirit form is taking shape. The spirit personality then emerges from the cabinet into full view of the sitters. Singing by the entire group helps to establish good vibrations for building up the forms.

In order to materialize, spirits must lower the vibrations of the spirit bodies to conform to the rate of vibration of the sitters. Using the spirit body of the medium as a framework upon which to build (while the physical body remains in the cabinet) the spirit entity molds a replica of himself which is seen by the sitters. The spirit body is connected to the medium's physical body by the pericord.[15] Spirit helpers assist in all aspects of this phenomenon. Materialized forms should not be touched without permission of the spirit controls, since it can do great harm to the medium if the ectoplasm should spring back too suddenly into the physical body of the medium.[16] (King, 37-38)

---

14. For a definition of "ectoplasm," see Appendix C for a glossary of relevant terms.
15. The word "pericord" comes from the root *peri* which means "about, beyond or around." The cord refers to the "ethereal string attached to the astral body in an astral projection, stretching as far as the projector desires to go; ethereal energy, breath, and 'spirit' runs back and forth through this thread while bodies are detached; can be perceived clairvoyantly..." (Bletzer, 135, 462)
16. This is a common belief among Spiritualists, but there has never been any documented case where a medium was killed (or even severely injured) from someone touching him/her when materialization was in the process of occurring. In the latter part of the 1800's onward, sitters would often pounce upon the spirit entity when it was thought to be fraudulent. Often was the case that instead of a materialized entity, it was in fact a human masquerading as a spirit. Genuine materializations tend to look ethereal, according to mediums, and sitters today can certainly tell the difference.

Transfiguration

Somewhat related to materialization is the phenomena of transfiguration. This type of phenomena occurs when the face of the medium transforms and transfigures into the face of a spirit entity. The actual face seems to change appearance, transfiguring into that of spirit entities, sometimes in quick succession. This type of manifestation occurs when ectoplasm covers the body of the medium, transfiguring it to resemble the form of a manifesting spirit entity.

Another form of transfiguration is called "etherealization." "This phase is not often witnessed. The spirit forms which appear in the séance room lack the density that is apparent in full materialization. They are more etheric in nature. However, because of the lack of density, the forms usually disappear very quickly. The appearance is ephemeral; it makes a fleeting impression." (King, 35-36)

These types of materializations—transfiguration and etherealization—offer a demonstration to those present during such manifestations of the innate connection between the spirit and earth planes. Although hard to comprehend to those who have not yet experienced such phenomena, they are quite extraordinary to those who have, offering them visual proof of spirit communication between those in the here and now with those who have passed over to the other side.

Direct Voice

During a séance or healing circle, a spirit can speak through "direct voice" (sometimes called "independent voice") which is seemingly separate from that of the medium's voice (meaning the actual voice of the medium); this is unlike what occurs in "trance mediumship" where the medium's voice is used, but changes in tone and style. What does occur, however, is the medium's voice box is used to draw from it the necessary ectoplasm to form the voice heard by those in attendance. Spiritualists maintain that this is why the voice sometimes resembles that of the control medium. Usually, though, the voice is said to be quite distinct of that of the medium; depending upon the entity coming through, the voice can be masculine, feminine, childlike, and even with a foreign accent.

During such phenomena a "trumpet" is sometimes used. This is a long, narrow conical object made out of tin that is used as a tool by the spirit entity to communicate the message. It is open at both ends, constructed in sections with tiny seams that allow the trumpet to be reduced in size for easy storage. It is used as a sort of megaphone by the spirit-world to make the voice coming through stronger, louder and clearer. The sound is created from a makeshift voice box that is formed at the end of the trumpet with ectoplasm. As with direct voice, ectoplasm is a necessary part of this type of manifestation which aids in lifting the trumpet up off the table so the spirit entity can use it to send the message to those present.[17]

> The spirits usually indicate their presence in the room by moving the trumpet about and touching the sitters with it, its movements being seen in the dark by coating it with luminous paint. Sometimes luminous faces are faintly seen in the dark and floating spirit lights.[18] If the conditions are good and there are several sitters, all sorts of conversations with spirit friends may be heard. Different spirits not only speak with different voices and accents, and in every language, but remarkable good singing and whistling are often heard.
>
> Apparently the *modus operandi* of the spirits when communicating with the direct voice is to materialize sufficiently to be able to speak. They evidently create a larynx or its equivalent, from ectoplasm withdrawn from the medium or sitters, just as they do at materialization séances when they show themselves fully formed and talk to the sitters. (Holms, 45-46)

Curiously, many dubiously inspired tests were performed in the early decades of the Spiritualist movement to ascertain the validity of the medium performing such manifestations. One such test involved a sitter who would sit next to the medium and place his/her hand tightly over the medium's mouth; another test procedure included sealing the medium's mouth shut with plaster so that if the lips moved in any way, or if the mouth was opened even slightly, the plaster would quickly breakaway. Sometimes the medium would be required to take a big gulp of water from a glass and asked to hold the water in his/her mouth throughout the trumpet and direct voice manifestation (the glass was physically removed from the séance room or placed out of reach of the medium); afterward, he/she would spit the mouthful of water into an empty glass to prove that it was not him/her speaking, but in fact authentic direct voice (Holms, 46).

---

17. This researcher attended a number of séances and healing circles where trumpets were displayed for the use of the spirit entities, but on no occasion did a direct or independent voice come through these objects.
18. "Spirt lights" are "dancing globules or sparks of light filling the air in a séance room or psychic development circle, [indicating] that etheric world entities are in the room, ready to bring help to psychic manifestations." (Bletzer, 582)

Apports

Apports are basically objects that are presented as gifts to sitters in a circle from one location to another, and even from the spirit realm. These can consist of almost anything: jewelry, flowers, coins (money), flowers, relics, precious and non-precious stones, *etc.*

The following testimonial regarding apports is taken from an interview with The Reverend John Lilec:

> TJL: Have you had any experience with apports?
>
> RJL: Yes, when I walked up the stairs from the séance room, where I was sitting as a student, coming up the stairs and all the lights were on at Rev. Tingley's[19] house, and right behind me and in front of me, I could hear these popping noises and they were apports following right into the light. And they were just...pop, pop, pop...and everyone was just following and picking these things up.
>
> TJL: What type of objects were they?
>
> RJL: They looked liked diamonds, rubies, garnets, precious and semi-precious.
>
> TJL: Now, did these things stay in the physical, and people could take those as souvenirs with them?
>
> RJL: Yes, they can use them as souvenirs and also they would tell them that they are meant for the energies drawn and as healing stones for themselves; if anything, a souvenir of that event. I have heard many stories now of different apport mediums and a lot of charlatanism, but I have seen the apport delivered two different ways now; right in through, passing through the medium's solar plexus, before it must reach that individual or location. And so it's difficult to try to explain to people how this works, but we understand the science—that's the beauty of it.
>
> But I have seen another instance when I was in séance with Rev. Tingley, and we got a red light right over him and he was in trance, at an angle where I could see him but the sitters couldn't. We had about 17 or 20 people in there. All of a sudden, I saw a man's hand throw these objects out into the audience, out into the sitting room. But Rev. Tingley, both of his hands, and being a

---

19. Rev. Tingley, who is now in spirit, was the mentor and teacher of Rev. Lilec when he was a student studying mediumship in development and unfoldment classes.

scientist and trained to study every little detail, I realized his arms were right on the table. So I went to a private séance and asked the spirit doctor,[20] Dr. Taylor, without being doubtful or pessimistic, and trying to be respectful at the same time—Dr. Taylor knew that I was edging to the words and he just said, "Well, that was Dee Dee Ho." And it was, a little man that projected right out of Rev. Tingley, actually throwing these objects. I had never seen this before. I always thought they were delivered through a trumpet.

Many Spiritualists relate similar experiences regarding apports and the appearance of objects seemingly out of thin air into the laps of sitters or onto the table of the healing circle or séance. Skeptics and debunkers of Spiritualism and physical phenomenon maintain that instead of the spirit world, these objects come from a very earthbound source—the medium himself/herself—through elaborate hoaxes and fakery.

Throughout the history of Spiritualism, there have been countless instances of fakery and trickery associated with mediumship and physical phenomena—some rather sophisticated, others rather unrefined.

4.3 Fraud and Trickery within the Spiritualist Movement

The history of Spiritualism is checkered, at best, with numerous allegations of fraud surrounding it from its earliest beginnings to contemporary times. The year 1848, when the Fox sisters allegedly made their first contact, is widely regarded as the start of psychic phenomenon, mediumship and Spiritualism. Even their spirit communication came under suspicion years later when they alleged that it had all been a hoax from the beginning. This was after they had been paraded about the country for many years doing mediumship-related demonstrations by P.T Barnum who could see an opportunity for making money, thus helped in making them nationwide celebrities and household names.

> The fame of the Fox Sisters and their tour to promote their "Spiritualist" society encouraged others to discover their own talents for communicating with the dead. It wasn't long before other "mediums" started to appear; and only a

---

20. Spiritualists believe that each person has five main spirit guides: Doctor-Teacher, Master, Chemist, Indian Guide, and Joy guide. Each guide has a distinct role in the medium's work and assists him/her with messages, readings, and spiritual matters. See Appendix P for a detailed explanation of "spirit guides."

short time before most started charging money for their services. These services were rendered in sessions called séances, which typically took place in a darkened room with the participants sitting in a circle holding hands. The purpose for holding hands was clear; it prevented anyone from using their hands to falsely produce ghostly phenomena, and, often, the medium would be tied to the chair with his or her legs secured as well. Under these circumstances, sounds were heard, the medium would talk in different voices and languages, and small physical objects would appear and disappear, furniture would levitate or move, and, occasionally, a spirit would "materialize" in a temporary physical form. (Haslam, 2003)

Within the first decade of the movement there were literally millions of believers and followers. This, in part, had to be due to the humanistic desire to want to believe in the supernatural and metaphysical, which no doubt provided an excellent avenue for frauds and charlatans to capitalize on this widespread trend by sowing their seeds of deception to make quick money off the unsuspecting multitudes who sincerely believed in the idea that loved ones could make contact with those left behind. Because the movement attracted people from all walks of life—the rich and poor, educated and unschooled, skeptical and devoted—people were very much interested in "proving" beyond any doubt the existence of spirit communication by scientific means.

Initially, regular mediumship (like clairvoyance and clairaudience) was enough, but as the ordinary adherents began demanding more and more proof, the pressure to produce phenomena for financial gain became a worrisome trend for Spiritualism as a religion. Sitters in a séance who paid good money to see a deceased parent, aunt, uncle or grandparent appear to give a message became the norm; people not only wanted a message from the medium, they wanted to see, touch, and talk to the apparition.

The result was an influx of elaborate trickery that was used to mimic phenomena (and which would guarantee "physical phenomena" just in case the spirits were not being cooperative with the medium); further complicating the situation were medium imposters who wanted to get in on this potentially profitable trend that was sweeping the country by administering séances under the guise of Spiritualism, but without the mediumship skills to do it. These were the ones that were most creative in conjuring up apparent phenomena using the "tricks of the trade" popular with magicians and conjurers of the day.

In 1921, Harry Houdini penned a book entitled *Miracle Mongers and Their Methods* which set out to debunk clearly all of the techniques and methods used to create illusions and magic. Later, Houdini would become Spiritualism's most famous and unrelenting critic as he sat out to debunk once and for all any pretense of spirit communication that was natural and not manipulated. It was in the above mentioned book, however, that he made his first ever printed comment on his feelings about the occult and Spiritualism (he referred to it as spiritism):

> The great day of the Fire-eater—or, should I say, the day of the great Fire-eater—has passed. No longer does fashion flock to his doors, nor science study his wonders, and he must now seek a following in the gaping loiterers of the circus side-show, the pumpkin-and-prize-pig country fair, or the tawdry booth at Coney Island. The credulous, wonder-loving scientist, wringing from Nature her jealously guarded secrets, the knowledge of which benefits all mankind, he gravely follows that perennial Will-of-the-wisp, spiritism, and lays the flattering unction to his soul that he is investigating "psychic phenomena," when in reality he is merely gazing with unseeing eyes on the flimsy juggling of pseudo-mediums. (Houdini, 96; Polidoro, 58)

The idea that "science" could categorically prove or disprove spirit communication gave many people hope in thinking that all they experienced and saw was absolutely authentic and true. It took a magician, like Houdini, though, to point out obvious tricks that the average person could not see. What seemed authentic was not always the case, as many would soon learn.

In collaboration with the magazine *Scientific American*, Houdini challenged mediums to demonstrate their mediumship under controlled conditions that could be scientifically verified in the December 1922 edition of the magazine. A prize of $5,000 was offered to anyone who could successfully demonstrate psychic phenomena to Houdini, the greatest illusionist and trickster of the day, under normal test conditions. If the medium could convince Houdini, Spiritualism's greatest skeptic, then he/she would receive the prize.

The only medium that came close to winning the cash prize was the wife of a well-to-do Boston doctor, Marjorie Crandon. She claimed to be in contact with the spirit of her deceased brother, Walter. During her séances, she would have objects fly across the room, ectoplasmic hands jutting out of places, ringing bells—all the while writhing around in her chair as if possessed. During her long career, she allegedly produced some of the most outstanding phenomena of the movement—ectoplasm that covered her body, spirit hands protruding from between her legs and many other physical phenomena that involved the moving of furniture and objects.

During the actual séance attended by Houdini, Marjorie would learn just how different from the average sitter he was. First, Houdini cleverly placed the bell that Walter was fond of ringing under his chair; he also bound his leg beforehand to make it sensitive to touch. During the séance, just as the bell rang, Houdini indeed felt the medium's leg pass his to ring the bell. Furthermore, as a distraction, Crandon asked a sitter to get up to get a pencil and some paper. Up to this point, the sitters had their hands joined in a circle, and each of the medium's feet were being pressed upon by the person on either side of her (a sitter on her right and Houdini on her left). This break in the circle allowed Crandon to reach around with the foot that the sitter (who was retrieving the paper and pencil) had been in charge of guarding, placing it under a large screen directly behind her; also, she used this opportunity to place a black megaphone on her head (the séance room was so dark that no one could see her do this). All of this occurred in a split second; she quickly put the free hand that the sitter was holding who went to fetch the paper onto Houdini's to make it appear that she was not free to produce any fraudulent phenomena. Suddenly, with a kick of her foot she was able to knock the screen over and in "Walter's" voice asked Houdini where he wanted the megaphone to be placed; Houdini answered in front of him, so she tilted her head, allowing the megaphone to fall off in front of Houdini.

Initially, it all transpired so flawlessly that it did appear that a spirit-manifestation had made these things happen. Houdini only knew for sure how she was able to ring the bell. Not convinced of her mediumship, he sneaked back into the séance room the next day and recreated all of the phenomena Marjorie Crandon produced in broad daylight. Her upper-middleclass demeanor and gentile behavior made it easy for her to trick many people.[21] Needless to say, she did not win the $5,000. Surprisingly, with multitudes of psychics all over the United States producing phenomena everyday in their séance rooms, not one medium was able to collect the prize money. All who claimed to produce fantastic phenomena, and who went before Houdini, were found to be frauds.

Spiritualism was exported to England in 1852 by an American, Mrs. Hayden. Quickly, this new religion gained in popularity, and another American, Henry Slade, decided to travel across the Atlantic in 1876 in hopes of capitalizing upon this emerging market. His specialty was "spirit-writing" or slate-writing—this is where a spirit writes a message on a miniature chalkboard for the sitter. His technique involved using two small framed chalkboards. First, he would have the sitter come in and he would show clearly that the boards were indeed blank with no

---

21. The stories contained in this section have been adapted from a television documentary entitled *Secrets of the Super Psychics*, Sebastian Cody (Executive Producer) (1995). [Television broadcast]. For the Learning Channel, an Open Media Production for Channel 4 in association with Discovery Channel.

writing on either one. He would place the boards together, slate to slate, and ask the spirit to write a message. The sitter would audibly hear the sound of chalk striking the slate. Next he would pull the chalkboards apart and a message would be visible. Often the messages were vague (*i.e.* "Time will tell.").

Two medical students who suspected fraud wanted to expose him. During their reading, they caught Slade handing the chalkboards to an accomplice behind a curtain. Initially, he had written a message on a separate chalkboard which fit snuggly on the back of the top board. When he placed the two boards together, the loose one (from the back) would fall down over the blank portion of the bottom board. The accomplice would then mimic the sound of chalk writing on a slate from behind a curtain. When Slade lifted the top board, a pre-existing message would be visible from the loose slate that now fit on top of the bottom board.

Slade was immediately arrested and taken to the Old Bailey for a very public trial. Because Spiritualism, mediumship, and psychics had become so popular in Great Britain by this time, the public was divided between those who believed in spirit communication and those who knew it was done through trickery. Slade narrowly escaped going to prison, but his trial did reveal the deep division which existed between scientists over the authenticity of Spiritualism. In fact, Charles Darwin (the creator of the Theory of Evolution) contributed the substantial some of $15 toward the prosecution. Alfred Russell Wallace (who had developed a Theory of Evolution alongside Charles Darwin's theory), however, served as a key witness for Slade's defense. This demonstrates how science and religion clashed during the late 19th century—those who believed fervently in mediumship and those who worked tirelessly to disprove it—and never have the twain met. Still today, although unable to prove spirit communication scientifically enough to convince the most ardent skeptic, a high percentage of people around the world do believe in ghosts, spirit communication, and phenomena.

It is interesting to note that Spiritualists were very well aware of the fakery being perfected against unsuspecting people and wanted to right these wrongs. Many Spiritualists worked hard to expose frauds in order to bring those duped back into the fold of the true mediums who worked honestly and genuinely.[22] The insatiable appetite for the public to see fantastic and magnificent physical

---

22. For an actual letter written to the editor of a journal by a practicing Spiritualist who was calling for more rigid standards in exposing fraudulent mediums, see Appendix O.

phenomena is where Spiritualism took a turn for the worse—evidently dating back to the originators of the movement—the Fox Sisters.

> By 1855, Spiritualism claimed to have two million followers....Also in 1855, Margaret Fox converted to Catholicism. She and her sister Catharine were both alcoholics, and Margaret had become disillusioned with the whole idea of Spiritualism. She continued to do the stage act with her sister for two more years due to family pressure, but when her older sister Leah quit as their manager after her marriage to a wealthy businessman in 1857, Margaret also left the act. Catharine continued to make irregular appearances, regaining some of her waning fame by producing automatic mirror-writing (messages written so they were only readable in a mirror).
>
> During this time, Spiritualism was condemned by leaders of organized religions, who attempted to get laws passed banning the movement. Many mediums were ostracized by family and friends, mainly because of the religious ban. Starting in the 1850's in [Great] Britain, and in the 1880's in America, investigators began looking into and exposing the many fraudulent mediumship schemes that were operating in both countries, further sullying Spiritualism's image.
>
> More damning still, in 1888, the Fox Sisters made a public appearance in New York in which Margaret stated that Spiritualism was a fraud and an evil, and that herself and Catharine had been faking phenomena all the years they had been in practice. The sisters went on tour to expose the fakery of Spiritualism...even though Catharine continued to work as a medium. In 1889, Margaret recanted her confession, but her inconsistent behavior had already damaged Spiritualism's public image deeply. (Haslam, 2003)

Trickery and fakery certainly caused a lot of consternation among many Spiritualists from the movement's beginning...and still does today. Sadly, and especially with the advent of technology and more sophisticated ways of deception, there are mediums who try to defraud the public with wondrous fake phenomena in the séance room. Fortunately, however, technology to detect fraud has also improved and charlatan mediums are usually found out.

In the early years, the methods were very crude and the flimsiest of evidence was interpreted as absolute proof. Today's standards are much higher and the average person much savvier in detecting fraud and trickery. People of the 21st century are naturally skeptical and inquisitive; people are not so easily duped and are much less likely to accept supernatural occurrences without first logically examining them intently. Critics maintain that psychic phenomenon and mediumship is dependent only upon the gullibility of the believer. Interestingly, though, every culture from around the world since ancient times has had mediums and a strong belief in the supernatural. Could all of this be attributed to fraudulent tactics by the mediums?

Perhaps those who perpetrate fraud actually started out with noble intentions and with true gifts of mediumship, but the attraction of not only financial gain, but also the adulation by those who witness their marvelous phenomena, caused them to lose sight of their spiritual calling and to take the spiritual low-road; the temptation to cheat was too great, the lure of fast money too enticing. Those who allow the ego to take over do detract from legitimate work in this field by mediums who work honestly and sincerely. Whether or not one believes in spirit communication is almost a non-issue; it is quite apparent that those who practice mediumship with pure hearts do believe in what they are doing and have legions of sitters to attest to their work.[23]

4.4 The Séance, Clairvoyant Circle and Healing Circle

If the heart of Spiritualism is the medium, then the soul is the "séance," which is not to be confused with a "clairvoyant circle" and/or a "healing circle."[24] The word *séance* comes from the French word meaning "to sit." Basically, and in the simplest of terms, a "séance" is where an outside spirit naturally uses the physical body, mind, and/or higher-self of the medium to speak to and give messages to

---

23. One interesting observation I made during my research was how mediums will often seek out readings themselves from other mediums. If one is connected to spirit, why then must one seek out the mediumship of another person? Why not give a reading to yourself? It was explained to me that just as a medical physician should not doctor or medicate himself/herself, so it is with mediumship. Mediums have difficulty separating their personal-selves from that of their spiritual-selves when it comes to giving a self-reading. Also, I noticed quite often that practicing mediums would recommend other mediums to their own siblings, parents and children for readings (just as a doctor should not attempt to diagnose a family member because of the emotional attachment involved that can detract from the professionalism of the person). This suggested to me that what the average medium does is genuine, at least in his/her own mind and heart, because if it were patently based on fraud, why would they then seek out mediums for themselves and their families if it were all based on an elaborate hoax? Why would they pay money to another person knowing that it was all bogus information? In my research, I have found that the overwhelming majority of Spiritualist mediums are sincere in their work and in their beliefs, honestly attempting to make a difference in people's lives by offering them hope in the hereafter.

the people sitting (sitters) at the séance using direct voice. The medium is often in some type of trance (either deep or light) and is dependent upon his/her "control" spirit or "gatekeeper" to guide the other spirits accordingly while conducting the séance.

In a "clairvoyant circle" the medium is in an artificially lighted room (*i.e.* with lamps) and gives messages to the people in attendance. The medium calls in those in the spirit world and gives messages to the sitters from the other side. The "healing circle," albeit different, does most resemble a séance. A healing circle consists of people sitting together of one accord for either a specific healing or of the general healing of the people in attendance, and for others of the world, through the use of spiritual or divine healing. Regardless of whether it is a séance, clairvoyant circle or a healing circle, there are some very necessary steps and basic precautions the medium must take in order to conduct the gathering of sitters successfully and safely.

The séance or circle is conducted by a medium with as few as one or two other people, up to practically any number of people who wish to sit and participate in it. Setting the space and clearing the energy is very important in the preparation portion of having a séance or circle. In a séance, a darkened room is preferred to create an enclosed space that resembles a "cabinet."[25] Of course, each medium has his/her own particular style when conducting a séance or a circle, but in general, there are some basic rules that are followed (albeit adapted to the medium's own, personal preferences).

A personalized ritual helps the medium to raise the vibration of the room and to set the scene and it helps to clear the space of any unwanted or stagnant energy. A sacred book, such as the *Holy Bible*, is often used during a séance or healing circle. This is to bring into the circle the energy surrounding the purity of spiritual knowledge that a sacred text contains. A candle symbolizes the light of

---

24. While doing onsite research for this study, I attended a number of séances and clairvoyant and healing circles to observe and experience this very essential and unique aspect of Spiritualism, mediumship and spirit communication. As a result, I was asked to write a series of modules on this and other topics for the Universal Spiritualist Association's *College of Religious Education*. The material included in this section is an abridged version of this work. (Universal Institute for Holistic Studies, College of Religious Education, Level IV, Module 1, *Introduction to Spiritualism*, "The Séance, Clairvoyant Circles, and Healing Circles," pp. 24-29; Muncie, IN: The Universal Institute for Holistic Studies, 2001)
25. A cabinet is an enclosed space that allows for the build up of energy by the medium in order to produce phenomena. Also, see Appendix C for a list of terms.

God, because where there is light, dark forces may not dwell. A bell or another type of musical device (Tibetan cymbals, a singing bowl, *etc*) helps to raise the room's vibration. In fact, any item that has spiritual significance to the medium—music, flowers, incenses—is also used to help raise the overall vibration of the room. Like people, objects also carry energy (good and bad) as well as *karma*; it is important for the medium to choose items to introduce into the circle which reflect positive energy and pure intentions.

The ideal number for a séance or circle is between six and twelve people. The reason for this is that it is important that all of the members are able to concentrate clearly and deeply; also, member compatibility makes a huge difference in having a successful séance or healing circle. If there is a self-serving member of the group, a "message hog," or worse, a skeptic, then it will lower the vibration rapidly and will ultimately distract from the task at hand of having spirits enter and give messages.

Of course, genuine mediums who take pride in their work welcome healthy discernment within a séance or circle; this is a necessary part of having authentic communication with the spirit world when joined in a gathering of sitters. But, mediums generally do not appreciate people who are merely thrill seekers or Spiritualist "tourists" who do not sincerely believe or do not genuinely want to make contact (*i.e.* only participate in order to see a "ghost") because these people bring to the séance or circle an energy that will lower the vibration and ultimately scare away any positive disincarnates that may want to make contact and communicate with the other sitters.

Needless to say, trust between the members is vital, as well as a mutual level of understanding and sensitivity. Spiritualists try to avoid inviting these types of negative thinkers or those who will bring the energetic vibration down, or distort it, into their séance rooms or circles. The Universal Law of "Like Attracts Like" lies at the core of a séance or healing circle, and a person who is experiencing a negative emotional trauma, or is negative in deeds or actions, has a tendency to attract negative energy from the spirit world. In these cases, what tends to happen, according to practicing mediums, is that the person who is living in the negative tends to usurp the positive energy of the other members, which in turn can invite and/or attract unwelcome spirits who are disturbed in some way, are tricksters, or are of lower vibrations. These entities can cause harm if the medium is inexperienced or is not in complete control of the séance.

In addition, mediums point out that the sitters who are participating should do so with pure hearts, because spirits will sometimes broach topics and issues that may be sensitive to some of the people in the circle—family secrets or other information that a person may not feel comfortable having shared with a lot of strange people sitting in a darkened, nearly pitch-black room. Again, a high level of trust and comfort between the members is most preferable for mediums doing séance-type of work.

Once the area has been cleansed with sage or another type of tool (feather, incense, *etc.*) then the circle may be opened. Each member usually sits in his/her own chair in the circle. The medium has the responsibility to monitor and to be aware of what is happening at all times—psychically, spiritually, energetically, and physically—in the circle and in the room. Once the medium is in a trance-state, it is vital that he/she has a firm and working relationship with the control or gatekeeper spirit. This spirit entity will monitor and guide the séance appropriately while the medium is in trance, through the medium. Spiritualist mediums tend to call in regularly, and have a mutually beneficial working relationship with, all of their spirit guides and spirit teachers.

In all of the séance and healing circles attended in the course of the research for this study, the medium used some type of affirmation or prayer as a way to raise the vibration of the group. The "Lord's Prayer" was used the most and is something that usually all of the members can recite together. The reason for doing this, according to Spiritualists, is that there is power in the spoken word, so the prayer and/or affirmation is said loudly, clearly and forcefully with power and determination that reflects sincerity and confidence. It was common for this to be said at least three times, and this is because repetition builds up the vibration of the room from the group effort. At times, the medium, along with the séance or circle members, said the prayer/affirmation four times looking Northward, Eastward, Southward and Westward. This acts as a protection from all sides from any type of malevolent entity or force that may try to enter.

In addition, after calling in God, the Light, and the spirits into the circle, the medium sometimes then covered the room and circle with a robe of white light to seal the area with a "psychic shield." The intention of the séance or circle is clearly stated unequivocally, asking that only the highest and best be allowed to enter the séance or circle. The medium asked the Archangels—Michael, Raphael, Gabriel, and Uriel—for their presence to guard the four corners of the area, and to protect all of those present. At this point, the medium invited his/her spirit teachers and guides, as well as angels and loved ones to enter the séance or circle. The reason for all of the cautionary protection, as explained to me by mediums that hold séances and healing circles, is that there are trickster and prankster spirits who rove the hereafter looking for chances to be naughty. The mediums I interviewed said that it is necessary to beware of entities who claim to be high up entities, a common prank by disturbed spirits. Hence, they are quite careful in what they bring forth.

The closing of the séance or circle is of equal importance. Failing to close the area properly by cutting the energy, and thanking the spirits for coming, is like leaving a telephone partially off the hook after a telephone call—the connection, albeit with static, is still open and receiving. So it is with Spirit. If the connection is not broken, the medium's guides, angels, loved ones in spirit, will continue to try to make contact. Also, a channel left open indefinitely will attract unwanted entities.

Entities in spirit, as well as the medium's own guides and angels, do not understand or have the same concept of time that humans do. The medium is always in charge and must set the ground rules for contact. It is up to the medium, as the séance or circle leader, to tell them that it is time to vacate the space in order to allow for the séance or circle to be closed. Even in everyday life, mediums find it necessary to remind them that they are human and that as a human being they need their "human" time to go about their everyday business of living and working. Mediums maintain that just as it is important to respect the role the spirits play in their lives; it is of equal importance that those in the spirit world have respect for the mediums' concept of time and need for space.

In closing, the medium will often ask all of the members to join in a closing affirmation or prayer before extinguishing the candle, and closing the sacred text. Afterwards, often times, sitters want to talk about the séance or circle that they just experienced, as well as their impressions (both spiritual and physical). This period of time immediately following communication with the spirit world, allows the sitters to put the experience into perspective and to think more clearly and deeply about the messages given. It is often the case that after all is said and done, it is the time immediately after and even much later, that the information given makes sense and can be better understood by the intended recipient. Ultimate interpretation, however, is left up to the individual.

4.5 Summary

In this chapter, a survey of Spiritualism and mediumship was rendered, focusing on the various types of spirit communication and methods of doing it. Specifically, mental and physical mediumship were introduced, offering a variety of illustrations and detailed explanations of the various types of phenomena. As well, the fraudulent side of Spiritualism and mediumship was explored, citing historical instances where trickery and jugglery were used on unsuspecting sitters, and how in-depth investigations uncovered the deceptions. Finally, the séance and clairvoyant and healing circles—the heart of spirit communication—were researched, delineating extensive detail regarding these fascinating and essential aspects of mediumship.

Many aspects of mediumship are misunderstood. Mediums are at once reviled and rejoiced, depending upon the mood of society. The work of mediums is a very hazy area that naturally opens itself up to ridicule. Those who have experienced phenomena (whether it is mental or physical) have no qualms about accepting the idea that spirits exist and certain people are adept at communicating with them. Those who have not experienced any supernatural occurrences find it hard to believe in the possibility of spirit communication. These two camps of thought probably will never come to any mutual conclusions, except, perhaps, to agree to disagree.

Although mediumship has been around for eons, Spiritualism is rather new when considering the entire scope of human history. The idea of a religion that is based upon "talking to the dead" makes outsiders suspicious of the motives and purpose of the adherents. Especially perplexing is when people posing as mediums surreptitiously dupe unsuspecting believers by preying upon their grief for a loved one with only financial gain as a motive. This despicable behavior gives the entire movement a bad name; even if one does not accept the idea of spirit communication, one must accept the fact that there are honest and sincere mediums that wholeheartedly believe in spirit communication and feel what they are doing is in service to humanity.

5

Statement of the Problem and Purpose of the Study

5.1 Introduction

Ever since the Hydesville Rappings of 1848, when the Fox sisters, Katie and Maggie, devised a system of raps to make intelligent communication with a disincarnate entity they affectionately called "Mr. Splitfoot," people from all walks of life, backgrounds and economic means, have been intrigued with the possibility of communicating with loved ones who have passed away. There is a seemingly innate need, or longing desire, "to know" what awaits us earthlings once the transition called "death" occurs. What is the basis for this need to know? Why are people's curiosities so aroused at the possibility of what lies beyond this life? This fascination has been a part of collective human consciousness since time immemorial—every culture and religious tradition, from the beginning of time, has wondered what lies beyond this life.

Added to this desire to know is the idea that a goodly number of people are generally titillated with the mere prospect of communicating with those who have passed over, leading many to attempt actively some sort of communication with those on the other side of the veil; or to seek out some type of guidance relating to their future prospects and life. The majority of people, perhaps, will not necessarily or readily admit to seeking out the counsel of a medium or psychic—but with all of the psychic hotlines available, tarot readers advertising in trade magazines, and the recent surge of television mediums like James Van Praagh, John Edwards and Sylvia Brown (making this a multibillion dollar industry), tend to suggest otherwise. Many people, as "entertainment" or as a fun diversion, will religiously read their horoscope included in daily newspapers. Even those who profess not to believe in it will often read what is in store for them for the day. It is a part of human nature to wonder what the future holds, and if another person has an inside track on how to foretell the future, a significant number of people are more than open to hearing what they have to say.

Adding to this desire, is the fact that most every person alive has had some sort of paranormal experience, or knows someone who has (or has at least been told of another's ghostly encounter), in which there is no obvious explanation that can logically explain it away; a large number of people have indeed visited a psychic or medium in hopes of getting a glimpse of their future or in contacting a loved one who has died. Hasn't every person, at one time or other, contemplated (if even casually) the possibility of loved ones on the other side communicating with those left behind in life? Even those who categorically deny the feasibility of any existence of apparitions must have a small part within them that questions the possibility of a hereafter where those who preceded them in death can be found.

The religion of Spiritualism purports to have the answers to all of these questions, basing its entire belief system on the idea that people do not die, bodies do, with the spirit of the person continuing on in another dimension, waiting patiently for a chance to make contact with those left behind. Spirit communication is at the center of Spiritualism with Spiritualists placing their belief in the hands of a medium's ability to commune with entities that have passed over.

Not long after the Fox sisters made their alleged "spirit contact," legions of people became fascinated with the idea of talking to the dead. This occurred at a time when the United States was experiencing spiritual growing pains, with a number of new movements popping up around the Eastern seaboard. People were searching for new and less constricting belief systems, while questioning many of the Puritanical rules that controlled their lives (which had been the norm for centuries). The fact that spirit communication was even remotely possible changed all prior held beliefs concerning entrenched and undisputed teachings of mainstream religions—the prospect of a new religion that was based on Natural Law and spirit communication, with undertones of a philosophy and science, and that which denied original sin, vicarious atonement, the physical resurrection of Jesus, as well as preaching positively about the redemption of all people no matter how sinful they were, appealed to a growing number of citizens who had grown tired of the fire and brimstone sermons of mainstream religions. Interestingly, however, many newly converted adherents to the various movements brought with them many of the engrained ideas of their own Christian religious traditions, trying to fuse the belief systems of their childhood with that of the new religions. This was of no matter, because the modest mediumship of the Fox sisters was about to explode into a full-fledged movement to be called "Spiritualism."

Gradually, as more and more people claimed to be connected to and able to communicate with the spirit world, self-proclaimed mediums were suddenly holding living room séances from coast to coast. From the very initial stages of the Spiritualist movement, however, self-enrichment sometimes became a motivating factor for a number of the mediums who soon began charging for their spiritual services. All of this served to muddle what was indeed genuine from what was mere fakery and deception. If the United States was experiencing spiritual growing pains, Spiritualism was experiencing severe growing pains.

Initially, the idea of this new religion was to be void of dogma, church tenets, creeds and doctrines. People were to be "free thinkers" accepting the truths from all religious traditions and sacred texts, allowing a free flowing of ideas and beliefs to transpire. It was not long, though, until infighting began to occur and it became painfully clear that some type of organization had to be created in order for the movement to develop fully. Several independent Spiritualist-based organizations began cropping up, making it increasingly difficult to manage. Added to this is the fact that in the very early days, mediums were basically itinerant preachers who traveled from city to city to give tent demonstrations of mediumship via messages in the form of mental and physical phenomena. Since many of the early Spiritualists had been Christians, many leaned toward organizing the movement modeled on Christian organizations because this is what many were comfortable with and the only system they knew personally (churches, services, use of the Holy Bible, hymns, *etc.*).

Critics and cavilers abounded as the movement started to gain momentum. Mainstream churches were losing parishioners to Spiritualism, and they were not about to give up without a fight. Many of these critics attempted to tie Spiritualism to the work of Satan, trying to instill fear and guilt into those who were following the new religion's teachings. Regardless of the criticism by nonbelievers, and even being aware of the potential for fraud by charlatan mediums, people swarmed to Spiritualist meetings and the movement grew in leaps and bounds. The young movement boasted millions of followers in the early 1850s, just a few years after the Fox sisters' revelation. This is all the more amazing when considering the population of the United States at the time was just around 30 million. (Buescher, xi)

> ...the New England Spiritualists Association estimated the number of spiritualists[1] in the United States as 2 million, and *The North American Review* gave its opinion that the figure was reasonable. The *Spiritual Register*, a popular annual serial compiled by spiritualists, estimated the number of spiritualists in

1860 as 1,600,000 but suggested that the number of nominal believers was 5 million.² (Buescher, x)

At the heart of Spiritualism, though, is the medium—a person sensitive to the vibration of spirit entities who can interpret through a variety of means intuitive visions, feelings, sounds or voices, and smells, interpreting these as messages by those on the other side to those in the here and now. Mediums and mediumship, in many aspects, have come a long way since the early days of the Spiritualist movement when anyone could claim to be a Spiritualist medium. A spiritualist medium today, one that is board certified and thoroughly tested, goes through a rigorous course of study including (but not inclusive of) Spiritualism's history, belief system, and notable personas associated with the movement; metaphysical training; the Bible (as well as other sacred texts); healing; public speaking; platform decorum; ministerial ethics, and most importantly, perhaps, mediumship unfoldment and development.³

Becoming a certified Spiritualist medium requires dedication, commitment and perseverance. What criteria are used to determine effective mediumship competency? What are the mediumship competencies that are relevant to working as a medium? How does one develop mediumship ability? What selection process is

---

1. Some authors always keep "spiritualist" and "spiritualism" in the lowercase. This author has consistently capitalized it throughout this study just as one would use the uppercase for "Christianity," "Buddhism," or "Judaism."
2. Since Spiritualism was not yet organized into a denominational religion (in that churches and ministries were formed offering some semblance of an organization and body to the movement), a number of people maintained their own religious traditions outwardly, but practiced and/or participated in spirit communication in private. For these reasons, it is impossible to know exactly how many adherents there actually were at the time. Even today, the real number of practicing Spiritualists is at best misleading in that there are a number of people who do not openly subscribe to Spiritualism, but in private are quite open and receptive to its beliefs and practices (*i.e.* those who seek guidance and counsel from a medium in the form of a reading, attending séances and healing circles, and believing in spirit communication through personal, experiential instances that lead people not to categorically deny the plausibility of spirit communication). I found in my research that people are a bit hesitant and even embarrassed to admit that they believe in spirit communication for fear of being labeled unkindly by those who do not believe—a form of spiritual bullying, of sorts.
3. See Appendix Q for a sample course of study to become a certified Spiritualist medium via the Morris Pratt Institute of Milwaukee, Wisconsin in association with the National Spiritualist Association of Churches (NSAC).

in place to accurately measure and validate one's mediumship skills? The answers to these questions can be found in the process that Spiritualist organizations require for people to become certified mediums, as identified by existing Spiritualist associations, most notably the National Spiritualist Association of Churches (NSAC), the Indiana Association of Spiritualists (IAOS), the Southern Cassadaga Spiritualist Camp Meeting Association (SCSCMA), and the Universal Spiritualist Association (USA).[4]

Aspiring mediums who wish to be certified by an accredited Spiritualist organization generally must complete an extensive mediumship developmental program, as well as a battery of tests given in stages throughout the study course—both written and oral in the form of evidential demonstrations of mediumship. First, the novice medium must enroll in and successfully complete a specified number of classes related to Spiritualism and mediumship. Second, the medium must participate in message services, séances, and church services to demonstrate his/her platform work.[5] This serves as a type of "apprenticeship" in that older, more seasoned mediums will often critique the novice's work, style and ability, commenting on the presentation and accuracy of the message. In addition, the older medium will offer suggestions and advice on how to improve the aspiring medium's ability to give messages more clearly and accurately. Third, the novice medium must give messages in the form of genuine spirit communica-

---

4. Lake Pleasant, Massachusetts was home to the largest of the 19th century Spiritualist camps; established in 1874 with tents, it grew rapidly and by 1890 had "500 cottages, a grocery store, and a hotel, and offered band concerts, dancing, and refreshment stands as well as a variety of mediums, fortune tellers, magnetic and electric healers, and inspirational Sunday lectures." (Guthrie, *et al*, 17) It is important to note that by far the most renowned of these organizations was the NSAC located in Lily Dale, New York (known earlier as the Cassadaga Lake Free Association and renamed "Lily Dale" in 1879); the IAOS was formed in 1886 in Chesterfield, Indiana and is affectionately known as "Camp Chesterfield" by the locals; the SCSCMA originally was created as a winter retreat for the northern Spiritualists escaping the harsh winters of New York and Massachusetts and was established in 1894; the USA no longer has a Spiritualist camp of its own (it did have a camp at one time called "Maple Grove," but it is no longer in use) as it was an offshoot of the IAOS, being established in 1956. The USA is unique in that it was the first to modernize, embracing modern technology like the internet to reach more people; it developed the first on-line ordination and certification system by distance learning with a yearly residence session at its annual symposium. The Morris Pratt Institute, located in Milwaukee, Wisconsin, offers courses by distance study also (it is affiliated with the NSAC, its parent organization) [See Appendix Q for a course of study for the Morris Pratt Institute.]

tion as a type of evidential testing to a panel of sitters who are all certified mediums; this is to ensure that the aspiring medium is indeed making actual spirit contact. The members on the panel will judge the novice's ability based on whether or not he/she is able to give messages that can be confirmed definitively by the panel (*i.e.* a name of a loved one in spirit and/or a description as well as a message that a panel member can recognize and concretely identify).

As a rule, this process takes anywhere from a couple to several years to complete. During this period of time, the novice studies about Spiritualism, esoteric studies, in addition to developmental and unfoldment classes which serve to instruct the aspiring medium on how to not only develop his/her mediumship skills, but how to hone them. They also learn practical aspects of mediumship involving outside tools that can aid them more readily in connecting them with spirit (*i.e.* astrology, tarot, numerology, *etc.*). Throughout the course of their studies, aspiring mediums are required to take periodic written exams comprising the material they studied up to that point.

During the developmental phase of mediumship, often the novice is assigned a certified medium who acts as a mentor in guiding and advising the aspiring medium. After successfully completing this course of study, the novice's are assigned various duties to not only further their mediumship skills, but also to familiarize them with the workings of the church service and all other related aspects of being a Spiritualist medium. Throughout this tenure, the probationary medium is exposed to as many of the necessary elements of being a medium as possible, therefore gaining valuable experience in the process. Upon completion of the "apprenticeship" and testing, the novice medium is then formally allowed to practice as a Spiritualist medium, endorsed by the parent organization that certified him/her, complete with papers suitable for framing.

Mediumship has certainly had its ups and downs since its widespread acceptance in the mid-1800s, once enjoying throngs of followers to a period when it practically became nonexistent. Interestingly, after each major war (the US Civil War and World Wars I and II), a surge in popularity occurred due to sudden interest by grief stricken families who lost young soldiers in the fighting, ever hopeful that some type of contact can be made to put their minds at ease, knowing that those who perished were indeed all right and happy in the afterlife.

---

5. "Platform work" refers to the medium standing in front of the congregation for the purpose of giving messages from the spirit world to those in attendance. This term most likely has its roots in the old days when Spiritualists traveled the countryside as itinerant mediums, standing on a raised platform to do their work. This is a common phrase used by Spiritualists when referring to doing a message service.

In general, though, interest in Spiritualism has gradually waned over the past century and a half. Today, formal membership is modest in comparison to the heady days of yesteryear. Interest does pique occasionally, most recently with the proliferation of celebrity mediums that write books, appear on television, radio, and who write columns in newspapers and magazines. Spiritualism, not unlike most other religions that have also experienced a decline in membership recently, is struggling to survive in some ways. It may not thrive like it once did, but it will continue on, even with fewer adherents, because there is still more than a casual interest by a certain cross-section of the population who may not believe wholeheartedly in spirit communication, but do believe enough to seek counsel and guidance by practicing mediums and psychics to have a reading (just in case, on the off chance, there is something to it). For those who have experienced spirit communication through a Spiritualist medium, there is no need for convincing—they are firm believers who trust completely the experience of what they saw, felt, heard or learned from the spirit message as indisputable proof and truth.

Unlike the more traditional or mainstream religions, however, the public demands proof of spirit communication and clamor to see physical phenomenon, reducing Spiritualism, somewhat, to a form of mere entertainment or thrilling diversion rather than the religion that it is, followed and believed in as fervently by Spiritualists as any adherent of any other denomination or religious tradition. For Spiritualists who are sincere in their beliefs and in their mediumship work, and who live their lives in accordance to the Declaration of Principles,[6] they find it disheartening to be constantly confronted by those trying to debunk their mediumship skills or by those who criticize their belief system without the proper knowledge of knowing what they are saying due to a lack of understanding and tolerance. No other religion is made to offer definitive proof of its belief system through evidential means; people believe what they believe based on a deep faith that comes from within—a knowing that is divine in origin.

In contrast, no other religion had placed itself in such an untenable situation as Spiritualism had done, especially in its founding days. Spiritualism initially was founded on the basis that it was not only a religion but also a philosophy and a science. The "science" aspect of Spiritualism, and the early attempts to harness spirits and apparitions using crude technological devices of the day, hurt the movement in that it was not able to live up to the expectations of the people who wanted to see scientific proof, demanding that the medium be correct 100% of

---

6. See Appendix I for a list of the Declaration of Principles.

the time in his/her readings (with physical phenomenon appearing each and every time a séance was conducted).

According to the Universal Spiritualist Association's Constitution and Bylaws (1998) its aim is threefold: the glorification of God through the act of worshiping, service to others, and religious education. It also has an expressed purpose to "preach, teach, promulgate and practice the Religion, Science, and Philosophy of Spiritualism." (1998) The areas of interest that the Universal Spiritualist Association supports and encourages include psychic phenomena, extra-sensory perception, consciousness expansion, parapsychology, occultism, esotericism, mysticism, hermeticism, cabala, tarot, astrology, numerology, transcendentalism, and "other kindred subjects." (1998) This list is seemingly much more inclusive of a wider variety of areas than other Spiritualist organizations. Of course, the Universal Spiritualist Association also includes mental and physical phenomena as being a central part of its purpose; mediumship involving mental phenomena includes impressional channeling, prophecy, inspirational channeling, psychometry, clairvoyance, clairaudience, clairsentience, cartomancy, skrying, pyromancy, geomancy, trance speaking and xenoglossis. (1998) Mediumship involving physical phenomena includes rapping, parakinesis, telekinesis, precipitation, direct writing/drawing, direct voice (both independent and trumpet), transfiguration, materialization, apport, and spirit photography. (1998) The association's mediums are basically allowed to use any of the above tools or types of mental and physical mediumship in their work, but it was my observation that during readings and message services, the mediums relied solely on their mediumship abilities to contact the spirit world.

The National Spiritualist Association of Churches, as a rule, prohibits the use of outside tools like astrology, numerology, tarot, *etc.* by mediums sanctioned by them in their mediumship work. Mediums must do their mediumship solely based on their connection with spirit, using their mediumship skills which in essence include all of the examples previously listed for mental and physical mediumship. This rule is in place, in part, to make certain that the mediums working are doing so honestly and are not employing any outside assistance or gimmicks to give readings.

Each Spiritualist organization regulates its mediums by providing specific guidelines regarding mediumship when giving readings and messages. For example, during the high season (early summer to early autumn) at the Spiritualist camps, mediums follow the same fee scale; many camps and churches have a formal dress code (women wear long gowns or dresses and men wear suits) when doing platform work. In general, mediums are discouraged from attempting to bring in full-form materializations; in the past, the pressure to perform upon command, coupled with the adulation a medium received when presiding over a service or séance that had materializations, caused some mediums to mimic and create phenomena through artificial means. This type of trickery, of course, is not tolerated by the parent organization. Hence, many organizations have done away with allowing this type of phenomena to occur.

This researcher found that allegations of fraud and deception were promptly investigated and taken very seriously by the leaders of the Spiritualist camps that were personally observed. The governing bodies always took steps immediately to insure that the mediumship offered was authentic and genuine. As it was explained to me by a Spiritualist who had a position of authority at a camp, it behooves the camp or church to keep the religion (as a whole) and the particular association, free from imposters and deceivers in order to maintain a high sense of integrity within the organization. Not to do so would be self-defeating as a scandal involving trickery or fakery would be ruinous for the entire movement. Mediums found to be in noncompliance of the rules of mediumship engagement are usually promptly asked to desist; the membership and certification papers are often revoked; as well, any privileges associated with working as a medium under the association's directive are taken away.

Mediums that are formally and properly trained by established Spiritualist associations tend to have similar mediumship skills and techniques. This is most likely due to not only the structured portion of the training period, but is also a result of the "apprenticeship" aspect where novice mediums study under older, more experienced mediums. Each medium, however, approaches mediumship based on a much more individual style using a type of mental phenomena that is most comfortable to him/her. The primary research data gathered for this study reveals this clearly as each subject had a very personal connection to the spirit world that was uniquely his/her own. All of them employed similar techniques, but each tended to have a personal aspect that was used while doing readings and giving messages.

A detailed fieldwork questionnaire[7] and personal interviews[8] were conducted by this researcher and author of this treatise. The purpose in so doing was to gather as much data as possible regarding specific mediumship skills, backgrounds, experiences and competencies relevant to Spiritualist mediums and their work (as identified by 48 certified Spiritualist mediums who are currently practic-

---

7. See Appendix R.
8. See Appendices G and H.

ing some form of mediumship). Some of the topics contained in the fieldwork research included questions on the mediums' religious backgrounds prior to becoming a Spiritualist medium; when and why they actively pursued mediumship; what type of certification they possess; years of service as a medium; first recognition of mediumistic gifts; positive or negative mediumship experiences; outside tools used in their mediumship work; personal daily routine and ritual used to connect to the spirit world; type of mediumship experienced (mental and/or physical); reasons why people seek the counsel of a medium; and how the medium responds to criticism of spirit communication.

The criteria for the gathered data on the mediumship of the surveyed mediums was largely based on the experiential aspects of their work as well as pertinent background information that was directly, and indirectly, related to their mediumship. To gain a broader understanding of the requirements and the duties of being a medium, information was collected on several levels, including conducting site visits, interviews, attending séances and healing circles, and attending message services at Spiritualist churches and camps; in addition, it was necessary to examine documentation and artifacts (spirit portraits, apports, and historic photographs of materializations) of mediums, as well as distributing, collecting, and analyzing a comprehensive questionnaire.

5.2 Origins and Rationale

Initially, interest in this topic had its genesis in my master's work which dealt with Sephardic Jewish history. Although seemingly unrelated at first glance, the seed was sown for further study of religion and its history. I had visited a medium and was given a reading which piqued my interest in this most unusual slice of American religion that I scarcely knew existed. As I began to research Spiritualism, I found that it was very controversial in its belief system, especially amongst Christians, but had achieved widespread acceptance in its early years, but was deeply marred by scandal and fakery throughout its flowery history. Primarily, I was most intrigued by the lack of modern research on the topic of mediumship and how it relates to Spiritualism, and I was astonished that there were very few recent fieldwork studies done on the aspect of the mediumship and mediums themselves. Completely ignorant of Spiritualism and its history in the beginning, I began reading what I could and found that the majority of the available literature on the subject was a century old, dating back to the late 19th century and early 20th century. Although recently published literature on Spiritualism does exist, there is little information on mediumship and mediums that is current and up-to-date. It was at this time that I realized I had happened upon a potential subject area in which to pursue my PhD.

Admittedly, I initially had no concrete hypothesis about Spiritualism or mediumship, only a vague idea based on stereotypical accounts of psychics and fortunetellers. Fortunately, early on, I was able to make the acquaintance of a Spiritualist medium, who is also an ordained minister, which aided me tremendously in focusing my research and devising a research plan. As I began collecting data from my fieldwork in the beginning stages of my dissertation, my knowledge of Spiritualism and mediumship gradually developed in tandem with the data collection process and subsequent analysis of the gathered data. To quote a description offered by Wilcox (1982) in Parmenter (1997) sums up my personal experience in initiating my research:

> One begins fieldwork not with a *tabula rasa* but with a foreshadowed problem in mind. However, the problem is of necessity general in scope. Because one is attempting to understand a system in its own terms, according to its own criteria of meaningfulness, one cannot predict in advance precisely which aspects of the system will have significance or the kind of significance they will have…. It is crucial to begin the research without specifically predetermined categories of observation, questionnaires, precise hypotheses, and so on. (459)

It became clear to me that I had fallen into this research trap of having a preconceived idea of what it was I wanted to determine—a foreshadowed problem. Since I had examined Sephardic Jewry in my previous graduate work systematically, with a historically linear approach, I realized early on that for this study I needed to go directly to the source, divorcing myself from any preconceived perceptions in order to stretch the parameters of my research plan, focusing on the actual circumstances, rather than depending upon an obsolete criterion that was not current with the reality of mediumship today.

In the beginning, I thought that I would focus solely on modern mediumship. It became apparent soon after that this approach was flawed as it limited the scope of the study by disallowing the true roots of Spiritualism to be explored completely, and it failed to take into proper account the religious history that led up to the creation of the movement in the mid-1800s. I decided I had to fill in the missing pieces by researching religion back to ancient times, showing how the layering of traditions helped to make the situation right for the development of a number of new religions that have their roots—not from across the Atlantic in Europe—but homegrown in the United States. Furthermore, I realized that this background information was indeed necessary for the lay reader to be able to gain a clear understanding of where mediumship came from and how it gradually developed over the past 150 years. It was apparent that I had to rethink my foreshadowed problem and include sufficient research to make the study coherent and organized.

From the beginning until the end of my fieldwork, then, the theme of mediumship in spiritualism remained constant, but the result of the study is much different from the one I set out to do in the beginning. The narrow scope in which I initially approached the subject made it impossible to continue as it lacked depth and an understanding of the whole. My original concern over the foreshadow problem, therefore, was never completely abandoned but was merely amplified beyond my initially narrow interpretation to include it in a more complete context. After all, Spiritualism arose partly because the times and attitudes had metamorphosed from a layering of religious traditions throughout the history of the United States, allowing opportune conditions both socially and spiritually for it to develop—during a time when people were open and inviting of such radically new ideas and beliefs. Without the background research included in the review of literature in Chapters 1-4, the topic would not have been fully developed and understood on its own merits in an appropriate historical context.

5.3 Research Questions

The following research questions are presented:

1. What types of religious upbringings, and their effects, did persons who chose Spiritualism have on them; and what type of person trains to become a certified medium?

2. What relative factors exist to prompt mediums initially to pursue Spiritualism as a religion?

3. What types of mediumship are most common among Spiritualist mediums?

4. How do Spiritualist mediums connect to spirit and how and what kinds of tools do they employ in their work?

5.4 Statement of the Problem

There are ample sources and extensive literature dealing with Spiritualism and mediumship, but currently, however, there are no studies that focus directly on the medium as a person and a professional with regards to his/her mediumship. No study, to my knowledge, has focused on how and why a person first realizes or chooses to become a medium. Related to this is the background of the medium and the type of spiritual upbringing and experience the person had previously which led him/her to seek out Spiritualism and mediumship (if in fact the person was not raised in a Spiritualist church). For these reasons, the topic of mediumship as it relates to Spiritualist mediums is explored, emphasizing the type of mediumship practiced by the medium.

5.5 Purpose of the Study

The purpose of the study is threefold; first, to determine the specific backgrounds and training done by those seeking to become certified mediums; second, to identify the process and techniques used by mediums in their work; third, to qualify the process used in preparation for a spirit message to take place.

5.6 Hypotheses

The research hypotheses are as follows:

Sub-hypothesis 1: Mediums who converted to Spiritualism were predominately raised in or came from Christian backgrounds. It is hypothesized that a low percentage of practicing Spiritualists were actually raised as Spiritualists; instead, due to a spiritual void in the religious tradition in which they were raised, a majority of practicing Spiritualist mediums who come from Christian backgrounds, converted to Spiritualism. Currently, there are no data to support or deny this conclusion that an overwhelming percentage of Spiritualist mediums are converts to the religion.

Sub-hypothesis 2: Mediums were drawn to Spiritualism due to a lack of understanding and flexibility by their former churches. Unhappy with the spiritual opportunities afforded to them, many sought out Spiritualism as a way to fill a spiritual void not fulfilled by mainstream religions.

Sub-hypothesis 3: Spiritualist mediums are trained similarly and predominantly employ similar techniques and tools in their work. Formal study and training are central to a medium's ability to be an effective medium. This training and mediumistic education are predictive factors in being a successful medium.

Sub-hypothesis 4: Mediums constantly hone their abilities through daily ritual and through years of experience. Practicing mediums nearly always use some type of centering technique to prepare them for a reading or message service that is a part of their daily spiritual ritual.

5.7 Significance of the Study

The significance of the study is to contribute to the existing research on modern mediumship and Spiritualist mediums. First, the study detailed the religious backgrounds of practicing Spiritualist mediums, identifying the religious backgrounds and denominations of the respondents, as well as the reasons for converting to Spiritualism. Second, it evaluated the results of the questionnaire regarding these points and additional relevant data related to mediums and mediumship in the context of their professional life. Third, it analyzed the data in order to develop an overall understanding of the work of contemporary mediums. Finally, this study determined how mediums work professionally, and what means they use to give readings, and the types of phenomena that appear during spirit communication. The results of this study show how mediumship has evolved over the past century and a half, and may suggest the direction mediumship is headed in the future.

5.8 Limitations of the Study

This study has the following limitations:

1. The design of this study was largely limited to Spiritualist camp resident mediums. Because the respondents were mainly selected from mailing addresses for resident mediums in Spiritualist camps, practicing Spiritualist mediums outside Spiritualist camps were few in number and not fully represented in this study.

2. This study is applicable to certified Spiritualist mediums; mediums or psychics who are not formally trained and who are not members in good standing of a Spiritualist association were not considered, even though their mediumship ability may be as valid as that of Spiritualist mediums.

3. Although completely anonymous, respondents may exhibit bias in answering the questionnaire due to a desire to give what they perceive to be the desired answers to the questions; and due to the nature of their work, they may offer answers that offer seemingly more examples of spirit communication and phenomena than actually took place.

4. Due to strict guidelines set forth by some Spiritualist organizations, respondents may have hesitated to respond completely in the areas of spirit phenomenon or outside tools for fear of being chastised later once the results are public.

5. The design initially did not quantify a set number of respondents but instead generated analysis from only the data received; as well, a distinction between ordained Spiritualist ministers who are certified mediums and mediums who are not ordained ministers was not made initially, but was noted in the analysis once the fieldwork data was collected.

6. Because of the small number of non-native American respondents (N=5) in this study, the results cannot necessarily be generalized to other foreign Spiritualist mediums.

7. Because of the small number of male respondents (N=9) in this study, the results of the study cannot necessarily be generalized to other males who are practicing Spiritualist mediums.

8. The study will not attempt to predict the success of mediums' abilities in mediumship.

9. The study will not determine or evaluate the preparation or training of Spiritualist mediums.

5.9 Basic Assumptions

This study makes the following assumptions:

1. The mediums used in this study have sufficient experience and knowledge of mediumship to respond adequately to the research questions.

2. Given the guarantee of anonymity, the respondents did respond honestly and objectively, offering information that is relevant and true.

3. The mediums used in this study are all duly certified and are practicing mediums with ample experience to comment intelligently on the topics covered on the questionnaire.

5.10 Definitions

In general terms, most Spiritualist associations have a multi-tiered system of certification. These usually consist of 4-5 levels of certification; for instance, the Universal Spiritualist Association (USA) has five levels: Cleric, Missionary, Deacon, Minister, and Healer. The Indiana Association of Spiritualists (IAOS) has four levels: Healer, Medium Missionary, Associate Minister, and Minister. This study evaluates those that have attained certification to practice mediumship (for the USA this is from the "Missionary" level or higher and for the IAOS this is from the Medium Missionary level or higher). These associations' certification levels are representative of the majority of Spiritualist associations' certification systems. It should be noted that the majority of the respondents (81%) were ordained Spiritualist ministers as well as practicing mediums.

A medium is defined officially as "one whose organism is sensitive to vibrations from the spirit world and through whose instrumentality, intelligence in that world are able to convey messages and produce the phenomena of Spiritualism." (Morris Pratt Institute, 1997)

The study examines Spiritualists only. A Spiritualist "is one who believes, as the basis of his or her religion, in the communication between these and the spirit world by means of mediumship and who endeavors to mould his or her character and conduct in accordance with the highest teachings derived from such communication." (Morris Pratt Institute, 1997)

Spiritualism, hence, is defined as the "Science, Philosophy, and Religion of continuous life, based upon the demonstrated fact of communication, by means of mediumship with those who live in the spirit world." (Morris Pratt Institute, 1997)

Mental and physical phenomena of Spiritualism, for purposes of this study include (but are not limited to) clairvoyance, clairsentience, clairaudience, independent voice, independent writing and paintings, materializations, spirit photography, psychometry, and trance channeling, as well as other forms of spirit communication that are specifically demonstrated by Spiritualist mediums.

5.11 Summary

People seemingly have an innate desire to want to know their future and to make contact with loved ones who have passed away by seeking the guidance of mediums. This need to know is a part of human consciousness and effects everyone at some point in their lives, whether as a fleeting thought or as a personal crusade.

The medium is the conduit between those on earth and those who inhabit the spirit world.

In the early years of the Spiritualist movement, many people claimed to be mediums without any real qualifications other than saying that they could commune with the dead. Gradually, associations formed which tried to legitimize the movement by requiring certain criteria to be met before one could practice mediumship. Eventually these organizations began certifying mediums, which helped establish mediumship and ultimately Spiritualism as a religion.

This chapter introduced the actual origins and rationale for this study. It was decided early on that a more comprehensive approach had to be taken with regards to the topic in order to offer a complete background of the history of religion that served to make the conditions right for Spiritualism (and other American-made religions) to be founded, all around the same geographic area and roughly around the same time. Interest to pursue this topic was based on two main criteria; first, a sincere desire to learn more about Spiritualism and mediumship. There is scant information on the subject that is recent and academically researched. Most of the literature is quite dated and largely deals with the history of the movement and mediumship, but not on the mediums themselves. And second, I wanted to make a contribution to the existing literature on the subject, and to offer new insight into this most interesting segment of American religious history.

The research questions, as well as a statement of the problem, were presented in this chapter along with the purpose of this study. The limitations of the study were outlined and basic assumptions made about the design of the study.

6

Research Methodology, Procedures, Design, and Data Collection

In this chapter, the research procedure and design is presented, as well as a description of the data collection and data analysis procedures, and concludes with the ethical decisions involved in this study.

6.1 Research Design and Procedures

With regards to methodology and the research design, after careful deliberation, a decision was made to use a combination of "quantitative" and "qualitative" techniques of data collection in order to garner more extensive and comprehensive research as a way to proceed confidently forward in this study. For the historical research sections that comprise the literature review of this dissertation, a more *qualitative* technique was utilized. A "grounded theory" study was employed with the primary data collected in the field (as it was not available in published research literature on the subject). Although primarily a historical research study, this technique was useful in the social science aspect of the study as it allowed a more practical observation of the mediums' behaviors and interactions in their mediumship work which was more open and free.

In addition, "content analysis" of portions of the data was done to be more objective and systematic in some of the research material gathered in the form of surveys. A combination of case studies, ethnography, phenomenological studies, as well as the already mentioned grounded theory and content analysis style of research, was employed depending upon the specific aspect of the data gathered (*i.e.* case studies = observing mediums doing their work at Spiritualist camps and churches and interviewing them in their homes where they do readings and have séances; ethnography = visiting Spiritualist church services, message services, séances, and healing circles, as well as attending Spiritualist sponsored symposiums, museums, and libraries to understand more deeply how their work in mediumship was reflected in their church and camp culture; phenomenological study = sampling a representative portion of the population (Spiritualist mediums) to research their lives, work, and attitudes toward Spiritualism more deeply; grounded theory study = interviewing in person and by telephone Spiritualist mediums to get a clearer understanding of their lives and work in a natural setting that is comfortable for them; and content analysis = researching descriptive statistical analysis in the form of specific characteristics of Spiritualist mediums in general.

For the social science aspects of the study, a *quantitative* approach was used, more specifically, a "descriptive research design" was employed which included survey-generated data in the form of questionnaires, as well as telephone and personal interviews. Simultaneously, and in conjunction with the descriptive research design technique, observational study techniques were also employed through participation in séances, healing circles, message services, symposiums, and seminars which dealt directly with the area of research being pursued.

6.2 Population Sample of Subjects and the Selection Process

As pointed out by Hammersley and Atkinson (1983) and Fetterman (1989) in Parmenter (1997), access to the target group focusing on ethnographic research can be troublesome; this was partially the experience I encountered. Initially, the Spiritualist mediums were somewhat hesitant (and even unwilling in some cases) to assist in the fieldwork study. In part, this was most likely due to long held suspicions of non-mediums wishing unfettered access to their work only to publish an unflattering exposé about their religion, belief system and mediumship work. It seems that in past experience when an outside researcher wished access and it was granted, it was only to portray the mediums negatively in an effort to debunk their work publicly.

From the beginning, it was made clear that the purpose of this study had nothing to do with trying to "prove" or "disprove" the mediumship abilities of the Spiritualist medium; instead this study wished to approach the subject matter as objectively as possible from a historical perspective that was based in the study of social science. The purpose of this study was not to make value judgments on their belief system or to criticize their activities, but solely to garner research about the religion of Spiritualism and the mediumship of Spiritualist mediums on an individual, personal level. During the course of my research, I converted to spiritualism; the fact that I am a practicing Spiritualist helped tremendously in allowing me access to all facets of the mediums' activities.

When approaching the mediums, at no time did I refer to them personally as "subjects," "informants," or "respondents." These terms tend to suggest a formalized relationship between the participants and the researcher, sometimes disallowing a free flow of information to occur. In no way did I want to have any tension with the mediums (who were so crucial and integral to my study); I wanted to avoid the potential uneasiness that can sometimes arise unwittingly between a researcher and a subject because of a perceived power struggle where the researcher is in the "power" position and the subject is relegated to a weak position (or worse, the subject feels the researcher is superior, and he/she is inferior). As noted by Spindler (1982) in Parmenter (1997):

> Too often social scientists have assumed (though usually unintentionally) a superior stance in relation to their "subjects." In ethnography, people are not subjects; they are experts on what the ethnographer wants to find out about and accordingly are treated with great respect and always in good faith (490).

Indeed, the mediums that graciously agreed to assist me in gathering the needed data for this study were definitely the "experts" and without their participation and involvement, there would have been no study. It was imperative, in my estimation, to ensure that they felt comfortable, at ease, and uninhibited in offering to me their honest and sincere opinions and views on Spiritualism and on their lives as mediums.

As a "descriptive study," I determined that attempting to survey *every* practicing Spiritualist medium would be a Herculean, if not impossible, task to achieve. Considering the sheer demographic numbers of potential subjects, not to mention the logistics of reaching each and every one, made this unfeasible. So, instead of studying the entire Spiritualist medium population, I decided to select a subset, or sample, of the subject population to survey. By employing this data collection technique, I could make representative generalizations about the entire population with confidence. Hence, a cross-section of selected practicing Spiritualist mediums was made.

The representative group consisted of mediums that are certified and practicing, residing in a Spiritualist camp or are members in good standing of a Spiritualist association. This microcosm of the whole of practicing mediums was carefully and deliberately chosen in order to allow for the general characteristics of the total population to be observed in their responses. It is hoped that enough care and planning was taken to allow the conclusions of the study to be free of bias and distortion. By having a representative sampling of the total population in real-life settings, it is hoped that the external validity of the research is indeed sound and well-grounded.

The participants were all Spiritualist mediums who were duly certified by a functioning and legitimate Spiritualist association. The majority of the subjects were ordained ministers, in addition to being practicing mediums. The population sample was selected using two main criteria: 1) the medium had to be a Spiritualist and a resident of a Spiritualist camp; or 2) the medium had to be a member in good standing of a Spiritualist organization. The list of participants were generated from official mailing lists for Spiritualist camps (Camp Lily Dale, Camp Cassadaga, and Camp Chesterfield); a National Spiritualist Association of Churches list of ministers and mediums published on the internet; and a contact list of mediums associated with the Universal Spiritualist Association distributed at a yearly symposium sponsored by the said association.

6.3 Data Collection Instruments

The subjects, once onboard with the study, were generally very forthcoming with information and materials, assisting greatly in my research task. Oftentimes they offered much more detail than was originally sought. The survey was medium-sized in length with 20 questions[1] in order not to be too tedious in scope for the respondents. As it was, in hindsight, perhaps a shorter questionnaire might have elicited more people's responses. The interviews generally lasted an hour (for the formal taped interviews) and sometimes longer for the conversational-style interviews that were done in the form of casual discussions.

Although the fieldwork questionnaire (the primary instrument) consisted of 20 questions, these were actually subdivided into several smaller sections in the original design of the study, unbeknownst to the subjects: personal background, including age, sex, religion, years as a Spiritualist; certification and qualifications; mediumship experience; outside tools; personal ritual; client or reader related requests; and response to criticism and general comments. The questionnaire did not incorporate rating scales (*i.e.* a checklist scale—"please check the items that pertain to you"; or a Likert scale—"please mark accordingly: strongly agree,

---

1. See Appendix R.

agree, neutral, disagree, and/or strongly disagree"). Instead, an open-ended questionnaire was utilized in this study.

In retrospect, some sort of rating method for gathering research might have made it easier to collocate and analyze the data generated, but ultimately I decided to use an open-ended configuration in the question design in order not to limit the subjects in their responses and not to assume to know what possibilities exist. It was hoped the questionnaire would elicit more detailed and complete results that were accurate, honest and sincere. This certainly was the case, because the responses in many instances covered areas and activities that I would never have thought to have included in a checklist or Likert format. The responses tended to be lengthy and complex, making the interpretation of the data tedious and difficult, but rich with research. The "thick description"[2] aspect of designing the study, in this case, proved to be invaluable.

The instrument was sent by regular post to a total of 170 participants who primarily resided in Spiritualist camps. A nominal number of questionnaires were requested by subjects to give to friends with whom they were acquainted. This pleased me greatly, as several mediums took the initiative to assist me above and beyond my initial request. Written instructions were included with the questionnaire, as well as a self-addressed, stamped envelope in which to return the survey. A total of 55 surveys were received back (roughly 34%); of these, 7 had to be discarded because the subjects did not fit the study's criteria (mostly because they were not certified Spiritualist mediums).

Initially, I had contemplated generating a survey via the internet using e-mail to gather the research data. This idea was quickly abandoned as a higher than average number of practicing Spiritualist mediums (many quite elderly) was not computer literate or internet savvy. Hence, I felt that the best way to get an accurate sampling of the target group was to generate the research using the regular postal system. In the end, the questionnaires proved to be a valuable source of information exploring mediumship and the mediums' opinions and thoughts which would have been nearly impossible to acquire solely by observation or in casual conversational interviews. The anonymity of the survey allowed the mediums to be completely candid in their answers without fear of recrimination or criticism.

The second instrument used was personal interviews, both in person and by telephone.[3] One interview, in particular, was with an ordained minister (male)

---

2. This is where "the situation is described in sufficiently rich, 'thick,' detail that readers can draw their own conclusions from the data presented." (Leedy, 106)

who had been a practicing Spiritualist for over 20 years (but in fact felt he had been a Spiritualist since childhood due to his experiences with phenomena). This interview largely concentrated on the aspects of mediumship that included mental and physical phenomena, primarily experiential in content. Another interview was with an ordained minister (female) who also had been involved with Spiritualism for over 20 years, but had been exposed to similar beliefs as Spiritualism since childhood. This interview consisted mainly of the history, belief system, and philosophy of Spiritualism as a religion and science.

Often the formal interviews did not offer the subjects a comfortable form in which to discuss openly their mediumship and Spiritualist experiences. The tape recorder on the table, the notepad of questions, and the atmosphere made these types of interviews somewhat strained. Even though the interviews were usually conducted in locations that offered a relaxed and non-threatening atmosphere, the subjects appeared to be nervous and tense (sometimes asking me to turn off the tape recorder so they could gather their thoughts more coherently).

Many of the interviews, then, took the form of casual conversations where the subjects felt totally at ease and non-threatened (without the pressure of a tape-recorder and fixed list of questions). This configuration allowed for more dialogue and more in-depth information being provided. Through these "mini-interviews" I was able to further clarify areas of my research that I had observed prior but did not completely understand. Also, it allowed me to receive alternate opinions and interpretations of Spiritualist practices which were relevant to mediumship. As Parmenter (1997) notes, quoting Fetterman (1989), "…informal interviewing feels like natural dialogue but answers the fieldworker's often unasked questions (49)." On numerous occasions I engaged Spiritualist mediums in discussions that served to further assist me in my fieldwork, garnering much needed information and understanding from these informal, but very important interviews which ultimately became integral parts of my research.

Much data was collected by "participant observation." Parmenter (1997) quotes Taft (1998) in defining the role of participant observation within ethnography in the following way:

> The investigators' involvement in the normal activities of the group may be treated as a case of partial acculturation in which they acquire an insider's knowledge of the group through their direct experience of it. These experiences provide them with tacit knowledge which helps them to understand the significance to group members of their own behavior and that of others and

---

3. To see transcripts of two of the taped interviews, see Appendices G and H.

enables them to integrate their observations about that behavior with information obtained from other sources such as interviews with informants and documentary material. (59)

I had extensive opportunities to attend Spiritualist services, séances, healing circles and other activities throughout the fieldwork portion of this study over a period of nearly four years. Although not completely a "participant insider," I was able to participate in the above mentioned areas as a Spiritualist which allowed me firsthand access to realms that non-Spiritualist outsiders rarely have the chance to see and experience. In this role as a quasi-participant, I was able to observe freely, ask any questions I wanted to, interview a number of people, and participate in many of the assemblies, conferences, and workshops held in Spiritualist churches and camps.

In general, I was quite fortunate in that I was able to develop and foster amicable relationships, and even friendships, with many of the subjects I used for this study. Their openness and willingness to help me made the task all that much easier. Had I been severely challenged in my research, denied access, or unduly obstructed by any of the mediums in positions of authority, I would not have been able to gain the insight into their lives and work that I did.

Even though I tried to break down any barriers that existed between myself and the subjects, I sometimes felt some reticence on the part of a few mediums initially to open up to me; I was told later that this was due to the fact that although I was a PhD student doing research, I also had a professional title—professor—from my regular career as a university educator. I would have preferred that the subjects not know this, and if I were to do it all over again, I would take greater care in keeping this unrelated aspect private. Of course, I immediately attempted to play this fact down when introduced, emphasizing my "student" status as not to put any pressure on the medium "to perform for the visiting professor." Fortunately, it was the pattern that after a few minutes of conversation, the mediums would feel relaxed enough with me as a person to be themselves without consciously thinking about my professional status.

Finally, the other technique of collecting data I utilized actively was from Spiritualist generated documents in the form of printed material, magazines, books, and articles written by, and primarily for, Spiritualists. Although dated in many instances, this type of documentation still offered valuable insight into mediumship.

Regarding all of the research techniques employed for the fieldwork portion of this study, I am sure that more time and care could have been taken which would have made the study comparatively better. In retrospect, if I had collected better data, surveyed more mediums, as well as gathering the data in a more logical manner and conducting more in-depth interviews, having better informed observation, and utilizing a more succinctly designed questionnaire, the results would have been more absolute. Certainly, my data collection techniques, the data I collected, and the analysis are not perfect by any means, and if I were to do it again, I surely would improve upon these areas. However, these caveats aside, I do feel that the research gathered does offer sufficient depth and scope in which an informed analysis can be made about Spiritualism, Spiritualists, and mediumship.

6.4 Ethical Decisions

One of the ethical aspects of this study was the anonymity afforded the participants, since the questionnaires were filled out in their homes and sent to me via mail. To ensure honest and accurate answers, anonymity was strictly enforced; once the questionnaires arrived, letters from the alphabet (first single letters—1-26; and then double letters—27-48) were assigned to each questionnaire. If a name had been included on the questionnaire, it was promptly removed. All envelopes with the postmark were discarded before the questionnaire was closely examined. All of this was to insure complete anonymity.

Informed consent was gained by the subjects willing to participate; if they chose not to, they just ignored the written request. Since I had no position of power within the Spiritualist community, where one might feel compelled to participate because of my position, there was no duress, unfair inducement or manipulation of the subjects to participate. Even for the interviews, since many of the subjects did not know me personally at that time, there was no element of pressure for them to participate. The participants, who agreed to assist me, participated on their own merit and volition.

All of the people who I interviewed and who I spoke to informally were aware that I was in the process of gathering research for a PhD dissertation. Sometimes this fact was soon forgotten as the subjects let their guards down in the course of the conversation, and subsequent meetings, but initially, everyone I spoke to about mediumship and Spiritualism were well aware of my research and fieldwork.

It could be argued, then, that each and every time I spoke to someone regarding Spiritualism I should have said that this potentially could be used in my research. In this sense, I did not gain informed consent, per se, but as mentioned before, each and every subject I spoke with was well aware of my research plan and study intent. Since I was not at all sure how the information would or could be used that was about to be given to me, made it impossible to actively seek informed consent for much of the information given in these "mini-interviews."

In my case, the fact that I am a practicing Spiritualist often overshadowed the fact that I was in the process of conducting academic research. But since I held no power position within the Spiritualist organizations in which the subjects were associated, my presence did not pose any problem of undue influence being exercised over the subjects in the study. It was my utmost concern during the entire fieldwork phase of this study that the subjects trust me and feel comfortable in telling me their honest opinions and feelings about Spiritualism and mediumship. My experience mirrors that of Parmenter (1997):

> Trust is the basis of human relationships with people involved in research, and those relationships are essential to the development and completion of the study. Trust leads to its own ethical minefield, however. It is unlikely that people were always aware of my role as a researcher when speaking to me, and some things they said were undoubtedly intended to be heard as private opinions rather than to be made public knowledge. At the same time, it would have imposed a strain on the relationship for me to start asking "Excuse me, but did you say what you said as a friend, or can I use it for my study?" As far as possible, then, I used my own judgment, and did not record any comments which were obviously intended as private information. The basic principle of not causing any harm or betraying the trust of the people I was involved with guided this judgment.

Finally, confidentiality was a primary concern of mine as I gathered research for this study. I felt a keen responsibility to the subjects and Spiritualist associations that assisted me in my work. I employed the lettering system for specific references to mediums that completed the questionnaires, and only used names of those mediums who agreed to a tape-recorded interview. I did not have to resort to using pseudonyms as it was unnecessary, even though a large portion of this study is qualitative in nature.

6.5 Summary

This chapter dealt with the methodology and design of the study, the subjects as a sampling of the overall Spiritualist medium population, and the instruments used in the data collection phase of this study. The techniques employed in this pursuit encompassed a variety of methods, ensuring a wider selection of material and research generated. Although some aspects certainly could have been approached and implemented differently, as a novice researcher this is all a part of the learning process. I have tried to highlight the areas where the study is flawed and has obvious limitations in this chapter. I am confident, however, that the years of fieldwork spent on gathering this research, is valid enough to offer a contribution to the existing research on the topic.

7

Presentation, Analysis, and Discussion of the Data and the Results

7.1 Introduction

The purpose of this study was to determine what the present population of Spiritualist mediums' religious and spiritual backgrounds was, and why they decided to pursue Spiritualism as a religion, and mediumship as a vocation? In addition, the study endeavored to learn the process that encompasses becoming a medium, the types of mediumship (mental and/or physical) the medium actually practices, and the techniques and/or tools used by contemporary mediums in their work. The intention of the study was also to qualify the process and ritual used in spirit communication.

The results of the study, which are described in the following sections, provide clear information that definitively supports the conclusions of this study focusing on the mediumship of contemporary Spiritualist mediums.

7.2 Descriptive Statistics of the Participants' Demographic Data

The study was conducted on Spiritualist mediums who either reside in Spiritualist camps or who are members in good standing of a recognized Spiritualist association. The participants had to be certified mediums, or higher. An overwhelming majority of the participants were ordained ministers (over 80%). One hundred seventy questionnaires were sent out to Spiritualist mediums using mailing lists for resident mediums residing in Camps Lily Dale, Cassadaga and Chesterfield; an internet list of addresses of mediums associated with the

National Spiritualist Association of Churches; also, a mailing list containing names for mediums associated with the Universal Spiritualist Association which was circulated at their annual symposium in the year 2002.

The majority of the questionnaires were sent out in June 2002, with additional questionnaires being sent out to the mediums affiliated with the Universal Spiritualist Association in July 2002; the bulk of the completed questionnaires were received back between July 2002 and September 2002. Although the amount of time needed to complete the questionnaires varied, it is estimated that (on average) it took the respondents between 15-30 minutes to complete the survey in its entirety.

Statistics on the Age and Sex of the Participants

The age of the participants ranged from 43 to 88; the mean was 62. Their sex was predominantly female (82%) with a smaller percentage being male (18%). Within the female group, the youngest subject was 43 and the oldest was 88 (with a mean of 65 years of age). Within the male group, the youngest subject was 52 and the oldest was 74 (with a mean of 59 years of age).[1]

Figure 5.

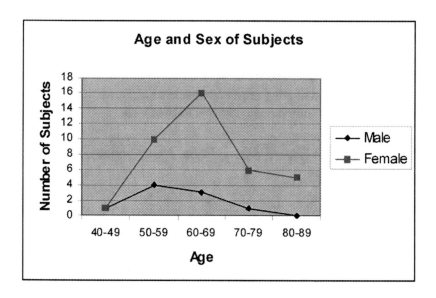

---

1. See Figure 5.

As Figure 5 illustrates, the data is especially telling in that it suggests that the religion is predominantly made up of women. Historically, this is also true from its inception. Spiritualism and spirit communication, first started by the young Fox sisters, eventually served to offer women an active voice in religion, as well as positions of authority in churches, at a time when women were largely relegated to doing housework and to raising a family. Eventually, Spiritualism would give women a vocation—a career—in which they could nurture a profession that was separate from their dependence upon any male figure (whether it be a husband, father, brother, uncle, grandfather, or son).

Until Spiritualism became a religion, women had to be satisfied with secondary and subordinate roles—not only in society, but also in church leadership, church services, and even in church politics. Women were generally not allowed to preach from the pulpit, and were largely forbidden from becoming ordained. Spiritualism as a religion and belief system offered women equality by changing many of the steadfast, traditional rules that had governed women, religion, spirituality, and equality. Goldsmith (1998) points out:

> Perhaps the most startling discovery was the extent to which Spiritualism and the inception of woman's rights were intertwined. At a time when women had no power to achieve equal rights, they relied on the "other powers" provided by Spiritualism to sustain their efforts. Through the mouths of trance speakers came words of wisdom from long-dead seers, and from the spirits came the courage to go forward. (xiii-xiv)

The data gathered for this study suggests that Spiritualist women still find great comfort in the movement and enjoy an equality of the sexes still denied many other women who adhere to mainstream religions. Spiritualism not only offers them a voice, but an opportunity to be heard on equal footing with men. Also, Spiritualism seems to still be "intertwined" with many social issues of the day, offering an alternative view to and acceptance of marginal members of society, from all races, creeds, economic and social backgrounds, and sexual orientations.

Through interviews, onsite research, as well as discussions with a number of Spiritualist mediums, I found a rather high percentage of male (and to a lesser degree, female) mediums and ordained ministers to be homosexual. The sampling was rather limited, and because this question was not included in the original questionnaire, these assumptions cannot be regarded as scientifically sound. But from the data I gathered which can be regarded as significant, it can be generally deduced, perhaps, that this trend can be loosely compared to that of women in the early days seeking out Spiritualism as an alterative to other mainstream religions: it offered no religious or spiritual restrictions based on gender or sex; hence, regarding the issue of sexual orientation also as a non-issue in relation to participating in and taking leadership roles in the church.

The fact that Spiritualists are "free thinkers" and place no moral judgment upon the actions or personal lives of other people (this is to be worked out between the individual and God once the person makes his/her transition to the spirit world), allows homosexuals a place in which to develop and nurture their spiritual selves. Spiritualism seems to offer this stratum of modern society, just as it did for women in Victorian times, an avenue in which to practice their religion freely and openly (as homosexuals) without fear of being judged; it allows homosexuals a haven in which to worship and practice their faith, regardless of their sexual orientation.[2] Also, it is interesting to note that since the majority of mediums are women, and many of the male mediums I interviewed and spoke with were gay, it leads me to wonder if "mediumship" work is somehow connected to a type of feminine energy (this is not to suggest the men are "feminine," but that perhaps the spiritual aspect and vibratory energy needed to make spirit contact is somehow feminine in nature). This was explained to me in the following way by a Spiritualist minister:

> When you do this kind of work, we are all electromagnetic, and we all have male/female energy—which is not sexual. When you do mediumship, you use the "feminine" energy more than the "male" energy. Many straight men are uncomfortable with tapping into this female energy. Gay men are more comfortable tapping into it, so more male mediums tend to be "gay." Straight men are often conditioned from childhood to deny their feminine energy-side, so they do not tap into it very much. Society tends to emphasize to men that they

---

2. This aspect of modern Spiritualism intrigued me, so I inquired further to a number of Spiritualist mediums, both homosexual and heterosexual, as to the reasons for the attraction of gays to Spiritualism and vice versa. It was pointed out to me that this was not always the case. There was a time when Spiritualist mediums and ministers (who were gay or lesbian) had to hide their sexuality from the majority, fearing they would be asked to leave the movement. Spiritualism, however, does view issues from a more progressive point of view, and usually does precede everyday society in the general acceptance of current issues and controversies. Just as Spiritualism embraced women and women's rights at a time when society was fighting issues of equality with a vengeance, so does Spiritualism today embrace those searching honestly and purely for their own spiritual truth and place in society—regardless of their sexual orientation.

are not supposed to "feel," for instance, "real men don't cry." You can't be a medium without being able to feel deeply. (Brown, 2004)

Conclusive results of this assumption will have to await further research in the future, as data on this aspect was not adequately collected to form a theory in which to make a definitive deduction on the subject.

Spiritualism is an "old" religion, and this is not in reference to the number of years since its founding. Many Spiritualist mediums, both men and women, are elderly and this is a troubling prospect for the religion: attracting younger men and women to carry the Spiritualism banner into the next century. The youngest medium in the study was in her 40's; the oldest in her late 80's. The average age of all the women subjects was 65 (and the men 59), which suggests that it is a "graying" religion with the majority of Spiritualists being older. It can be deduced, then, that if younger people do not embrace the religion, and soon, it has the potential of becoming defunct (perhaps even within the next twenty years) if the membership numbers do not begin increasing with those in their twenties and younger.

Spiritualism has historically been a "feast or famine" religion with periods of great crowds of people clamoring to attend Spiritualist churches and camps for services and séances, to times when the religion nearly faltered completely. Buescher (2004) offers the following to explain this phenomenon:

> One became a Spiritualist simply by trying the spirits and being encouraged by the results. In this respect, Spiritualism was a volatile, charismatic movement that spread across denominational lines. But individuals' interest in Spiritualism often waxed and waned. Many who devoted their attention to Spiritualism when it emerged in the late 1840s and early 1850s had cooled in enthusiasm by the mid 1870s. And by the 1880s, many followers had drifted into other newer movements that had historical ties to Spiritualism...(xi)

As mentioned earlier in this dissertation, interest seemed to pique after great wars, prompting people to seek out mediums to contact loved ones in the spirit world to make sure they were all right. Hazelgrove (2000) echoes this by offering:

> The experiences of the trenches eluded conventional theological explanation, and legends concerning the supernatural abounded. In civilian circles bereavement was to become a national experience, mourning a community activity. In this emotional climate, stories of the return of the dead were common. Some observers at the battlefront saw strange figures who, after tending the wounded, instantly and inexplicably disappeared. (13)

Experiential accounts are the basis for many people's belief in spirit communication; especially when grieving, these experiences by others offer hope to those who wish to know where their loved ones are. It was (and is) during these times that Spiritualism tends to become revived.

The movement seems to have always had a tumultuous history that "ebbed and flowed" as a sign of the times and with the mood of the people. Now seems to be no different, except that the religion as a whole is aging quickly without any real prospect of younger people taking over the reigns of the movement that will ensure it makes it into the next century. Spiritualism has survived over its century-and-a-half tenure from periods of being nearly extinct to eras of burgeoning prosperity. It will most likely overcome the current concern of an aging membership by reviving itself as it always has. As long as there are people who want to believe, who actively seek spiritual guidance about their futures, and who wish to commune with the dead, Spiritualism will endure.

Statistics on the Ethnicity of the Participants

The majority of the subjects (83%) were Americans (born and raised in the United States). Of the 16% who indicated they were a nationality other than American hailed from Canada, Sweden, and Puerto Rico. Six percent of the subjects either failed to indicate or refused to divulge any nationality.[3]

Spiritualism is one of only a few religions that was not "imported" to the United States, but instead was "exported" to other parts of the world. Early on, it made its way to Great Britain where it flourished. It eventually spread to other countries in Europe, Australia, and even to South and Central America, but it never did reach the masses outside the United States like Mormonism or Christian Science did—two other American-made religions that were exported from the shores of the United States.

This lack of proliferation is largely due to the fact that Spiritualism is not a "missionary" religion and its adherents do not actively evangelize or try to convert people to it. Spiritualists believe that it is available and accessible to all people, so if it is in the divine order of things, people will be led to it and discover its attributes on their own. This is part of the reason why it is currently having a membership crisis.

As shown in Figure 6, the nationality of the subjects used in this study was overwhelmingly American, with a small percentage coming from outside the United States. This figure is probably representative of the entire Spiritualist

---

3. See Figure 6.

movement in that each association has a nominal percentage of foreign members, with the majority being born and raised in the United States.

Figure 6.

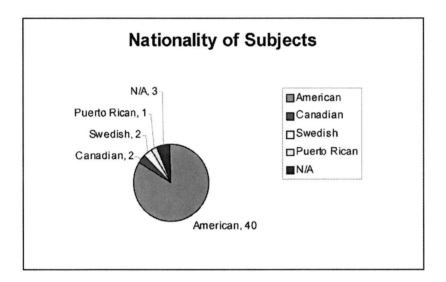

Statistics on Years as a Spiritualist

The years of formal affiliation in Spiritualism as a religion ranged from 7 years to 85 years. The mean average of years as a practicing Spiritualist (not a medium) was 31 years. The number of "lifelong" Spiritualists (the criterion being that the person practiced Spiritualism for at least half of their entire life) was 50%. Those practicing Spiritualism from 1-19 years was 26% of the total; 20-29 years was 35% of the total; 30-39 years was 19% of the total; and 40 years or more was 20% of the total.[4]

These statistics further illustrate the fact that Spiritualism is an aging religion, with the majority of the participants being elderly; since the average number of years attributed to being a Spiritualist is over thirty, the percentage of "lifelong" Spiritualists is exactly half of the total number of participants. This suggests that the percentage of younger ministers or recently certified mediums is significantly less than those who have been practicing Spiritualist mediums for decades. Again,

---

4. See Figure 7.

without younger mediums to take over the work of the older ones, Spiritualist mediumship as we know it will eventually reach a state of extreme crisis.

Figure 7.

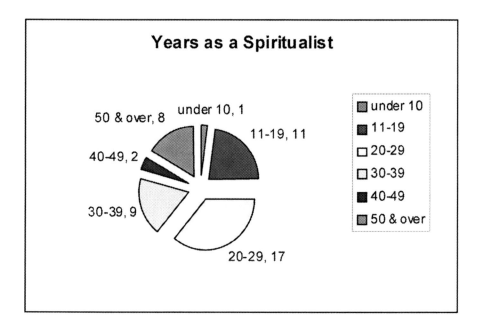

Statistics on the Years Participants were Certified and the Age of Mediumship Awareness

The participants in the study indicated that they had become certified as early as 1952 up to as recently as 2000. Six percent of the respondents had received certification between the years 1961-1970; 19% from 1971-1980; 31% from 1981-1990; 25% from 1991-2000; and 17% of the subjects did not indicate an exact certification date in their response.[5]

The statistics reveal that the mediums who participated in this study, many longtime Spiritualists, were not necessarily certified when they first became Spiritualists, but instead became certified later in life. A quarter of those surveyed indicated they had been certified as recently as the last decade. This suggests that although they were older in age, a decision was made to seek certification later on

---

5. See Figure 8.

in their Spiritualist experience. Not included in the study, however, was data relating to the percentage of these people who may have been practicing mediums for a longer period, but who were not certified by a Spiritualist organization until much later. As is delineated in Figure 9, a significant number of the respondents were well aware of their mediumship gifts from early childhood. This, then, would make it appear that although the respondents were not "certified" they may well in fact have been involved in some sort of mediumship activities.

Figure 8.

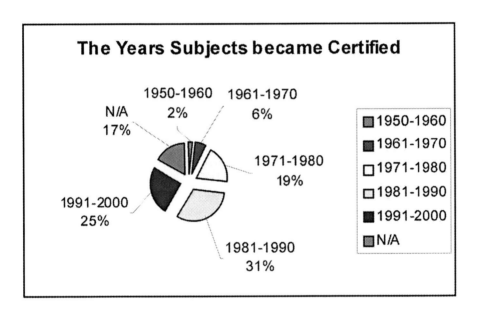

Forty percent of the respondents indicated that they were aware of their mediumship gifts under the age of 6 years old; 10% between the ages of 21-30; 13% between the ages of 31-40; 4% between the ages of 41-50; and 2% over the age of 51. Seventeen percent of the subjects could not accurately recollect when they were first aware of their mediumship abilities, or chose not to respond to this question.[6]

---

6. See Figure 9.

Figure 9.

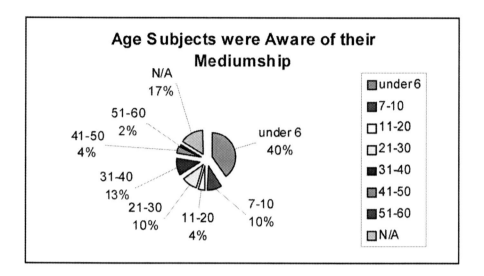

A number of respondents who claimed to be aware of their mediumship abilities as a child referred to seeing, talking and playing with "spirit" children. At the age of six, *Respondent H* notes, "I recall seeing, hearing, feeling a small spirit boy. Today I know him as my spirit guide. He came to me as a child so I would not be afraid." *Respondent C* relates this experience: "I remember seeing spirit-playmates, playing Indians, in the trees...." *Respondent DD* offers, "As a small child with a handicap, my playmates were spirit children who were invisible to others."

Many Spiritualists believe strongly that small children, especially babies, are gifted with seeing spirits before they reach an age where distraction with more mature endeavors causes them to lose this ability. Perhaps "make believe" friends that children often have are in fact "spirit children" who are communicating with them.

In response to the question "What was your first experience?" *Respondent P* explains, "...seeing spirit people and children and speaking with them. The adults brought children to play with me and the situation to me at that time seemed quite natural and normal." "As far back as I can remember, perhaps 2 years old, I saw spirits, heard them speak and answered them," says *Respondent SS.*

Other respondents, as children, recall communicating with spirits, sometimes strangers, and sometimes with family members who had passed over:

Respondent Q (aged 9 at the time)
A spirit entity (woman) sat on the side of my bed—I sat up, and she gently told me not to be afraid, tucked me back under my covers and kissed me on the forehead. At that time in my life, I had to share my parents' bedroom. I looked over and they were both in their bed, asleep.

Respondent T (aged 6 at the time)
…seeing my grandmother, who had passed away…very aware and very alive and communicative. [She] appeared almost nightly for a year, at the foot of my bed…

Respondent EE (age not given)
I had a spirit playmate as a child. My great-grandfather had died 11 years before I was born. We moved in with my great-grandmother when I was a baby. I often saw him around the house.

Respondent UU (early childhood, under 6)
…when the full-figured spirit of my sister appeared to me. She was killed in a train/car accident a short time previously.

Respondent M (early childhood)
I was aware of "imaginary friends" from the time I can remember. Of course, it didn't have the name "mediumship." I also usually knew who was on the phone when it rang, was very intuitive. My mother was diabetic and I learned to read her so well that I often knew when she was in a diabetic reaction before she did. I first became aware of mediumship at about the age of 39-40, being able at that time to put a label on it. I do remember going to the Gettysburg battlefield after high school with my grandparents and picking up all kinds of impressions then, but again, not able to label what was happening.

Statistics on the Participants First Experience with Spirit Communication

Regarding the first paranormal experiences of the subjects, three primary categories were indicated: seeing spirits as a child (44%); seeing and hearing spirits as an adult (23%); and through mediumship development classes as an adult (15%). Eighteen percent of the subjects either could not recall the exact moment or first experience of spirit communication, or they chose not to answer this question.[7]

Nearly 40% of the subjects surveyed experienced their first spirit communication as an adult. Some of the respondents indicated that there first experience with spirit entities were through "channeling." Others indicated that they heard,

---

7. See Figure 10.

felt or saw apparitions as an adult. *Respondent B* relates, "My mother was in spirit when I had channeled her spirit while in a meditative trance." *Respondent D* offers, "Someone that passed came to me and explained the circumstances of [their] death and asked me to comfort the family and explain[it to them]." "About 40 years ago, I had a premonition that my son was going to become very ill. Not long after, he ended up in the ICU with diabetes," related *Respondent Z*. Respondent BB tells about knowing what her sons are doing, "After my sons were born, I became aware of things they were experiencing many miles away. Spirit also made me aware of the boys' 'questionable activities.'"

A number of respondents noted that their first experience with receiving spirit communication occurred while participating in mediumship development or unfoldment classes. These people related how, as adults, they were able to develop mediumship abilities. It seems, then, that unlike the other respondents who had intuitive premonitions or who had experience with some type of mental or physical phenomenon, these particular people were able to train their mediumship through instruction. Spiritualists maintain that everyone has the ability to become a medium—some are more gifted than others—and this can be achieved naturally or can be developed in classes over a period of time.

Figure 10.

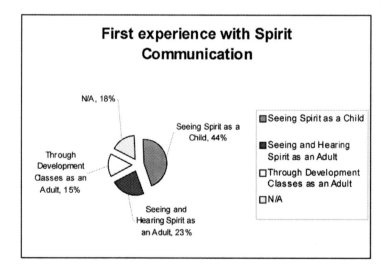

7.3 Findings and Discussions

Sub-hypothesis 1:

The first sub-hypothesis of this study was to determine whether there was a significant correlation between mediums that were predominantly raised in or came from Christian backgrounds and those who were raised as Spiritualists. This sub-problem was included in the questionnaire that was completed by the subjects.

Ninety-six percent of the subjects indicated that they had some type of religious upbringing when they were children. Of this percentage, 87% indicated that their religious backgrounds consisted of one or more denominations of Christianity.

The percentage of subjects that indicated that they were raised with only one main Christian tradition was 50%; the percentage of subjects that indicated they were raised in two or more Christian traditions was 38%; the percentage of subjects that indicated that they were raised as Spiritualists was 8%; and the percentage of subjects that indicated they had no type of religious upbringing was 4%.

In total, the subjects indicated 63 different affiliations (there were only 48 subjects). This suggests that a number of the subjects did a fair amount of "religion hopping"—the phenomenon where a person will seek out a religion, try it for a while realizing that it does not offer them what they are looking for, then try another, and sometimes another, until they finally end up with one they like, in these cases, embracing Spiritualism.

The participants indicated 15 times that they had followed Catholicism, the most of any of the Christian-based religions. This figure does not mean that 15 people *only* followed Catholicism before converting to Spiritualism, but that 15 of the 48 core subjects—at one time or other in their religious life—considered themselves to be Catholic, hence wrote "Catholicism" on the questionnaire. It should be noted that 19% of the total number of participants considered themselves to be only "Catholic" before converting to Spiritualism. Thirteen percent of those who marked that they had been "Catholic" at one time had converted to Catholicism before converting to Spiritualism.

One possible reason for the interest in Spiritualism of traditionally raised Catholics—and those who converted to Catholicism as adults before becoming Spiritualists—has to do with the ritual involved in the ceremonial aspects of the two religions. A Catholic Mass has a very ritualistic liturgy; Spiritualism and mediumship are also comprised of a lot of ritual in the form of chanting and singing to raise the vibration, concentrated meditation or mantra recitation similar to that of those who practice saying "The Rosary," the use of incense during the services, prayer, and the spiritual cleansing of the space where the service takes place.

Perhaps people who first felt a need to search for a new religion happened upon Catholicism because they were seeking ritual, tradition, and religious conformity in their lives. Also, many Protestant denominations' belief systems, although loosely connected, vary widely from one another. Catholicism is quite uniform, no matter where one goes in the world.

In addition, Catholicism advocates spirit communion with the anointed saints which is similar to Spiritualism's belief in spirit communication—the difference being that Catholics only speak to anointed saints who have been designated by the Church as being holy, and Spiritualists will talk to any benevolent spirit that wishes to make contact.

Spiritualists who identified themselves as former Methodists was the second most common Christian denomination and the most widely practiced of the Protestant denominations; third place goes to Lutherans; fourth place to Baptists; fifth place to life-long Spiritualists; tied at sixth place were Presbyterians and Church of God followers; in seventh place were the Nazarenes and Congregational Church followers; and the Unity, Pentecostal, Christian Science, and Episcopalian traditions had one person each who at one time in his/her life had followed these belief systems.

Interestingly, 38% of the total number of subjects indicated two or more religious affiliations while growing up and as adults. This implies that a number of people indeed went searching for a religion that made them feel accepted and comfortable before settling on Spiritualism as their religion of choice. To give an overview of this phenomenon, the following testimonials from the subjects are offered:

> *Respondent A* (age 68, female)
> ...baptized Baptist, attended Church of Christ, was Methodist, but raised by an agnostic mother and had an atheist brother...
>
> *Respondent C* (age 53, female)
> ...I was raised Spiritualist. I was sent to the Methodist [Church] with my friends in order to appear normal. My mother tried to protect me from those who were dyed in the wool [Methodists]...[8]
>
> *Respondent D* (age 59, female)
> ...brought up Lutheran; was never really happy with it. I looked elsewhere...

Respondent H (age 60, female)
...raised Baptist, but converted to Catholicism at age 20; [I followed] metaphysical studies all my life; a practicing Spiritualist since [the age of] 41...

Respondent K (age 52, male)
...raised Presbyterian, became agnostic, then Baptist, Methodist, and now Unitarian-Universalist (became a Spiritualist in 1985)...

Respondent M (age 52, Male)
...Before becoming a Spiritualist, I tried to be a practicing Christian, but with a lot of doubts and questions. I started as a Methodist, which is what the family was, all the way back to when Wesley came to Georgia. At age 19, I followed a girlfriend into the Lutheran church, drawn by the ritual and forms. Realized Luther had a lot of prejudices that I could not handle. During my university years, I had a Roman Catholic phase and a Jewish phase, neither one of which came to anything. After college, was married and remained in the Lutheran Church until about age 38, then went to a very liberal church called Pilgrim's United, where the sermons spoke of chakras and reincarnation. During this time, from 1989 forward, I was also attending church in Cassadaga and taking development classes, so Pilgrim's became my transitional church. The two pastors encouraged me to go to Cassadaga fulltime and study mediumship and to study the ministry.

---

8. A surprising aspect of this research indicated that a certain percentage of current Spiritualist mediums do not necessarily embrace their religion openly, like this subject suggests while growing up. It is difficult to discern concretely, then, how many of the subjects actually openly discuss their religion in public and society, and how many try to hide it. This is a most perplexing aspect because if the medium believes in his/her religion sincerely, then why fear repercussions from non-adherents, unless it is for fear of physical harm coming to them because of their belief system and mediumship work. Research was not gathered in the form of raw data in the area of "religion bashing," verbal threats or physical violence of nonbelievers toward the Spiritualist mediums used in this study; it is an interesting question, however, that could be researched in the future to attempt an answer, in part, as to why some Spiritualist mediums prefer to keep their religious affiliation private, even to the point of attending another denomination's church in an attempt to hide the fact that they are practicing Spiritualist mediums:

> When I first attended a Spiritualist church, it was usual for it to be an afternoon or evening service. One would hear the comment "I go to my real church in the morning."
> (*Respondent FF*)

Respondent P (age 60, female)
...raised both Lutheran and Spiritualist. I am a 5th generation Spiritualist and minister, medium, healer; my mother was a healer; grandmother, minister-medium—both physical phenomenon mediums.

Respondent Q (age 55, female)
...Baptist as a child, Methodist as a teenager, Presbyterian as a young adult—a Spiritualist as soon as I found it in 1977. [I] had always believed and been raised with Spiritualist beliefs, just didn't realize it was a religion.

Respondent R (age 75, female)
...[I] was raised in the South to attend the church that was the closest because there was no transportation. Weather was also a factor—sometimes the closest was not preferred...my mother always said that "any church was better than no church."

Respondent S (age 49, male)
...raised Baptist, converted to Nazarene (adult); as a teen, explored Methodist, Catholic, Church of God, Pentecostal, [and] joined a Spiritualist church at the age of 35.

Sub-hypothesis 2:

The second sub-hypothesis of this study was to ascertain what prompted the subjects initially to pursue Spiritualism as a religion, and to become mediums. This sub-problem was included in the questionnaire that was completed by the subjects.

A number of participants in this survey cited simple reasons for pursuing Spiritualism. For instance, *Respondent F* had read the *Declaration of Principles* of Spiritualism and believed them to be true, so she decided to become a Spiritualist. *Respondent J* had simply visited a Spiritualist church service and was impressed enough to follow it as a religion. "Not satisfied with other religions" was the reason given by *Respondent HH*. "Curiosity" was offered by *Respondent II*.

The majority of the respondents, however, had a more spiritually-based need, ideological reason, or a personal experience with the spirit world that offered them proof (sometimes a religious epiphany of sorts) of spirit communication which prompted them to pursue Spiritualism:

Respondent MM:
I don't think of it as a 'religion'...I think of it as a gift from God and I feel blessed that He has chosen me to help and guide people to a better understanding of themselves and the people around them.

Respondent QQ:
...[I] studied 7 different religions and couldn't find the answers I needed. I wanted to know how to heal, like Jesus did. The scriptures say we can do all things like he did....also, [I wanted to know] what happened to my 2-year-old son who had died...

Respondent NN:
...going to a Spiritualist for a reading when I was in my mid-20's, observing public platform work and then being urged to "try my hand" at psychometry. Within a few years, I had my own clairvoyant experiences which provided indisputable proof...

Respondent OO:
After a private reading, I went to a local Spiritualist church and found their views most like mine...

Respondent PP:
I don't consider it to be a religion, but a science and philosophy...

Respondent M:
I was prompted to pursue Spiritualism the first time I went to Cassadaga for a reading. I realized that there was a religion that was love and I really did not have to believe in Hell and all the contradictions. I also enjoyed the fact that I could read, study and practice what I was lead to, such as Buddhism. I do A LOT of Buddhist practice and teach Vispassana meditation, as well as Spiritualist development.

Respondent EE:
My father passed away when I was 8-years-old. My mother followed him one year and three days later. I was 9-years-old when my mother passed on. I was going to Catholic school and as I would walk to and from school, I knew my mother was walking with me. She would tell me things like, "Hurry home tonight and maybe Aunt Mary won't be in a bad mood..." I had wanted a religious life from the age of 5 and I fully intended to become a nun. In high school, this changed through my husband-to-be and his aunt and uncle who were Spiritualist mediums. I fully believed in life after death and the ability to communicate with [spirits]. I then became a Spiritualist.

Respondent GG:
Family problems. I needed help and the Lutheran minister was no help. A friend that attended a Spiritualist church listened and helped.

Respondent W:
...a search for a non-judgmental, love-based religion. A desire to remove "fear" as a spiritual motivator. Disgust with power-based righteousness.

Respondent Z:
A friend passed and I wanted to know where he was and what he was doing. A mutual friend took me to a Spiritualist service and I've been going ever since.

Respondent Q:
My first exposure came when I heard a Spiritualist minister and medium speak at a local college. The Declaration of Principles and philosophy of Natural Law and personal responsibility felt as if I had come home.

Respondent E:
No dogma or creed, but a set of principles we follow. Also, continuity of life and communication with the "so called dead" which I experienced at age 13 when my father passed.

Respondent B:
I had my first vision when I was 8-years-old, but did not take my gift seriously until my late twenties. My dreams, upheavals in my home life and relationships drove me to pursue Spiritualism.

Respondent C:
I was taught at a very early age about spirit communication, through my mother's example (mediumship). I have always accepted the concepts and didn't realize there was controversy. When I was young, I just thought this must be something new that others hadn't found out about yet.

Other respondents mentioned the openness of the religion, the "free-thinking" aspect, the desire to believe that life goes on, and actual personal proof of spirit communication that prompted them to look further into the religion and ultimately adopt it as their own. Several subjects mentioned feeling comfortable with the philosophy of Spiritualism which drew them to the belief system. Others admitted that "curiosity" motivated them initially to seek out Spiritualism. Seemingly, though, the majority of people were somehow introduced to the religion by a family member, friend, work colleague, or spouse.

Since Spiritualism is not an evangelistic or missionary based religion in the same sense as other mainstream religions where people actively seek out and try to convert new souls to the congregation, this trend makes sense: it is a "by word of mouth" religion in that people who have a connection to it, experience with it, or an interest in it tell others; these people in turn have their curiosity piqued and decide to experience it for themselves.

Historically, when the movement first started, it was at a time when mass-communication was a distant dream. Today, with a click of a button, one can turn on a radio, television, computer, or phone that allows access to a myriad of information, sources, and people in a matter of seconds. The fact that Spiritualism was able to become such a huge movement in its early days without the benefit of these modern modes of communication (just books, journals and newspapers) made Spiritualism largely a "by word of mouth" religion from its inception. Although more modern modes of information dissemination are currently used by Spiritualist associations around the country, it seems to still be largely a "by word of mouth" religion.

The subjects' interest in Spiritualism and mediumship, as delineated in the previous testimonials, seemed to center around several primary areas: 1) a need or desire to know what lies beyond; 2) restlessness in the religious tradition they were following; 3) the freedom to follow Spiritualism in tandem with other belief systems and religious traditions.

Initially, a number of subjects had their first experience with Spiritualism by being introduced to it by a family member or friend, getting a reading from a Spiritualist medium, and by pure happenstance. Of course, Spiritualists do not believe in "coincidence" and maintain that everything is in divine order and happens for a reason—hence, the people were either drawn to, exposed to, or happened upon Spiritualism because it was the right time for them spiritually, personally and emotionally to be able to handle the beliefs and principles of this religion. A number of these people, then, were seeking some type of "proof" of life beyond or were interested in contacting a loved one that had already passed over. This goes back to the premise that as human beings, there is an innate need or desire to know what lies beyond; people want to believe that the people they loved did not merely turn to dust, but actually live on in another form somewhere beyond.

The overwhelming majority of people in this study seemed dissatisfied with the religion they grew up with, and even with the religions that they dabbled in as adults, prompting them to search for the one that resonated most profoundly and deeply from within them. Reasons for being unhappy with religious traditions that were fundamentally-based or mainstream focused largely on the lack of tolerance or flexibility from within the religion to accept beliefs and traditions from outside. The subjects used words like—openness, free thinking, flexible, tolerant, nonjudgmental, holistic, comfortable, love-based, hopeful, and understanding—to describe Spiritualism and its attraction.

Perhaps the most cited reason for converting to Spiritualism, though, was the freedom that Spiritualism allowed them in worshiping as they pleased and what they pleased. They could incorporate other spiritual traditions and belief systems with those of Spiritualism. Because of this phenomenon, there are Christian-Spiritualists, Buddhist-Spiritualists, New Age-Spiritualists, Native American-Spiritualists, Islamic-Spiritualists, as well as any number of other combined religious traditions that are practiced around the world. Spiritualism allows its adherents to accept and utilize the "truths" from all religions and spiritual traditions as long as they are benevolent, from the light of God (or whatever the name of the higher power the belief system is centered upon) and advocates "right living."

The idea of "right living" is open for interpretation as many fundamentalist Christians would categorically disagree with some of the more liberal and progressive attitudes of Spiritualists regarding personal responsibility, freedom of choice, and "free-thinking;" however, this is left to the individual person to decide and he/she will be made to atone for his/her indiscretions as an individual once in the spirit world. No matter how terrible of a life the person lived on earth, that person's soul is redeemable and must continue to work through these soul issues toward further enlightenment—if not on the earth plane, then when on the other side.

When asked to explain the differences between Spiritualism and mainstream religions, The Reverend Sarah Brown (2004) described it in the following way:

> ...we are free thinkers. We don't—and this sounds rather self-serving—but I don't think we are as judgmental. You see, moral living is hoped to be obtained by all of us, but what is right for me may not be right for you. As long as I'm not hurting anyone, it is not my right or your right to judge.... What I consider to be moral you may not, but of course, morals differ from culture to culture, country to country and generation to generation. We, as Spiritualists, do not have a set of rules; of course, abiding by Natural Law...and the Ten Commandments are good rules to live by, but a lot of religions go places, that in my opinion, they don't belong—you shouldn't drink coffee, you shouldn't do this, you shouldn't do that—they get into rule making and that's where I have the freedom as a Spiritualist....I must strive for a high moral character, but what that means to people varies from person to person. A good thing, above all, is do no harm....

This echoes many of the subjects' feelings, in large part, of why they find Spiritualism to be liberating and attractive—they are allowed to incorporate their religious traditions, belief systems, and lifestyles into Spiritualism without having to change, abandon, or deny what they hold deeply. Very few, if any, religions offer its adherents such wide-ranging flexibility in belief and practice as does Spiritualism. These are alluring aspects of the religion that people who are unhappy in their former religion find most appealing.

Sub-hypothesis 3:

The third sub-hypothesis of this study was to identify the process in which a medium becomes certified and to identify the tools that mediums employ in their mediumship work. This sub-problem was included in the questionnaire that was completed by the subjects.

Statistics on Certification Levels and Affiliations of the Mediums

The medium and/or ministerial certification and affiliation with Spiritualist organizations of the participating subjects were as follows: 81% were ordained ministers, with 19% not ordained.[9] All of the subjects, however, had received certification papers to practice as a medium from a Spiritualist organization. Of the total number of subjects in this study, 30% were certified by the National Spiritualist Association of Churches (NSAC); 16 % were certified by the Indiana Association of Spiritualists (IAOS); 15% were certified by the Universal Spiritualist Association (USA); 10% were certified by the Southern Cassadaga Spiritualist Camp Meeting Association (SCSCAMA); 13% indicated certification by other Spiritualist organizations; and 16% of the respondents either failed to answer this question or chose not to disclose their affiliation and certification organization.[10]

---

9. See Figure 11.
10. Possible reasons for the subjects choosing not to disclose the Spiritualist organization where they received their credentials are: 1) they inadvertently failed to fill in that portion of the questionnaire; 2) for privacy reasons, they wished not to divulge this information to ensure complete anonymity; 3) they were hesitant or embarrassed to admit which association certified them (the organization may no longer exist or they are currently at odds with the association); or 4) the respondents failed to renew their certification papers, and although they are trained and were at one time certified, technically were not certified when filling out the questionnaire. See Figure 12.

Figure 11.

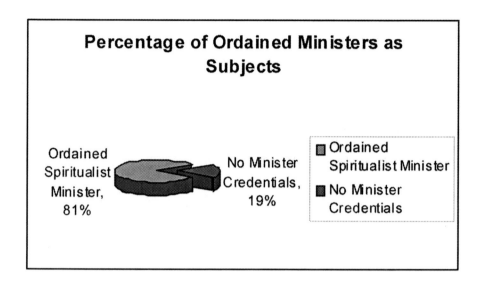

Figure 12.

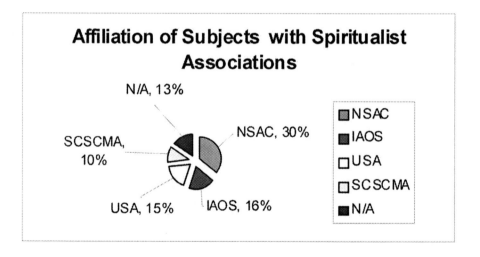

The high percentage of Spiritualist mediums that were also ordained as ministers reflects a tendency of Spiritualists to pursue further more education within their parent organizations. One could easily be a medium without the added exertion of becoming a minister, which involves a much more rigorous curriculum and battery of tests that is not necessarily rewarded financially (the majority of Spiritualist ministers do not have their own churches and congregations and usually have a career besides that of "minister"). This statistic, then, can perhaps be interpreted as a way to measure a person's seriousness, self-discipline, and genuine desire to enhance one's knowledge and skills in the field of mediumship. It is a general assumption, in all areas of academic education, that the further one studies in his/her field, the more expert and serious about the subject the person becomes. Hence, it can be deduced that the majority of Spiritualists who continue their education to become ministers (the overwhelming majority in this study) are interested in and committed to the field of mediumship for reasons other than financial gain or a desire to deceive others through trickery and fakery.

Persons motivated by greed for financial gain, or who set out to be deceptive in their mediumship, merely would have to study up to the level that allows them to be certified mediums. There would be no obvious gain, either financially or in masking deception, to continue on through ordination as a minister. As previously stated, the percentage of Spiritualist ministers who have churches is quite low in comparison to the number of ordained ministers without individual churches who are practicing mediums; so a financial motive is unlikely in this case. Also, it seems unlikely, then, that a person would put himself/herself through the rigors of becoming ordained if he/she were not sincere and honest in his/her mediumship and ministry. Unless, of course, the person is motivated by a sense of ego in anticipation of the added status one might receive upon ordination by those who are not a part of the clergy.

Of course, these assumptions are based largely on presumption as there is no scientific or verifiable way of learning the true motivation of why a person wants to become a medium or ordained minister. For critics, though, who may wish to question the sincerity or validity of Spiritualist mediums and/or mediumship, these points can be of service in logically contemplating the motivation (if other than a genuine ability to communicate to spirits) of those continuing on past the level of "medium" to become ordained ministers.

The certification categories in which the subjects indicated they were certified included: commissioned healer, missionary, medium, licentiate minister, associate minister, and minister.[11] In addition to the official certification process, a number of respondents indicated that they were involved in a variety of other spiritual or service related areas that may or may not be sanctioned by their Spiritualist association: Spiritualist teacher, social worker, Reiki Master,[12] licensed astrologer, hypnotherapist, licensed psychic, Karuna Reiki Master, intuitive healer and visionary artist.

As a general rule, it was found that the process to become a certified Spiritualist medium by recognized Spiritualist associations resembled quite closely one another. Each association had a different class listing or course title, but it generally covered the same material. Also, the actual titles given for each level of study differed somewhat, but were largely equivalent in scope and context.

Within the context of the Spiritualist mediums' actual work in mediumship, the subjects noted a variety of tools they used to make a clearer vibratory or mental connection to the spirit world. Some of the subjects, however, indicated that they use nothing except their mental mediumship ability. Many of the mediums who studied under the direction of the National Spiritualist Association of Churches (NSAC) implied that due to association rules, they were not allowed to use any outside tools in their mediumship work. Some of the responses are as follows:

> *Respondent A:*
> I start with tarot and use limited astrology…sort of eclectic, as I believe I tap into other's sub-consciousness, the collective unconscious, and see and feel spiritual beings…

> *Respondent B:*
> I now work clairvoyantly, but when I first began my work I did numerology and palmistry. Also, I still interpret dreams.

> *Respondent C:*
> I have used tarot. I love to write a page or letter from Spirit to the one receiving. I write while in meditation. I have done some voice from trance…interestingly I have seen images and glimpses in the crystal ball, not my everyday practice, but something yet to pursue.

> *Respondent D:*
> Tarot. I heal people and help them overcome hardships.

---

11. Each organization's certification process varies somewhat regarding actual levels and titles associated and assigned to the various degrees leading up to and becoming a medium, and higher (ordination as a minister).
12. Reiki is a "laying of hands" healing technique that utilizes the life force energy of the universe to promote healing of the body, mind, and soul.

Respondent H:
Tarot, a little numerology, some astrology; these are just tools to assist Spirit to get through.

Respondent I:
...tarot, animal cards, angel cards, healing and working with auras, absent healing.

Respondent R:
Tarot with some numerology and astrology.

Respondent BB:
A good medium will (should) use everything at his/her disposal to make a connection with the client. I use numerology and astrology to enhance clairvoyance, clairgustance, clairaudience, clairsentience, *etc*.

Respondent CC:
I occasionally use astrology to reinforce information given mediumsistically.

Respondent QQ:
After prayer opening, I ask the name of the person and hold hands for a moment to get their vibration. I use their voice vibration, too. I can see every cell in their body, or into anything they might want to know. I know a little bit about numerology, colorology, astrology, *etc* but use intuition to combine all else.

Respondent E:
I am a mental medium and do not use tools. Spiritual counseling is very strong.

Respondent F:
No tools except for meditation.

Exactly 50% of the subjects maintained that they used nothing in their mediumship work other than straight, mental mediumship. This percentage includes those that indicated that they used meditation (like *Respondent F*) or another similar method of connecting to the spirit world. The other 50% of the subjects indicated that they used some type of physical tool (*i.e.* tarot, astrology, numerology, psychometry, crystal ball, *etc.*) to assist them in connecting and in giving a reading.

Largely, the use of outside tools depended upon the association to which the medium belonged; the NSAC seemingly forbids any outside tools, so those mediums reiterated, over and over, that they did not use any additional help other than their mental mediumship to give a reading. Some of these subjects, however, did indicate that outside the confines of the camp, they do use some type of tool occasionally, but when doing readings for the association, they do not.

The subjects that maintained they did not use any additional tool other than their mental mediumship offered some very interesting insights into why they do not use any outside tools: "What I see is what I tell…no tools used." Another offered, "No! As an NSAC member, I can't and didn't." Another indicated, "In my professional working camp, I am not allowed to use other tools. It is strictly mental mediumship. However, at home, I do some tarot (self-taught and taught by my son-in-law, a pagan) and very little palmistry." Very candidly, another related: "Absolutely not. As a medium, I was taught that if properly trained these appliances are not necessary. You are relating a message from a spirit person to someone on the earth plane. It's like answering a phone for someone else and simply relating what is being seen, felt or heard. The rest are unnecessary crutches or a means of entertainment which detracts from the religion. Mediumship is a sacred faculty and should be treated as such." Similarly, another added: "No. I have learned a little about tarot and astrology and numerology, so I can talk about them when people ask. But I do not use these for readings—I enjoy pyschometry, but nothing is as glorious as real spirit communication. It comforts people and reassures them that their loved ones are all right, and they will be too, after their own physical death. I do some transfiguration which is particularly evidential." A medium offered: The NSAC does not permit such devices. I have never done anything but straight mediumship! [Outside tools] are psychic tools and they have their place, but not in mediumship."

At best, "to use" or "not to use" has divided the two sides on whether or not a Spiritualist medium should or should not use outside tools in his/her work. Mediums who do mediumship at Spiritualist camps must follow strict procedures and rules concerning what type of mediumship they are allowed to practice (usually mental mediumship only). Those that are not affiliated with a camp or those who maintain multiple dwellings (one on camp and another outside of camp) often do utilize some type of outside tool in their mediumship.

Basically, using a form of tarot, astrology, or numerology helps to focus the medium; it also assists the medium in tuning into the person's vibration more easily. Neophyte mediums tend to use these more consistently than older, more seasoned mediums that have been practicing mediumship for many years. Although similarly trained in their vocation, mediums do vary widely in how they use their mediumship, and if they do or do not employ some type of outside tool to assist them.

Furthermore, the subjects were asked what type of divination method that they regularly used in their personal and private life. The most common responses were tarot, numerology, and astrology. Thirty-five percent of the respondents indicated one of these as a method they used in their private life. In addition, the mediums indicated that they used Reiki (which is not a divination method, but can be used as a method for clearing the mind), journaling, dowsing, pendulums, and drinking magnetized water.

Sub-hypothesis 4:

The fourth sub-hypothesis of this study was to classify how they prepare and center themselves before giving a reading. This sub-problem was included in the questionnaire that was completed by the subjects.

This sub-hypothesis was further divided into three additional areas: personal routine when giving readings, personal connection with Spirit on a daily basis, and the manner of receiving messages from the spirit world. The preparation a Spiritualist medium did before giving a reading to a client included simple acts such as sitting in silence, deep breathing exercises, meditation, concentrated prayer, singing; and more complicated routines including spiritual cleansing of the space, burning candles and incense, and by invoking the divine by clothing the area in white light.

The majority (52%) of the respondents used some type of prayer to connect to the spirit world. A few mediums mentioned using the "Lord's Prayer" to raise the vibration, making it easier for the spirit entities to assist in the reading. Thirty-one percent of the respondents indicated that they used some form of meditation before a reading to connect with the spirit world. A large proportion of the subjects indicated that they utilized both—prayer and meditation—in preparation for their work.

Having a clear mind and making a sincere intention to do good seem to be the predominant factors in preparing for a reading. Interestingly, a small number of respondents admitted that they did nothing special to prepare for a reading, except to just start doing it. Over 89% of the subjects, however, indicated that they initiated some type of preparatory ritual before embarking on their mediumship work.

It stands to reason that when one is to give a reading for another, especially to a stranger, that a clear mind would be a prerequisite to doing any type of mediumship work. Critics maintain that mediums do not connect to anything from the other world, but instead, are masterful at reading a person's body language, mannerisms, and personality by fishing for information that they can mirror back to the person sitting in such a way that it seems like new information. Perhaps this may be true for some mediums, but if it were the norm throughout the Spiritualist movement then eventually there would be no new information to offer, and the client would realize the person is using a means other than spirit communication to offer messages. This does not explain, either, how the medium will often offer actual names to the client sitting that are recognizable and correct. A discerning mind is the most important aspect for a sitter to possess in order to deduce intelligently and logically what is true and what is not from a personal, experiential point of view.

The Spiritualist mediums used in this study indicated that the manner in which they connect with Spirit before doing their mediumship work mirrors what they do as a personal ritual on a daily basis. The majority indicated that prayer and meditation were viable parts of their daily spiritual routines. In order to do this type of work, it is necessary to be centered and clear-headed, hence the need for the medium to exercise some sort of personal ritual to achieve these things.

When giving a message, all of the subjects indicated that they use a form of mental mediumship to receive spirit messages. The percentage of subjects using mainly clairvoyant mediumship was 78%. The second most common form of mental mediumship was clairsentience; and the third most common was clairaudient. Most of the subjects indicated that they indeed used a combination of all of these. In addition, several subjects mentioned "smells," "colors," and "direct voice" as areas of mediumship that they regularly experience.

7.4 Summary

This chapter presented the results of the study, analyzed the data gathered from the questionnaire, and discussed and interpreted the results. The participants' demographic data was provided in order to give a clear overview of their ages, sexes, backgrounds, training, and experience with mediumship. I tried to make explicit some of the basic assumptions regarding mediums and their demographic data by utilizing charts and graphs. The data revealed a few surprises in that Spiritualism is a rapidly "graying" religion, and the overwhelming majority of Spiritualists are converts to the religion from a variety of Christian-based denominations. The reasons for this high percentage of conversion were explored, as well as the attraction of the subjects to Spiritualism initially. Also, an inordinate amount of Spiritualist mediums seem to be women. This could be related to the fact that mediums must tap into a more "feminine" based energy, one which men are in possession of but often times (due to societal pressure and social mores) deny. Related to this is the supposition that there is a high disposition of homosexual men who are Spiritualist mediums.

Analysis of the data was performed according to the stated hypotheses that were presented earlier. The four sub-hypotheses were delineated in detail offering evidential research to further substantiate the assumptions related to them.

Conclusions and Recommendations

The study was undertaken in part to determine whether Spiritualist mediums were raised in the religion or if they converted from another religion; in addition, another aim was to discover what reasons or motives they had to pursue Spiritualism and mediumship if, indeed, they had converted to the religion. Also, this study endeavored to find out what formal training the Spiritualist mediums were required to fulfill before becoming certified, and what if any, ritual they used in their mediumship work and daily life. Four research questions were examined as sub-hypotheses to offer more in-depth analysis on the factors that relate to the mediums and their mediumship. All four sub-hypotheses consisted of a content analysis approach using a questionnaire. The analysis of the data supported the stated sub-hypotheses.

The first half of this dissertation served as a literature review by focusing upon the historical background of Spiritualism and mediumship as a technique to offer sufficient grounding on the subject as a forerunner to the actual study. The linear approach in the first four chapters was purposeful and deliberate; without these basic details and facts, the results would have had less meaning. These qualifications were presented chronologically, offering a complete history of mediumship from ancient times through to the advent of Spiritualism in the mid 19th century. It was decided that this historical background was necessary and an integral component in the understanding of contemporary Spiritualist mediums.

The second half of the dissertation was centered upon the actual results of the empirical study. Many examples were delineated which supported the stated sub-hypotheses. The findings of this study have led to a number of conclusions, some that were expected and others that proved to be rather surprising, concerning the unique population sampling used in the main part of the study.

Discussion

The first research question that was posed and answered was—What types of religious backgrounds and upbringings did persons who converted to Spiritualism have (and the effects on them); and what type of person trains to become a certified medium? The answers were more complex than anticipated, but basically corroborated the stated sub-hypotheses: Mediums who converted to Spiritualism were predominantly raised in or came from Christian backgrounds; and mediums were drawn to Spiritualism due to a lack of understanding and flexibility by their former churches. The majority of the subjects in the study were in fact converts to the religion; nearly all of the subjects had been raised, or at least exposed to, some type of religion while growing up. Of those, a high percentage of the respondents had practiced Christianity or had been exposed to some type of religious upbringing that followed a Christian denomination of a Catholic or Protestant tradition.

Interestingly, it was discovered that the majority of Spiritualist mediums—both men and women—had engaged in a phenomenon I labeled "religion hopping" before settling on Spiritualism as a religion. A number of the subjects experienced multiple belief systems, religions, and spiritual practices (throughout their lives) before decisively converting to Spiritualism. This phenomenon is a process related to an individual's desire to "find himself/herself," hoping to experience a spiritual epiphany, of sorts, that would ultimately be a spiritual self-awakening that the individual would intuitively know to be "the one" religion he/she must follow.

These assumptions are derived from the theory that these people felt they lacked the necessary elements they wanted or needed on a spiritual level from the religious traditions and belief systems they adhered to during the formative years of their lives. This created a profound need from within to search for a spiritual path by dabbling in a wide variety of traditions, practices, and belief systems, searching for the one spiritual path that afforded them the essentials of a spiritual life that were flexible and tolerant enough to allow them the freedom to worship in a way that was fulfilling and comfortable to them. Many of the subjects commented on the rigidity of mainstream, fundamentalist-based religions, which ultimately impelled them to search elsewhere. Spiritualism was attractive to these subjects because it allowed a mixing of traditions, practices, and belief systems, as well as combining, adapting, and incorporating those they liked and felt contented in pursuing.

A striking discovery was made regarding the ratio between men and women who are certified Spiritualist mediums—overwhelmingly, women out numbered men (5 to 1). In addition, the majority of the women subjects were ordained ministers; this is in stark contrast to mainstream religions where church elders are predominantly men, and where many fundamentalist religions prohibit women from holding any leadership positions and bar them from becoming ordained ministers, basing this prohibition on biblical teachings.

Spiritualism is certainly a religion that offers women complete equality in all facets of the movement. This trend has clear historical roots that date back to the beginning of the movement where women were at the forefront of the religion holding leadership and ministerial positions. Spiritualism attracted women then, as it does today, due to its egalitarian policies. Women are, and always have been, allowed to be full and equal members to men, and enjoy any and all facets of the religion on equal footing. It was noted, but not researched formally in the main part of the study, that this equality of the sexes extends to "sexual orientation" as well. A significant number of male mediums are homosexual and as a rule are completely accepted within their Spiritualist communities and churches. This, as outlined in Chapter 7, may have something to do with the type of energy needed to conduct the work of mediumship; mediums tend to use more of a female generated energy while doing mediumship work, rather than a male-based energy. Gay men tend to be more comfortable than straight men in tapping into this energy source. Partly, this is due to societal pressures placed upon straight men to act and behave "manly;" straight men have a more difficult time than gay men, it is presumed, to delve into this female-energy source.

The gay men interviewed in this study found Spiritualism to be an attractive alternative to mainstream religion for many of the same reasons that the women of yesteryear did—a tolerance and openness that offered them a level of respect, a feeling of equality and complete acceptance within the religion. Few mainstream religions even recognize, let alone accept, gay and lesbian parishioners into their flocks. As one female Spiritualist medium commented to me, quoting the leader of a Spiritualist camp, "This camp was built on the backs of gay men…" which clearly suggests that homosexual Spiritualists have had a very positive and productive influence on the movement, just as women have had, throughout its long history.

Also revealed in the fieldwork data was the finding that Spiritualism is a rapidly "graying religion." This term is used to describe the current phenomenon of the statistics on aging within the religion. The majority of the participants were elderly, with the youngest respondent being middle-aged. This is a troubling prospect for the religion as it is in danger of literally "dying out" within the next couple of decades unless an influx of young blood is infused into the movement to serve as the new torchbearers to carry the religion's banner on, and into, the next century.

One possible reason for the recent decline in membership and lack of dedicated interest in the religion by more young people has to do with "choice'—there are so many more spiritually-based movements today than there were in the past that competition has become quite keen in attracting new members searching for a belief system outside the confines of mainstream religions. This influx of "choice" between religions has also taken its toll on the mainstream religions; people are following a number of belief systems that do not necessarily precipitate becoming a member of or attending a church on a regular basis. So, in many ways, Spiritualism has become a part of the "mainstream" over the years, adopting a system that is still on the fringes of the more traditional belief systems but "churchified" enough to be considered somewhat mainstream. Many younger people currently prefer more freedom of choice and flexibility in their religious proclivities, choosing belief systems that offer even less structure and dogma than Spiritualism.

The New Age movement has gained in popularity in recent years, attracting many younger people, because of this lack of structure and dogma; although Spiritualism maintains that it is a creedless religion, it still requires a certain amount of time and dedication to be an adherent (*i.e.* attending church/message services, volunteering, contributing monetarily, *etc*). The main difference between the New Age movement and the Spiritualist movement is that "Spiritualism" is a religion, and the "New Age" movement is still but a trend. Spiritualists are very quick to point out that Spiritualism is not "New Age" but "Old Age," and generally they do not appreciate being categorized as a "New Age" religion. Although similar in their teachings and philosophies, allowing a mixing of traditions, practices and belief systems and "free thinking," the New Age movement does not have a centralized or organized belief system, incorporating a system with regulations and principles. It is all encompassing of anything that is not "mainstream," and is more culturally than religiously based, focusing on spirituality as it pertains to various peoples and traditions, rather than to a singular belief system.

Spiritualism requires a certain degree of dedication and perseverance, and not mere dabbling. Ironically, it was for the same reasons that people initially developed Spiritualism as a religion that people today follow New Age ideas and practices—a desire for a less regimented, more flexible and open attitude toward spirituality. Because Spiritualism is organized and maintains principles and a specified set of beliefs and practices, perhaps young people today find it too constricting and prefer to have more spiritual freedom, even though many of the practices and beliefs overlap, and in essence, are the same. Spiritualist churches must work to devise a way to attract these "spirituality searchers" if they are to survive the current crisis of being a "graying religion."

The research question, "what types of mediumship are most common among Spiritualist mediums?" was hypothesized as: Spiritualist mediums are trained similarly and predominantly employ similar techniques and tools in their work. This was found to be true because the certification process, although varying slightly between the Spiritualist associations, generally follow similar curriculums and training periods that lead to certification.

As shown in Figure 8, the subjects were largely certified more than twenty years ago. Over 50% of all the subjects realized their mediumship gifts as a child and had their first encounter with spirit communication at that time. Once a decision was made to convert to Spiritualism, these aspiring mediums then trained formally through a Spiritualist association to receive certification. The vast majority of the subjects continued on past the level of "certified medium" to become an ordained minister. Very few Spiritualist ministers maintain their own church, but do work and minister at special functions, Spiritualist camps, and privately.

The results of this study, however, indicate that the years of being a certified medium is not a significant factor in predicting the types of mediumship performed. Almost all mediums use clairvoyance in their work, as well as clairaudience, and clairsentience. The majority indicated that "mental" mediumship was their primary forte, with a small number relating experiential events involving "physical" phenomenon and mediumship.

It was found that some of the certifying organizations frown upon "physical" mediumship in the form of materializations due to a questionable past where unscrupulous mediums would manufacture such phenomena. Also, a number of mediums indicated that the association to which they were connected did not allow them to use any outside tools in their mediumship work. A number of mediums, however, did admit using astrology, numerology, and tarot to assist in connecting with the spirit world.

The data dictated that, in general terms, the Spiritualist movement is quite uniform in its basic policies, rules, beliefs and practices. Even though each association is largely independent of the other, they all tend to maintain a semblance of regularity and constancy.

Limitations

A number of limitations affected the ability of general conclusions to be drawn from this study. The participants who participated were all certified Spiritualist mediums, but were mostly limited to those who resided in Spiritualist camps; therefore, the results cannot necessarily be generalized to draw inferences about other certified Spiritualist mediums who may be working as ministers and mediums in their own communities.

The number of participants in this study also could have been increased. Although the years as a medium indicated an aging population, it is mildly suspected that an increase in the number of participants could alter the results of the analysis slightly. It is not known, then, if a significant number of Spiritualists are younger in age as the subjects used in this study indicated the opposite.

Recommendations for Further Research

Several areas of potential research arose out of the need for continued studies of Spiritualist mediums and mediumship. The first area would expand the study of participants who do not live inside a Spiritualist camp more fully. A small number of respondents most likely lived outside of a recognized camp, but no specific data were gathered to ascertain the validity of this assumption definitively. This recommendation would provide a broader spectrum for evaluating Spiritualist mediums in more detail and with more conclusive evidence. Also, breaking down the subjects into more specific categories would generate more significant data regarding their personal lives and motivation; specifically, a study that included sexual orientation as a component would offer valuable insight into this area of the study.

A second area in need of study would be what percentage of Spiritualist mediums hail from countries other than the United States; how prevalent the Spiritualist movement in these countries is; and what religious backgrounds do these people have (if converts to Spiritualism). There are significant numbers of Spiritualists in Great Britain and Australia, so it would be interesting to investigate how their associations are faring in contemporary times in comparison to their American counterparts: Are they a religion mostly of "religion hoppers"? Is the religion "graying" as rapidly as it is in the United States? What type of training and certification process do they require to become licensed mediums? These questions were well beyond the scope of this study, but would be of value in future research studies on this topic.

Finally, the propensity of spiritualist mediums sometimes to feel the need to hide their religious affiliation and mediumship work from outsiders is an area in need of more in-depth investigation. What are the reasons behind this hesitation to be open and honest about their religion? Is it related to embarrassment, shyness, a need for privacy, or is it out of a sense of fear? What percentage of Spiritualist mediums has actually experienced an overt form of "religion bashing" (either verbally or physically)? Future research could serve to uncover the answers to these questions (as well as generating further, more relevant research data on Spiritualist mediums and their mediumship).

This ethno-religious study of Spiritualist mediums offers new insight into the movement, in general, and more so into the motivations and personal lives of the mediums themselves. Although Spiritualism is a rather new religion in comparison to its Christian-based cousins, it has a long and vibrant history that affords the researcher of religion a most fascinating area of exploration in which to pursue.

Bibliography

Albanese, C.L. (1992) *America Religions and Religion.* (2nd ed.). Belmont, CA: Wadsworth Publishing Company.

Alper, Dr. F. (1986) *Universal Law for the Aquarian Age.* Phoenix, AZ: Arizona Metaphysical Society.

Andrews, T. (1998) *Psychic Protection.* Jackson, TN: Dragonhawk Publishing.

Austin, B.F. (n.d.) *The A.B.C. of Spiritualism: One Hundred of the Questions most Commonly asked about Spiritualism, Answered Tersely and Plainly.* Lily Dale, NY: National Spiritualist Association of Churches (NSAC) (Stow Memorial Foundation).

Awtry-Smith, Rev. M.J. (1985) *The Sunflower: The Symbol of Spiritualism.* Wauwatosa, WI: Morris Pratt Institute Association.

Awtry-Smith, Rev. M.J. & Vogt, P.M. (Eds.) (1981) *Who's Who in Spiritualism of Yesteryear, Volumes I & II.* N.p.: SAM, INC. Psychic Research Consultants.

Baer, Y. (1961) *A History of Jews in Christian Spain.* Philadelphia: The Jewish Publication Society of America.

Bailey, A.A. & Djwhal Khul. (1953) *Esoteric Healing.* London: Lucis Press, Ltd. (14th printing 1998).

Bailey, A.A. & Djwhal Khul. (1971) *Ponder on This.* London: Lucis Press, Ltd. (9th printing 1996).

Bailey, A.A. & Djwhal Khul. (1972) *Serving Humanity.* London: Lucis Press, Ltd. (6th printing 1999).

Barnes a, P. (n.d.) *Alone With God: Day by Day In the Silence*. Lily Dale, NY: National Spiritualist Association of Churches (NSAC) (Stow Memorial Foundation).

Barnes b, P. (n.d.) *A Way of Life: A Course of Study*. Lily Dale, NY: National Spiritualist Association of Churches (NSAC) (Stow Memorial Foundation).

Barnes c, P. (n.d.) *"Lo, I Am With You Always*. Lily Dale, NY: National Spiritualist Association of Churches (NSAC) (Stow Memorial Foundation).

Barnes d, P. (n.d.) *Prophets, Seers and Religions: Ancient and Modern*. Lily Dale, NY: National Spiritualist Association of Churches (NSAC) (Stow Memorial Foundation).

Barnes e, P. (n.d.) *Psychic facts: A Series of Fifteen Lessons on the Laws Governing Mental and Physical Mediumship*. Lily Dale, NY: National Spiritualist Association of Churches (NSAC) (Stow Memorial Foundation).

Barnes f, P. (n.d.) *Self-Realiziation: A Series of Fifteen Lessons Covering the Third Year's Work of the Institute of Universal Science*. Lily Dale, NY: National Spiritualist Association of Churches (NSAC) (Stow Memorial Foundation).

Barnes g, P. (n.d.) *The Chemistry of Thought: Mental Science Revised*. Lily Dale, NY: National Spiritualist Association of Churches (NSAC) (Stow Memorial Foundation).

Barnes h, P. (n.d.) *The Christian Bible: Its Prophets and Mediums*. Lily Dale, NY: National Spiritualist Association of Churches (NSAC) (Stow Memorial Foundation).

Barnes i, P. (rev. 1997) *The Fundamentals of Spiritualism*. Lily Dale, NY: National Spiritualist Association of Churches (NSAC) (Stow Memorial Foundation).

Barnes j, P. (n.d.) *The Laws of Spirit Mediumship*. Lily Dale, NY: National Spiritualist Association of Churches (NSAC) (Stow Memorial Foundation).

Barnes k, P. (n.d.) *The Story of Healing: From Primitive to Modern Methods*. Lily Dale, NY: National Spiritualist Association of Churches (NSAC) (Stow Memorial Foundation).

Barnes l, P. (n.d.) *The Trinity of Spiritualism: The Science, Philosophy and Religion of Spiritualism*. Lily Dale, NY: National Spiritualist Association of Churches (NSAC) (Stow Memorial Foundation).

Barnes m, P. (n.d.) *The Questionnaire: For the Teacher and Investigator*. Lily Dale, NY: National Spiritualist Association of Churches (NSAC) (Stow Memorial Foundation).

Barrow, L. (1986) *Independent Spirits: Spiritualism and English Plebeians—1850-1910*. London: Routledge & Kegan Paul.

Berger, R. (2002) *They Don't See What I See—How to Talk with Loved Ones Who Have Crossed Over*. Boston: Weiser Books.

Besant, A. (1892) *Reincarnation*. Adyar, India: The Ind-Com Press for The Theosophical Publishing House (12th ed. 1999).

Besant, A. (1897) *The Ancient Wisdom*. Adyar, India: Vasanta Press for The Theosophical Publishing House (15th ed. 1998).

Besant, A. (1892) *The Spiritual Life*. Wheaton, IL: The Theosophical Publishing House (republished in 1991, 2nd printing 1993).

Bias, Rev. C. (with Nichols, Rev. E.; Ed.) (rev. 2000) *Physical Mediumship*. Muncie, IN: Universal Spiritualist Association.

Bias, Rev. C. (n.d.) *The Liturgy and Ritual of the Universal Spiritualist Association*. (n.p.): Universal Spiritualist Association.

Blavatsky, H.P. (1889) *The Key to Theosophy: A Simple Exposition Based on the Wisdom-Religion of All Ages*. Passadena, CA: Theosophical University Press (republished in 1995).

Blavatsky, H.P. (n.d.) *The Voice of Silence: Being Extracts from 'The Book of Golden Precepts.'* Wheaton, IL: The Theosophical Publishing House (republished in 1992).

Bletzer, J.G. (1998) *The Encyclopedic Psychic Dictionary*. Lithia Springs, GA: New Leaf Distributing Company.

Boddington, H. (1938) *Materialisations*. London: Psychic Press (this edition published in 1992).

Braude, A.D. (2001) *Radical Spirits: Spiritualism and Women's Rights in Nineteenth-Century America*. Bloomington, IN: Indiana University Press (2nd ed.; original work published in 1989 by Beacon Press).

Brown, Rev. S. (2002) *Personal Interview*. July 24, 2002, Chesterfield, Indiana.

Brown, Rev. S. (2003) *Telephone interview*. July 20, 2003, 10:00 pm-10:45 pm, Japan Time.

Brown, Rev. S. (2004) *Personal interview*. January 13, 2004, Chesterfield, Indiana.

Buchanan, J.R. (1850) "Spirituality—Recent Occurences," *Bucahnan's Journal of Man* (New York), February 1850: 489-492. Retrieved from http://www.spirithistory.com/buchanan.html on October 6, 2002.

Budge, E. A. Wallis. (1967) *The Book of the Dead: The Papyrus of Ani*. New York, NY: Dover Publications (2nd ed.; original work published in 1895).

Buescher, J.B. (2004) *The Other Side of Salvation: Spiritualism and the Nineteenth-Century Religious Experience*. Boston: Skinner House Books.

Bunts a, E. B. (n.d.) *New Testament Mediums: Spiritualism in the Bible*. (n.p.) (affiliated with the National Spiritualist Association of Churches (NSAC)).

Bunts b, E. B. (n.d.) *Old Testament Mediums*, Indianapolis, IN: Summit Publications (affiliated with the National Spiritualist Association of Churches (NSAC)).

Burroughs, H.G. (1962) *Becoming a Spiritualist* (5th printing 1999). Lily Dale, NY: National Spiritualist Association of Churches.

Cadwallader, M.E. (1917) *The Hydesville Cottage: Hydesville in History*. Lily Dale, NY: SAM, Inc. (reprinted in 1979).

Cadwallader, M.E. (1917) *Hydesville in History*. Lily Dale, NY: National Spiritualist Association of Churches (NSAC) (Stow Memorial Foundation, reprinted in 1992).

Campbell, E. & J.H. Brennan. (1994) *Body, Mind & Spirit: A Dictionary of New Age Ideas, People, Places, and Terms.* Rutland, VT: Charles E. Tuttle Company, Inc.

Carpentar, A.E. (1888) "Exhibitions of Tricks as Demonstrations of Spirit Power," *Religio-Philosophical Journal,* July 14, 1888. Retrieved from *Spirithistory.com* "Spirit Brides and Rag Babies" at http://www.spirithistory.com/carpent.html on October 6, 2002.

Carrington, Dr. H. (1920) Your *Psychic Powers and How to Develop Them.* New York, NY: Dodd, Mead and Company (republished by Health Research, Pomeroy, WA).

Carroll, B.E. (1997) *Spiritualism in Antebellum America.* Bloomington, IN: Indiana University Press.

Chaudhuri, H. (July 21, 2001) "Spiritualism," *Religious Movements Homepage.* Retrieved from http://religiousmovements.lib.virginia.edu/nrms/Spiritism.html on May 26, 2003.

Chernow, B. & Vallasi, G. (Eds.) (1993) *The Columbia Encyclopedia* (5th ed.). New York, NY: Columbia University Press (distributed by the Houghton Mifflin Company.

Cieslak, Rev. B. (1995) *Minister's Service Book.* Nepean, Canada: Daisy Publishing.

Cody, S. (Executive Producer) (1995) *Secrets of the Super Psychics.* [Television broadcast]. For the Learning Channel, an Open Media Production for Channel 4 in association with Discovery Channel.

Colville, W.J. (n.d.) *A Catechism of Spiritual Philosophy: A Series of Questions and Answers Designed to Confer Light Upon Many Interesting Topics.* Cassadaga, FL: National Spiritualist Association of Churches (NSAC).

Colville, W.J. (1906) *Universal-Spiritualism.* New York, NY: R.F. Fenno & Company (republished by the Morris Pratt Institute, Wauwatosa, WI in 1987).

Cooke, G. (1994) *The New Mediumship.* Liss, UK: The White Eagle Publishing Trust (originally published in 1965).

Cowan, T. (1994) *The Book of Séance: How to Reach Out to the Next World*. Chicago: Contemporary Books.

Crites, S. (1997) *Lively Ghosts Along the Potomac*. Martinsburg, VA: Butternut Publications.

Crookes, W. (1874) *Researches in the Phenomena of Spiritualism*. London: Reprinted from The Quarterly Journal of Science, republished by Health Research, Pomeroy, WA.

Crow, J. (1985) *Spain: The Root and the Flower*. Berkley, CA: University of California Press.

Davis, K.C. (1998) *Don't Know Much About the Bible*. New York, NY: Avon Books.

Davis, A.J. (1979) *Clairvoyance and How to Do Good: Reprints*. Jamestown, NY: SAM, Inc. Psychic Research Consultants.

Davis, A.J. (1923) *The Harmonial Philosophy: A Compendium and Digest of the Works of Andrew Jackson Davis—The Seer of Poughkeepsie*. London: William Rider & Son, Ltd. (republished by Health Research, Pomeroy, WA).

De Swarte, L. (1999) *Principles of Spiritualism*. London: Thorsons (an imprint of HarperCollins Publishers).

Dowling, L. (1907) *The Aquarian Gospel of Jesus the Christ* (16th printing 1997). Marina del Rey, CA: DeVorss & Company.

Doyle, Sir A.C. (1985) *The History of Spiritualism: Volume One & Two*. New York, NY: Arno Press (reprinted ed.; original work published in 1926 by George H. Doran Company).

Dreller, L. (1997) *Beginner's Guide to Mediumship*. York Beach, ME: Samuel Weiser, Inc.

Eddy, M.B. (1875) *Science and Health*. Boston, MA: Christian Scientist Publishing Company.

Eldred, Rev.G. (1984) *Spiritualism: Esoteric Lectures—The Key of Knowledge through the Mediumship of George Eldred.* Boronia, Australia: Caravel Exhibition Services.

Eldred, Rev. G. (1995) *Spiritualism: Esoteric Lectures—The Key of Knowledge through the Mediumship of George Eldred—Book 2.* Boronia, Australia: Caravel Exhibition Services.

Eldred, Rev. G. (1998) *The True Meaning of Life: 150 Questions and Answers on the World of Spirit.* Boronia, Australia: Caravel Exhibition Services.

Farrington, K. (1999) *The History of Religion.* New York: Quadrillion Publishing, Inc.

Faubel, R. (n.d.) *What You've Always Wanted to Know About Spiritualism.* Lily Dale: NY: National Spiritualist Association of Churches (NSAC).

Fetterman, D.M. (1989) *Ethnography: Step by Step.* Newbury Park, CA: Sage Publications.

Fortune, D. & Knight, G. (1999) *Spiritualism and Occultism.* Loughborough, Great Britain: Thoth Publications.

Fortune, D. (2001) *What is Occultism?* York Beach, ME: Samuel Weiser, Inc.

Fraser, C. (2002, November 21) "The Mormon Murder Case." *The New York Review*, pp. 18-21.

Friedlander, J. & Hemsher, G. (1999) *Basic Psychic Development: A User's Guide to Auras, Chakras & Clairvoyance.* York Beach, ME: Samuel Weiser.

Goldfarb, R.M.; & Goldfarb, C.R. (1978) *Spiritualism and Nineteenth-Century Letters.* Cranbury, NJ: Associated University Presses.

Goldsmith, B. (1998) *Other Powers: The Age of Suffrage, Spiritualism, and the Scandalous Victoria Woodhull.* New York, NY: Alfred A. Knopf, Inc (reprinted in 1999 by First HarperPerennial.

Guiley, R.E. (1991) *Harper's Encyclopedia of Mystical & Paranormal Experience.* New York, NY: HarperCollins Publishers, Inc.

Greer, Rev. S. R. (1994) *Stop, Look, Listen, and Sense: Spirit Calls.* Chesterfield, IN: self-published.

Grumbine, J.C.F. (1917) *Beckoning Hands From the Near and Beyond: Concrete Facts and Laws of Conscious Spirit Communion and Communication.* London: L.N. Fowler & Co.

Grumbine, J.C.F. (1897) *Clairvoyance: Its Nature and Unfoldment.* Republished by Pomeroy, WA: Health Research.

Guthrie, J.J.; Lucas, P.C.; & Monroe, G. (Eds.) (2000) *Cassadaga: The South's Oldest Spiritualist Community.* Gainesville, FL: University Press of Florida.

Hall, T. H. (1962) *The Spiritualists: The Story of Florence Cook and William Crookes.* New York, NY: Helix Press/Garrett Publications.

Hammersley, M. & P. Atkinson. (1983) *Ethnography: Principles in Practice.* London: Routledge.

Haslam, G. (2002) *Spiritualism: A Brief History.* Anomalies Articles. Retrieved April 26, 2003, from http://anomalyinfo.com/articles/ga00005.html.

Hare, R. (1855) *Spiritualism—Scientifically Demonstrated: Experimental Investigation of the Spirit Manifestations, Demonstrating the Existence of Spirits and their Communion with Mortals.* New York, NY: Partridge & Brittan (reprinted, 1963, Elm Grove, WI: The Sycamore Press).

Harris, E. (1995) *Spiritualism: A Way of Life.* (n.p.)

Harrison, P.D.; Kennedy, P.J.; Srogi, A.W.; Srogi, S.; Ward, W.W. & Williams, B.R. (1986) *Chesterfield Lives! Spiritualist Camp: 1886-1986—Our First Hundred Years.* Chesterfield, IN: Camp Chesterfield: Indiana Association of Spiritualists.

Harrold, R. (1979) *Cassadaga: An Inside Look at the South's Oldest Psychic Community with True Experiences of People Who Have Been There.* Miami, FL: Banyan Books.

Hart, C. (1998) *Doing a Literature Review: Releasing the Social Science Research Imagination.* London: Sage Publications (reprinted in 2002).

Hazelgrove, J. (2000) *Spiritualism and British Society between the Wars.* Manchester, UK: Manchester University Press.

Heyrman, C.L. (2002) "Puritanism and Predestination—The 17th and 18th Centuries: Divining America, Part I." *The National Humanities Center.* Retrieved May 26, 2003, from http://www.nhc.rtp.nc.us/tserve/eighteen/ekeyinfo/puritan.html.

Holms, A. C. (n.d.) *The Fundamental Facts of Spiritualism.* Lily Dale, NY: Stow Memorial Foundation.

Holy Bible. King James Version (KJV). (1970) Camden, NJ: Thomas Nelson, Inc.

Houdini, H. (1993) *Miracle Mongers and Their Methods: A Complete Exposé.* Buffalo, NY: Prometheus Books (original copyright, 1981).

Hultkrantz, A. (1994) "Religion before History" in *Eerdman's Handbook to the World's Religions* (2nd ed.; Pat Alexander, organizing editor). Grand Rapids, MI: William B. Eerdman's Publishing Company.

Indiana Association of Spiritualists. (2002). *Welcome to a Spiritual Center of Light: Historic Camp Chesterfield—What is Spiritualism?.* [Brochure]. Chesterfield, IN: Indiana Association of Spiritualists, Camp Chesterfield.

Jack, A. (Ed.) (1990) *The New Age Dictionary.* New York: Japan Publications.

Jackson, Jr., H.G. (1972) *The Spirit Rappers.* Garden City, NY: Doubleday & Company.

Kardec, A. (1874) *The Book of Mediums: Guide for Mediums and Invocators.* (Republished in 1970) York Beach, ME: Samuel Weiser, Inc.

Kardec, A. (n.d.) *The Spirits' Book.* (Republished in 1989) Las Vegas, NV: Brotherhood of Life Publishing.

Keeves, J.P. (Ed.) (1988) *Educational Research, Methodology and Measurement: An International Handbook.* Oxford: Pergamon Press.

King, M.L. (n.d.) *Mediumship and Its Phases.* Indianapolis, IN: Summit Publications (N.S.A.C. and the Stow Foundation).

Krakauer, J. (2003) *Under the Banner of Heaven—A Story of Violent Faith.* New York, NY: Doubleday (a division of Random House, Inc.).

Larabee, W. H. (1960) "Spiritualism, Spiritualists." *Encyclodpedia of Religious Knowledge,* Vol. XI, pp. 51-52. Grand Rapids, MI: Baker Book House.

Leadbeater, C.W. (1903) *Clairvoyance.* Adyar, India: Vasanta Press for The Theosophical Society (17th printing 1998

Leedy, P.D. & Ormand, J.E. (2001) (7th ed.) *Practical Research: Planning and Design.* Upper Saddle River, NJ: Merrill-Prentice Hall (originally published in 1974).

Leonard, T.J. (1994) "Jews Throughout Spanish History." *Bulletin of Hirosaki Gakuin University,* Vol. 30, pp. 37-57. Hirosaki, Japan: Hirosaki Gakuin University Press.

Lilec, Rev. J. (2002) Personal interview. July 29, 2004, Ball State University, Muncie, Indiana.

MacDonald, Rev. R.J. (n.d.) *Service Book: National Spiritualist Association of Churches.* Cassadaga, FL: National Spiritualist Association of Churches.

Maffly-Kipp, L. (2000) "African-American Religion in the Nineteenth Century: Divining America." *The National Humanities Center.* Retrieved May 26, 2003, from http://www.nhc.rtp.nc.us:8080/tserve/nineteen/nkeyinfo/nafrican.html.

Melton, J. G. (1978) "Spiritualism." *Encyclopedia of American Religions, Volume 2.* Wilmington, NC: McGrath Publishing Company.

Milburn, E. (Ed.) (2000) *Trail of Religion.* Chesterfield, IN: Indiana Association of Spiritualists (IAOS) Camp Chesterfield.

Miller, P. (1943) *Cavalcade of the Spirit.* London: Psychic Press.

Morris Pratt Institute. *History, Philosophy, and Information.* Retrieved from http://www.morrispratt.org/info.html. March 26, 2004.

Morse, E.B. (1933) *The 'Whys' of Spiritualism.* Summit, NJ: Stow Memorial Foundation.

Myers, Rev. A. A. (n.d.) *Spiritualism: Science, Philosophy, Religion*. Lily Dale, NY: National Spiritualist Association of Churches (NSAC) (Stow Memorial Foundation).

National Spiritualist Association of Churches. (1999). *Foundation Facts Concerning Spiritualism as a Religion*. [Brochure]. Lily Dale, NY: Stow Memorial Foundation. Author.

National Spiritualist Association of Churches. (2001). *Spiritualism: Social Policy Statements: Consensus Resolutions on Current Issues*. [Brochure]. Lily Dale, NY: Stow Memorial Foundation: Author.

NSAC Spiritualist Manual. (1998). Lily Dale, NY: National Spiritualist Association of Churches of the United States of America.

Nelson, R. (ed.) (1999) *The Handy History Answer Book*. Canton, MI: Visible Ink Press.

Ostling, R.N. & J.K. Ostling. (1999) *Mormon America: The Power and the Promise*. New York: NY: HarperSanFrancisco (an imprint of HarperCollins).

Overlee, V.W. (1983) *Psychics: Past—Present*. Canaan, VT: Mora Press.

Owens, E. (2001) *How to Communicate with Spirits*. St. Paul, MN: Llewellyn Publications.

Pakenham, M. (2001, April 29). "The love-hate ties between Houdini, Conan Doyle." *The Daily Yomiuri*, p. 18.

Parker-Wakefield, M. (1995) *The Facts About Orthodox Religions and Spiritualism Explained*. London: Regency Press Ltd.

Parmenter, L.K. (1997) *Becoming International in a Japanese Junior High School: An Ethnographic Study*. Unpublished doctoral dissertation, University of Durham, Great Britain.

"Photographing Heaven." *Spirit History*. Retrieved from http://www.spirithistory.com/Photos/html on October 6, 2002.

Plum, Rev. A. (2001) *An Interfaith Minister's Manual* (3rd ed.). Alexander, NC: Mountain Church.

Podmore, F. (2000) *Modern Spiritualism: A History and Criticism.* London: Routledge/Thoemmes Press (original published in 1902 by Charles Scribner's Sons, New York).

Polidoro, M. (2001) *Final Séance: The Strange Friendship between Houdini and Conan Doyle.* Amherst, NY: Prometheus Books.

Richards, C. (Ed.) (1997) *The Illustrated Encyclopedia of World Religions.* New York: Barnes and Noble—Element Books.

Rogge, M. (1996) The *Roots of the New Age: Part One.* Retrieved from http://www.xs4all.nl/~wichm/newage3.html on October 30, 2000.

Royce, Rev. C.M. (1975) *To the Spirit…From the Spirit: A Self Help Service Book and Ministers' Manual.* No place listed: International General Assembly of Spiritualists of America.

Scher, F. (1981) *Spiritualism and Mediumship Studies.* N.p.

Schoenfield, E.A. (n.d.) *The Spiritualist Minister and His Work.* Lily Dale, NY: National Spiritualist Association of Churches (NSAC).

Schneider, H.F. (1980) *Writings of Andrew Jackson Davis: A Resume.* Indianapolis, IN: Summit Publications, N.S.A.C.

Scott, D. (2000) "Mormonism and the American Mainstream: The 19th Century—Divining America." *The National Humanities Center.* Retrieved May 26, 2003, http://www.nhc.rtp.nc.us:8080/tserve/nineteen/nkeyinfo/nmormon.html.

Shaw, E. (1995) *Divining the Future: Prognostication from Astrology to Zoomancy.* New York: Gramercy Books.

Smith, J. Jr. (1932) *History of the Church.* 7 Vols. Salt Lake City: Desert News Press.

Smith, U. (1896) *Modern Spiritualism: A Subject of Prophecy and a Sign of the Times.* Hagerstown, MD: Review and Herald Publishing Association (this out of print book was retrieved on April 26, 2003 at http://ourworld.compuserve.com/homepagesclt4/mstoc.htm).

Spindler, G. (1982) *The Ethnography of Schooling.* Illinois: Waveland Publishing.

Spong, J.S. (1991) *Rescuing the Bible from Fundamentalism: A Bishop Rethinks the Meaning of Scripture.* New York, NY: HarperSanFrancisco (an imprint of HarperCollins).

Stefanidakis, Rev. S. (1998) *Forerunners to Modern Spiritualism: Emmanuel Swedenborg.* Retrieval date N/A: http://www.fst.org.

Stefanidakis, Rev. S. (1998) *Forerunners to Modern Spiritualism: Andrew Jackson Davis.* Retrieval date N/A: http://www.fst.org.

Stefanidakis, Rev. S. (1998) *The Hydesville Events, March 31, 1848.* Retrieval date unknown: http://www.fst.org.

Swan, I. (1969) *The Bang Sisters and their Precipitated Spirit Portraits.* Chesterfield, IN: Hett Memorial Art Gallery and Museum (Camp Chesterfield) (rev. 2nd printing, 1991).

Taft, R. (1988) *Ethnographic Research Methods.* In Keeves (Ed.) pp. 59-63.

The Origin of Modern Spiritualism: Statements of Witnesses Regarding the Mysterious Noises Heard in the House of John D. Fox in Hydesville, N.Y. (1979) Lily Dale, NY: SAM, Inc.

"The Story of Spiritualism." *New Age On-Line Australia.* Retrieved October 15, 2000 www.newage.com.au.

Tuttle, H. (1900) *Mediumship and Its Laws: Its conditions and Cultivation.* Cassadaga, FL: National Spiritualist Association of Churches (NSAC) (100th edition 1974).

Universal Spiritualist Manual: The Liturgy and Ritual of the Universal Spiritualist Church (rev. ed., n.d.) Muncie, IN: Universal Spiritualist Association.

Universal Spiritualist Association. (1998 rev.) *Constitution and By-Laws.* Muncie, IN: Universal Spiritualist Asociation.

Universal Spiritualist Association, College of Religious Education (CORE). (2001) "The Séance, Clairvoyant Circles and Healing Circles," *Introduction to Spiritualism*, Level IV, Module 1 (pp.24-29). Muncie. IN: Universal Institute for Holistic Studies (for the Universal Spiritualist Association).

Wallis, E.W.; and Wallis, M.H. (republished 1968) *A Guide to Mediumship and Psychical Unfoldment*. Mokelume Hill, CA: Health Research.

Washington, P. (1995) *Madame Blavatsky's Baboon: A History of the Mystics, Mediums, and Misfits Who Brought Spiritualism to America*. New York, NY: Schocken Books.

Webster's New Collegiate Dictionary. (1973) Springfield, MA: G. & C. Merriam Company (revised ed: 1979).

Wetley, L.E. (1979) *The Secret of Psychic Phenomena*. Jamestown, NY: SAM, Inc. Psychic Research Consultants.

Wilson, A. (Ed.) (1995) *World Scripture: A Comparative Anthology of Sacred Texts*. St. Paul, MN: Paragon House.

Wilson, Rev. P. D. (1979) *Modern Psychic Phenomena: Volume 1*. Indianapolis, IN: Summit (Stow Memorial Foundation).

Wilson, Rev. P. D. (1979) *Modern Psychic Phenomena: Volume 2*. Indianapolis, IN: Summit (Stow Memorial Foundation).

Wilson, Rev. P. D. (1981) *Modern Psychic Phenomena: Volume 3*. Indianapolis, IN: Summit (Stow Memorial Foundation).

Woelfl, G. (1976) *Psychic Experience: An Introduction to Spiritualism*. Menlo Park, CA: Redwood Publishers.

Appendix A

An Abridged Timeline of Modern Spiritualism from 1848-1920

1848

The birth of Modern Spiritualism takes place in Hydesville, New York with the "Hydsville Rappings" that occurred in the cottage of the John Fox family, on March 31.

1849

-The first public demonstration for a small group of devotees of the mediumship of Margaret Fox was held in Corinthian Hall, Rochester, New York on November 14.

1851

-A team of professors from the University of Buffalo Medical School came to critical and negative conclusions regarding the validity of Spiritualist claims of mediumship and phenomena.

-By 1851, more than 150 regular circles were functioning in New York City and 60 in Philadelphia, with thousands of others functioning around the United States.

1852

-Mrs. Maria Hayden traveled from the United States to Great Britain and was the first Spiritualist medium to work in England.

-Beginning in 1852, state and regional Spiritualist conventions began to be held regularly. These were often filled with strife and internal conflict as the attendees could rarely agree on anything of true substance.

-The Spiritual Telegraph, published in New York, began circulation; it lasted until 1860 and was the most widely circulated Spiritualist periodical of the 1850s.

1853

-Judge John Edmonds (1816-1874) was an influential Spiritualist in America during the early years of the movement. He enjoyed a long career in politics, in both houses of the State Legislature of New York. He served as President of the New York Senate and was appointed to the New York Court of Appeals. He eventually was forced to resign his judgeship due to his Spiritualist beliefs and outward support of the Fox sisters because of the public's denunciation of his beliefs.

-A British subject, David Richmond (1816-1891) became a Spiritualist while living in the United States; upon returning to his native Darlington, England, he tried to start a Spiritualist church but was ran out of town by the very conservative Quaker townsfolk. He then fled to Keighley, in Yorkshire, and successfully established the first Spiritualist church in Great Britain. This church is still referred to as the "Mother of all Spiritualist churches" in Great Britain.

1854

-Robert Owen (1771-1858), the noted British social reformer and socialist, was a pioneer in the cooperative movement. He converted to Spiritualism in 1854 after sitting in séance with Mrs. Marie Hayden. After his transition, Emma Hardinge Britten channeled his spirit where he dictated *The Principle of Spiritualism* through her mediumship. Robert Owen's son, Robert Dale Owen, also converted to Spiritualism and was a statesman in Indiana, where he championed women's rights and the emancipation of slaves; he also was instrumental in the founding of the Smithsonian Institution as a member of Congress (1843-1847).

-The Society for the Diffusion of Spiritual Knowledge (SDSK) was formed in New York City and was led by a group of wealthy and socially prominent Christian Spiritualists; it soon folded amid a wave of hostile essays and letters written against it.

1855

-Daniel Dunglas Home (1833-1886) was one of the greatest mediums to have ever lived, experiencing in the presence of others nearly all types of physical and mental phenomena. He discovered his mediumsistic gifts while living in America; upon returning to his native England in 1855, he sparked great interest among the public with his mediumship skills.

-Prominent Philadelphia chemist, Robert Hare, initially dismissed spirit manifestations as fraud and delusion. Converting to the movement, Hare became a publicist for Spiritualism, publishing Experimental Investigation of the Spirit Manifestations in 1855; he tried repeatedly to persuade, ultimately unsuccessfully, the American Association for the Advancement of Science to address the topic.

-Dr. Henry Slade, an American medium, was tested by a panel of eminent investigators regarding his slate-writing mediumship (where messages are written by spirit on sealed slates). He was pronounced to be genuine.

-The first Spiritualist newspaper was published in Keighley, *The Yorkshire Spiritual Telegraph*.

-Alexander N. Asakof (1832-1903), an imperial councilor to the czar of Russia, is considered to be a Spiritualist pioneer in Russia. A Swedenborg enthusiast, he was introduced to Modern Spiritualism after reading Andrew Jackson Davis' *Nature's Divine Revelations* in 1855.

1856

-Allan Kardec (1804-1869) published his classic, *Le Livre des Esprits* [*The Spirit's Book*], which had a profound impact upon the Spiritualist movement.

-James Martin Peebles (1822-1922) was known as the "spiritual pilgrim" because of his travels around the United States and the world, and his writings that helped to spread the philosophy of Spiritualism more widely. He claimed to have had a "band of angels" from which he received spiritual guidance and inspiration.

1857

-A team of prominent Harvard Scientists investigating spirit communication and phenomena debunked the movement with its critical conclusions to Spiritualist claims.

-Boston Spiritualists started the periodical *Banner of Light*.

1860

-By 1860, the movement had spread as far as New Orleans, Texas and San Francisco.

-The federal census listed 17 Spiritualist churches in the United States.

1863

-Andrew Jackson Davis (1826-1910) established the first Sunday Spiritualist Lyceum in New York. By far one of the most famous and revered mediums in the Spiritualist movement, he developed and then initiated Lyceum-based education through his out-of-body experiences and visits to "Summerland." He is regarded as the "Father of the Lyceum Movement."

-Professor Augustus de Morgan (1806-1871) was one of the first British scientists to investigate Spiritualist physical phenomena and was convinced of their occurrence.

-Robert James Lees (1849-1931), a journalist, philanthropist, novelist and medium, believed that his psychic experiences began before his third birthday, at a stage of mental development when children are learning and maneuvering the physical world. He is alleged to have been a confident of Queen Victoria who desperately wanted to contact the spirit of her late husband, Prince Albert. He was also allegedly involved in the on-going investigation to find the serial killer, Jack the Ripper.

1865

-The first "National Organisation of Spiritualists" was attempted in Darlington, England

-*Religio-Philosophical Journal* (1865-1907) was established in Chicago.

1866

-This year marks the return to England from the United States of Emma Hardinge Britten; she quickly gained notoriety for her gifted mediumship, and was possibly the most renowned and most respected medium and advocate for Spiritualism in the early decades of the movement.
-The first Spiritualist Lyceum was held in Nottingham, England.

1869

-A report submitted by an investigative committee for The Dialectical Society on Spiritualism found the movement to be genuine.

-The first Spiritualist minister, The Reverend James H. Powell, was ordained.

1870

-The federal census listed 95 Spiritualist churches in the United States.

1871

-Florence Cook (1856-1904), a gifted medium who is most well-known for her physical phenomenon materialization of Katie King. This phenomenon was investigated by Sir William Crookes and he allegedly proved that the Katie King spirit was indeed distinct from that of the medium.

-Emma Hardinge Britten (1823-1899) received *The Principles of Spiritualism* from Robert Owen (1771-1858) while he was in Spirit. These are as follows:

1. The Fatherhood of God

2. The Brotherhood of Man

3. The Communion of Spirits and the Ministry of Angels

4. The continuous existence of the human soul

5. Personal responsibility

6. Compensation and retribution hereafter for all the good and evil deeds done on earth

7. Eternal progress open to every human soul

-Sir William Crookes (1882-1919) reported on Spiritualism to the Royal Society and published his findings in the quarterly, *Journal of Science*. Initially, he undertook the task of investigating Spiritualism in order to expose it as nonsense. However, during his research he became convinced of spirit communication and for the rest of his life he remained completely convinced of it.

1872

-A second attempt to form a national organization in England failed. It did, though, stimulate widespread interest and it was recognized that such a body to oversee Spiritualism in Great Britain was indeed needed.

1873

-Dr. A. Russell Wallace (1823-1903), co-discoverer of the Theory of Evolution with Charles Darwin, had investigated Spiritualism deeply over a number of years; in 1873, he declared that spirit phenomena were proven scientifically.

-A conference in Liverpool, England led to the formation of the British National Association of Spiritualists with its headquarters located in London.

1874

-The Spiritualist camp, Lake Pleasant, was established in 1874 and consisting of tents; by 1890, it had five hundred cottages, a grocery store, and a hotel, offering band concerts, dancing and refreshment stands as well as a variety of mediums, fortune tellers, magnetic and electric healers, and inspirational Sunday lectures.

1875

-Helena Petrovna Blavatsky (1831-1891), also called "Madame Blavatsky," a former devotee to Spiritualism, founded the Theosophy movement.

-Frank Podmore (1856-1910), initially an opponent to Spiritualism, he became a convert after experiencing personally a number of supernormal occurrences while studying at Oxford University. He was a frequent contributor to *Human Nature* on Spiritualistic subjects. His reoccurring doubts were finally put to rest through his experiences with the medium, Henry Slade.

-Thomas Lake Harris established the mystical Fountain Grove community near santa Rosa, as a sort of Spiritualist utopia.

1878

-Emma Hardinge Britten toured Australia and New Zealand promoting Spiritualism.

1879

-The Cassadaga Free Lake Association, later renamed Lily Dale Assembly (in 1906), was established in Chautauqua County, New York. At its height in the early 20th century, this 80 acre camp was comprised of several hundred cottages, indoor and outdoor meeting places, a hotel, a store, a post office, a library, athletic fields, and a fire department.

1882

-John B. Newbrough publishes *Oahspe* which tells of humanity's origins on a lost Pacific continent and predicts a coming utopian age.

1885

-The American Society for Psychical Research was started.

1886

-*Indiana Association of Spiritualists* is established as Camp Chesterfield, Indiana.

1887

-An unfavorable report by the Seybert Commission which investigated Spiritualism under the auspices of the University of Pennsylvania at the bequest of wealthy Philadelphia Spiritualist Henry Seybert.

-The *Two Worlds* periodical was launched as a weekly newspaper by Emma Hardinge Britten.

-The *British Lyceum Manual* was published for the first time. Its co-authors were Mr. H. A. Kersey of Newcastle Upon Tyne, England, Mr. Alfred Kitson, and Emma Hardinge Britten.

1888

-Fox sisters claimed to have manipulated the "rappings" with their toes, damaging the movement tremendously with their confession (later, this was recanted by Kate Fox).

1890

-The federal census listed 334 Spiritualist churches in the United States.

-The *Sunflower* was started as a Spiritualist newspaper (1890-1909) by the Cassadaga Free Lake Association.
-Formation of the *National Spiritualists Federation* and *Spiritualists Lyceum Union* (the name was later changed to *British Spiritualists Union* in 1894).

1892

-*Cassadaga* (1892-1897) was a periodical produced by the Cassadaga Free Lake Association.

1893

-Foundation of *National Spiritualists Association of America*.

1894

-*The Southern Cassadaga Spiritualist Camp Meeting Association* was established in Florida as a counterpart to the New York site, which offered mediums a warmer climate to work in during the cold winter months.

1901

-Foundation of *Spiritualists National Union Limited*.

1902

-The *Spiritualists National Union* acquires the rights, assets and obligations of the *National Spiritualists Federation*, obtaining legal status whereby it could hold real property.

1906

-The federal census listed 455 Spiritualist churches in the United States, with total memberships in the tens of thousands

1907

-The *Progressive Spiritual Church* was formed by several members who withdrew from the *National Spiritualist Association* because they wanted to move from an emphasis on psychic research to establish an organization dedicated to the religious aspect of Spiritualism.

-Levi H. Dowling publishes *Aquarian Gospel of Jesus Christ*, containing alleged events of Christ's life, including travel to India during the time in the Bible that is suspiciously lacking in information regarding the life of Jesus.

1916

-The Fox cottage (where the initial movement had its genesis) was moved to the Spiritualist camp of Lily Dale, in New York.

1918

-Sir Arthur Conan Doyle proclaimed his belief in Spiritualism. He was regarded as the "St. Paul" of Spiritualism because of his positive and prolific writing on the subject, as well as being an avid proponent.

1920

-William McDougall, professor of psychology at Harvard University and author of *Body and Mind and Social Psychology*, was a keen but reserved investigator who took great care not to commit himself as to the genuine occurrence of the supernormal and agencies of an extra-terrene origin.

Nota Bene: The material used in this timeline was compiled from the following sources:

Chernow, Barbara A. and George A. Vallasi (editors), *The Columbia Encyclopedia* (5th Ed.), New York, NY: Columbia University Press (distributed by Houghton Mifflin Company), 1993.

Chesterfield Lives: 1886-1986—Our First Hundred Years, Chesterfield, IN: Camp Chesterfield, 1986.

De Swarte, Lyn G. *Thorson's Principles of Spiritualism*, London, England: Thorsons, 1999.

Guthrie, John J., Phillip Charles Lucas and Gary Monroe (editors). *Cassadaga: The South's Oldest Spiritualist Community*, Gainsville, FL: The University Press of Florida, 2000

Hamilton-Parker, Craig. *The History of Spiritualism*, http://www.spiritualists.org (accessed on April 26, 2003.

Harrold, Robert, Cassadaga: *An Inside Look at the South's Oldest Psychic Community with True Experiences of People Who Have been There*, Miami, FL: Banyan Books, 1979.

The History of Modern Spiritualism, New Age On-Line Australia, www.newage.com.au (accessed November 13, 2000.

Appendix B

Hydesville in History: Testimony of Eye-Witnesses

Statements of Witnesses regarding the Mysterious Noises Heard in the Home of John D. Fox in Hydesville, NY

The following statements were made by the different persons whose names are signed to them, and taken down in writing as they made them; after which they carefully read and signed them. They comprise but a small number of those who heard these noises, or have been knowing to these transactions; but they are deemed sufficient to satisfy the public mind in regard to their truthfulness.

Certificate of Mrs. Margaret Fox, Wife of John D. Fox, the Occupant of the House

"We moved into the house on December 11, 1847, and have resided here since that date. We formerly lived in the city of Rochester, N.Y. We were first disturbed by these noises about a fortnight ago. It sounded like some one knocking in the east bedroom, on the floor; we could hardly tell where to locate the sounds, as sometimes it sounded as if the furniture was moved, but on examination we found everything in order. The children had become so alarmed that I thought best to have them sleep in the room with us. There were four of us in the family, and sometimes five.

"On the night of the first disturbance we all got up, lighted a candle and searched the entire house, the noises continuing during the time, and being heard near the same place. Although not very loud, it produced a jar of the bedsteads and chairs that could be felt when we wee in the bed. It was a tremulous motion, more than a sudden jar. We could feel the jar when standing on the floor. It continued on this night until we slept. I did not sleep until about twelve o'clock. On March 30th we were disturbed all night. The noises were heard in all parts of the houses. My husband stationed himself outside of the door while I stood inside, and the knocks came on the door between us. We heard footsteps in the pantry, and walking downstairs; we could not rest, and then I concluded that the house must be haunted by some unhappy, restless spirit. I had often heard of such things, but had never witnessed anything of the kind that I could not account for before.

"On Friday night, March 31, 1848, we concluded to go to bed early and not permit ourselves to be disturbed by the noises, but try and get a night's rest. My husband was here on all occasions, heard the noises, and helped search. It was very early when we went to bed on this night—hardly dark. I had been so broken of my rest I was almost sick. My husband had not gone to bed when we first heard the noise on this evening. I had just lain down. It commenced as usual. I knew it from all other noises I had ever before heard. The children, who slept in the other bed in the room, heard the rapping, and tried to make similar sounds by snapping their fingers.

"My youngest child (Cathie) said: 'Mr. Splitfoot, do as I do,' clapping her hands. The sound instantly followed her with the same number of raps. When she stopped the sound ceased for a short time. Then Margaretta said, in sport: 'Now do as I do; count one, two three, four,' striking one hand against the other at the same time, and the raps came as before. She was afraid to repeat them. Then Cathie said, in her childish simplicity: 'O, mother, I know what it is: tomorrow is April-fool day, and it's somebody trying to fool us.' I then thought I would put a test that no one in the place could answer. I asked the noise to rap my different children's age, successively. Instantly each one of my children's ages was given correctly, pausing between them sufficiently long to individualize them until the seventh, at which a longer pause was made, and then three more emphatic raps were given, corresponding to the age of the little one that died, which was my youngest child. I then asked: 'Is this a human that answers my questions so correctly?' There was no rap. I asked: Is it a spirit? If it is, make two raps, which were instantly made, causing the house to tremble. I asked, "were you injured in this house?' The answer was given as before. 'Is the person living that injured you?' Answered by raps in the same manner. I ascertained by the same method that it was a man, aged thirty-one years; that he had been murdered in this house, and his remains were buried in the cellar; that his family consisted of a wife and five children, two sons and three daughters, all living at the time of his death, but that his wife had since died. I asked: 'Will you continue to rap if I call my neighbors that they might hear it, too?' The raps were loud in the affirmative. My husband went and called in Mrs. Redfield (our nearest neighbor). She is a very candid woman. The girls were sitting up in bed clinging to each other and trembling with terror. I think I was as calm as I am now. Mrs. Redfield came immediately (this was about half-past seven), thinking she would have a laugh at the children; but when she saw them pale with fright, and nearly speechless, she was amazed, and believed there was something more serious than she had supposed. I asked a few questions for her, and was answered as before. He told her age exactly. She then called her husband, and the same questions were asked and answered. Then Mr. Redfield called in Mr. Duesler and wife, and several others. Mr. Duesler then called in Mr. and Mrs. Hyde, also Mr. and Mrs. Jewell. Mr. Duesler asked many questions, and received answers. I then named all the neighbors I could think of, and asked if any of them had injured him and received no answer. Mr. Duesler then asked questions and received answers. He asked, 'were you murdered?' Raps affirmative. 'Can your murderer be brought to justice?' No sound. 'Can he be punished by law?' No answer. He then said: 'If your murderer cannot be punished by the law, manifest it by raps', and the raps were made clearly and distinctly. In the same way Mr. Duesler ascertained that he was murdered in the east bedroom about five years ago, and that the murder was committed by a Mr. ___, on a Tuesday night, at 12 o'clock; that he was murdered by having his throat cut with a butcher knife; that the body was taken down the cellar; that it was not buried until the next night; that it was taken through the buttery, down the stairway, and that it was buried ten feet below the surface of the ground. It was also ascertained that he was murdered for his money, by raps affirmative. 'How much was it, one hundred?' No rap. 'Was it two hundred?' etc.; and when he mentioned five hundred the raps replied in the affirmative. Many called in who were fishing in the creek, and all heard the same questions and answers. Many remained in the house all night. I and my children left the house. My husband remained in the house with Mr. Redfield all night. On the next Saturday the house was filled to overflowing. There were no sounds head during the day, but they commenced again in the evening. It was said there were over three hundred persons present at the time. On Sunday morning the noises were heard throughout the day by all who came to the house. On Saturday night, April 1st, they commenced digging in the cellar; they dug until they came to water, and then gave it up. The noise was not heard on Sunday evening nor during the night. Stephen B. Smith and wife (my daughter Maria) and my son, David S. Fox, and wife, slept in the room this night. I have heard nothing since that time until yesterday. In the forenoon of yesterday there were several questions answered in the usual way, by rapping. I have heard the noise several times today.

"I am not a believer in haunted houses or supernatural appearances. I am very sorry that there has been so much excitement about it. It has been a great deal of trouble to us. It was our misfortune to live here at this time; but I am willing and anxious that the truth should be known, and that a true statement should be made. I cannot account for these noises; all that I know is, that they have been heard repeatedly, as I stated. I have heard this rapping again this (Tuesday) morning, April 4. My children also heard it. I certify that the foregoing statement ha been read to me, and that the same is true; and that I should be willing to take my oath that it is so, if necessary.

(Signed) "Margaret Fox.

"April 11, 1848."

Statement of John D. Fox

"I have heard the above statement by my wife, Margaret Fox, read, and hereby certify that the same is true in all its particulars. I heard the same rappings which she has spoken of, n answer to the questions, as stated by her. There have been a great many questions besides those asked, and answered in the same way. Some have been asked a great many times, and they have always received the same answers. There has never been any contradiction whatever.

"I do not know of any way to account for these noises, as being caused by any natural means. We have searched every nook and corner in and about the house, at different times, to ascertain if possible whether anything or anybody was secreted there that could make the noise, and have not been able to find anything which would or could explain the mystery. It has caused a great deal of trouble and anxiety.

"Hundreds have visited the house, so that it is impossible for us to attend to our daily occupations; and I hope that, whether caused by natural or supernatural means, it will be ascertained soon. The digging in the cellar will be resumed as the water settles, and then it can be ascertained whether there are any indications of a body ever having been buried there; and if there are, I shall have no doubt but that it is of supernatural origin.

"April 11, 1848." (Signed) "JOHN D. FOX"

Statement of William Duesler

"I live in this place. I moved from Cayuga County here last October. I live within a few rods[1] of the house in which these sounds have been heard. The first I heard anything about them was a week ago last Friday evening (March 31). Mrs. Redfield came over to my house to get my wife to go over to Mr. Fox's. Mrs. R. appeared to be very much agitated. My wife wanted me to go over with them, and I accordingly went. When she told us what she wanted us to go over there for, I laughed at her and ridiculed the idea of there being anything mysterious about it. I told her it was all nonsense, and that we would find out the cause of the noise, and that it could easily be accounted for. This was about nine o'clock in the evening. There were some twelve or fourteen persons present when I left them. Some were so frightened that they did not want to go into the room. I went into the room and sat down on the bed. Mr. Fox asked a question and I heard the rapping, which they had spoken of, distinctly. I felt the bedstead jar when the sounds were produced. Mr. Fox then asked if it would answer my questions if I asked any; and it rapped three times. I then asked if it was an injured spirit, and it rapped. I asked if it had come to hurt anyone who was then present. It did not rap. I then reversed the question, and it rapped. I asked if my father or I had been injured by it (as we had formerly lived in the house), and there was no noise. 'If we had not injured you, manifest it by rapping,' and we all heard three distinct raps. I then asked if such or such a one had injured it (meaning the several families who had formerly lived in the house), and there was no noise. Upon asking the negatives of these questions the rapping was heard. I then asked if Mr. ____ (naming a person who had lived in the house at a former period) had injured it; and if so, to manifest it by rapping, and it made three raps louder than usual; and at the same time the bedstead jarred more than it had before. I then inquired if it was murdered for money, and the sounds were heard. Questions and answers as to different sums of money were then given as stated by Mr. Fox. All in the room said they heard the sounds distinctly.

"After that I went over and got Artemus W. Hyde to come over. I then asked nearly all the same questions, and got the same answers. Mr. Redfield went after David Jewell and wife, and Mr. and Mrs. Hyde also came in. After they came, I asked the same questions over again, and got the same answers. I asked if it was murdered by being struck on the head, and there were no sounds; I then reversed the question, and the rapping was heard. I then asked if it was stabbed in the side, and there was no answer. Upon asking the negative of this the rapping was heard.

---

1. A "rod" is a measure of length equal to 5 ½ yards (or 5.02 meters).

It usually rapped three times in giving affirmative answer to my questions. I then asked if it had its throat cut, and it rapped as usual. Then, if it was with a butcher knife and the rapping was heard. In the same way it was ascertained that it was asleep at the time, but it was awakened when the knife entered its throat; that it struggled and made some noise and resistance. Then I asked if there was anyone in the house at the time but him, and it did not rap. I then asked if they were two alone, and the rapping was herd. I then asked if they two were alone, and the rapping was heard. I then asked if Lucretia Pulver was there at the time, and there was no rapping. If she had gone away that night, and if Mrs. ____was gone away also, and the rapping was heard each time. There was no rapping heard only when we asked questions. I then asked if anyone in Hydesville knew of the murder at the time except ____, and it rapped. Then I asked about a number of persons, if they knew it, and there was no rapping until I came to Mrs.____, and when I came to her name the rapping was heard. Then if anyone but ____ and his wife knew of it, and I got no rap. Then if they were all that knew of the murder, and it rapped. I asked if the body was put into the cellar, and it rapped. I then asked if it was buried in different points of the cellar, and to all my question there was no rapping until I asked if it was near the center, and the rapping was heard. Charles Redfield then took a candle and went down to the cellar. I told him to place himself in different parts of the cellar, and as he did so I asked the question if a person was over the place where it was buried, and I got no answer until he stood over a certain place in the cellar, when it rapped. He then stepped one side, and when I asked the question there were no noises. This we repeated several times, and we found that whenever he stood over the place the rapping was heard, and when he moved away from that one place, there was no rapping in answer."

Statement of Miss Lucretia Pulver

"I lived in this house all one winter, in the family of Mr. ____. I worked for them a part of the time, and a part of the time I boarded and went to school. I lived there about three months. During the latter part of the time I was there I heard these knockings frequently; in the bedroom, under the foot of the bed. I heard it a number of nights, as I slept in the bedroom nearly all the time that I stayed there. One night I thought I heard a man walking in the buttery. The buttery is near the bedroom, with a stairway between the two. Miss Amelia Losey stayed with me that night. She also heard the noise, and we were both much frightened, and got up and fastened down the windows, and fastened the door. It sounded as if a person walked through the buttery, down cellar, and part way across the cellar bottom, and then the noise ceased. There was no one else in the house at the time except my little brother, who was asleep in the same room with us. This was about twelve o'clock I should think. We did not go to bed until after eleven, but had not been asleep when we heard it striking. Mr. and Mrs. ____ had gone to Loch Berlin, to be gone till the next day. One morning about a week after this Mrs. ____ sent me down cellar to shut the outside door which fastens on the inside. In going across the cellar I sank knee deep in the center of the cellar. It appeared to be uneven and very loose. After I got upstairs Mrs. ____ asked me what I screamed for. When I told her, she laughed at me for being frightened, and said it was only where rats had been at work in the ground.

"A day or two after this, Mr. ____ carried a lot of dirt into the cellar, just at night, and was at work there some time. Mrs. ____ told me he was filling up rat holes.

"A few days before I first heard the noises, or anything of the kind had ever occurred, a foot-peddler called there about two o'clock in the afternoon. Mrs. ____ then told me that Mr. ____ thought they would not want me any longer, and that I might go home; but if they wanted me again they would send for me. Mrs. ____ was going to Loch Berlin to stay that night. This was the first I had heard of it. I wanted to buy some things of the peddler, but had no money with me, and he said he would call at our house the next morning and sell them to me. I never saw him after that. Three days after this they sent for me to come and board with them and go to school. I accordingly came, and went to school about one week, when she wanted I should stay out of school and do housework, as she had a couple of coats to make over for her husband. She said they were too large for her husband, and out of fashion, and she must alter them. They were ripped to pieces when I first saw them. I should think the peddler was about thirty years old. I heard him conversing with Mrs. ____ about his family. He told her how many children he had, in answer to her inquiry. I do not recollect how many he said he had. Mrs. ____ told me that he (the peddler) was an old acquaintance of theirs. A short time after this Mrs. ____ gave me a thimble, which she said she had bought off the peddler and paid him 50 cents for. Some time after I had left her I visited her again, and she said the peddler had been there again, and showed me another thimble which she said she had bought off the same peddler. She said he had cheated her; that he had sold it to her for pure silver, but it was only German silver.[2] She also showed me some other things which she said she had bought off him.

"I did not (and do not now) know what to think of the noises I have heard. The dog would sit under the bedroom window and howl all night long. Mr. and Mrs. ____ appeared to be very good folks, only they were quick tempered.

"This peddler carried a trunk and a basket, I think, with vials of essence in it. He wore a black coat and light-colored pants.

"I am willing to swear to the above statement if necessary.

Lucretia Pulver.

"April 11, 1848."

Mrs. Anna Pulver

"I was acquainted with Mr. and Mrs. ____. I called on them frequently. My warping bars[3] were in their chamber, and I used to go there to do my work. One morning when I went there Mrs. ____ told me that she felt very badly; that she had not slept much the night before. When I asked her what the matter was, she said she didn't know but it was the fidgets; she thought she heard something walking about from one room to another and that she and Mr. ____ got up and fastened the windows down. She felt safe after that. I heard her speak about hearing sounds after that which she could not account for.

"April 11, 1848."   "Anna Pulver."

[Taken from: Cadwallader, M.E. (1917) *Hydesville in History*. Lily Dale, NY: National Spiritualist Association of Churches (NSAC); pp 25-34 [Reprinted by the Stowe Foundation in 1992].

---

2. "German silver" is nickel silver (a silver-white alloy containing a mixture of copper, zinc, and nickel).
3. Tools used to weave threads lengthwise in a loom.

Appendix C

A Glossary and List of Terms and Definitions Associated with Mediumship and Modern Spiritualism

Astral projection or travel: This is an action where the spirit leaves the body during a sleep state or through a conscious effort, and travels into a spiritual dimension or an area on the earth plane different from where the physical body is located.

Cabinet: This is an enclosure within a room, sometimes portable, usually with a curtain drawn across the entrance, in which a medium goes into a trance state while seated. The confinement of the medium's energy within the cabinet aids her or him to build up energy for the purpose of producing phenomena.

Chakra: This is a Sanskrit word meaning "something that rotates." Chakras are seven conically shaped rays of energy, with the main energy centers located along the body's vertical axis. They are the root, which is at the base of the spine; the sacral, two inches below the belly button; the solar plexus, in the waist area; the heart; throat; third eye, which is slightly above the eyebrows in the center of the forehead; and crown, the very top of the head.

Circle: To sit in a circle is a term used to describe an action where people gather regularly to meditate for the purpose of contacting spirits, usually in someone's home. There may or may not be a teacher present.

Development Class: This is a class where a person may learn to enhance his or her psychic and mediumistic abilities under the tutelage of an experienced teacher who is a psychic or medium.

Ectoplasm: This is a Greek word meaning "exteriorized substance." This cloudy substance streams out of mediums when they are demonstrating phenomena, usually from the mouth or nose, and frequently from the solar plexus, but can emanate from any orifice. Generally it forms around the spirit to give the entity a visible shape when a spirit is manifesting during a séance to afford the participants the opportunity to see a spirit. Ectoplasm may also surround a spirit when the entity manifests in daily life, outside of a séance sitting.

Going to the light: This is a term used to describe when a person ceases to live on the physical plane, and his/her spirit makes the transition into the spirit side of life. A brilliant white light has been reported being seen, according to people who have had near-death experiences, when a person is dying and entering the spirit world. It also has connotations of a higher spiritual presence, such as God.

Karma: This could be referred to as lessons in life. Some religions and many people believe our souls come to the earth to work through specific issues, or karma, so that we may grow spiritually.

Kundalini: This is a storehouse of vital energy, or creative life force, located at the base of the spine, symbolized as a coiled snake. It is the serpent of life, fire and wisdom. When this power of the spirit is awakened, it opens the chakras and can produce psychic powers.

Manifest: This is the appearance of a spirit through numerous means, such as a visible form, by sound, or touch.

Materialization: Materialization is when a spirit appears either during a séance or chooses to manifest in front of someone under ordinary circumstances.

Medium: A medium is a person who is sensitive to the vibrations from the spirit world. He or she is able to communicate with those on the spirit side of life through various means, delivering information and assistance to those who ask. All mediums are also psychics.

Messages: messages can be greetings, information, warnings, comfort, and advice that one might receive through the mediumship of an individual from a spirit. Usually these messages are brief and delivered to a group of people individually for the purpose of demonstrating the continuity of life. Spiritualists conduct message services as part of their religious services.

Mini-reading: This is an activity where a person sits for a reading with a medium for a short period of time, such as fifteen minutes, at a reduced fee. Frequently many mediums will offer this service to the public as a fundraiser for a church.

Natural law: These are principles that are operating in nature that include what is the innate within us and throughout all life, forming the orderly condition of things in nature. The understanding of these principles can often determine our actions and/or the consequences of our actions. In other words, we can create our own happiness or unhappiness by the choices we make.

Nature spirits: Nature spirits are spiritual beings, frequently invisible to the human eye, titled fairies, gnomes, salamanders, etc., who are involved with nature. They are also referred to as spirits of water, air, fire, and earth.

Other side of life or other side: This is the spirit world where one goes after passing away.

Physical phenomena: This is used as a means to demonstrate the continuity of life. Some examples would be the materialization of a spirit from a cabinet, a trumpet rising, a table moving, or voices emanating from a person or object.

Platform: A stage used by mediums for the purpose of delivering messages or lectures.

Psychic: A knowing, sensing ability. This is a mental act, such as knowing who is calling on the telephone before answering, or sensing from a distance that your children are in danger. Everyone is psychic to a certain degree. All professional psychics are not necessarily mediums.

Reader: A reader is someone who gives mediumistic or psychic readings or counseling, often referred to as a medium or spiritual counselor.

Reading: This is an activity where a person visits a medium or psychic for the purpose of receiving information/assistance regarding his or her life. This term could also apply to someone who would offer tarot card services. Not all means of receiving a reading necessarily offer communication with spirit, as would that received from a medium.

Séance: This term was popular in the 1880s and early 1900s when people would gather in a darkened room to contact spirits through various means. A more accurate definition currently would be when people sit in classes for development purposes. Technically, when one sits in a circle during classes, they are participating in a séance.

Silver cord: The silver cord is an ethereal conduit or "pipeline" through which the energy or soul life flows to the physical body. It is like the umbilical cord that goes from a mother to her baby, providing the child a soul gateway and physical energy line from the mother. (See Ecc. 12:6-7.) In full-form materializations, it is what bonds the spirits to the medium, thereby providing energy to the spirit.

Skotograph: This is a phenomenon used to demonstrate the continuity of life by using photographic paper during meditation and placing it in solutions for development. Spirit faces appear when the film has developed.

Spirit: This is a word that has several meanings. Spirit can be defined as a luminous, ethereal form, once human that now is deceased, living in another plane of existence. It is also a term used for God or to denote a higher spiritual power.

Spiritualism: Spiritualism is a religion, science, and philosophy that believes in continuous life, based upon communication with those who live in the spirit world, as demonstrated through mediumship. Through such communication one is able to receive guidance in mundane and spiritual matters from spiritual beings that are knowledgeable. They embrace personal responsibility and the belief that the doorway to reformation is never closed. Like all other positive religions, Spiritualism also teaches that we should follow the Golden Rule.

Spiritualist: This is a person who believes, as the basis pf his or her religion, in the continuity of life and personal responsibility, and endeavors to mold his or her character and conduct in accordance with the highest teaching derived from communion with the spirit world. He or she may or may not be a medium.

Symbol: This is where an interpretation can be deciphered from seeing an object depicted during meditation or in a dream state.

Synchronicity: Events that happen, appearing to be coincidental, as in simultaneous events.

Third eye: This is one of the energy centers each person posses, also referred to as a charka. It is located between the eyes and slightly above the eyebrows. It is sometimes referred to as the all-seeing eye.

Trumpet: An instrument used to demonstrate physical phenomena. It is usually made of lightweight aluminum, cone-shaped, and collapses into itself for storage.

Unfoldment: The hoped-for end result of sitting in circles or classes for the purpose of learning to communicate with the spirit world and, eventually, "unfold" mediumistic abilities.

White light: This is representative of God or a higher spiritual power, filled with love and protection from all harm.

[Taken from: Owens, Rev. E. (2001) *How to Communicate with Spirits*. St. Paul, MN: Llewellyn Publications (pp. 181-188)]

APPENDIX D

The Symbol of Spiritualism: The Sunflower

By
Rev. Marilyn J. Awtry-Smith, N.S.T.

Excerpt from
The New Educational Course

On
Modern Spiritualism

The symbol of Spiritualism is the Sunflower.

Time often obscures many things. Hopefully, some sincere investigator of modern Spiritualism will uncover the complete story of the Sunflower.

Somehow in the early days of the movement, the records were lost or perhaps not even recorded. Therefore, it is unknown at this time as to who first suggested the Sunflower as a suitable emblem of modern Spiritualism. However, we do know that for centuries long before the Christian era, the Sunflower was regarded as the emblem of truth and Constancy. Since the days of mythological fables, the Sunflower has been a favorite emblem of constancy....

From the Sunflower, the bright color "yellow" also became, among the ancients, the symbol of Truth and Constancy. For this very reason, it was adopted by the Women Reformers of the 1800's.

In our search for knowledge as to the adoption of the Sunflower by Spiritualists, we do know that it has been the emblem of Spiritualism at least since 1892.

The Association of Spiritualists at the Cassadaga Lake Free Association at Lily dale, New York, adopted the Sunflower as its seal as shown in its Constitution and By-Laws developed in 1892 and adopted in early 1893.

In 1900, Mr. W. H. Bach manufactured the first pins bearing the emblem of the Sunflower. He also produced buttons, brooches, and watch fobs[1] faced with the Sunflower. The design was a white background edged in gold with a yellow sunflower in the center.

Also on November 16, 1900, Mr. N. F. Raulin, Speaker of the "First Assembly of Spiritualists of Philadelphia" formed the "Young people's Twentieth Century Sunflower Club."

In 1928, the Sunflower was adopted as the official badge of "International Spiritualism" at the Conference of International Federation of Spiritualists. This followed with the Sunflower Song" being composed by Mrs. Grace Linn Sandy of Indianapolis, Indiana. The song was adopted as the Association's Song by the Delegates at the Convention held in Indianapolis in 1928. A copy of the words or music of the song cannot be located.

However, at the 92nd Annual Convention of the N.S.A.C., on October 11, 1983, a new song was presented by Linda N. Alden of Rochester, new York entitled "Like the Sunflowers."

Chorus:

*And I shall try to be
like the sunflowers that I see—
Turning my mind to the light
that always shines for me.*

*We are like he tiny mustard seed
that grows so strong and tall
And with Spirits Teaching us the*

---

1. A "fob" is a short ribbon or chain attached to a pocket watch.

truths our faith will never fall.

Spirit brings to us the truth
of love's eternal light
Through 100 years and sweat and tears
they've brought daylight to the night.

◆ ◆ ◆

Why was the Sunflower selected as the international representative of Spiritualism?

The **Sunflower** is native to the soil of the United States; however, it has been transplanted to many other soils all over the world. In 1948, **Spiritualism** was recognized as a religion in thirty-eight nations.

The **Sunflower** is like a magnet. It attracts selectively! The uncommon nectar of **Spiritualism** is very similar to its official flower. Spiritualism appeals not to the masses, but to the individual who seeks reason—the individual who substitutes something beyond mere faith.

The **Sunflower** rests upon a strong stalk. **Spiritualism** also demonstrates to mankind that peace and understanding here and hereafter depends upon a strong character.

The **Sunflower** with its long reach protects the weaker plants and flowers and helps shield them from the angry winds. It tends to balance the natural forces to give protection to the plants it is near. And, **Spiritualism** can be expressed in the same light. It protects man from superstition that prohibits his spiritual growth and provides him with a solid foundation upon which he can base a firm groundwork of understanding why he is here, what he must do and where he is going.

The **Sunflower** also provides a great medicinal value and contains almost a complete balance of all the natural vitamins and minerals. **Spiritualism** stresses the value of spiritual and physical healing.

Thus, with this comparison of the **Sunflower** and **Spiritualism**, it becomes very apparent the sunflower is an excellent emblem for the representation of Spiritualism followed with the motto,

> "As the **Sunflower** turns its
> face to the Light of the Sun—
> So let **Spiritualism** turn the face
> of humanity to the light of Truth.

[Taken from: Awtry-Smith, Rev. M. J. (1985) *The Sunflower: The Symbol of Spiritualism*. Wauwatosa, WI: Morris Pratt Institute Association (pp. 1-5).]

APPENDIX E

The Hydesville Cottage

The original Fox Cottage in Hydesville, N.Y. was purchased by B.F. Bartlett of Cambridge Springs, Pennsylvania and it was moved to Camp Lily Dale in upstate New York, the headquarters of the National Spiritualist Association of Churches. This occurred in 1916, almost seventy years after the first rappings were heard inside the house by the Fox sisters, Katie and Maggie, and their parents.

For obvious reasons, this house held a dear and special place in the hearts of Spiritualists as it was the structure where the first spirit-communication was heard that started the entire movement. The original house was furnished authentically to the time period in which the Hydesville Rappings occurred; even the tin trunk that the itinerant peddler, Charles B. Rosna, had with him when he was murdered was prominently displayed in the house.

Sadly, in the early morning hours on a day in 1955, the cottage burned to the ground. Fortunately, though, the peddler's trunk containing artifacts from the Fox family (*i.e.* the Fox family Bible) were saved from the fire. These items are now on display at the museum at Camp Lily Dale.

Figure: The original Fox Cottage

APPENDIX F
Natural Law

Natural Law is the law of God set into motion to govern all. It is immutable and unchangeable. There is no record of it ever having been changed to suit the whim and desire of anyone. There is law that controls organic life and a law that controls spiritual life. Both are so correlated that one reacts upon the other. Today we are coming to a realization of the fact that we may control our destiny by understanding and complying with Natural Law. Through right thinking, we may create health, happiness and for ourselves prosperity.

Using destructive thinking, we may create disease, unhappiness and poverty for ourselves. All indications point to the fact that sooner or later Natural Law and its reaction in our life will be a part of our education. The Spiritual Law is the highest because it enables us to live upon a higher plane of existence. Through our contact with the Spiritual and its manifestations, we are able to live more harmoniously and constructively with the great forces of Nature. Through our knowledge of the law, we have been able to utilize the great forces of nature for our own sustenance and comfort; to conquer time and space, and to overcome the Law of Gravitation.

A knowledge of the **Law of Cause and Effect** is quite essential for progression. We must realize that every cause brings about its certain effect, and if we would seek to better our lives we must be careful of the causes we create. We create by thinking; thought becomes deed, the deed sets in motion the immutable law that brings the effect into our lives, be it constructive or destructive. Through the power of constructive thought, men and women with their finite mind contact God or Infinite Intelligence, and begin into realization that which they have thought about. As Emerson says, "Thought makes everything fit to use."

The **Law of Attraction** states we attract to ourselves that which we are. As we vibrate mentally, as we desire through physical sensation, so we attract to our lives those of a like nature and desire. How true the saying, people may be judged by their associates. By creating with the spiritual power we set into motion the vibrations that, in accordance with the law, will attract things and people of a higher and better type. We see in others only that which is within ourselves. Therefore if you see only the error in those you contact, there is something radically wrong within yourself.

The **Law of Life** is the law that controls the relationship of God and humanity. Our understanding of that relationship, and our ability to adjust ourselves to it, depends on the power of the Infinite that is expressed through us. We are Infinite within ourselves if we only allow perfect life to have full expression.

The **Law of Love** is the most important of all laws; it is the creative force of all life. Down through the ages, love has been the light that has led thousands of sould to great achievement. History tells us that there are many instances where love has made or marred kingdoms. It is the constructive force and the highest vibration that can be attained.

The **Law of Truth** is the knowledge of what constitutes right thinking, right acting, and right living. It is accessible to all who seek it, and truth will eventually rise again triumphant over wrong doing.

The **Law of Compensation** is that law which metes out to us the payment for our deeds. As we sow, so shall we reap, and when we transgress God's law, compensation sets in automatically in one form or another.

The **Law of Freedom** gives to us a full realization of our unlimited power of choice. It brings to us the knowledge that we can build our own life in accordance with our desires. We will suffer or be rewarded in the hereafter for so doing. Knowing these laws and the absolute certainty of the results, gives to humanity an unlimited power, and we can truly say, "Knowing the truth has set me free."

[Taken from: Barnes, P. (rev. and edited 1997) *The Fundamentals of Spiritualism*. Lily Dale, NY: National Association of Spiritualist Churches (NSAC) (Stow Memorial Foundation), pp. 43-45.]

◆ ◆ ◆

*In addition to the above basic laws, there are a number of other Natural Laws:

Law of Vibration—positive thoughts and positive actions produce and create a positive (or higher) vibration in the person;

Law of Thought—both positive and negative thoughts affect one's vibration; these patterns are a part of one's being and essence. Thoughts are powerful, and the feelings associated with them give the thoughts even more power. Thoughts centered around positive emotions of love, compassion and kindness produce a clear and clean vibration; thoughts which focus on negativity, like jealousy, anger, hatred and bitterness will sully the vibration and darken it.

Law of Harmony—allows the smooth flow of positive energy to be a part of one's daily life and routine. Maintaining harmony allows a blending of positive energy about one's entire being.

Law of Continuity—states that Natural law is continuous and applies to both the earth plane and spirit world. Life is continuous. One doesn't die; one's body does. The body is the physical vehicle in which one's spirit or soul-essence is housed.

[These additional laws have been obtained from personal conversations and interviews with Spiritualist mediums (during the course of this dissertation's research).]

APPENDIX G

Personal Interview with Rev. Sarah Brown, Spiritualist Medium

[Tuesday, January 13, 2004, at Camp Chesterfield, Indiana]

TJL: I am very interested in knowing about the Science, Philosophy and Religion of Spiritualism. I would like to begin with the "Science"…what can you tell me from the perspective of a medium?

RSB: Well, the fact that it is a science has been proven by physical phenomena. It is demonstrated through mediumship, in a physical way that absolutely is ruled by Natural Law. It is a religion because of our basic Spiritualist beliefs, primarily the belief in an Infinite Intelligence, not necessarily what we would call God—not a personal God, but an Infinite Intelligence—to me that simply means the Laws of Nature, which is connected to all three. It is a philosophy because of the thought, or the intellectual part of it.

TJL: Many of the older Spiritualist books illustrated contraptions to try to capture spirit…In the early years of Spiritualism, do you think the need to have a scientific aspect was important because the world was embracing new sciences?

RSB: Probably. But to me the most important part, of course, no matter whether it is the science, or the philosophy, or the religious part, is the proof of the continuation of life—the continuity of life—which was and is the ultimate lesson of Spiritualism.

TJL: As a medium, what convinced you as "proof" the continuity of life?

RSB: I had, what I now know were circles in my home, and we began to have phenomena in the form of materializations, trance, and clairvoyance, clairaudience, clairsentience—we began to experience these…we actually didn't even know the names of the phenomena we were seeing, we were just having phenomena because we were simply gathered as one accord, in a group, and to my way of understanding and my belief, as long as two or more are gathered as one accord, and their motives are pure, and the intent is there, eventually you will get physical phenomena. But that is not the purpose of Spiritualism—to have physical phenomena. The purpose is to prove the continuity of life, therefore giving people hope and proving that life goes on.

TJL: What about the philosophy of Spiritualism?

RSB: Our basic philosophy is the nine principles. That is basically our philosophy. As free thinkers, we are able to believe in our own belief system as long as we believe in those nine principles.

TJL: Spiritualists say that they have no real dogma, but wouldn't the nine principles be considered "dogma"?

RSB: I suppose it could be interpreted as being dogmatic, but they are very general. Actually to me they are not rules or regulations, they're beliefs actually in Natural Law and basic right living. You could be of any dogma, creed or religious background and it would not conflict with those principles. I don't think any belief system could conflict with those principles, unless you were a fundamentalist Christian, then you might have problems with the one where the doorway to reformation is never closed to any spirit here or in the hereafter. In other words, there is always hope for the restoration of that soul to right living here or hereafter.

TJL: What differentiates Spiritualism from Christianity? What are some of the main differences?

RSB: Well, first of all, we do not believe in vicarious atonement—the fact that Jesus, the Christ, did die (the politicians killed him) does not absolve us of any responsibility for our own actions. We do not believe that the only way into the light of God is through Jesus, the teacher. We believe all souls continue to progress no matter whether they are on earth or in spirit, and whether they believe in Jesus the teacher's philosophy, or not. Now, there are some Christian Spiritualists, but to me that is a contradiction of terms because it clearly states that we do not believe in vicarious atonement and that Jesus was the only son of God; we believe that we are all sons and daughters of God. He was a soul that had mastered life, in other words, he was simply one who has reached the stage and progression of mastership.

TJL: Do Spiritualists believe in and perform baptisms?

RSB: We do christenings of children sometimes, and even adults sometimes, dedicating them to Infinite Intelligence, and to right work. But not in the sense that they are being baptized to wash away their sins, since we do not believe in sins, what would be the point?

TJL: Do Spiritualists believe in original sin?

RSB: Absolutely not. At least this Spiritualist doesn't. In general, no they do not because that leads one to believe that you come in tainted before you even get started. Well, we know that we are human, and if you believe in original sin, you believe you were tainted by Adam and Eve, which to us is just a metaphor for the beginning of life on earth. It really wasn't one man and one woman…and them eating the apple of wisdom, and being removed from the Garden of Eden, and the serpent and so forth, is just a story to express our state of un-enlightenment. It isn't factual.

TJL: How do Spiritualists regard the Christian belief in the physical resurrection of Jesus Christ?

RSB: Well, we believe that he came back as spirit as all of us can. He may have materialized, which I think he did, as a full materialization. They did see him and there were many reports of him being seen, but that is true of any of us. I have seen full materializations of humans and the fact that they called it "resurrected," I believe he continued as we all do, in or out of the body. Occasionally, when spirit wants to appear to someone, they will materialize through mediumship, into the physical. This is what I believe was meant by the resurrection.

TJL: In your own mediumship work, do you use the Holy Bible or another sacred text?

RSB: I use all sacred texts, not just the Holy Bible. Of course, I was raised in North America and Christianity is the predominant religion. I love the stories of the Bible. I think there are good rules for right living, at least some of them in there. But we believe it was written by man. Perhaps inspired in part by God, but it is not the absolute word of God. And plus, it has been through so many translations and I suppose that so much of it has been lost, misconstrued, or translated wrongly or differently. It's also in my opinion that it has been edited and twisted a little bit to suit the needs of the patriarchs and the ones in charge at that time.

TJL: What is the difference between the Christian Christ and the historical Jesus?

RSB: Well, Christ was not his last name. Christians mistakenly, in my opinion call him "Jesus Christ," thinking that is part of his name. If you ask most Christians what that word [Christ] means, they usually tell you that it is his name. What has happened is the "Christed" state is when one reaches a state of perfection. The Christ Spirit is when you have attained the ultimate of human life; you are in a "Christed" state. I think that the historical Jesus actually lived, and most Spiritualists do. We never argue the fact that he existed and was a great prophet and that he was a master-teacher and had attained that "Christed" state…but I still think that he was human. I don't think that we are getting the full picture of how he really lived. Being in the human state, he may well have been married, and may have well lived a human life like we all do, even traveling and learning other religious traditions.

TJL: What is meant by "principle before personality"?

RSB: That is a saying that a lot of people use that is part of the "detachment." The ultimate lesson that all masters teach is the lesson of detachment from the physical and detachment from the emotional. Putting principle before personality is just being able to detach, which I don't think any of us do to perfection because we are human. But in our work, we must always put principle before personality. I may not care for your personality or for your actions, but the fact that who you are and what you are has to come first.

TJL: Are there any other differences between Spiritualism and mainstream Christianity that you would like to add?

RSB: Just that we are free thinkers. We don't—and this sounds rather self-serving—but I don't think we are as judgmental. You see, moral living is hoped to be obtained by all of us, but what is right for me may not be right for you. As long as I'm not hurting anyone, it is not my right or your right to judge each other. What I consider to be moral you may not, but of course, morals differ from culture to culture, country to country and generation to generation. We, as Spiritualists, do not have a set of rules; of course, abiding by Natural Law…and the Ten Commandments are good rules to live by, but a lot of religions go to places, that in my opinion, they don't belong—you shouldn't drink coffee, you shouldn't do this, you shouldn't do that—they get into rule making and that's where I have the freedom as a Spiritualist. Now, I must abide by the laws that I am living in, and I must strive for a high moral character, but what that means to people varies from person to person. A good thing, above all, is do no harm, in my opinion.

TJL: How does the notion of "Divine Order" affect how people live their lives?

RSB: I do believe that there is a Divine Order and a Divine Plan, but that does not take away our freedom of choice and our freewill. Otherwise, we would just be robots. I do believe that all is in Divine Order until we, with our freewill and free choice, change that. And if it is divine it must be of the highest and the best. Where I get into trouble is when I step in and insert my own will and freewill. But it is not always wrong. I am not saying that. As we evolve, hopefully our choices and our freewill lead to a higher level. I make mistakes.

TJL: But isn't that a part of Divine Order also?

RSB: Of course, how else would I learn? I do not believe that God tests us. I do not believe that God punishes us. I think we do quite a fine job of that for ourselves. But, I think things happen in Divine Order because I was supposed to learn for some reason. Of course, some of this is very mysterious to me because I don't know what Divine Order is all of the time.

TJL: What are some of the tenets of the Spiritualist movement—not dogma—but some of the other beliefs that you haven't commented upon yet?

RSB: They are not really written. I can't speak as a Spiritualist, I can only speak for myself because we don't have dogma and we don't have a set order of beliefs. I am free to believe and think as I will. There are certain beliefs that tend to be quite common amongst us. For instance, a lot of us believe in reincarnation that we live over and over again, striving to attain progress and to progress into the light of God when we reach the state of perfection or mastership. But then there are Spiritualists who do not believe that, and that we live one life only.

TJL: Do you think that the early Spiritualists, more than today, tended to have that belief based on the Christian influence many had at that time?

RSB: Of course. It wasn't until the Eastern philosophies began to be more widely accepted among us.

TJL: So, with that said, do you consider Spiritualism to be an evolving religion?

RSB: I think so, but with the main premise being to prove through mediumship the continuity of life. Of course, if you hope to evolve you are going to search. We are "chelas," the Sanskrit word for "seekers."

TJL: What is the general interpretation by Spiritualists of the term "New Age" and how do Spiritualists feel about being put into this category by mainstream religions?

RSB: We kind of laugh at that because I think New Age is a catchall phrase for anything that is not mainstream. We like to think that we are "Old Age" because mediumship has been demonstrated since the beginning of the history of humans. They have always sought contact with spirit until organized religion taught them that that was wrong and they shouldn't do that—or some of the mainstream religions taught them that—at least in this country, that they should not contact spirit.

TJL: How accepted do you think Spiritualism is by mainstream religions? Does it depend upon the denomination?

RSB: I don't think that we are very much accepted by mainstream Christianity, but there are individuals, for instance, we have Catholic nuns who come to [our Spiritualist] camp on retreat. Of course, they are always in civilian clothes; they don't advertise who they are. We have Tibetan monks that come to Spiritualist camp. We have one ordained Methodist minister who is also an ordained medium, but that is an exception. There are people from all religions to see the

Spiritualists. Most of them are curiosity seekers. Some of them, though, are seriously seeking because maybe something is missing from their own religion. If you ask mainstream, especially clergy, they are going to tell you to stay away from Spiritualists.

TJL: Why do you think that is? Is it a lack of understanding on their part or…?

RSB: I can't speak for them, but I think it is largely because people fear what they don't understand. They have been taught to fear. You most often hear it referred to as "consorting with spirit." They will pray to the spirits of the father, and Son, and Holy Spirit, and they will accept the spirit, even the Catholics talk about the communion of saints and the other world. They are talking about spirit. For some reason it is OK to talk to martyred or anointed or sanctified spirits, but it is not Ok to talk to your mother or grandmother. I think mostly it is fear and a lack of understanding. Ignorance breeds fear. They love to quote from the Bible that you are not supposed to seek out mediums and fortunetellers. We are not fortunetellers; we are prophets and mediums. But there is something that draws them to us. They slip and seek us out. Maybe it is curiosity, I don't know. We welcome them…anyone who is interested or seeking…we are not going to turn them away or judge them, or even ask them what religion they are. It is none of our business.

TJL: Critics of Spiritualism maintain that the continuity of life has not been proven scientifically and that it is all a bunch of poppycock. How do Spiritualist mediums respond to those types of accusations? And as you well know, there are a lot of fraudulent occurrences in this type of work…

RSB: Anytime you have the real thing, you are going to have imitators. I don't respond, usually, we do not evangelize—I don't want to seem harsh—but it doesn't matter to me whether people believe it or not. I see what I see; I hear what I hear. I know what I know. Spirit has proven their existence to me, beyond a shadow of a doubt, over and over and over. My job as a medium is simply to give people what spirit gives me, and if they can accept that, that's wonderful; and if they can't then they should leave it there. I don't worry about whether they believe or not. I've never ever tried to convert anyone. And any medium worth his salt or her salt is not going to try to convert you anyway. Convert you to what? So, it doesn't really matter to me. I don't defend and I don't try to make people to believe my way. It is there if they want it, great, and if they don't, that's their choice.

TJL: Then why do you suppose that of the three American-made religions, that Mormonism and Christian Science have really succeeded, and Spiritualism has not...is it because they evangelized?

RSB: Yes, they evangelized and they advertised. And that is fine.

TJL: Also, do you think that another reason, in part, could be because those two religions had personalities in which the religions were formed around, and Spiritualism didn't have a recognizable personality like that?

RSB: Well, to me that is the difference between a religion and a cult. A cult is based on a personality and a religion is based on a philosophy, and we certainly are not based on a personality. Although there have been, like the Fox sisters and other mediums, well-known ones, we have never had a primary personality that you could say "here is the founder of Spiritualism or here is the founding father." However, I don't think that Christian Science is holding up too well. They are like all American churches, I may be wrong but, they are seeing a decline in membership. I do think that organized religion has fallen to the wayside and contrary to popular belief; I think we have outgrown it. I know that some people say we have fallen into a state of moral decay, but I simply think that a lot of people are going out and are seeking on their own and have outgrown it. It works for some people, but for others it doesn't work anymore.

TJL: Could you describe a typical Spiritualist church service?

RSB: There is usually a lecture...

TJL: Based upon a sacred text or scripture?

RSB: No. That's a sermon and those are rather rare in Spiritualist churches; they usually have a lecture which is not based on scripture or holy writings, but is informative like a lecture should be. Then there is usually a demonstration by two to three mediums of their mediumship, whether it is trance or clairvoyance, where they give messages from the spirit world.

TJL: In you r Spiritualist community, what are some of the types of mediumship demonstrations that are done in the church services?

RSB: Clairvoyance, which is the ability to see clearly. You actually stand between the two worlds and act as the medium. A medium is simply someone whose body, mind and spirit is sensitive to the world of spirit. She or he may use different tools to demonstrate that, like flame messages, or flower messages, or spirit art…

TJL: And that is where the medium draws what?

RSB: The medium draws a picture of the spirit that is around you. Flowers are when he or she brings a bouquet of flowers and spirit tells them which flower to give to whom and the message to give with it. Flame messages are when spirit precipitates a picture or a symbol on a piece of paper and tells you what the message is to give with the picture. Trance, which is the easiest and purer form, is where the medium goes into a trance and allows spirit to speak through him or her.

TJL: What is "cabinet" work?

RSB: This is when the medium sits in the cabinet to give messages.

TJL: Why is it important to sit in a cabinet?

RSB: It holds the energy in. It makes it easier on the medium. But they are getting away from it. They don't do it much anymore. They don't need the cabinets; they can go into trance without it. I think this sort of work is easier now because the vibration of the world is different. This is my opinion only—you are finding more and more of the younger mediums working in the light, instead of working in the dark and in the cabinet. It is easier to work now than it used to be. The New Age people call it "channeling." It is not the same, however, in my understanding. There is a tendency now for Spiritualism, rather than it being something that people sought out when they wanted to contact a loved one that had passed away, I think nowadays people are seeking out Spiritualism…we have to be more things to more people now; I think they expect the religious part of Spiritualism more. Than used to, they would just simply come in to see the demonstration or to have a reading, or go to a séance, and now I think they want a worship service, information, instruction. I find our job is becoming broader, and I do find being accepted into the ministry of our community more readily as far as doing church services, and weddings and funerals, and so forth. I think more and more people are finding that Spiritualism is not something you do as a lark, or go to a séance to talk to dead people, but seeking it out to be their religion and their philosophy—not just an adventure like so many people did during the last century.

TJL: It seems to me that the people in the last century were very concerned with the "science" part of Spiritualism. It is almost a non-issue today, isn't it?

RSB: You see, we don't find it necessary, and not because I accept it on blind faith, because I don't, but I don't worry about proving my religion in a scientific way. I have just seen phenomena and I have seen it happen and I know what I see and I know what I hear and I know what I smell, and I don't find it necessary to prove it. It seems that, in order for it to be accepted in the last century, that they prove that scientific part of it.

TJL: Hasn't it gotten a lot easier to scientifically prove, considering that one can have a photo of their aura taken, and one can't see microwaves, but we know they are there?

RSB: I think that maybe science is finally catching up with us. We don't set ourselves up to be tested anymore as much as the old mediums did. That was not unusual at all for a poor thing to subject herself to betide up or stripped naked, to prove that what she was doing was real. Well, the American public is sophisticated enough now that they are going to pretty well know if what you are doing is genuine or fraudulent. I don't find it—and I don't mean to be rude—necessary to be tied up or stripped naked to prove my mediumship. If you believe what you see, fine; if you don't fine. I just don't—maybe I'm not dedicated enough to Spiritualism, but I just don't find that necessary.

TJL: What about those who do precipitate fraudulent acts in the name of spirit?

RSB: Maybe they are teaching discernment. It doesn't excuse them for doing it, but any time you have the real thing, you are going to have imposters. I would certainly not do anything to perpetuate that practice, nor would I participate in that practice, but if you have a scam committed on you or a con artist gets hold of you, maybe you had better stay away from it until you can discern the difference. I know that sounds cold-hearted. But if you are that easily duped.... They [imposters] had to have something to imitate; their imitations must be based on some real phenomena, in my opinion. Take what you need and leave the rest of it there, but don't throw the baby out with the bathwater because you get a bad apple, it doesn't mean they are all bad. You have got to use your own discernment. That is sad you have to do that and I am always embarrassed if there is an imposter, but I am not the medium police.

If you go to a medium, number one, make sure you know what is happening before you react too quickly—that this one is not genuine or that the gift is not genuine—do your homework and make sure you know what you are hearing and what you are looking at. Keep an open mind but use your discernment. If you run across one that is not in close touch with spirit, or not in touch with spirit at all, don't go back.

Spirit doesn't care who they use. That is one thing that throws people off. They think a medium has to be someone above reproach and the he or she is perfect and wonderful, and one step below the master. That is not true. Spirit will use anybody that says "I am open, here I am, use me." And people think well that couldn't mean anything coming out of him or her because he or she is too human. Well, God knows we are human. If they waited for the vessel to be perfect, then nobody would be used—at least not on the earth plane—that I know of.

I approach Spiritualism as a personal religion more than that of a science. It's my religion; it's my church. I know that sounds odd because I have said we have no dogma and we have no creed, but those nine principles all that I really need. Maybe I do approach it too emotionally. Maybe I don't detach enough from it. Scientifically and philosophically, the main thing I love about Spiritualism is that I am allowed to believe what I want to believe. I have never had that freedom before—I have been Protestant, I have been Catholic, I have been agnostic, and I have never had freedom, and not been judged or threatened by the belief system itself: "If you don't believe this then you are going to do this." The idea that: "You are going to pay!" I don't have this in Spiritualism. It is a comfort zone for me, which don't you think that is what we seek in a religion—comfort and hope. It has proven the continuity of life to me, so I have hope. The spiritual healing, which is an intricate part of our religion—and I have been the personal recipient of that over and over and over through my life—so I have the healing, the hope, the comfort. Maybe I am too simplistic, maybe I should delve more into the scientific and philosophical areas of my religion, but to me…you know when something just feels right? And I didn't accept it unquestioningly. I didn't just follow like a little sheep. In fact, I had been going to camp and been around Spiritualists for three or four years before I even became a member. And if I want to talk to Buddha, I can talk to Buddha.

We believe that there is truth in all religions. And basically all religions teach the same things about right living: "Do unto others as you would have them do unto you." That's in every religion. I love the Native American connection with nature. After all, that is God too. When I was sick, I found myself dancing to East Indian music in front of my little altar raising the vibration of my body, and getting well, you know. And I can use the truths that are true for me from any religion, and it is accepted. I won't ask you believe it or use it, but to me it is real.

I have a problem when mainstream religion categorically renounces other traditions or belief systems because it shuts down independent thinking or independent opinions. My father, and even my mother, always taught me to investigate and to form my own opinions. I was given freedom of thought. I just have a problem when I am told that I must believe something or else…or else what? I am going to burn in hell and all that is doing is instilling fear, and my God doesn't sentence people to burn in eternal fire. We would never sentence our own beloved children, no matter what my daughter did—even if she were an ax murderess—I would never sentence her to burn in a fire. I might not approve of her actions, but she would still be my daughter, and I would still love her and care for her, and do the very best I could for her. Well, if I could love my earthly child like that, how much must God love me? I can't imagine. I don't believe in a God that would sentence you to a fiery pit for an eternity.

TJL: So, your idea of Heaven and Hell are not locations but conditions?

RSB: Yes, states of consciousness. I have created dandy hells for myself on earth and now I am concentrating on creating a heaven. This is heaven to me; this is beautiful. I am free.

TJL: Thank you Reverend Brown for this interview.

APPENDIX H

Personal Interview with Rev. John Lilec, Spiritualist Medium

[Monday, July 29, 2002, at Ball State University, Muncie, Indiana]

TJL: I am interviewing Rev. John Lilec from Ohio who will be commenting upon his experiences as a Spiritualist and mediumship. First, before becoming a Spiritualist, did you have any other religious affiliation?

RJL:…Russian Orthodox, Roman Catholic, Southern Baptist…garden salad variety.

TJL: What religious tradition were you basically raised in?

RJL: Russian Orthodox.

TJL: What first prompted you to pursue Spiritualism?

RJL: it just happened…life leads you in that direction. I can't precisely pinpoint it. It is a series of events, pieces of a puzzle that must fall into place before one recognizes what's true, knowing where we belong.

TJL: Did you have any opposition from family?

RJL: For me, being an Aries, it just doesn't matter. But, [to answer your question] yes, I did. Especially with a cousin who is a Pentecostal minister, a sister whose husband is a Southern Baptist minister…[sarcastically] we had the best of times, let me tell you.

TJL: How were you able to deal with their not accepting your religion…by talking with them, or were they unwilling even to talk about it?

RJL: I tried to talk with them, asking intelligent questions referring to fundamental beliefs, usually they were arguments though, so I casually just said "goodbye." Nothing spectacular

TJL: How long have you been a Spiritualist?

RJL: To be honest, I believe I have been a Spiritualist all of my life. A searcher.

TJL: Perhaps what I mean is when did you become affiliated with Spiritualism as a religion?

RJL: Let's see, I was led in that direction, but there really wasn't really any Spiritualism in Cleveland, or Sandusky [Ohio], where things happened. I was led to Rev. Ann Heart through a series of events. She had a church, or attended a church, under the direction of Rev. Tingley in Toledo, Ohio. But many events led me to Ann—phenomena, the metaphysical and the physical, the master-teacher that appeared to me in broad daylight. From one end of the city to the other, you're driving, and you hit every green light. I'd pass this individual and you don't recognize him—a man in a long robe with long hair and a beard, a very peaceful demeanor about him. The walk, the look, everything…by the time I arrived at the restaurant, pull up, there he is manifesting again. In broad daylight with 50 other witnesses who witnessed this. I studied their faces and many were kind of unsure. There were a few skeptics. It was like I was taking a poll, mentally, scanning everything. At the same time, I find out later, Ann Heart had received and had that vision, too. Ann, with direct voice and in a séance with Rev. James Tingley, that spirit revealed himself as Master Nathan, revealing the date. And I asked this master-teacher point blank about the gifts of materialization; he appeared in broad daylight, and if I was his instrument, where as a newcomer, did that mean that perhaps I possessed the gift of daylight materialization, but had to uphold it. The odds are a million to one they will tell you. It requires the strictest discipline to that path. Many other events happened. The first time of sitting with physical phenomena, about 7 or 8 different manifestations all happened in one evening. There was a collage of spirit.

TJL: Can you give some more detail about that?

Personal Interview with Rev. John Lilec, Spiritualist Medium

RJL: Let me begin where it began with me losing a job in Sandusky, Ohio. I was working in a factory, and having to live in a car because I was too proud to go back to Cleveland for help, financially. Praying and having my whole life open up, being planned as far as going into business, the tools, and the investment everything. And what I'd do was opening up the power of visualization, unknowing what it was to Spiritualism.

TJL: You naturally, through a succession of events, came upon this technique on your own?

RJL: Yes, I would see the job and the tools, the amount of time involved, and this had become a daily exercise. Each day planning more and more challenges that was more complicated. Then that's what happened with Spiritualism where I sat for class with Rev. Heart. This was about 1986, and before that I can tell you about one instance, where I was sitting in my own apartment and all of a sudden with the television on, I felt like I was in a dead, deep trance. The deepest trance I have ever been in, but conscious, which was strange. It was like I was a sleep, but in a room, a totally dark room. And at the same time seeing all of these lights coming at me; I was in a chair, by myself, with millions of lights coming at me…one by one. We are told that our brain power uses only 3 or 4%, but I felt like an absorbent sponge taking in 80 or 90% of this…it was like in hyper-drive, and I was just a disk and all of this was being downloaded. Simultaneously, this still small voice telling me not to worry that I will be able to understand all of this when the time is right. This went on for about an hour and a half. After I came out of it, people were banging on the door, calling on the telephone, the television going, completely unaware of any of it. So then when I talked to Ann about Spiritualism—I knew Ann, but not as a Spiritualist, just as a friend—she started to teach me but I was a real hard case student for her. When she would describe or give me a statement on something—ectoplasm—I would have another terminology and I would it in the form of a parable, another scripture from the other side of the wall. All of this drove this poor woman crazy. I just kept going and going.

We sat for the first time, in her kitchen, it was partially lit from the neighbors light next door, and on the wall there were about 25 to 30 ectoplasmic blobs—a lot of people may not understand what they are, but in zymology it represents power; a power of the physical, representative of the spirit doctors. Six inch by six inch by six inch, a cube actually, light blue in color, with a white dot, bouncing around slowly and the whole box would go across the room, from right to left, very slowly. The eye of the hurricanes, or the Indian symbol of the high master…where these little fire, orange in color, swirl clockwise, and they 14-16 inches in diameter, each one. And these were symbolic of the power that was there. A silhouette of a trumpet, not the actual trumpet, a person, a spirit really dressed in white light, came out of the floor up to the lower torso and looked right up at both of us. A master-teacher, a man with a turban with a beautiful jewel, was where the wall and the ceiling meet; it turned out to be Master Omar, looking down, straight at us.

TJL: So, he manifested during this time with the others. Was it a full body manifestation?

RJL: No, it was just the head, but fully formed. Then on that evening, too, it looked like a fireball, but it was all done in white with the flames going out of the backside. It looked like a comet. Right away we knew exactly who that was. It was our founder [of the Universal Spiritualist Association], the man that came in and left on Haley's, the brilliant teacher, Clifford Bias.

TJL: Did you know The Reverend Clifford Bias personally?

RJL: Not personally on the earth plane, but through the séance room, yes. He has visited our circle many times.

TJL: You have affectionately referred to The Reverend Tingley several times. Was he a mentor to you?

RJL: Oh, yes. Rev. Ann Heart told me that the best I would ever see in this whole entire lifetime of physical mediumship would be from Rev. Tingley and boy was she right. I have seen the gifts of trumpet—multi-voice trumpets, and if that wasn't enough, trumpet in the red light, trumpet in the white light, in regular light attached to solar plexus', apports, materializations…

TJL: How do you define an "apport"?

RJL: The materialization of objects from one location to another. They could be objects that have long been in the earth for centuries, like Indian arrowheads or jewelry.

TJL: Have you had any experience with apports?

RJL: Yes, when I walked up the stairs from the séance room, where I was sitting as a student, coming up the stairs and all the lights were on at Rev. Tingley's house, and right behind me and in front of me, I could hear these popping noises and they were apports following right into the light. And they were just pop, pop, pop and everyone was just following and picking these things up.

TJL: What type of objects were they?

RJL: They looked liked diamonds, rubies, garnets, precious and semi-precious.

TJL: Now, did these things stay in the physical and people could take those as souvenirs with them?

RJL: Yes, they can use them as souvenirs and also they would tell them that they are meant for the energies drawn and as healing stones for themselves; if anything, a souvenir of that event. I have herd many stories now of different apport mediums and a lot of charlatanism, but I have seen the apport delivered two different ways now; right in through, passing through the medium's solar plexus, before it must reach that individual or location. And so it's difficult to try to explain to people how this works, but we understand the science—that's the beauty of it.

But I have seen another instance when I was in séance with Rev. Tingley, and we got a red light right over him and he was in trance, at an angle where I could see him but the sitters couldn't. We had about 17 or 20 people in there. All of a sudden, I saw a man's hand throw these objects out into the audience, out into the sitting room. But Rev. Tingley, both of his hands, and being a scientist and trained to study every little detail, I realized his arms were right on the table. So I went to a private séance and asked the spirit doctor, Dr. Taylor, without being doubtful or pessimistic, and trying to be respectful at the same time—Dr. Taylor knew that I was edging to the words and he just said, "Well, that was Dee Dee Ho." And it was, a bitter man that projected right out of Rev. Tingley, actually throwing these objects. I had never seen this before. I always thought they were delivered through a trumpet.

TJL: So, getting back to an earlier question I asked, when would you say you became a Spiritualist?

RJL: Probably 1986, officially, but I think it started as early as 1980 because of my way of living. There were many aspects that helped to bring me to that way of life, like the independence and the ability to go to different places and to adapt. I was always a free spirit. I think the Navy had a lot to do with that as far as the different locations; I would plot in the back of my mind, if I went AWOL here in Spain, or Athens, Greece, could I survive by learning the language. So, I believe that is kind of like a Spiritualist seeking like an initiation itself, like a master.

TJL: When and where were you ordained?

RJL: I was ordained in 1992, in the First Spiritualist Church of Toledo, Ohio. And by sanction, in I believe July of 1992, at the Universal Spiritualist Association at Maple Grove [Anderson, Indiana].

TJL: When did you become a certified medium?

RJL: I had practiced…that is kind of hard to say. Probably the late 80's.

TJL: At what age were you aware of your mediumistic gifts?

RJL: I remember the sensitivity. I remember never being able to walk the walk of society or to talk the talk. I was always open to a different direction.

TJL: What was your first experience with mediumship?

RJL: Rev. Fred Felix met through me, back when I was a little child in Cleveland. And I was told this later on, having talks with him later on that I was predestined to go to Toledo and to study.

TJL: What would you say was the most fantastic experience, in a positive way, in mediumship?

RJL: I believe the turning point was where I sat in séance and heard Rev. Tingley's direct voice, apport, materialization, healings, master-teacher séances; there are like four different types of séances. I believe the most memorable was when I was in a séance with just a few sitters, his health was still fairly good yet, and my father came out of the cabinet and Mabel Riffle attending the cabinet called me over, and I stood near the cabinet and she told me where to stand, and all of a sudden out of the cabinet walked the spirit of my father, fully formed with a light-bluish ectoplasm. We looked at each other, eyeball to eyeball, and he looked a little bit younger but I certainly could tell that it was my father. There was no more stress or pain that he had in the physical; you could see that he was rejuvenated in his eyes. We looked eyeball to eyeball and he reached out and we shook hands and I could feel that grip, a generally cool energy and it was like the last closing seen in *Ghost*. Where you break down and cry and say "Oh, my God, how great thou art!" This is beautiful. And you realize the practicality that you'd like to live in this part of the world. If you could freeze this second right now, you'd like to live it over and over or with new people, but you realize you are attached to the physical world but you have your proof, so you drop this big, heavy overcoat off yourself as you go through you life. After you experience something like that, you now realize that there are people through ego try to destroy this part of the religion by denying it. Many will try to cast doubt by telling you about charlatanism, but when you have seen for yourself, and you must not let no man or woman—anyone—take that away from you.

TJL: What was your most frightening experience?

RJL: I was told to follow my intuition and when I was [inaudible] I would have to claim it three times and at the third time, with all the lights on, with white walls, all of these tiny little black flecks of light, silvery black, were coming out of the carpet as negative energy. Anyway, it was coming toward me and I remembered what my teacher, Ann Heart, had told me about pulling up the right hand and visualizing intense white light going right towards where ever you want it to go. After doing this, I stood there and the black mass collected and sort of hovered, and this was about eight feet away from me, and this was huge, like seven feet tall. All of these dots, they were coming closer, they went half-way around the corner of the hallway of the apartment and then just dissipated like into another portal or another dimension. So, I realized that evil can come in many forms, just as good can come in lights, all the way to full formed shapes and masses. So I don't know if that was really frightening, scary, but as far as séances, I never really ever was frightened.

TJL: Do you use any divination tools in your work?

RJL: Nothing.

TJL: You are a healer. Could you explain a little bit about that?

RJL: I am drawn more to the holistic way, the natural way, using your hands and energy. I had noticed for many years that I am a person that could not sleep with my arms and legs crossed. There was always a jolt of energy. I had visualized and I would do little tests through the years, like offering Rev. Tingley healings. He was sitting in a chair and I would visualize, and I would call in my guides and I have some guides that are a little bit ornery like Tulip. I would visualize a lot of power, intense power, and I would have my chakras open, fully, with the electricity, the light blue shaft that goes right through you, and it so clear like you can see each other right here. It coursed through my right hand right down Rev. Tingley's crown, jolted down, shot down, through his body. He jumped out of his chair, and being a scientist, an ornery scientist, I asked him, "What did you see?" He said, "Where's the blue light…it jolted me out of this chair!" So, he taught me how to open up and use the third eye, so we could direct energy and actually move objects. So we had exercises with witnesses' years ago, in opening and closing doors from across the room. He had a kitchen door in this house, all of the doors and windows closed this door would open and close. Rev. Tingley would open it, and I would close it. We would get a kick out of watching television; you would see studies where people were just straining to bend that spoon, like they are in overdrive and any minute they are going to blow their eye out.

TJL: How do you personally connect with spirit when doing mediumship work like giving readings or doing a healing?

RJL: It is usually a prayer right there, feeling those present, one by one. Many Spiritualist churches and other organizations will tell you it is not necessary to know the identity of the spirit. I have always been a believer that you sit for an hour before, like for physical phenomena, in the morning and I call each and every name, and I tell students to call each and every name of their guides; you only have one joy guide, one Indian, one doctor. You may find yourself 25 or 30 guides and other specialists coming in and out to help you with your mediumship. But all in all, I would say I would call on an average of 75-100, especially during a séance, call upon all of the great doctors, like Dr. Salk. From what I understand, we have the main ingredient that we are told is for AIDS that Dr. Salk has given over a decade ago, but it can't fall into the hands of these greedy pharmacists that keep it only for the rich. If we could get it on paper, that they agree that if they gave the main ingredient the serum is derived from that they would make it available to the poor.

TJL: On a daily basis, what do you do as a general routine or ritual to connect with spirit?

RJL: I meditate in the morning, every morning, breathing exercises. No matter if it has been a terrible day, I do breathing at night also. Breathing in, and out, seven times. I also meditate in the evening and reflect about what the day has meant. I give thanks to God. Thank your spirits for another day of seeing you through it and for giving you the wisdom and the strength.

TJL: When giving messages, how do you receive them from spirit?

RJL: It is a combination of both clairvoyance and clairaudience. Sometimes Tulip, my joy guide, will whisper in my ear, but many times it will be in the voice of the spirit itself. I'll see them in my third eye. I always teach students that spirit doesn't train you, you must train your spirit guides to present the symbolism, to learn to simultaneously not just to receive but asking the questions mentally, too. It goes in a flash, and a lot of people think we need to speed up our vibration to make a connection; so, spirit has to slow down to make that connection. When we are going at snail's pace, it is very hard for an individual to keep that message flow going.

TJL: What are three most common reasons people come to see you as a medium?

RJL: Many times, a percentage of readings are prophecies before that have proven themselves or through others. I prefer serving in churches messaging, teaching, but I have taught many private groups outside of churches.

TJL: What was the most unusual request from a client during a reading?

RJL: Many times a client thinks you just turn on a switch for materialization or that you can do 17 or 20 readings accurately in a row. They don't realize that you are a human being and that just takes everything out of you. We can't guarantee that anything is going to happen; we don't know when phenomena are going to happen. We are thankful if we see a spirit light or get one impression. Many times people feel that if you attended classes then you are a master-medium.

TJL: How do you respond to harsh criticism by people who are out to debunk it?

RJL: Well, they haven't seen the truth. Like an imitation rose, whether it is out of velvet or plastic, it was modeled after an original in the first place. I would ask them questions about their own religion; I don't believe in arguing, but I'd like to present things and challenge their minds intelligently. We will always find criticism and we will always be knocked down, being accused of this and accused of that. But all you do is hold your head high and be dignified and realize you are a representative of that religion, but defend it. I will not roll over and be insulted.

TJL: How would you sum up your own mediumship in your own words?

RJL: I am thankful for what I have, and to be the best that I can be—not trying to sound like an Army commercial. We are striving for perfection, knowing full well that we will never achieve it [completely on the earth plane], but as long as we keep striving we are all that much closer to achieving it.

TJL: How would you some up Spiritualism in your own words?

RJL: Spiritualism is the most beautiful religion in the world. Perhaps it is the oldest religion in the world when that first connection was made. This is a religion where impressions are given, ideas, inventions and cures. Healing is as old as the ages and so is Spiritualism. It is a combination of the best that all religion has to offer. Isn't true when you study about all of the different religions, you are going past Christianity into Hindu, Buddhism, after all wasn't it all founded on similar ideas? If we dig deep enough we could present the common person where all religion was founded upon.

TJL: Is there any closing comment that you would like to make?

RJL: May God bless Spiritualism and all those people who make it happen and may find the wisdom before our time is over in helping to bring about new faces with new torches for the future. May Spiritualism never die, never cease, for this would be a sad, sad world if that were to happen.

TJL: Thank you, Rev Lilec; I really appreciate the time you have given me today.

APPENDIX I

Selected Versions of the "Declaration of Principles" as Used by Spiritualist Organizations throughout the United States and Great Britain

There are literally hundreds of Spiritualist societies and associations across North America, Europe, and Australia. The *National Spiritualist Association of Churches* (NSAC) is by far the largest such organization with affiliated churches and associations. The nine principles listed in the Declaration of Principles for the NSAC are the most widely used and accepted. There are, however, a number of Spiritualist offshoots that have based their principles loosely on those of the NSAC.

The original "Principles of Spiritualism" were channeled from the spirit world by Emma Hardinge Britten in 1871 from her friend and colleague, Robert Owen, a notable "free thinker", humanitarian, and philanthropist in England.

1. The Fatherhood of God

2. The Brotherhood of Man

3. The Communion of Spirits and the Ministry of Angels

4. The continuous existence of the human soul

5. Personal responsibility

6. Compensation and retribution hereafter for all the good and evil deeds done on earth

7. Eternal progress open to every human soul*

*These principles were later adopted by the Spiritualists' National Union (SNU), the recognized religious organization representing the religion of Spiritualism in Great Britain. (*Principles of Spiritualism*, by Lyn G. De Swarte, 5)

◆ ◆ ◆

"…in Great Britain there are many independent organizations, such as the Greater World Christian Spiritualist Association (GWCSA), formerly the League, started by Ms. Winifred Moyes on 30th May 1931, at the behest of her special Guide from the spirit world, known as Zodiac, who gave his first public address through her trance mediumship in August 1928." (*Principles of Spiritualism*, by Lyn G. De Swarte, 6)

1. I believe in one God who is Love;

2. I accept the Leadership of Jesus Christ;

3. I believe that God manifests through the Illimitable Power of the Holy Spirit;

4. I believe in the survival of the Human Soul and its individuality after physical death;

5. I believe in the Communion with God, and His Angelic Ministers and the souls functioning in conditions other than in life;

6. I believe that all forms of life created by God intermingle, and are interdependent and evolve until perfection is attained;

7. I believe in the perfect justice of Divine Laws governing all life;

8. I believe that sins committed can only be rectified by the sinner himself, or herself, through the redemptive power of Jesus Christ, by repentance and service to others;

9. I will, at times, endeavor to be guided in my thoughts, words and deeds by the teachings and example of Jesus Christ.*

*Many early Spiritualists had a difficult time with not placing Jesus in a prominent position within the movement. As these principles illustrate, some of these Christian-Spiritualists needed to have Jesus more prominently placed within the religion. This is likely due to the fact that many Christian Protestants and Catholics had pangs of guilt from being raised strictly within the Christian tradition, so a compromise suited their needs more—accepting the basic ideas of Spiritualism, but including aspects of Jesus' divinity and role as the Son of God, vicarious atonement, etc. that mainstream Spiritualism denied. The "free thinking" aspect of Spiritualism allowed these adjunct organizations to take root. All Spiritualists consider themselves to be non-conformists, which they are when compared to mainstream religion, but these spin-off groups are the true non-conformists as they rejected, in some way, the conformity of the nationally recognized organizations in both America and Great Britain.

◆ ◆ ◆

The *Indiana Association of Spiritualists*, the organization that runs the Spiritualist camp, Camp Chesterfield, as well as the other well-known Spiritualist camp in Florida, Cassadaga, operated by the *Southern Cassadaga Spiritualist Camp Meeting Association*, use the Declaration of Principles as outlined by the NSAC.

The *Universal Spiritualist Association*, founded by The Reverend Clifford Bias in 1956, was formed after a dispute occurred with the Indiana Association of Spiritualists. This organization adopted a set of precepts, a confession of faith and acts of faith very different from those of the NSAC:

The Precepts of Faith

1. The Lord is Almighty God.

2. Thou shalt worship the Lord thy God.

3. There is a natural world and there is a spiritual world.

4. Divine Law is holy, just, and good.

5. The gift of God to all people is eternal life.

6. Those in the natural world and those in the spiritual world can communicate, one with the other.

7. All humanity shall turn to righteousness and dwell in the house of the Lord forever.*

Profession of Faith

We Believe In the Creatorship of God, the oneness of all life everywhere, the leadership of The Christ, salvation by character, and the progression of humanity upward and onward forever.*
[These are taken from the official Universal Spiritualist Association's website (www. spiritualism.org).]

The Acts of Faith

1. We believe that God is Love, and Power, and Truth, and Light; that perfect justice rules the worlds; that all His sons shall one day reach His feet, however far they stray. We hold the Fatherhood of God, the brotherhood of man; we know that we do serve Him best when best we serve our brother man. So shall His blessing rest on us and peace evermore. Amen.

2. We place our trust in God, the holy and all glorious Trinity, who dwelleth in the Spirit of man.

We place our trust in Christ, the Lord of Love and wisdom, first among many brethren, who leadeth us to the glory of the Father, and is Himself the Way, the Truth, and the Life.

We place our trust in the Law of Good which rules the worlds; we strive towards the ancient narrow path that leads to life eternal; we know that we do serve our Master best when best we serve our brother man. So shall His blessing rest on us and peace forevermore. Amen.*

* This is taken from *The Liturgy and Ritual of the Universal Spiritualist Church* (revised edition) by Clifford Bias, published by the Universal Spiritualist Association (n.d.), p.5.

APPENDIX J

Professor Hare's Spiritual Telegraph

◆ ◆ ◆

Julia Schlesinger, "Robert Hare, M. D. Professor of Chemistry in the University of Pennsylvania, Graduate of Yale College and Harvard University, Associate of the Smithsonian Institute, and Member of Various Learned Societies." *The Carrier Dove* (Oakland), May 1886: 101-104.

◆ ◆ ◆

Professor Hare held an eminent position in the ranks of the scientists of America and Europe. His "Brief View of the Policy and Resources of the United States," was published in 1810, and was followed by more than a hundred publications from his pen, some of the political, moral, or financial nature, but mainly on the subject of chemistry and electricity. He was the inventor of several ingenious machines for use in scientific investigations, and when his attention was called to the—as he then thought—delusion of Spiritualism, he invented some very complete machines—two of which we give illustrations of—to demonstrate the fallacy of table rappings and turnings. Like many other scientists who have undertaken that task, he was hoisted "by his own petard," but, unlike many of his co-workers in the scientific field of labor, he was honest enough when thoroughly convinced of the Spiritual origin of the phenomena, to publicly avow his belief, and shared the usual fate of persons who run counter to the ordinary, popular current. Materialism is considered excusable in scientists, but let one avow his belief in Angelic communion with humanity and the dogs of denunciation and vituperation are let loose. In a letter published in July, 1853, Prof. Hare said: "I recommend to your attention, and that of others interested in his hallucination, Faraday's observations and experiments, recently published in some of our respectable newspapers. I entirely concur in the conclusions of that distinguished experimental expounder of nature's riddles." In his book entitled "Experimental Investigation of the Spirit Manifestations," published in 1855, from which we draw for this sketch, he frankly says, referring to that letter, "I allege it to be an exemplification of wise ignorance, which is about equivalent to folly. The wisest man, who speaks in ignorance, speaks foolishly to the ears of those who perceive his ignorance. The great mass of men of science appear in this light to Spiritualists when they argue against Spiritualism." Shortly after the publication of that letter, Prof. Hare was induced to sit at a private house where spirit rappings were produced; all his ingenious devices to account for the raps by mundane agencies failed to produce the expected result, and he soon learned there were many things in Heaven and earth heretofore "undreamed of in his philosophy."

His first investigations were with rapping mediums and he soon became satisfied as to the honesty of the worthy people, who were themselves under a deception if these sounds did not proceed from spiritual agency. Visiting another medium, in the company of a legal friend, he received communications from the tippings of a table which indicated the letters to form messages as the fingers were passed over an alphabet. When the medium's eyes were directed away from the alphabet his companion received the following communication: "Light is dawning on the mind of your friend; soon he will speak trumpet-tongued to the scientific world, and add a new link to that chain of evidence on which our hope of man's salvation is founded."

He invented a machine intended to demonstrate that the "manifestations attributed to spirits could be made without human agency. (See engraving of apparatus accompanying this: Sketch, A.) It will be readily seen that the tray upon which the medium's hands were laid, rests upon balls, making it impossible for the medium to move the table, or produce any action of the index upon the dial. Having this apparatus at the residence of a lady by whom it had been actuated on previous occasions, he says: "This lady sitting at the table as a medium, my sister reported herself. As a test question, I inquired 'What was the name of a partner in business of my father, who, when he left the city with the Americans during the Revolutionary War, came out with the British, and took care of the joint property?" The disk revolved successively to letters correctly indicating the name to be

Warren. I then inquired the name of the partner of my English grandfather, who died in London more than seventy years ago. The true name was given by the same process. The medium and all present were strangers to my family, and I had never heard either name mentioned, except by my father."

Possibly a case of mind reading, which is the wise explanation that has been given in connection with our slate writing experience published in the last number of this magazine. We live in a progressive age, and if the mind can revolve a disk, or write without human contact with the agents employed, we may yet develop its powers to a state wherein we can enjoy our *otium cum dignitate* in our easy chairs, and direct insensate matter to perform our manual labor. Why not? If it be true, as our Mind Cure friends assure us, that a fractured or dislocated limb can be restored to a sound condition by silent prayer.

Professor Hare's ingenious method of testing the power of the unseen intelligences is very interesting, affording conclusive evidence of an invisible power acting in response to his desires (See B in plate of illustrations of apparatus, which is similar to machines used by Professor [William] Crook[e]s in his investigations.) Referring to these trials he says: "My much-esteemed friend, Professor [Joseph] Henry, having treated this result as incredible, I was induced to repeat it with the greatest precision and precaution. A well-known medium was induced to plunge his hands, clasped together to the bottom of the cage, holding them perfectly still. As soon as these conditions were attained, the apparatus being untouched by anyone excepting the medium as described, I invoked the aid of my spirit friends. A downward force was repeatedly exerted upon the end of the board appended to the balance equal to three pounds' weight nearly. It will be perceived that in this manifestation, the medium had no means of communication with the board, besides the water. It was not until he became quite still that the invocation was made.

Nevertheless, he did not appear to be subjected to any reacting force. Yet, the distance of the hook of the balance from the fulcrum on which the board turned was six times as great as the cage in which the hands were situated. Consequently, [102] a force of 3 x 6 = 18 pounds must have been exerted. The board would probably have been depressed much more, but that the water had been spilled by any further inclination of the base.

"This experiment has since been repeated again and again, but on a smaller scale, when, not only the downward force was exercised, but the spelling of words was accomplished. On one occasion, when no result ensued, it appeared to arise from the water being so cold as to chill the medium, because on warming it up to a comfortable temperature, the desired manifestations were obtained."

A practical illustration of the necessity for proper conditions for the medium, or, that the mind needs warmth for the exercise of its powers. A "crumb of comfort" for those in doubt as to their final destination. Many of the experiments made by Professor Hare, through the agency of his dials, operated by different mediums, effectually expose the fallacy of the mind theory, so frequently advanced as a refutation of spiritual agency. Some of his interviews with Mrs. [Maria] Hayden—one of our first and best public mediums—are very conclusive on this point. He says: "While in Boston, having read to a friend a communication from my father through a writing-medium, I placed it in one of my pockets and proceeded to the Fountain Inn. When there, I felt for it without success. Unexpectedly I went to Salem by the cars, and returned the same evening. On undressing myself the scroll was missing, and I inferred that it had been lost between the place where it had been read and the inn above named, where I felt for it unsuccessfully. In going next morning to Mrs. Hayden's, and my spirit father reporting himself, I inquired whether he knew what had become of the scroll. It was answered that it had been left upon the seat in the car on my quitting it at Salem. Inquiring of the conductor, who was on duty in the car where it had been left, he said that it had been found on the seat, was safe at Portland, and should be returned to me the next day. This promise was realized.

On one occasion, sitting at the disk with Mrs. Hayden, a spirit gave his initials as C. H. Hare. Not recollecting any one of our relations of that name precisely, I inquired if he was one of them. The reply was affirmative. 'Are you a son of my cousin, Charles Hare, of St. Johns, New Brunswick?' 'Yes' was spelled out. This spirit then gave me the profession of his grandfather, also that of his father…. Subsequently, the brother of this spirit made us a visit in Philadelphia, and informed us that the mundane career of his brother, Charles Henry, had been terminated by shipwreck, some four years anterior to the visit made, as mentioned to me.

A spirit of the name of Powel tendered his services and undertook to spell Cato, but instead of that name, Blodget, my friend, occupied the disk, and spelt his own name, and afterward Cato. On the same occasion Blodget spelt out and designated words without the medium seeing the alphabet. The employment of letters to express ideas neither existing in the mind of the medium or in mine, cannot be explained by any psychological subterfuge."

Professor Hare became developed as a medium sufficiently to enable him to converse with his spirit friends, and says in this connection: "I am no longer under the necessity of defending media from the charge of falsehood and deception. It is now my own character only that can be in question." This being the condition the following test is only explicable by one of two theories: either Professor Hare—a man "Sans peur, san reproche"—was culpable or idiotic enough to make public a false statement, which, even if true, would only bring his good name and reputation into disrepute among his scientific associates; or, intelligent beings, outside of any human organization, exist and have to the power to communicate with mortals.

Being at the Atlantic hotel, Cape May, about one hundred and thirty miles distant from Philadelphia, on the third of July, 1855, at one o'clock, Prof. Hare requested his spirit sister to convey a message to Mrs. Gourlay, in Philadelphia, asking her to induce Dr. Gourlay to go to the Philadelphia Bank to ascertain the time when a note would be due, and to report to him at half-past three o'clock: she did report at the time appointed.

Prof. Hare states: "After my return to Philadelphia, being at the residence of Mrs. Gourlay, I inquired of her whether she had received any message from me during my absence. In reply, it was state that while a communication from her spirit mother was being made to her brother, who was present, my spirit messenger interrupted it to request her to send her husband to the bank to make the desired inquiry. Her husband and brother went to the bank in consequence. With the idea received by the latter, my sister's report coincided agreeably to his statement to me. All this proves that a spirit must have officiated, as nothing else can explain the transaction. The note-clerk recollects the application, but does not appear to have felt himself called upon to take the trouble to get the register, which was not in his hands at the time. Hence, the impression received by the applicants was not correct, but corresponded with the report made to me by my sister, which differed from the impression on my memory, and, of course, was not obtained from my mind.

Wishing to make this transaction a test, I was particularly careful to manage so that I might honorably insist on it as a test; and, until I learned the fact from Mrs. Gourlay and from the note-clerk, that the inquiry was made, it did not amount to a test manifestation. I submit these facts to the public, as proving that there must have been an invisible, intelligent being with whom I communicated at Cape Island, who bore my message to Mrs. Gourlay, so as to induce the application at the bank. Otherwise, what imaginable cause could have produced the result, especially within the time occupied of two and a half hours?

The existence of spirit agency being thus demonstrated, I am justified in solemnly calling on my contemporaries to give credence to the important information which I have received from spirits, respecting the destiny of the human soul after death. They may be assured that every other object of consideration sinks into insignificance in comparison with this information and the bearing it must have upon morals, religion, and politics, whenever it can be known and be believed by society in general, as it is by me."

Had Professor Hare—the man of scientific attainments which placed him in the front rank of scientists in Europe and America—published a monograph on the cerements of an unusual character, found on the body of a mummy, decayed and sanctified by the dust of three thousand years, he would have been accorded a hearing by his scientific dry-as-dust contemporaries, and his scientific treatment of the matter would have been lauded by them as evidence of his remarkable acumen and powers of scientific research.

Alas! The honorable man and renowned scientist had made a grand mistake, in the estimation of his compeers, in turning from his chemical investigations to the study of the evidences of immortal life, and all its unspeakable grandeur of progression. He cast his pearls before learned swine, and swinishly did they turn and rend him. His earnest appeals to his learned confreres to listen to the evidences of the immortality of the human spirit, which he had demonstrated through strictly scientific methods of investigation, was contemptuously thrust aside, and the wise men continued in the more congenial pursuits of watching the wonderful developments of nature in the transformation of tadpoles' tails and bugology.

Professor Hare gives the experience of many other investigators of the phenomena, as corroborative evidence to support [103] his own statements; among them that of [homeopathic] Dr. W[illiam] Geib [of Philadelphia], which we give to illustrate some of the wonderful phases of mediumship now being daily exercised in our midst. The medium referred to is Mrs. Ada Foye, of San Francisco.

Dr. Geib says: "Being subsequently in the city of New York, I visited the public circles of a medium for automatic writing and the sounds. Being requested, as the rest had been, but without response, to ask if any of my spirit friends were present, my interrogation was answered by three distinct raps upon the table. 'Now ask who it is: a father, mother and so on'; and I was informed it was a son. 'Is your sister with you?' 'Yes.' 'Will you spell his name?' 'Yes;' and it was correctly given. 'Is her little son with her?' 'Yes.' 'Will you spell his name?' 'Yes;' and a name of seventeen letters was correctly spelled out by the card, the letters being indicated, when pointed to, by three raps. My spirit son also informed me when he had died, and of what disease. It will be observed that my son's name had not been mentioned, reserving it for a test. Three raps had replied in the affirmative to my question, when the medium spasmodically seized a pencil, extended a sheet of paper toward me, and wrote upside down, so that I might read it as written: 'We are looking forward for you to join us, when we shall be more so;' and to my perfect delight and astonishment, signed my son's name to the communication, asking whether the name was correct.

On a subsequent occasion, when a large and respectable company was present, I remarked to the medium that she had reported the fact that foreign languages had been written by her hand. 'All kinds of language; but I don't know anything about them,' was the reply. 'If you have no objection, I should like to get a communication from my son, in a foreign language. 'Oh, not in the least; if he knew it in this world, he will know it in the next.' 'My son, will you give me a communication in a foreign language?' Answer, three raps. The company were all intent on this striking and convincing test of spiritual intercourse. 'In French?' 'No;' one rap. 'In Spanish?' Three raps. The medium's hand, as before, seized the pencil, and wrote upside down a communication in correct Spanish, though we all accepted her declaration that she was not acquainted with one word of the Spanish language."

We have presented some of Professor Hare's experiments with the phenomena of Spiritualism, and will close our sketch with some of the conclusions to which he arrived in consequence thereof.

Professor Hare says: "Confining the range of my philosophy to the laws of motion, magnificently illustrated by the innumerable solar systems, but no less operative in every minute mechanical movement, I hold that I could only come to the same conclusion as Faraday, that if tables when associated with human beings moved, it must in some way be due to those beings, since, agreeably to all experience of the laws of matter in the material world, inanimate bodies can not originate motion. But as when the planetary motions are considered, any hypothesis fails which does not account for the rationality of the result, and therefore involves the agency, not only of a powerful but a rational cause; so the manifestations of Spiritualism, involving both reason and power, might consistently justify me in looking for agents endowed with the reason and power manifested by the phenomena. This power being invisible and imponderable, and at the same time rational, there was no alternative but to consider it as spiritual, no less than that to which the planetary motion is due. In its potentiality the power thus manifested might be extremely minute as compared with the potentiality of the Creator, still it had to be of the same spiritual nature.

It has not appeared unreasonable to infer that the soul in assuming the spirit form should acquire a power of which material beings are destitute, and of which they can only conceive an idea from its necessity to the operations of God. Parting with its material attributes, were the soul not to acquire others, even if it could exist, it would be perfectly helpless. Hence, in becoming an immaterial spirit, it must acquire powers indispensible and appropriate to that state of existence."

Although Professor Hare's efforts to induce his scientific friends to investigate Spiritualism were met with contempt or indifference, his interest continued unabated and he continued his communions and investigations to the end of his earth life, deriving great comfort therefrom. Writing in 1858, he says: "Far from abating my confidence in the inferences respecting the agencies of the spirits of deceased mortals, in the manifestations of which I have given an account in my work, I have, within the last nine months, had more striking evidence of that agency than those given in the work in question."

Illustration of Apparatus Used by Prof. Hare

Description of the instrument by which spirits were enabled to move a table under the influence of mediumship, yet in no wise under the control of the medium employed, even clairvoyance being nullified. (A)

The table is about six feet in length, and sixteen inches in width, so contrived as to separate into three parts for convenience of carriage.

The pair of legs under the right side are upon castors. Those of the left side upon an axle, passing through perforations suitably made for its reception. The axle serves for two wheels of about six inches diameter, of which one is grooved. A disk, is secured upon a pivot, affixed to a strip of wood, which is made to slide between two other strips attached to the frame of the table just under the top board. By this means the band embraces both the hub of the disk and the wheel; when this turns in consequence of the shoving of the table horizontally along the floor, the disk turns with the wheel, and as much faster as the circumference of the groove in the hub, is less than that of the groove in the wheel.

Any mortal having due hold of the table, may, by shoving it one way or the other, bring any letter under the index, so as to spell out any desired word. But no person, sitting as the medium is in the engraving represented to sit, with the plate on two balls, can actuate the disk so as to spell out words. Utterly incapacitated from moving the table, it were manifestly impossible to actuate the disk, or to interfere with the movements otherwise imparted.

Description of Apparatus Illustrated, Marked B.

Representation of an experiment, in which the medium was prevented from having any other communication with the apparatus, actuated under his mediumship, excepting through water. Yet under these circumstances the spring balance indicated the exertion of a force equal to eighteen pounds.

A board is supported on a rod so as to make it serve as a fulcrum, as in a seesaw, excepting that the fulcrum is at the distance of only one foot from one end, while it is three feet from the other. This end is supported by a spring-balance which indicates pounds and ounces by a rotary index.

Upon the board, at about six inches from the fulcrum, there is a hold into which the knob of an inverted glass vase, nine inches in diameter, is inserted.

Upon two iron rods proceeding vertically from a board resting on the floor, so as to have one on each side of the vase, a cage of wire such as is used to defend food from flies, of about five inches diameter, is upheld (inverted) by the rod within the vase concentrically, so as to have between it and the sides of the vase an interstice of an inch nearly, and an interval of an inch and a half between it and the bottom of the vase.

The vase being filled with water until within an inch of the brim, the medium's hands were introduced into the cage and thus secured from touching the vase.

These arrangements being made, the spirits were invoked to show their power, when repeatedly the spring-balance indicated an augmentation of weight equal to three pounds. The relative distances of the vase and balance from the fulcrum being a 6 to 36, the force exerted must have been $3 \times 6 = 18$ pounds; yet the medium did not appear to be subjected to any reaction, and declared that he experienced none.

It was on stating this result to the Association for the Advancement of Science, that I met with the same reception as the King of Ava gave to the Dutch Ambassador, who alleged water to be at times solidified in his country, by cold, so as to be walked upon.

The belief in spiritual agency was treated as a mental disease, with which I, of course, had been infected; those who made this charge being perfectly unconscious that their education has associated morbid incredulity with bigoted and fanatical credence.

Although Prof. Hare mentions the receipt of communications through the instrumentality of apparatus B, he fails to give the method of obtaining them, which was probably by the substitution of an alphabetical dial and index in place of the spring-balance, as shown in the illustration.

(Retrieved from http://www.spirithistory.com/hare.html on October 6, 2002.)

Appendix K

Spirit Manifestations of the Bible

From Genesis to Revelation, the nearness of the spirit world, and the inter-communication of spirits and mortals runs like a golden strand.

Not only spirit communion, but every phase of manifestations distinctively known as Modern Spiritualism, is represented on many occasions, often hundreds of years apart. This similarity of expression shows that the same psychic laws held then as now, and there has been no change. Spiritualism furnishes the key whereby the mysteries of the Bible and its miracles are explained with a clearness commentators have not been able to attain for want of knowledge it furnishes. Though angels are understood to be special creations, and spirits to have ascended through mortal bodies, the words are used by the writers of the Bible as interchangeable as shown by the following passages:

"Yea, while I was speaking in prayer, even the man, Gabriel, whom I had seen in the vision." Dan. IX-21. He previously says that this spirit "stood before me as the appearance of a man.: Chapter VIII-15, "He maketh his angels spirits," Psalms, CIV-4, Luke places departed spirits on a level with angels, XX-36: "Neither can they die any more, for they are equal unto the angels," etc.

The terms are indiscriminately used: "And as Peter knocked at the gate, a damsel came to harken—then said they it is his angel" (spirit). Acts XII-13, 15: "I am he that liveth and was dead, and behold I am alive forever more." Rev. I-18: The soul of a man separated from his body. Matt. XIV-26; Luke XXIV-37.

Spiritual Body

There is a natural body and a spiritual body." I Cor. XV-44.

Physical Manifestations

The angel unloosed Peter from chains in prison: —"When they were past the first and second ward, they came to the iron gate that leadeth into the city, which opened to them of its own accord, and they went out." Acts XII-7-10.

"And when they came unto Lehi, the Philistines shouted against him, and the spirit of the Lord came mightily upon him, and the cords that were upon his arms became as flax that was burnt with fire, and his hands loosed from off his hands." Jud. XV-14. A fine physical manifestation is recorded in Ex. XIV-25, where the Lord "Took off the chariot wheels" of the Egyptians. An angel went before them in a cloud. Ex. XIV-19. The moving of a table now, is paralleled by an angel rolling back the stone from the door of the sepulcher. Matt. XXVIII-2.

Inspiration and Mediumship

"For to one is given by spirit the word of wisdom; to another the word of knowledge by the same spirit." I Cor. XII-8. "And the spirit entered into me when he spake unto me, and set me upon my feet, that I heard him that spake unto me." Ezek. II-2. "To whom has thou uttered words, and whose spirit came from thee?" Job XXVI-4.

Speaking Unknown Tongues

"To another divers kinds of tongues; to another the interpretation of tongues." I Cor. XII-10. "And they were filled with the Holy Ghost, and began to speak with other tongues, as the spirit (which controlled them) gave them utterance." Acts II-4. "If any man speak in an unknown tongue, let it be by two or at the most by three, and that by course, and let one interpret." I Cor. XIV-2,27. If there was no interpreter they were to keep silent, for "the spirits of the prophets are subject to the prophets." It appears that they had a great deal of trouble in the meetings, or St. Paul would not have cautioned them to have all things "done decently and in order."

Materialization, and Clairvoyant Appearances

An angel appeared to Hagar, Gen. XVI; three came to Abraham so perfectly materialized, that "they did eat,": Gen. XVIII; and again to restrain him from sacrificing his son; to Lot, Chap. XIX; an angel wrestled with Jacob, XXXII, 24; an angel spoke to all the people, Jud. II; came and sat under an oak and talked to Gideon, Jud. VI; to Monoah, XII; the spirit of Samuel conversed with Saul, I Sam. XXVIII; an angel came to feed Elijah, I Kings XIX-5-8; protected the three Hebrew children from fire, Dan. III. An angel appeared to Joseph in a dream, Matt. 5; an angel appeared to the two Marys at the sepulchre [sic]; to Zacharias, Luke I; to Mary, Luke I; to the shepherds, Luke II; to Mary Magdalene, John XX; opened the prison doors, Acts V; to Cornelius, Acts X; to Peter in prison,

Acts, XII; to Paul in "vision," Acts XVI and XVII; and see Deut. IV-12. A "materialized" book was shown, Ezek. II-9. Joshua saw and conversed with a spirit who held a drawn sword in his hand, Josh. V-13; and in Amos, it is said the "Lord stood upon a wall made by a plumb line with a plumb line in his hand." Samuel appeared "covered with a mantle." A spirit appeared to Daniel "clothed in linen, whose loins were girded with fine gold." Dan. X. Feeding the multitude of 5,000 on five loaves and two fishes. Luke IX, 12-17. Making wine at the marriage feast. John II, 1-9. And lastly the several materializations of Christ after the crucifixion.

Trance

"How he was caught up into Paradise and heard unspeakable words which it is not lawful for man to utter." II Cor. XII-2, 4. Like all those who have fallen into trance, he did not know "whether in the body, or out of the body." "Which saw the vision of the Almighty, falling into a trance, but having his eyes open." Num. XXIV-16.

Ministry of Angels

"And the angels ministered unto him." Mark I-13. "And the angel of God called to Hagar out of heaven,: when she was deserted in the wilderness. Gen. XXI-17. "The angels of the Lord encamp round about them that fear him, and delivereth them." Psalm XXXIV-7. "For he shall give his angels (spirits) charge over thee, to keep thee in all thy ways. They shall bear thee up in their hands, lest thou dash thy foot against a stone." Psalm XCI-11, 12; Matt. XXVI-53; Acts V-18, 19, and VII-26 to 29. A man (spirit) appeared to Paul and said unto him, "come over into Macedonia and help us." Acts XVI-9. "Are they not all ministering spirits, sent for to minister for them who shall be heirs to salvation?" Heb. I-14. Paul had a clear understanding of spiritual agencies. "Likewise the spirit also helpeth our infirmities." Rom. VIII-26.

Direct Spirit Writing

On the walls of Babylon: "In the same hour came forth fingers of a man's hand, and wrote over against the candlestick upon the plaster of the wall of the king's palace, and the king saw the part of the hand that wrote." Dan. V-5.

David received the plan of the temple from a spirit: "And the pattern of all he had by the Spirit, of the courts of the house of the Lord." David gave to Solomon: I Chron. XXVIII. The 19th verse says: "All this said David, the Lord made me understand in writing by his hand upon me, even all the work of this pattern."

"There came a writing to him (Jehoram) from Elijah the prophet." II Chron. XXI-12. According to the chronology, Elijah had been for some time dead, and hence it must have been by his spirit.

Levitation

"And when they were come up out of the water, the spirit of the Lord caught away Philip and the eunuch saw him no more—but Philip was found at Azotus." Acts VIII-39, 40. The meaning intended, evidently is that Philip was transported by spirit power. This is clearly expressed in Ezek. III-14. "So the spirit lifted me up and took me away." And more explicit, VIII-3, "And he put forth the form of an hand, and took me by a lock of mine head; and the spirit lifted me up between the earth and the heaven, and brought me in the visions of God to Jerusalem,_____." I Kings XVIII-12. Elisha causes iron to swim. II Kings VI-6. Christ walked upon the sea. Mark VI-49.

Clairvoyance

"Come see a man who told me all things I ever did: Is not this the Christ?" John IV-16 to 29. Stephen, Acts VII-55, 56. "Behold I see the heavens opened and the son of man standing at the right hand of God." Paul was clairvoyant. Acts XXVII, Samuel is consulted as a seer by Saul. I Sam. IX-10 to 20.

Clairaudience

"And he fell to the earth, and heard a voice saying unto him: Saul, why persecutest thou me? And the men which journeyed with him stood speechless, hearing a voice but seeing no man." Acts IX-4, 7. The apostles heard the voices of Moses and Elias on the mount. Matt. XVII-3-5; also Rev. I-10. "Now the Lord has told Samuel in his ear a day before Saul came." I Sam. IX-15, 16. Peter hears a spirit voice, Acts X-13. See Zech. I-9, 13, II-2, 7; V-5-10; VI-4. Job is addressed by a spirit, IV-12 to 16.

Dreams and Visions

Often messages can be given during sleep that cannot be given during the more positive state of waking. "Then was the secret revealed to Daniel in a vision." Dan. II-19. See Matt. I-20, II-12; Acts IX-10, X-13; Gen. XV-12; XX-3, 7, XXXI-24, XII-7; Jud. VII-13; Num. XII-6; Deut. II-1, IV-10, 18; Job. IV-13,

VII-14, XXXII-8; I Sam. XXVIII-6; Isa. XXIX-8; Dan. II-1, IV-18; Jer. XXVII; Joel II-28; Eccl. V-3; I Cor. XIV-15. The entire Book of Revelation is professedly the utterance of one in trance.

Speaking Through Trumpets

Exo. XIX-13, 16, 19; Rev. I-10.

Healing by Magnetized Articles or at a Distance

"Take my staff in thine hand and go thy way—and lay it on the face of a child." II Kings IV-29; Acts XIX-12.

Healing

"They shall lay hands on the sick and they shall recover." Mark XVI-18. "And Jesus put forth his hand and touched him—and immediately his leprosy was cleansed." Matt. VIII-3. Paul recovers his sight. Acts IX—17; Peter cures the lame man, Acts III-1 to 8; Elisha restores the life of the Schunammite child." II Kings IV-33-35; the leper is cured, II Kings, V-10, 11; healing the damsel, mark V-42. See Dan. X-18; Luke VII-21; VIII-46; Mark V-30; VI-56; I Kings XVII-19-22; Math. X-1; Luke X-9; James V-14, 15. Jesus healed by magnetic touch: "and the whole multitude sought to touch him; for there went virtue out of him and healed them all." Luke VI-19.

Independent Spirit Voices

Deut. IX-12, 13; I Sam. III-3, 9; Ezek. I-28; Math. XVIII-5; John XII-28-30; Acts VII-30-31, IX-4, 7; XI-7, 8,9.

Lying Spirit

God used a lying spirit to persuade Ahab that he may go up and fall at Ramoth-gilead, I Kings XXII-19-23.

[Taken from: *NSAC Spiritualist Manual.* (1998) Lily Dale, NY: National Spiritualist Association of Churches, pp. 56-60.]

Appendix L

Definitions of Clairvoyance

NOTE: Clairvoyance literally means "Clear Seeing," but in Spiritualism it has a technical meaning and refers to psychic sight. Clairvoyance may be either Subjective or Objective. It is often difficult, if not altogether impossible, for even the clairvoyant to distinguish between the two.

Six definitions of clairvoyance are here given, to-wit Subjective, Objective, X-Ray, Cataleptic, Trance-Control and Telepathic Clairvoyance. The first two definitions pertain to the two distinct forms of clairvoyance; the other four deal with phases of these two forms.

1. **Subjective clairvoyance** is that psychic condition of a human being, who thereby becomes a medium which enables spirit intelligences, through the manipulation of the nerve centers of sight, to impress or photograph upon the brain of the medium, pictures and images which are seen as visions by the medium without the aid of the physical eye. These pictures and images may be of the things spiritual or material, past or present, remote or near, hidden or uncovered, or they may have their existence simply in the conception or imagination of the spirit communicating them.

2. **Objective clairvoyance** is that psychic power or function of seeing, objectively, spiritual beings, objects and things by and through the spiritual sensorium which pervades the physical mechanism of vision, without which objective clairvoyance would be impossible. A few persons are born with this power; in some it is developed, and in others it has but a casual quickening. Its extent is governed by the rate of vibration under which it operates; thus, one clairvoyant may see objectively spiritual things which to another may be invisible, because of the degree of difference in the intensity of power.

3. **X-Ray clairvoyance** is a form of clairvoyance which partakes of the characteristics of the X-Ray, and seems to be objective. The clairvoyant who possesses this power is able to see physical objects through intervening physical matter, can perceive the internal parts of the human body, diagnose disease and observe the operations of healing and decay.

4. **Cataleptic clairvoyance** occurs when the body is in a trance state, resembling sleep, induced by hypnotic power exercised by an incarnate or discarnate spirit, or it may be self-induced. When in this state, the spirit leaves the body, and is able at its own will or the suggestion of the hypnotists to travel to remote places and to see clearly what is transpiring in the places it visits and to observe spiritual as well as material things in its environment. While in this state it sometimes happens that the thoughts of the spirit in its travels are expressed by the lips of the physical body, and that thought waves are conveyed to it through the physical body. This may be due to the fact that there is a spirit cord which connects the body and the spirit and transmits vibrations is not severed, the spirit may return to the body, but should it be severed, then what we call death would at once ensue. Under this form of clairvoyance there is an interblending of subjective and objective spiritual sight.

5. **Trance control clairvoyance** is that psychic state under which the control of the physical body of the medium is assumed by a spirit of intelligence and the consciousness of the medium is, for the time-being, dethroned. In this case the controlling spirit is really the clairvoyant and simply uses the medium's body as a means of communicating what the spirit sees and, therefore, the question of subjective or objective spiritual sight, in so far as the medium is concerned, cannot be raised. To some persons who go to mediums for consultations and who may become witnesses in trials at law, it may not be known that under the trance control of the medium is, to all intents and purposes, absent; therefore, in dealing with definitions of clairvoyance to be used for enlightenment of judges and jurors, it seemed necessary for the protection of mediums to explain what is here termed trance-control clairvoyance.

6. **Telepathic clairvoyance** is the subjective perception in picture form of thought transmitted from a distance.

[Taken from: *NSAC Spiritualist Manual.* (1998) Lily Dale, NY: National Spiritualist Association of Churches, pp. 44-45.]

APPENDIX M

Testimonial by the Author Regarding his Experiences at Séances and Healing Circles

During the three years I actively gathered research data for this study, I attended a number of séances, healing circles, clairvoyant circles and message services at Spiritualist churches both as an observer and as a participant. On more than several occasions, I did witness various examples of mental and physical phenomena.

On one occasion in particular (early on in my research), while participating in a healing circle, the medium told me clairvoyantly that she had my "mother's mother" (maternal grandmother) and a young girl named "Evelyn" who were coming through for me. She asked if I could accept them and although I knew of my maternal grandmother, she had passed decades before I was born; also, I had never heard of an "Evelyn" in my family who had passed over to the other side. The medium reiterated to me that the spirit entity was coming through for me, and asked again if I could accept them. Being a novice sitter, I said that they must be mistaken as I had no idea who the "Evelyn" could be. The medium thanked them and sent them back to the spirit-realm and brought another spirit through for someone else. I have since learned, through trial and error, that it is best to accept whatever comes through from the spirit-world; later, after thinking about the message, one can interpret, digest and even reject the message if it does not pertain readily to one's life, family or experience.

Later that evening, I asked my mother if the name "Evelyn" meant anything to her. She immediately proceeded to tell me a story about her half-sister who died as a young girl before she (my mother) was born. According to my mother (who had heard the story from her mother as a young woman), her half-sister had been jumping rope continuously one day and later complained of having a sideache. My grandmother passed it off as being overexertion from playing jump rope all day. It worsened as the night went on and soon became apparent that it was more serious than a normal pulled muscle. The country doctor was summoned and an emergency appendectomy was performed on the kitchen table; the appendix had burst, however, and Evelyn later died from the toxicity of the burst appendix. Although not exactly sure, to the best recollection of my mother, this probably occurred circa 1910. My mother recalls her mother speaking fondly of Evelyn periodically while she was growing up, but had not thought of her half-sister (that she never knew personally) in many years.

This was more than mere coincidence I concluded. First, the name "Evelyn" is not that common of a name and for the medium to call her by the actual name was nothing short of amazing to me; second, the fact that "Evelyn" would have been my aunt, the medium nonetheless specifically said that my maternal grandmother had a "young girl" with her; third, since I had no conscious (or subconscious) knowledge of the existence of Aunt Evelyn precludes the possibility of my offering by accident hints or information that would have guided or encouraged the medium to say what she did during this reading.

In a subsequent séance, with another Spiritualist medium completely unrelated and unknown to the original one who brought my grandmother and Evelyn through the first time, my grandmother and Evelyn came through again for me. Of course, I apologized profusely for sending them back the time before.

An instance of physical phenomena I experienced while sitting in a séance occurred in a one-room schoolhouse that had been converted into a family dwelling. The owners had felt the presence of apparitions ever since they moved in and wanted to have a séance to see if any contact could be made. They were not afraid, nor did they want to drive the spirits away, they were just curious as to who they were.

The room chosen for the séance was sealed by covering the doors and windows with heavy blankets. The room was cleansed and prepared for the séance by the medium. Those in attendance cited the Lord's Prayer in unison to raise the vibration of the room. Once the séance started, it was not long until spirit messages were coming through. The first message was from a cousin of one of the sitters; the medium noticed a lot of red and asked the person why there would be so much red. The person said that the cousin had been brutally murdered and there had been a lot of blood. Immediately, the medium asked if he could send the entity back as there was too much trauma involved to deal with that particular spirit at that time; the medium did not feel comfortable allowing this energy into the circle.

Soon thereafter, I and another sitter (who was facing the same direction) saw clearly a form (not a materialization but an etherealization) of a spirit dart across the room. At that moment, many of us felt a distinct coolness around us that caused the hair on our necks to rise up. Above the head of one of the participants, there was an orb of light floating effortlessly about two-feet over her head. She was sitting with her eyes shut, almost meditating, when this occurred. This was what Spiritualists refer to as a "spirit light." It remained there for the duration of the séance. During this séance, the medium intuited the name "Luke," which he perceived to be a little boy who was present.

A total of three séances were done in this same venue and at a subsequent séance in this same house, the medium and the sitters physically felt the presence of a spirit. When a question was asked, one woman (not the medium) experienced clairsentience-like sensations where the right side of her body would feel a burst of cool air. A code was established where a "yes" answer would receive this sensation. The owner wanted to know a name, so each letter of the alphabet was recited by the medium; when a letter corresponding to the name was said, the sitter would feel the cool air sensation. Slowly the letters J-A-C-O…were realized. At this point, everyone assumed the name must be "Jacob."

The next week, the owner of the house did some research to find out if there had ever been a "Jacob" that lived in the house and was attached to it or had gone to school there a century before and met an untimely death there, etc. Immediately prior to the current owners living there, it was used as a dormitory for farmhands working on the adjacent farm. The last known occupant was an old man by the name of Clyde Jaco. He had lived there until he was moved into a nursing home, where he stayed until he died, more than twenty years before.

At a séance that included only three people, in the reading room (a room especially reserved for the medium to give readings to clients) a rather odd thing occurred. During the séance, which was lit by a variety of candles, it appeared that the face of the medium completely disappeared. At first, I thought my eyes were playing tricks on me, so I looked away, and then looked back, it really did look as if the medium's face had vanished. Later when I told the medium what I saw, she explained that it was possibly a form of transfiguration when a spirit was perhaps trying to come through. Although I cannot say I saw the face of another spirit, I can say that I saw her face appear to have vanished.

When I first began doing the primary research for this study, I was admittedly a skeptic. As a researcher, though, I tried diligently to remain objective, setting aside my own personal beliefs and opinions when trying to ascertain the possibility or existence of spirit-communication. But having experienced a variety of spirit-related phenomenon during the course of my research, I cannot simply dismiss these occurrences out of hand. I suppose the old saying "seeing is believing" has substance in this instance.

[This testimonial was put down on paper by Todd Jay Leonard, February 29, 2004 which includes the period from 2000-2003.]

APPENDIX N

Psychometry

◆ ◆ ◆

The Organ of Spirituality

◆ ◆ ◆

Joseph Rodes Buchanan (1814-1899) was born in Frankfurt, Kentucky. His father, Joseph Buchanan, was a mechanical inventor, physician, newspaper editor, and author. The younger Joseph learned printing in his father's newspaper office, and then studied medicine at Kentucky's Transylvania University. After graduating he became an investigator of, and public lecturer on, the brain. He dissected or measured thousands of heads, and "he discovered and demonstrated the psychic and physiological functions of the brain by direct experiment," in part by external electrical or magnetic stimulation of the various regions of the head. Mapping out what he inferred from his experiments was part of "the greatest discovery in the annals of physiology," according to a biographical sketch published by Julia Schlesinger in *Workers in the Vineyard*, "the discovery that the function of every portion of the human brain could be ascertained, accurately located, and described—thus revealing all the psychic powers of man, their relation to each other, and their relation to the body and their wonderful interaction of the psychic and physiological faculties—thus solving the great mystery of the age, which before the investigations of Dr. Buchanan, no one had ever attempted to explore."

From 1846-56, Buchanan was a professor of medicine at the Cincinnati Eclectic Medical Institute and authored *The Eclectic Practice of Medicine and Surgery* and other works, including the eight-volume *Buchanan's Journal of Man*. Buchanan was also the "discoverer" of what he called "Psychometry." He believed that humans leave psychic energy on objects they touch as a kind of residue, and that a sensitive psychic could read the collected energies on an object as an imagined narrative history of its use. This was used by psychics to produce descriptions of ancient civilizations through touching recovered artifacts. It was also used by psychic "healers" to diagnose the illnesses of people who had sent them a lock of their hair and a dollar in an envelope.

Buchanan was a leading physiological experimenter, but his mapping of the human mental faculties onto the brain, or his discovery (as he explained in the following article) that a person could be induced to see spirits through an electrical stimulus to a certain portion of the brain, did not exclude for him the possibility that spirits were in fact real. On the contrary, his own investigations eventually convinced him of the truth of spiritualism, and he became a mainstay on the spiritualist lecture circuit.

◆ ◆ ◆

Joseph Rodes Buchanan. "Spirituality—Recent Occurrences," *Buchanan's Journal of Man* (New York), February 1850: 489-492.

In the year 1841, I found that by exciting the marvelous organs, lying near the temporal ridge, the subject might be made sufficiently marvelous and imaginative not only to believe in ghosts, but to see them. Making this experiment upon an intellectual young lady at a social party, she became quite agitated as she beheld her deceased mother. In '42 [1842] an exact survey of this region demonstrated that there was a special organ of SPIRITUALITY at the junction of Ideality, Marvelousness and Imagination, by means of which we obtained rather definite ideas of spiritual beings, and also an organ of more extravagant functions, properly styled the organ of SPECTRAL ILLUSION, lying a little higher in the imaginative region, near the affections.

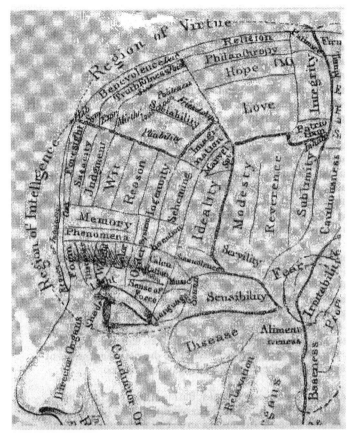

Under the excitement of Spirituality the mind is elevated to a more spiritual state. Its attention turns away from gross matter, and it acquires an extraordinary power of recognizing mind, until at length even disembodied mind is distinctly perceived. Thus the subject will enter communication with the dead and with various spiritual beings, of whom he will speak, and with whom he appears to hold an interesting intercourse. Sometimes he will report that he is too gross and incapable of this exalted communion—that spiritual beings are beyond his reach, and will not commune with him. Mr. _____, a man of fine talent, but of little religious faith, was astonished and overwhelmed when he first underwent this experiment, and perceived as holding an independent existence, what he had before regarded as mere creatures of his own mind. He at length communed with his deceased father, but reported that his father now withdrew from him with a stern countenance, as if he was unfit for such association. Mrs. _____, a firm disbeliever of christianity and of all spiritualism, was overwhelmed with wonder and delight when I excited her Spirituality, and soon entered into familiar communication with various spiritual beings. In some cases her spiritual vision was sufficient to enable her to describe correctly the appearance of deceased persons whom she had never seen or heard described. Many others, under these experiments, have reported communications held with the deceased, and sometimes messages of advice, etc., have been sent to their surviving friends. Some of my friends have prosecuted these spiritual investigations to a great length, believing that they might thus place the world in a more intimate relation to spiritual life, and exert a holy influence upon men. In my own limited experiments, however, I [490] have not seen those copious and satisfactory results of which others speak. The communications have generally been of a vague character, and such as might easily have originated in the imagination or reason of the subject, aided by their impressibility to the mental influences of the living.

I do not wish to discredit or check such investigations, which I have been compelled to postpone to a late period as regards myself, but I would mention the dangers of delusion. Spirituality is so closely connected with Imagination in the brain, that there is an extremely strong probability that its revelations will be either partly or entirely the product of imagination. The close proximity of the organ of Spectral Illusion, the indications of which we know to be false creations, renders it still more probable that the spectres arrayed before the mind, are but its own irregular shadows—fanciful embodiments of some principle or influence at work upon it. Hence there is a strong probability that those who investigate these matters, may be lost in a wilderness of romantic spiritual fictions.

The existence of the organ of Spirituality is illustrated by the belief in all ages, of the existence of spiritual beings, and of their communion with the living. Thousands have entertained the sincere belief, arising from their own consciousness, that they held communion with the spirits of departed friends and relatives. Occasionally this communion has led to practical benefit, by means of advice and warnings received from spiritual sources when awake or when dreaming, which would indicate either that a kind, spiritual being had communicated the intelligence, or that it was attained by an unusual exertion of the intuitive foreseeing faculty.

A lady of great intelligence, moral worth and practical energy, told me confidentially that she had for a great portion of her life been subject to spiritual visions which she dared not mention to any one, lest her sanity should be doubted. These celestial visitants came to her in the daytime when her mind was perfectly calm, clear and free from excitement, the communion was pleasant and elevating. They appeared to be angelic beings of an exalted nature, with whom she was conscious that she would in a future life become more intimate. Their visits occurred more frequently when her moral faculties were in their highest condition, and became very rare when she became too much engrossed in worldly affairs to the neglect of her duties. Dr. H., an intelligent practitioner of medicine in one of our Atlantic cities, believes himself to be in daily intercourse, of the most intimate character, with the spirit of a departed friend. There are many who entertain the persuasion that they commune with the departed, who are unwilling to speak of a matter which they regard as sacred, and which they would not desecrate by exposure to idle comment.

The belief in guardian spirits, which is expressed by poets and orators, with a half real, half metaphorical meaning, and which is to some a matter of religious sentiment, is sanctioned by the results [491] of many experiments upon subjects in whom the spiritual faculties have been excited. They have often spoken of guardian spirits, who preside over particular persons, and sometimes specified certain influences exerted by them for their benefit. The guardian spirit is most generally a deceased friend, and his influence is exerted through the minds upon which the spiritual influence operates.

A high excitement of Spirituality is not necessary to the spiritual vision. The sleep-waking state is generally quite spiritual and by a slight elevation becomes sufficient for spiritual communion. There is no impossibility in maintaining the organ habitually in sufficient activity for spiritual communion. On the contrary, if the organ be large and the circumstances of the individual's life favorable to its action, we may expect a spontaneous activity. Neurology renders it perfectly credible that an individual of active mind, may, during the greater part of his life, be in that state which is called spiritual communion of spiritual vision, but it does not sanction the idea that this mental power is limited to one, or to a very small number of persons. Whatever belongs to one individual, belongs to all of the race in varying degrees.

In all impressible persons the faculty of Spirituality may be excited. Even those who are decided materialists, may be convinced without argument, of spiritual existence, by thus making them perceive it. In experimenting upon letters, the spiritual power is often displayed. If the writer of the letter is dead, the subject, or investigator, will sometimes trace his character and career through life, recognize his death, and subsequent spiritual existence. In other cases, death will be his first perception, and he will forthwith describe him as a spiritual being.

The organ of Spirituality co-operates with the intuitive faculties, but is not a strictly intellectual organ itself. To arrive at truth in the investigation of spiritual subjects, we must rely upon the intuitive organs—they perceive the truth. Spirituality gives an ethereal and fanciful temperament, which may render the perceptions more vivid but may also give a definite embodiment to that which is only an abstraction, and mingle imaginative pictures with actual perceptions.

It requires no little care and patient investigation to arrive at a correct conclusion in reference to the vast mass of phenomena which have, during the past and present centuries, passed current as truly spiritual appearances. It may be safely assumed in advance, that so great an amount of evidence, of dispassionate statements, of popular belief, and of earnest excitement, could not have existed without an adequate cause, and therefore that there must be realities and laws which it is the duty of scientific men to ascertain. On the other hand, it may be assumed with equal certainty that all the real phenomena are intermingled with delusions and falsehoods, for there has been no greater source of delusion and imposture in all the history of man, than his relations to the spiritual world, in [492] reference to which the world is filled with the grossest falsehoods, by means of which the mass of mankind have been made the dupes and victims of the cunning despots, priests, jugglers and necromancers who profit by the fictions and superstitions which they uphold. From Nicholas of Russia to his sable majesty of Loango, in Africa, from the pow-wow-ing medicine-man of North America, to the high priest of Juggernaut, from Mahomet to Joseph Smith, one vast scene of imposture upon the many for the benefit of the few, assails our vision.

In view of these facts, we need not wonder that a determined spirit of skepticism now possesses the world, and prevails especially among the more influential and educated classes. If all that the most sanguine spiritualists claim were true, and the evidence easily accessible for all, it would be a groundless hope to suppose that such evidence as might be decisive upon any other scientific question would be satisfactory upon this. Such questions are predetermined in the popular mind, against the spiritualist, and the whole subject is buried beneath the conviction that all the facts upon which he relies as evidence, are the result of base imposture, credulity, ignorance, imagination or insanity. Evidence must be piled upon evidence, and one investigation after another must result in the overthrow of the most determined skepticism before any impression can be made upon the more intelligent portion of the community.

We should bear in mind that philosophy sanctions neither skepticism nor credulity; it requires simply a careful collection of evidence, extensive in proportion to the importance of the phenomena, and a patient suspension of our decision, until the accumulated facts present a harmonious consistency and indicate to the inductive reasoner the new laws of nature which they embody.

◆ ◆ ◆

Note that Buchanan located the "organ of spirituality" on what would be recognized today as part of the temporal lobes of the brain. The electromagnetic induction of spiritual experiences, including the vision of deceased spirits, through temporal lobe stimulation, has lately been re-discovered, and made the subject of scientific research, as described in various journals and magazines.

[Retrieved from http://www.spirithistory.com/buchanan.html.]

APPENDIX O

Spirit Brides and Rag Babies

Spirit Brides and Rag Babies

◆ ◆ ◆

John Curtis Bundy, Editor's note in *Religio-Philosophical Journal,* July 14, 1888

◆ ◆ ◆

Mr. A. E. Carpenter, one of the most experienced of Spiritualists and known in nearly every city and large town in the country as an expert mesmerist, has an interesting letter on another page. It is high time he and hundreds of other rational spiritualists in Boston should join in an organized effort to regulate the public practice of mediumship in that fraud-riddled city. The *Banner of Light* has shown its sympathy with swindlers and has condoned the offenses of incorrigible scamps so long that it cannot now have any reformatory influence even if it had the sense and courage to try.

◆ ◆ ◆

Albert Emerson Carpenter, "Exhibitions of Tricks as Demonstrations of Spirit Power," *Religio-Philosophical Journal,* July 14, 1888

◆ ◆ ◆

To the Editor of the Religio-Philosophical Journal:

I take up my pen to write from a sense of duty, feeling compelled to say something that ought to be said better than I shall be able to say it, and about which I shall be unable to express myself as strongly as I feel. Well do I appreciate the brave and sincere efforts that you have made to drag into the light and expose the vile impositions that have been practiced upon the public in the name of mediumship. Your fearless efforts in this direction are beyond praise, and ought to have called to your aid every honest and conscientious believer in spirit communion in the land. What are known as physical manifestations and materializations have furnished a fertile field for unscrupulous tricksters and deceivers to work. They have flourished and increased until their name has become legion. I think that it is safe to say that nearly all of the public exhibitions of so-called physical mediumship are nothing but tricks and most of them have not even the merit of being good tricks. A professional magician of any note would scorn to use many of the flimsy methods that are employed by these mediums (?) to deceive the people. Fifteen years ago a medium here in Boston, one of the first materializers, exhibited a bundle of rags draped in an old white skirt with a wire mask face at the top, as a spirit baby. A young man stopping at my house grabbed it out of her arms at the expense of being knocked down. It was captured, however, and we had it on exhibition for some time. Previous to this some ladies found concealed under the skirts of the same medium, two or three masks, a quantity of black jute that had figured as the long hair of an Indian maiden. These facts were published in the Boston papers at the time. The medium said that the rag baby had been brought there by her enemies, and carried away again. It was unfortunate for her, however, that the white skirt used to drape the baby was marked in indelible ink with the name of a friend who gave it to her.

The most remarkable part of it was that notwithstanding this exposure, she went on giving séances for years, and those who completed the expose lost caste among her credulous followers. Later [Henry] Gordon exhibited materializations in New York City, for nearly a year, exciting a great interest, until finally two level-headed Spiritualists sprang over the table which separated him from the audience and he threw down his draped image, "the spirit bride," and ran. On searching about they found two poorly constructed images dressed, one in male and the other in female attire.

Gordon had them so arrayed that he could remove their heads and change them for others. Something like a half-barrel of these heads were found at hand ready to be changed as occasion required. He had a stock company of spirits limited to the number of heads. It is a notable fact that most materializers are limited in the same way to a few devices for changes such as they have at hand. Lately we heard of a medium who marched out of the cabinet, followed by a spirit who kept just behind her, and seemed to move as she moved. Some close investigator discovered that she had a draped stick attached to her bustle; the present fashion of large bustles being especially convenient for such an arrangement. The dim light that pervades these séances makes it possible for these poor tricks to have the appearance of reality.

Then we must not forget that the minds of the observers are usually dominated with the idea that they are going to see a spirit. A state of mental expectancy may change in a poor light almost any object into a ghost. We are told that these conditions are absolutely necessary. Now no one is more conscious of the necessity of proper conditions for success than myself; but if the conditions are of such a character as to make accurate observation impossible, then the experiment becomes valueless. Until materializations can be presented under positive test conditions, it is but a waste of time to attend such séances. This statement, it seems to me, must commend itself to every intelligent person.

Let us look this matter squarely in the face. What we want to know is the truth, and knowing the truth we need not fear but it will lead us to the very best conclusions. I am confident that the majority of these fraudulent mediums are not even Spiritualists. They have no idea of what Spiritualism means in its best sense. They take up mediumship as a business, learn a few stale tricks, get the necessary equipment, and advertise. The more extraordinary and extravagant their claims the greater their success in drawing a crowd. I was talking with one of these wonder-workers a few days ago. I asked him how he came to be a medium. He quite frankly said, "Being out of a job I thought I would try the medium business, so I took it up as a profession." We shall find this is true of nearly all of these people whose exposes fill the columns of the daily press. They see an opening to make money, and being without principle, they do not hesitate to "coin our tears into dollars," as the New York *Herald* remarks in commenting on the Dis Debar trial.

◆ ◆ ◆

Anna O'Delia Salomon Messant, alias "Madame Dis De Bar," a con artist and adventuress who spent several years in New York City in the business of materialization and "the religion of Hanky Panky" (in John Bundy's phrase) for various rich cli-

ents, including Luther Marsh, a retired lawyer and 75-year-old widower. She was exposed and brought to court on fraud charges in 1888.

◆   ◆   ◆

The early mediums had a different history. They were developed in private home circles where members of the family gathered to invite the communion of their departed loved ones. Some one of the company peculiarly gifted proves to be a medium, and unexpectedly becomes the object of interest to all. With no thought of deception and no motive to deceive, her development goes on, and through her ministrations much joy is carried to sorrowing hearts. Many come to her until her time and strength is taxed to that extent that she is finally compelled to charge pay or cease to use her gifts. It is proper and right that she should do so. This is the history of true mediumship. It comes unsought and oftentimes has proved a source of poverty and martyrdom to its possessors. The record of the lives of our early mediums is a sad story of trial and persecution, and yet an imitation of the phenomena that occurred in their presence, and the confidence and faith which their honesty built up, has been the stock in trade of these vile impostors that have sprung up on every hand and flourished for a time "like a green bay tree."

Honest mediumship has been at a discount because of its modesty of claiming only what is true, while the blatant deceiver and trickster, claiming everything and doing nothing, wears broadcloth, silks and satins, and is covered with diamonds. Sometimes they meet with their deserts like the Dis Debars.

How do you suppose they regard the honest people who patronize them, and who often with tears and sobs, recognize their masks and images in the darkness as some loved friend whose body has been laid away? They laugh in their sleeves, do these wretches, while they spend the money of those whose "tears they have coined into dollars." They say, "What precious idiots these people are."

And those who endeavor to apologize and explain away the evidence of their fraudulent practices, instead of eliciting their gratitude, become still more the subjects of their contempt and ridicule. They brutally and recklessly play with the most sacred feelings of the human heart for paltry gain. To what depths of depravity have such beings sunk, and who can imagine a punishment superior to their deserts.

The end will be as the Religio-Philosophical Journal has predicted: that the law will step in and try to protect those who seem to be unable to protect themselves, as in the Dis De Bar case with Mr. Marsh. Finally statutes will be enacted against the practice of mediumship, and then the true as well as the false will be necessarily included.

◆ ◆ ◆

Bundy, the Editor of the Journal, distanced himself from many of his fellow spiritualists by lobbying the Illinois State Legislature for passage of a law combating fraudulent mediums—"Every person who for profit or in anticipation thereof for the purpose of presenting what is commonly known as spirit materialization, shall personate a spirit of a deceased person, or who shall by trick, device, or mechanical contrivance present anything to represent the spirit of a deceased person shall be guilty of misdemeanor, and upon conviction shall be subject to a fine of not less than $100 nor more than $300, or confined in the county jail not less than three months nor more than six months or both in the discretion of the court. This act shall not be deemed to apply to any portion of a scene or play in any theatrical presentation."

◆ ◆ ◆

Credulous old gentlemen have been continuously robbed, and some of them utterly ruined by the most shamefaced imposition practiced upon them in the name of mediumship. It is a pretty hard condition of things that compels an old-time worker in the field of Spiritualism like myself to make this statement, but it is unfortunately true. The worst of it all is that these bad people force themselves to the front and are supposed by outsiders to be genuine representatives of the spiritualistic movement, while it is true, as I have said, that they do not believe in Spiritualism, know nothing of its philosophy and many of them are on too low a spiritual and intellectual plane to learn anything about it. It is a notable fact that these people never seem to be impressed by the phenomena that occur in their presence, showing no interest in them, while others work in a perfect maze of wonder. This is because they know how cheap and ridiculous a trick they have played, and they naturally want to say as little about it as possible. The fact is that they and their tricks really have nothing to do with Spiritualism, *per se*, and no one outside can have the perfect contempt for them that fills the mind of the philosophical Spiritualist. Every expose that is made by such men as [magician Harry] Kellar and others is an unmixed blessing to the cause, and should be applauded by every sincere and honest believer in spirit intercourse.

The true man has no cause to defend except in the interests of truth, and if there is no foundation to our belief in spirit communion except that which rests upon trickery, collusion, and delusion, let it go by the board, and the sooner the better. For myself I am a believer in the possibility and reality of spirit communion, based upon facts in my own experience, which were of such a character as to convince the most skeptical person living. These exposes of frauds do not disturb my convictions in the least.

The true Spiritualist does not base his faith upon public exhibitions of phenomena, however wonderful they may seem to be. He depends upon his own observation of facts occurring among his personal friends and acquaintances, or with mediums that he has every reason to believe are honest. The phenomena that he relies upon are of such a nature as to put all possibility of deception out of the question. The honest mediums are anxious to make every condition possible to relieve the mind of the investigator from suspicion of themselves. The manifestations that occur in their presence may happen at any time and are often as unexpected to themselves as to others who may witness them. Their mediumship is not confined to the paraphernalia and equipment of the séance room or cabinet, nor their communications to a stock company of spirits in constant attendance.

Some of the best things I ever saw came unexpected and unsought. I have had occasion to mention some of these in my communications to the Journal. Many years ago, I was visiting at the house of Walter Currier, of Haverhill, Mass. His daughter Mary, then a slight girl eighteen years old, had been developed as a musical medium, and the demonstrations in her presence were of a marked and positive nature. Her father had fitted up a séance room, for the better accommodation of the friends who wished to see the phenomena. In it there was a piano and various musical instruments. Heavy blinds, when closed, caused a deep twilight to pervade the room even in the day time. Mary was a natural musician and a fine player on the piano. She spent much of her time in playing, and often went into the séance room for that purpose. It not infrequently happened that while she thus amused herself, the other musical instruments that were lying about would be taken up and played upon by invisible performers, keeping perfect time with music she was making. One day while she was thus engaged, and the other instruments had joined in, I quietly approached the door which was standing ajar and looked in. I saw several bells and a tambourine at one end of the piano moving about, and marking time to the tune that was being played. It was a curious sight, full of interest to the observer. I had a chance to see the effect of different degrees of light upon the manipulation of the instruments by the unseen operators. Occasionally the bells would be brought out from the shadows of the piano where the light was stronger, and when it became too strong the bells would drop to the floor. Then it would be pushed back again into the gloom and directly be lifted up and go on ringing as before. The medium went on playing without appearing to notice the efforts of her invisible aids. In this case our attention is called to the necessity of a certain amount of darkness or absence of light that was required for the handling of the instruments.

In the presence of this medium, I have often seen one end of the piano rise up and down and mark time to the tune that was playing upon the keys. Here we have the genuine phenomena, which the impostor fraudulently advertises to draw a crowd to his Sunday night exhibition in some theatre or hall:

"The piano will be lifted and float in the air. Spirit flowers will be brought. Forms of spirit friends will be seen and plainly recognized in full view of the audience," etc.

The crowd gathers, too often enhanced by numerous Spiritualists, and what they see is a few cheap rope tying tricks done in a cabinet. The impostor escapes through the back door and gathers up his ill-gotten gains, and leaves town on the night train. He waits a year and goes back and does the same thing over again.

Every Spiritualist in the land should give these people a wide berth, and never attend a theatre or hall exhibition advertised in the name of Spiritualism for they can be sure it is a swindle every time. Of course I am referring now to the physical manifestations. I could go on indefinitely with a record of the tricks and methods of those shameless impostors, but I have said enough, leaving the subject to the consideration of all honest people, believing that I have rendered some timely aid to the Journal in its noble efforts to drive out frauds from the ranks of Spiritualism.

A. E. Carpenter

[Retrieved from http://www.spirithistory.com/carpent.html on October 6, 2002; notes included are written by the website creator, Dr. John Buescher.]

APPENDIX P

Spirit Guides: Their Importance, Duties, Titles, and Place

Everyone has FIVE MAIN SPIRIT HELPERS. Some know these as guides, while others know them as GUARDIAN ANGELS, as spoken of in the Bible.

These were picked BY YOU and other heavenly helpers BEFORE YOU WERE BORN. Also, you had a prenatal period of training with them there, just as a blind man prepares and trains with his Seeing Eye dog before he takes the dog out into the world to be his constant aid and protector. There was a purpose in your birth, a commission you are to fill on this earth, a great lesson you must learn and carry back to your Great Oversoul to help it towards GOD BIND (the highest plane).

These guides helped you to prepare to come into an earth body in order that you might enter the schoolhouse (earth) for further training—to further the GROWTH OF THE DIVINITY within you. Therefore, they know the proposed plan of your life, its ultimate goal. True, you may find obstacles around which you must detour; but still, the ultimate goal, the very reason for your life remains the same. These guides are your ever-present helpers, your "go-betweens" to higher power (God Force). Isn't it a foolish waste of priceless power to walk life's path without cognizance of these helpers, even if never seeking mediumship?

Actually, too, in seeking mediumship, in activating the various Chakras and lifting Kundalini Power,[1] you open mighty reservoirs of power which, like electricity, can be either very helpful, if channeled rightly, or very destructive without proper governing.

Your INNER BAND, these five MAIN GUIDES, are your gurus (teachers, helpers), leading you through the maze and into the clear, placid pool of peaceful mediumship from higher, evolved souls which can and do help mankind, the kind who will not harm you in manifesting to and through you. Furthermore, they serve you in many ways through every day. It is utterly unwise to sit for development without knowing your band and HOW TO USE THEM.

Most of the unpleasant ridicule of mediumship would be avoided had the mediums themselves used their INNER BAND which is composed of all "good" spirits, as they sat. They (the mediums) would have been manifesting SPIRITUALISM instead of SPIRITISM, because spirits of a spiritual nature—helpful, kind, true, would be the only ones allowed to manifest. The unkind, the untrue, and the ridiculous, fantastic things could not have been spoken—things which in no way uplift to God and in no way help us to mold our characters and actions upon high principles. TEACHINGS WHICH ARE HARMFUL WOULD NEVER, NEVER COME THROUGH ANYONE WHOSE "INNER BAND" WAS WORKING.

Who and what are these guides?

First, there is your <u>DOCTOR TEACHER</u>. This is, perhaps, the one you will best know and who comes the closest to you through your entire life. He is the one who, without your knowing of his actually doing it, will, if you let him, screen so that the PRECISE, CORRECT PATTERN FOR YOUR SOUL DEVELOPMENT IS WHAT IMPRESSES ITSELF UPON YOUR THINKING AND, THEREFORE, CONTROLS YOUR ACTIONS. Each of you has a different pattern of development. What may be right for one machine may not be right for another. So it is with the most delicate thing in the world—SOUL DEVLOPMENT—and subsequent mediumship, if YOU are to be a medium. (Here, let me say that the ultimate aim of all students is that each learns to be his own medium so that he can hear directly from spirit, can pick up guidance directly, guidance which will accurately steer his ship of life to the highest Plans

---

1. The Kundalini is "a concentrated field of intelligent, cosmic, invisible energy absolutely vital to life; beginning in the base of the spine as a man r woman begins to evolve in their first incarnation; fed by chakras along the spine and by the cosmic energy entering through the feet from the earth; as WISDOM is earned in each incarnation, this electromagnetic, ultra potent energy moves slowly upward through the spine..." (Bletzer, 343)

of Heaven possible,) Each of us is manifesting on a different level of consciousness. Your Doctor Teacher knows just what level your soul is on. Therefore, what, in a book, may be the important message for one will not be important for you. Your Doctor will cause you to grasp what is important to you and to understand something that is to be another link in YOUR chain of knowledge. He has full supervision over your learning as to Soul Growth. You get so that you can sense the presence of your Doctor very easily. He comes with the feeling of loving warmth, very much as you would feel toward a kindly, loving parent.

Next, there is your <u>MASTER</u>. This one is usually a very highly evolved soul who has earned the title of Master. You can say, therefore, in a way that he is your control.... (Remember, ALL HAVE SOME FORM OF MEDIUMSHIP LATENT WITHIN THEM. IT IS A PART OF THE HEAVENLY HERITAGE WITH WHICH you were born.) In babies, before life thrusts them away from it, there is a close contact with the angel world. The Soul, that Divine part of you, is still aware of all that goes on in that place from whence it came. For quite a while, or until the cares of life and the ways of the world wean you away from your natural heritage of contact with the Angel World, that contact is still present. In after years, when you sit for spiritual development, you are just learning to use that contact again, just as you must learn again to use a limb which has broken. You must learn to use it again through exercise and FAITH.

Your Master Guide walks on the highest planes of any of your guides. He often takes the guise of a Far Easterner, showing his understanding of the occult or of the Esoteric things of the Angel World. (Esoteric means HIDDEN THINGS.) He will manifest to you on the very highest of spiritual matters, and he does not come often—as your Master.

Look to your Master for HIGHEST SPIRITUALITY. Work with him for a higher caliber of mediumship. He is the control of your FIVE GUIDE BOARD, also. (Just as a factory has a Board of Directors, so YOU have an INNER BAND which takes care of you and of the many, many "fringe" helpers which will be needed by you as you go through life. Just as the employees work under the directors in a factory, so all helpers for a specific purpose are called in to work under the right director or guide. YOU MAY HAVE A HUNDRED WORKING WITH YOU, BUT YOU HAVE ONLY FIVE GUIDES IN YOUR INNER-BAND, AND THEY REMAIN WITH YOU ALWAYS.

"Fringe" helpers come and go as needed, just as a attorney may come in, for a while, to assist you if you have legal problems on earth. After these specific problems are settled, the fringe helper will be thanked by YOUR DOCTOR TEACHERS and will return to his regular duties in the heaven world.

Then, you have a <u>CHEMIST</u>. This is your guide who helps you very closely on SPIRITUAL MATTERS, just as your Doctor Teacher helps on your learning. Also, this guide is the one who brings your own loved ones to you. Many of your loved ones, with the INTENSIFIED HEAVEN LOVE for you, look into your records to see what you are to do and how best to help you. In helping you from there, they WORK OUT PART OF THEIR OWN SOUL'S GROWTH in loving service to and for you. That is part of the reason why loved ones come back to us so often, along with their family ties to us. Naturally, they are more interested in their own kin than in others. So what is more natural than that they come to aid us? When a loved one is manifesting to you, it has been your Chemist who brought him or her in. That is a unique work of his, along with helping your spiritual side to grow.

You also have an <u>INDIAN GUIDE [PROTECTOR]</u>. This is the one from whom you draw your strength. He is the most earthy of your guides. Perhaps he remains closest to you and your mundane, everyday work. THEY LIKE TO BE ASKED TO ASSIST YOU IN EVERYTHING YOU DO, from finding a parking place for your car to finding a job for you on through the whole gamut of your needs for your physical help. YOU SHOULD USE THEM IN HUNDREDS OF WAYS DAILY. Every time you ask them to do something they grow Godward through their help to you, and they take keen enjoyment out of this material helping. IT IS UTTERLY AMAZING HOW MUCH THEY ACCOMPLISH IF YOU JUST ASK THEM TO HELP. Try it. What happens will add to your faith. Nothing is too trivial for them—just ask them.

Lastly, you have a <u>JOY GUIDE</u>. This is the one who becomes almost like one of the family, so close is he or she to you. It is as if you feel and her them; they make themselves felt in a million different ways. (This you will do soon after attaining mediumship.) They chatter to you constantly. Perhaps it will seem to be only an impression, but you will soon come to know their particular vibration which they bring. Usually, while they are very OLD SOULS and have great heaven-side training, they MANIFEST AS CHILDREN and give us the love of children. This manifesting as children—calling us Mamma or Daddy, Uncle or Auntie, makes for a sense of relaxation, breaking the tension so that spiritual manifestations can come through. They are, perhaps, the MOST BUSY of our guides. They bring manifesting spirits to us, monitoring the spirit in the use of controls so we can sense them, and screen the ones who can come to us in séance. You need to go to a few séances and hear these "Little Ones" talk to know what it means. They control your inner magnetic circle.

Each of your guides has his own particular position about you:

Your DOCTOR TEACHER will come in on your RIGHT SIDE.
Your MASTER will stand BEHIND you.
Your CHEMIST will come in on your LEFT SIDE.
Your INDIAN [PROTECTOR] will stand in front of you as your PROTECTION.
Your JOY GUIDE is all around you but usually places herself at your knee.

[Nota Bene: A note on this source is needed to clarify its origin, and facts contained herein. The original author is unknown as it has been passed down from medium to medium for a number of years. The original, which initially had been typed on a manual typewriter then carbon-copied and eventually photocopied, had many addendums and notes in the margins; portions had been blackened out and new information scribbled in above. A sincere attempt, however, was made to include the information as it appeared in the original text. This is an abridged version of the original as it was edited to some extent.

This explanation on "Spirit Guides" was most likely written in the form of lecture notes by a medium-teacher teaching development classes. The style of writing suggests that the person wrote them as he or she would have said it aloud, hence a number of grammatically incorrect sentences and a tendency for colloquialism can be found. This is included as it offers a glimpse to the type of lesson material used in development classes at Spiritualists camps today. This suggests that information is indeed passed down from teacher to student, and then reused, with updates and changes being added in each new generation of user.]

APPENDIX Q

Morris Pratt Institute Course Listing

The Morris Pratt Institute Association presents the Educational Course on Modern Spiritualism (1999 Revision)

The Correspondence Course on Modern Spiritualism

The Correspondence Course of Study on Modern Spiritualism consists of thirty lessons. Each lesson consists of study material (the lesson), a bibliography, recommended reading, and a set of questions for the student to answer. Written questions and answers are reviewed and graded by an assigned examiner.

The Correspondence Course provides the required educational information for certification in the Ministry of Spiritualism for the National Spiritualist Association of Churches, as Ordained Minister, Spiritualist Teacher, Licentiate Minister, Commissioned Spiritualist Healer, or Certified Medium.

Refer to the Application Form for the Course for further information.

Unit 1—The History of Spiritualism

Lesson 1—Psychic Events Prior to Modern Spiritualism

Generalities of Spiritualism
Miscellaneous Considerations
Forerunners of Modern American Spiritualism

Lesson 2—The Advent of Modern Spiritualism

Hydesville Background

The Fox Family
After Hydesville
The Fox Sisters
The Peddler and the Cottage
Spiritualism's Progression

Lesson 3—Spiritualism As An Organized Religion

History of the National Spiritualism Association
Principles and Definitions of the Association
Specific Growth of the Association
Certification from the Association

Unit 2—The Religion of Spiritualism

Lesson 4—Spiritualism as a Philosophy—Part I

Philosophy Defined
Spiritual Natural Laws
The Spiritualistic Philosophy
The Good Idea
Creation and the Philosophy of Spiritualism

Lesson 5—Spiritualism As a Philosophy—Part II

Attitudes Toward Death and Dying
Death, Dying and the Spiritualist Philosophy
The Reality of Life, Death and Dying

Lesson 6—Spiritualism As a Philosophy—Part III

Various Interpretations of Life After Death
What We Know About Life After Death
Considerations on Life After Death
Descriptions of the Spirit World

Lesson 7—Spiritualism's Teachings and Views

The Positive Aspects of Modern Spiritualism
Spiritualism's Views
Spiritualism and Christian Theology

Lesson 8—Spiritualism's Teachings & Views, Part II

Physical and Spiritual Nature of the Individual
The Individual's Duty
Life and Its Purpose

Unit 3—The Science of Spiritualism

Lesson 9—Spiritualism As Science

General Considerations
Relationship Between Science and Spiritualism
Some Early Scientists Who Studied Spiritualism
Some Early Scientific Research Organizations
Position of Science to Spiritualism—Spiritualism to Science

Lesson 10—Classification of Phenomena

Davis' Classification of Mediumship
Crookes' Classification of Mediumship
Sprague's Classification of Mediumship
Classification According to Parapsychology

Lesson 11—A Study of the Phenomena—Part I

Telepathy
Clairvoyance
Clairaudience

Lesson 12—A Study of the Phenomena—Part II

Retrocoguition
Precognition
Prophecy

Lesson 13—A Study of the Phenomena—Part III

Inspirational and Inspired
Inspirational Speaking and Writing
Independent—Automatic Writing
Trance

Lesson 14—A Study of the Phenomena—Part IV

Clairsentience
Psychometry
Spirit Photography

Lesson 15—A Study of the Phenomena—Part V

Materialization & Dematerialization
Teleportation & Apportation
The Status of Phenomena today

Lesson 16—A Study of the Phenomena—Part VI

The History of the Human Aura
Kilner, Kirlian and the Aura
Science/Parapsychology & the Aura
Spiritualism and the Aura

Lesson 17—a Study of the Phenomena—Part VII

Levitation
Out-of-the Body Experiences (OOBE)
Independent Voice (Direct Voice)

Lesson 18—Practice & Application of Phenomena—Part I

Awareness and Self-Realization
General Introduction to Meditation
The Practice of Meditation
The Application of Meditation

Lesson 19—Practice & Application of Phenomena—Part II

The Practice of Mediumship
Unfoldment of Mediumship

Lesson 20—Practice & Application of Phenomena—Part III

Mediumship and the Medium
Ethics, Education and the Medium
Mediumship and the Sitter
Benefits of Mediumship

Unsatisfactory Results of Mediumship

Unit 4—A Study Of Healing

Lesson 21—a History of Healing

Healing in Prehistory
Healing During Ancient History
Healing During the Middle Period
Healers of Modern Times

Lesson 22—The Theory of Healing

Healing Classifications
Spiritual Healing and the Spiritualist
Spiritual Healing and the Scientist

Lesson 23—Avenues of Healing

Contact Spiritual Healing
Absent Spiritual Healing
Psychic Surgery
Healing Without Sprit Intervention
The Healing Intelligence

Lesson 24—The Practice of Healing

General Considerations
The Practice of Healing
The Healing Experience
Activities for the Spiritual Healer
Steps for Certification

Unit 5—Comparative Religion

Lesson 25—Comparative Religion—Part I

The Beginning and Development of Religion
Religions of Some Ancient Cultures

Lesson 26—Comparative Religion—Part II

Buddhism
The Beliefs of China
Hinduism

Lesson 27—Comparative Religion—Part III

Zoroastrianism
Judaism
Christianity
The World of Islam

Unite 6—Representing Spiritualism

Lesson 28—Church Organization

The Parent Body
Stow Memorial Foundation
Spiritualist Benevolent Society
Certification
Auxiliaries
Incorporation of Auxiliaries
Organizing New Societies
Suggested Church Bylaws

Lesson 29—Serving Spiritualism

Serving the Platform
Platform Decorum
The Lecture Process
The Pastor
Special Observances
Suggested Platform Decorum

Lesson 30—Your Role in Spiritualism

The Importance of Image
Our Image—Our Future
A Brighter Future for Spiritualism—How?

Resource Units

In addition to the thirty lessons, Resource Units are available for purchase. The same lesson material as the Correspondence Course is presented in bound units and does not include the questions for each lesson. The Resource Units would be useful to current Ordained and Certified Workers who wish to be knowledgeable of the current information.

Unit 1—The History of Spiritualism
Unit 2—The Religion of Spiritualism
Unit 3—The Science of Spiritualism
Unit 4—A Study of Healing
Unit 5—Comparative Religion
Unit 6—Representing Spiritualism

[Retrieved from http://www.morrispratt.org on March 26, 2004.]

APPENDIX R

Fieldwork Questionnaire

Professor Todd Jay Leonard

Hirosaki Gakuin University
13-1 Minori-cho
Hirosaki-shi, Aomori-ken JAPAN 036-8577
E-Mail: tleonard@infoaomori.ne.jp   Tel/Fax: 81+172-34-7435

Dear Fellow Spiritualist,

I would like to enlist your help with a research project that I am working on. My name is Todd Jay Leonard and I am a university professor in northern Japan. Currently, I am gathering data for my doctoral dissertation which is focusing on Spiritualism and Mediumship.

I am a practicing Spiritualist and am interested in researching, in a positive way, the rich history of Spiritualism in America; and to gather fieldwork data, through surveys, to document definitively the current condition of mediums who are actively working with Spirit. There is certainly a noticeable void in the available literature and current research on this subject. There is an apparent need for academic research to take place in order to document categorically (for posterity and the future) the basics of this very American religion.

Much has been written about Spiritualism, both positive and negative, which largely focuses upon the need to "prove" or "disprove" the *ability* of the Spiritualist medium. This is not my focus. My study will be historical with a social science basis that will give an overview of Spiritualism with a concentration on the mediums themselves.

This is where your expertise comes in. I would greatly appreciate your kind assistance in helping me to gather data on this aspect of Spiritualism and mediumship. Enclosed is an anonymous questionnaire with 20 questions. I have included a self-addressed, stamped envelope in order for you to return the survey to me.

Any information you are able to give me will assist me tremendously in my research. I have included my e-mail and postal address, as well as, my phone and fax number in case you wish to contact me personally.

Thank you in advance with your assistance with this request.

Fieldwork Questionnaire for Doctoral Research Study by Prof. Todd Jay Leonard

The following questionnaire is designed to find out basic information about Spiritualism and Mediums. This is anonymous, so please be honest and forthright. I am planning to write my PhD dissertation on an aspect of Spiritualism and mediumship. Your assistance in my fieldwork data is greatly appreciated. Thank you for your time and assistance with this request.

AGE_____Male/Female_____Nationality_____

[Nota Bene: If you require additional space, please feel free to use extra paper to include with this survey; please write the number of the question next to the response.]

1. Before becoming a Spiritualist, what (if any) religion did you practice (or belief system did you follow)? (*i.e.* raised Baptist, but converted to Buddhism as an adult; baptized as a Methodist, but rarely went to church; devout Catholic all of my life, etc)
_____
_____

2. What first prompted you to pursue Spiritualism as a religion?
_____
_____
_____
_____

3. How long have you been a Spiritualist? _____

4. Are you an ordained Minister in a Spiritualist (or other) church? Please specify the denomination or organization. _____
_____
_____

5. If not an ordained Minister, do you have any Spiritualist credentials, qualifications, or certifications (other than Ministerial credentials). Please list these and the organizing body that issued them. _____

_____
_____
_____
_____

6. When did you become a certified medium? _____

7. From what age were you aware of your mediumistic gifts? _____

8. What was your first experience with mediumship? _____

_____
_____
_____
_____
_____
_____
_____

9. What was your most fantastic or memorable experience as a medium (in a positive way)?
Personally:_____

_____
_____
_____
_____

Reading for someone else:_____

_____
_____
_____
_____

10. What was your most frightening experience as a medium (in a negative way)?
Personally: _____
_____
_____
_____
_____

Reading for someone else: _____
_____
_____
_____
_____
_____

11. As a medium, and in your work, do you use any other tools (*i.e.* tarot, numerology, astrology, etc.) to assist you in giving people who come to you for readings? Other than giving messages, what is your specialty, so to speak? _____
_____
_____
_____

12. Please list any other divination methods you use regularly and personally in your private life? (*i.e.* tarot, astrology, numerology, etc)
_____
_____
_____
_____

13. What personal routine do you use to connect with Spirit when giving readings? _____
_____
_____
_____

14. How do you connect with Spirit on a daily basis? (*i.e.* prayer, meditation, trance-work, etc.) _____
_____
_____
_____

15. When giving readings, how do you mainly receive the messages? (*i.e.* direct voice, clairvoyant, clairaudient, clairsentient, etc.) _____
_____

16. Do you have, or have you ever had, any physical phenomena or materializations appear while conducting a séance or healing circle? Please describe these in detail. _____
_____
_____
_____
_____
_____

17. What are the <u>three</u> most common reasons people seek out your assistance as a medium or psychic?
1._____
2._____
3._____

18. What was the most unusual request by a client for your assistance as a medium?
_____
_____
_____
_____
_____

19. There is often harsh criticism of Spiritualism by orthodox and mainstream religions; also there are a number of groups who actively try to debunk mediumship as nonsense or creative fakery. How do you personally respond to such criticism?

_____
_____
_____
_____
_____
_____

20. GENERAL COMMENTS: Please feel free to include any additional information you may think of that may be of assistance to me in my research; please comment on any aspect of Spiritualism or mediumship.

_____
_____
_____
_____
_____
_____
_____
_____
_____
_____
_____
_____
_____
_____
_____
_____
_____
_____
_____
_____
_____
_____

978-0-595-36353-7
0-595-36353-9

Printed in the United States
71848LV00005B/43